THE PETERSON FIELD GUIDE SERIES®

A Field Guide to Western Birds

A Completely New Guide to
Field Marks of All Species
Found in North America
West of the 100th Meridian
and North of Mexico

Text and Illustrations by
ROGER TORY PETERSON

Maps by
VIRGINIA MARIE PETERSON

D0037214

• *Third Edition* •
Completely Revised and Enlarged

Sponsored by the National Audubon Society,
the National Wildlife Federation,
and the Roger Tory Peterson Institute

HOUGHTON MIFFLIN COMPANY
Boston   New York

to the memory of

CLARENCE BEAL

and

JAMES FISHER

―――――――――――

Text and illustrations copyright © 1990 by Roger Tory Peterson
Maps copyright © 1990 by Virginia Marie Peterson

For information about this and other Houghton Mifflin
trade and reference books and multimedia products, visit
The Bookstore at Houghton Mifflin on the World Wide Web
at http://www.hmco.com/trade/.

Library of Congress Cataloging-in-Publication Data

Peterson, Roger Tory, (date)
A field guide to western birds: a completely new guide to field
marks of all species found in North America west of the 100th
meridian and north of Mexico / text and illustrations by Roger Tory
Peterson; maps by Virginia Marie Peterson. — 3rd ed., completely
rev. and enl.
p. cm. — (The Peterson field guide series; 2)
"Sponsored by the National Audubon Society, the National Wildlife
Federation, and the Roger Tory Peterson Institute."
Includes index.
ISBN 0-395-91174-5   ISBN 0-395-91173-7 (pbk.)
1. Birds — West (U.S.) — Identification. 2. Birds — Canada,
Western — Identification. I. Peterson, Virginia Marie, (date). II.
National Audubon Society, III. National Wildlife Federation. IV.
Roger Tory Peterson Institute. V. Title. VI. Series.
QL683.W4P4   1989
598.2978 — dc20   89-31517
                         CIP

Printed in the United States of America
RIV 19 18 17 16 15 14 13 12 11 10

ROADSIDE SILHOUETTES

1. MOURNING DOVE
2. HOUSE SPARROW
3. BLUEBIRD
4. STARLING
5. COWBIRD
6. BLACKBIRD
7. KINGFISHER
8. SCRUB JAY
9. MOCKINGBIRD
10. LARK SPARROW
11. SHRIKE
12. FLICKER
13. MAGPIE
14. NIGHTHAWK
15. ROBIN
16. BURROWING OWL
17. PHEASANT
18. CALIFORNIA QUAIL
19. PURPLE MARTIN
20. BARN SWALLOW
21. CLIFF SWALLOW
22. KESTREL
23. SWIFT
    (VAUX'S OR CHIMNEY)
24. SCISSOR-TAILED
    FLYCATCHER
25. MEADOWLARK
26. KINGBIRD
27. HORNED LARK
28. PHOEBE
29. KILLDEER
30. CROW

THE PETERSON FIELD GUIDE SERIES®
Edited by Roger Tory Peterson

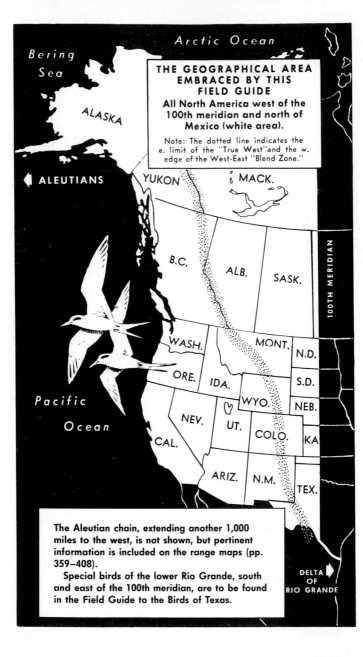

Bering Sea

Arctic Ocean

ALASKA

ALEUTIANS

YUKON

MACK.

THE GEOGRAPHICAL AREA EMBRACED BY THIS FIELD GUIDE

All North America west of the 100th meridian and north of Mexico (white area).

Note: The dotted line indicates the e. limit of the "True West" and the w. edge of the West-East "Blend Zone."

B.C.

ALB.

SASK.

WASH.

MONT.

N.D.

ORE.

IDA.

S.D.

Pacific Ocean

NEV.

UT.

WYO.

NEB.

COLO.

KA

CAL.

ARIZ.

N.M.

TEX.

100TH MERIDIAN

DELTA OF RIO GRANDE

The Aleutian chain, extending another 1,000 miles to the west, is not shown, but pertinent information is included on the range maps (pp. 359–408).

Special birds of the lower Rio Grande, south and east of the 100th meridian, are to be found in the Field Guide to the Birds of Texas.

Introduction

In 1934 my first *Field Guide* was published, covering the birds east of the 90th meridian in North America. Later this was extended to the 100th meridian on the Great Plains. This book was designed so that live birds could be readily identified at a distance by their "field marks," without resorting to the bird-in-hand characters that the early collectors relied on. During the following half century the binocular and the spotting scope have replaced the shotgun.

The "**Peterson System,**" as it now is called, is based on pattern-istic drawings with arrows that pinpoint the key field marks. These rather formal schematic illustrations and the direct comparisons between similar species are the core of the system, a practical method that has gained universal acceptance not only on this continent but also in Europe, where *Field Guides* now exist in 12 languages. This system, which is, in a sense, a pictorial key based on visual impressions rather than on technical features, has been extended to other branches of natural history and there are now about 40 titles in the Field Guide Series.

It was William Vogt, the first editor of *Audubon* magazine, who suggested that I put together a *Field Guide* using my visual approach to field identification, which I had already presented in articles in *Nature Magazine* and *Field and Stream.* After a preliminary draft of the book had been politely turned down by several publishers, Francis Allen, veteran editor of Houghton Mifflin, and a star birder himself, saw the validity of the new approach, and the rest is history. His successor, Paul Brooks, continued to carry on the editorial tradition.

Shortly after the first edition of the eastern *Field Guide* saw the light of day, Clinton G. Abbott, then director of the Natural History Museum at San Diego, asked why I didn't do a similar field guide for the West. I dismissed the idea at first, thinking that although the plan worked well for eastern North America, it would be a much more formidable task to attempt the same for the West. However, after prompting by Guy Emerson, then chairman of the National Audubon Society, I gave it a try. After tussling with a few of the problems, I concluded that field identification was not much more difficult in the West, and that most publications made things look more involved and clumsy than need be. There was already one excellent field handbook in use—Ralph Hoffmann's *Birds of the Pacific States*—but this covered only the states of Washington, Oregon, and California, whereas there was hardly anything of pocket size that was adequate for most other parts of the West.

This edition of *A Field Guide to Western Birds* is more than a revision; it is almost completely new, with 165 plates, as against 136 in the 1961 edition. None of the previous color plates of the western *Field Guide* has been retained. However, 24 plates have been borrowed from the latest eastern *Field Guide to the Birds* (1980), 30 others have been modified, and 111 plates are completely new. All species are now shown in color. The waterfowl are repeated in monochrome, because their flight patterns are more clearly diagnosed in that way.

There are also 441 three-color maps, a new feature. My wife, Virginia Marie Peterson, and I researched these together and she then carefully carried out their execution. Her trained hand and eye had previously been employed at the U.S. Coast Guard Research and Development Center, where she worked out critical methods for identifying oil spills by means of infrared spectroscopy. Virginia wrote the original *Infrared Field Manual for Oil Spill Identification.* She also prepared the 390 maps in the 1980 edition of the eastern *Field Guide to the Birds.*

With this new third edition, long overdue, the *Field Guide to Western Birds* has really come of age. Years ago I had concluded that for comparative purposes the ideal number of species per color plate would be about four (rather than ten or twelve, as in previous editions), but the cost factor prohibited this ideal format when we first broke ground. The success of the *Field Guide*, with its well-tested practical system, has grown steadily over the years, and the economics of distribution as well as technical advances in fine offset printing made it possible to surmount earlier restraints.

The *Field Guide* user will find one major format change that will be particularly helpful: species accounts, except in a few instances, now face the corresponding illustrations. Because of the success of this formula in the latest revision of the eastern *Field Guide*, many birders urged me to arrange text and plates of the western *Field Guide* in this way, and I have done so, but because of space limitations, maps are separate.

Area of this Field Guide: This guide covers North America west of the 100th meridian, as shown in the map on p. 2. Rather than a restrictive political boundary, an ecological one is more practical. In the U.S. the logical division of the avifauna is along the belt between the 100th meridian (midway across Oklahoma, Kansas, Nebraska, and the Dakotas) and the edge of the Rockies. This is by no means a sharp division, but people living in that ecological "twilight zone" will find that *A Field Guide to Western Birds* covers all species they are likely to encounter. In a general way, eastern birds follow the valleys west, while the western forms edge eastward along the more arid uplands. In Canada, eastern influences extend much further west, bridging the gap to the Rockies via the conifer forests north of the Great Plains.

The birds in the western third of Texas (the Panhandle and west of the Edwards Plateau) are covered in this *Field Guide.* Not so those in the lower Rio Grande Valley, where many western species reach their eastern outposts and a few very special Mexican species occur. These will be found in *A Field Guide to the Birds of Texas* (No. 13 in the Field Guide Series). Texas is the only state with its own *Field Guide.*

In the 1961 edition, I included a separate 32-page section on the Hawaiian Islands. Because of the excellent new *Field Guide to the Birds of Hawaii and the Tropical Pacific* by Douglas Pratt, Phillip Bruner and Delwyn Berrett, and also the latest edition of *Hawaii's Birds* edited by R.J. Shallenberger (published by the Hawaiian Audubon Society), I have chosen to omit that section and to devote those pages to a more in-depth treatment of Alaska, the Aleutians, and the Bering Sea area.

Drawings vs. Photographs: Because of the increasing sophistication of birders, I have leaned more toward detailed portraiture in the new illustrations while trying not to lose the patternistic effect developed in the earlier editions. A drawing can often do more than a photograph to emphasize field marks. A photograph is a record of a fleeting instant; a drawing is a composite of the artist's experience. The artist can edit out, show field marks to best advantage, and delete unnecessary clutter. He can also choose position and stress basic color and pattern unmodified by transitory light and shade. A photograph is subject to the vagaries of color-temperature (Kelvin), make of film, exposure, time of day, sunlight, open shade, use of flash, angle of view, skill of the photographer, and just plain luck. The artist has more options and far more control even though he may at times use photographs for reference. This is not a diatribe against photography; I am an obsessive photographer as well as a painter and therefore am fully aware of the pitfalls and the differences. Whereas a photograph can have a living immediacy, a good drawing is more instructive as a teaching device.

Subspecies: These simply represent subdivisions within the geographic range of a species. They are races, usually determined by morphological characteristics such as slight differences in measurements, shades of color, etc. These subtle subdivisions can usually be distinguished with accuracy only by collecting birds with a gun or a mist net and comparing them with museum specimens. The distinctions, often vague, are seldom apparent in the field. Subspecies have a meaning to the student of bird distribution and evolution and are of practical value to those involved in conservation and wildlife management practices. Should occasion demand, the scholar can refer to his copy of the older 5th edition of the Checklist of the American Ornithologists' Union (A.O.U.), which gave a detailed breakdown of races and their ranges. The 6th edition (1983) does so only in a very general way. However, in this new edition of the *Field Guide*, a few subspecies are recognized when field distinctions are obvious. One of the most controversial examples is the western "Bullock's" Oriole, which is now lumped with the eastern "Baltimore" Oriole under the new name Northern Oriole. "Myrtle" and "Audubon's" warblers are now lumped as the Yellow-rumped Warbler. Most of the juncos have also been lumped. The earlier names and a few others have been retained (in quotes) in deference to long-established usage. Names that were used in the 1961 edition of this book but which have since been changed by the Checklist Committee are in parentheses under the current name. We can expect further changes by the A.O.U.

The Ranges of Birds: A number of species have been added to the avifauna of western North America since the previous edition of this *Field Guide* was published in 1961. Notable is the Cattle Egret, which spread explosively after it arrived in the U.S. about 1952. Several eastern species are pushing west and a few exotic escapes, especially parrots, are doing well and may become established.

The ranges of many species have changed markedly during the past 50 years. Some are expanding because of decades of protection; others have diminished alarmingly or have dropped out of parts of their range due to environmental changes. The passion for bird feeding has had its effect on expanding the ranges of several species.

The Maps: Instead of detailed range accounts, maps are now employed; they have been conveniently assembled in a separate section (pp. 359–408). Because the projections are large enough to show state and provincial lines, ranges are now defined more critically. However, the Aleutians, extending more than 1,000 miles to the west of the Alaska Peninsula, are not shown, but any pertinent information about these islands is included in notes on the maps. For quick use, the map section is marked with a gray corner that serves as a thumb index. By grouping the maps we can update them more frequently without affecting the rest of the pagination. Our knowledge of bird distribution is becoming ever more exact because of the proliferation of field observers. Not only are some birds extending their ranges, but so are the birders.

Although many birds (waterfowl, game birds, seabirds) had already been mapped continentally in the *Handbook of North*

American Birds (edited by R. S. Palmer) and in other books, Virginia Peterson and I researched our own maps using state and regional sources, but we found these very uneven. Some western states already had good to excellent "latilongs," but only now are they becoming involved in more detailed atlasing.

Acknowledgments: The specimen material used in the preparation of the new color plates came almost entirely from the cabinets of the American Museum of Natural History in New York City. I am deeply grateful to the staff and curators of the Department of Ornithology of that institution for their assistance, and specifically to Dean Amadon, Allison Andors, Chris Blake, John Bull, Robert Dickerman, Eugene Eisenmann, John Farrand, Stuart Keith, Wesley Lanyon, Mary Le Croy, Allan O'Connor, Lester Shortt, and Françoise Villeumier.

Space prevents me from listing again the mass of ornithological literature digested in the preparation of the earlier editions of the *Field Guide to Western Birds*, as well as the regional works, checklists, papers, and periodicals that went into the compilation of this one. Assiduously I consulted them all and intentionally ignored none. A list of these sources is on file and available in my library.

Nor shall I list again the 200 or more field companions, correspondents, and others who contributed notes or helped in other ways in previous editions and those who were involved in their production. Their names are in the Preface of the second edition (revised and enlarged, 1961). However, I would like to acknowledge again two people who played especially important roles: Edgar Kincaid, who sharpened my critical senses, and Barbara Peterson, who typed and retyped the manuscripts a number of times, offered suggestions, and helped in many other tangible ways.

In preparing the new maps, Virginia Peterson and I consulted all of the pertinent state and regional books in the *Special Book Supplement* prepared by *American Birds*, and, equally important, the files of *American Birds*, which is published by the National Audubon Society, 950 Third Avenue, New York, New York 10022.

The breeding birds of Canada had already been mapped in *Birds of Canada* by Earl Godfrey, who generously made the updated version of these maps available to us prior to publication. Paul Johnsgard was also very generous, letting us see much of his own material prior to publication in several of his books. Don Roberson's scholarly *Rare Birds of the West Coast* was indispensable when dealing with casuals and accidentals, as was the *Distributional Checklist of North American Birds* by David De Sante and Peter Pyle.

The problem of covering Alaska adequately was solved when Pete Isleib, a peerless and indefatigable observer, prepared for us three albums of large-scale maps, based largely on years of research by his associates, Dan Gibson and Brina Kessel. They were then checked further by Peter Connors, James King, and John Wright. These maps cover every species known to have occurred in Alaska.

Before my wife, Virginia, finalized her cartography, she sent out a number of selected maps to the following authorities for fine-tuning: Stephen Bailey (Calif.), Mark Collie (Idaho), Phillip Detrich (Calif.), Jon Dunn (Calif.), Kimball Garrett (Calif.), Eugene Hunn (Wash.), Kenn Kaufman (Ariz.), Hugh Kingery (Colo.), Paul Lehman (Calif.), Guy McCaskie (Calif.), Joseph Morlan (Calif.), Vince Mowbray (Nev.), Dennis Paulson (Wash.), Don Roberson (Calif.), Oliver Scott (Wyo.), Arnold Small (Calif.), Ella Sorensen (Utah), Rich Stallcup (Calif.), Allan Stokes (Utah), Stephen Summers (Ore.), Daniel Taylor (Idaho), Thede Tobish (Alaska), Charles Trost (Idaho), R. E. Walters, Jr. (Utah), Ralph Widrig (Wash.), Kevin Zimmer (N.M.), and Dale Zimmerman (N.M.).

The following people gave us additional help on specifics concerning the maps: Frederick and Margarite Baumgartner, Stephen Bissell, Tom Cade, William S. Clark, James Grier, Donald Klebenow, T. E. Lebedz, Richard and Robert Lewin, Carl Mortis, Harry Nehls, W. J. Plowden-Wardlaw, Noble Proctor, J. V. Remsen, Jr., T. D. Reynolds, Chandler S. Robbins, Thomas Rogers, S. E. Senner, J. M. Scott, Brian Sharp, Alison Speirs, Sally Spofford, S. Sturts, J. F. Stetter, J. B. Tatum, Joseph Taylor, Dan Varland, Linda Westervelt, Miriam Westervelt, Herb Wisner, and C. Zeillemaker.

In addition, the following birders, through correspondence, reading portions of the text, or personal contact, made suggestions for this revision or helped in some other way: Peter Alden (who fine-combed the entire text), Jeff Altman, Elisha Atkins, Harold Axtell, Larry Balch, Benton Basham, Chuck Bernstein, Laurence Binford, Eirik Blom, Jon Boone, Kenneth Brandes, Don Bronk, Ted Chandik, Allegra Collister, Susan Roney Drennan, Bruce Duncan, Brian A. Evans, Robert Frisch, Frank Gill, John D. Goodman, Campbell Grant, William E. Grenfell, Jr., William W. H. Gunn, James E. Halferty, Theodora Halladay, Ed Harper, Donald S. Heintzelman, John P. Hubbard, Douglas James, Joseph R. Jehl, Jr., H. A. Kantrud, Robert E. Kennedy, Ben King, Edward A. Kutac, Greg Lasley, Gary R. Lingle, Steve Makara, David Messineo, Gale Monson, Ron Naveen, Kerry Pado, Ted Parker, Allan R. Phillips, Richard Rimmer, Terry Root, Gary Rosenberg, Margaret Rusk, Stephen Russell, R. A. Rylander, Fred Ryser, Paul T. Schnell, Ralph Shreiber, P. S. Skaar, Rich Stallcup, Robert A. Sundell, Paul W. Sykes, Jr., Ross L. Teuber, Florence J. Thornburg, Francis B. Vanslager, Richard Veit, Robert E. Walters, Lilia and Gordon Weber, Claudia Wilds, David Wolf, Bryce Wood, and Alan Wormington.

We owe special thanks to Seymour Levin, who devised a mapping system that protected the accuracy of Virginia Peterson's original cartography and saved her much time in preparing the final maps for the printer.

Putting a field guide together so that everything fits is a challenge comparable to a jig-saw puzzle or a game of chess. A thousand details were put in the hands of my secretary, Charles W. Schulze, who was helped by Jeannette Speirs and Dwight Macdonald, my studio assistants. In addition to handling an avalanche of correspondence, Mr. Schulze retyped the manuscript half a dozen times so that it would be in the best possible form for my editors.

At Houghton Mifflin, Harry Foster was on top of things from the beginning, working closely with Austin Olney and Jon Latimer. He was always just a phone call away and in turn relied on Barbara Stratton, a model of editorial thoroughness, who fine-tuned the manuscript and worked with Anne Chalmers, Brenda Lewis, Donna Muise, and Steve Pekich in readying everything for the typesetter and printer.

The quality of the color work is the result of close collaboration with the above people and the printer, Case-Hoyt of Rochester, N.Y., under the critical eyes of Dan Cooney, George Hannon, Jon Latimer, Brenda Lewis, Paul Nederlk, Wayne Oakley, Thomas Reetz, the color evaluator, Priscilla Sharpless, and Conrad Ward. In addition, Mrs. Peterson carefully checked all proofs of the maps with Dan Cooney, Brenda Lewis, Thomas Reetz, and Conrad Ward.

A field guide is a complex team effort, starting with the field observers and ending with the printer. I want to extend my deepest thanks to everyone involved.

Bird Songs and Calls

Not everything useful for identifying birds can be crammed into a single pocket-sized *Field Guide*. In the species accounts I have included a brief entry on **Voice**, and I have done this in my own way, trying to give the reader some handle on the songs or calls he hears. Authors of bird books have attempted with varying success to fit songs into syllables, words, and phrases. Musical notations, comparative descriptions, mnemonics, and even ingenious systems of symbols have also been employed. But since the advent of sound recording these other techniques have been eclipsed. A visual spin-off of the tape recording is the sonogram, but most people are not sufficiently oriented technologically to be able to interpret sonograms easily.

Use the recently revised *Field Guide to Western Bird Songs* (No. 2A in the Field Guide Series); it is available on records and cassettes. This comprehensive collection of sound recordings includes the calls and songs of more than 500 land and water birds—a large percentage of all the species found in western North America. They were recorded and prepared under the direction of the Laboratory of Ornithology, Cornell University. To prepare yourself for your field trips play the records or cassettes; then read the descriptions in this *Field Guide* for clues.

Birding by Ear: Eastern and Central (No. 38 in the Field Guide Series) by Richard K. Walton and Robert Lawson is another excellent shortcut to learning songs. These new cassettes, published by Houghton Mifflin, compare similar songs and analyze them for you. In learning bird voices (and some birders do 90 percent of their field work by ear) there is no substitute for the actual sounds. *Birding by Ear* will help you to systematize things and get your act together. It is basically for the eastern parts of the continent, but a companion volume for the West (No. 41) will soon be published.

Bird Nests

Most birders are not too skilled at finding nests. In most cases there would be an appalling gap between the number of species ticked off on their checklists and the number of nests they have discovered. To remedy this, Hal Harrison, the premier nest photographer, has prepared *A Field Guide to Western Bird Nests*. This *Field Guide* (No. 25 in the Field Guide Series) will expand your ornithological expertise.

Contents

CONTENTS

CONTENTS

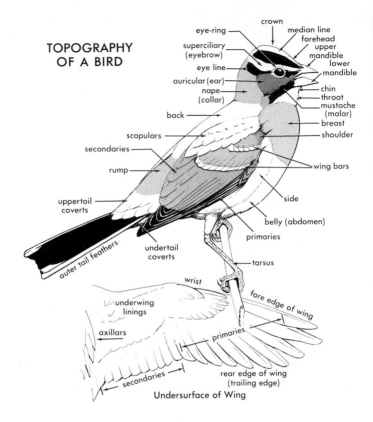

TOPOGRAPHY OF A BIRD

crown
eye-ring
superciliary (eyebrow)
eye line
auricular (ear)
nape (collar)
back
scapulars
secondaries
rump
uppertail coverts
outer tail feathers
undertail coverts

median line
forehead
upper mandible
lower mandible
chin
throat
mustache (malar)
breast
shoulder
wing bars
side
belly (abdomen)
primaries
tarsus

wrist
underwing linings
axillars
secondaries
fore edge of wing
primaries
rear edge of wing (trailing edge)

Undersurface of Wing

Other Terms Used in this Book

Sex symbols: ♂ means male, ♀ means female. These symbols are used frequently on the plates.

Accidental: In the area of this book, recorded fewer than a dozen times, far out of range (see maps, pp. 359–408). On the state level only one, two, or three records; might not be expected again.

Casual: Very few records, but might be expected again because the normal range of the species is in an adjacent state or province, or not too distant.

Introduced: Not native; deliberately released.

Exotic: Not native; either released or escaped.

In part: Subdivision of a family; or part of a species, such as a well-marked subspecies.

How to Identify Birds

Veteran birders will know how to use this book. Beginners, however, should spend some time becoming familiar in a general way with the illustrations. They are not arranged in systematic or phylogenetic order but are grouped in eight main visual categories:

(1) **Swimmers**—Ducks and ducklike birds
(2) **Aerialists**—Gulls and gull-like birds
(3) **Long-legged Waders**—Herons, cranes, etc.
(4) **Smaller Waders**—Plovers, sandpipers, etc.
(5) **Fowl-like Birds**—Grouse, quail, etc.
(6) **Birds of Prey**—Hawks, eagles, owls
(7) **Nonpasserine Land Birds**
(8) **Passerine (Perching) Birds**

Within these groupings it will be seen that ducks do not resemble loons, and gulls are readily distinguishable from terns. The needle-like bills of warblers immediately differentiate them from the seed-cracking bills of sparrows. Birds that could be confused are grouped together when possible and are arranged in identical profile for direct comparison. The arrows point to outstanding "field marks," which are explained opposite. The text also gives aids such as actions, voice, habitat, etc., not visually portrayable, and under a separate heading often discusses species that might be confused. The brief notes on general range are keyed by number to detailed three-color range maps in the rear of the book (pp. 359–408).

In addition to 160 plates of birds normally found in the area of this *Field Guide* there are five color plates depicting fifteen vagrants from Mexico and thirty-five strays or accidentals from Asia. With the exception of several parrots and two or three others unestablished escapes and exotics are not illustrated. However, if you see one, record it, so that if a pattern eventually emerges past information will not be lost.

What Is the Bird's Size?

Acquire the habit of comparing a new bird with some familiar "yardstick"—a House Sparrow, a Robin, a Pigeon, etc., so that you can say to yourself, "smaller than a Robin; a little larger than a House Sparrow." The measurements in this book represent lengths in inches (with centimeters in parentheses) from bill tip to tail tip of specimens on their backs as in museum trays. However, specimen measurements vary widely depending on the preparator, who may have stretched the neck a bit. In many cases the species accounts give minimum and maximum lengths, but in life, not lying in a tray, most birds are closer to the minimum lengths given.

What Is Its Shape?

Is it plump like a starling (left) or slender like a cuckoo (right)?

What Shape Are Its Wings?

Are they rounded like those of a quail (left) or sharply pointed like those of a Barn Swallow (right)? See also "Birds of Prey," pp. 168, 169.

What Shape Is Its Bill?

Is it small and fine like a warbler's (1), stout and short like a seed-cracking sparrow's (2), dagger-shaped like a tern's (3), or hook-tipped like that of a bird of prey (4)?

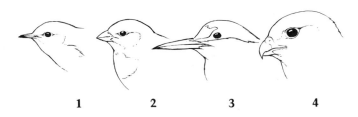

| 1 | 2 | 3 | 4 |

What Shape Is Its Tail?

Is it deeply forked like a Barn Swallow's (1), square-tipped like a Cliff Swallow's (2), notched like a Tree Swallow's (3), rounded like a jay's (4), or pointed like a Mourning Dove's (5)?

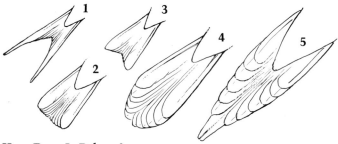

How Does It Behave?

Does it cock its tail like a wren or hold it down like a flycatcher? Does it wag, flick, or dip its tail? Does it sit erect on an open perch, dart after an insect, and return as a flycatcher does?

Does It Climb Trees?

If so, does it climb in *spirals* like a Creeper (left), in jerks like a woodpecker (center) using its tail as a brace, or does it go down headfirst like a nuthatch (right)?

How Does It Fly?

Does it undulate (dip up and down) like a Flicker (1)? Does it fly straight and fast like a Mourning Dove (2)? Does it hover like a Kingfisher (3)? Does it glide or soar? See also "Birds of Prey," pp. 168, 169.

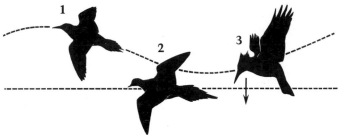

Does It Swim?

Does it sit low in the water like a Loon (1) or high like a Moorhen (2)? If a duck, does it dive like a deepwater duck (3) or does it dabble and up-end like a Mallard (4)?

Does It Wade?

Is it large and long-legged like a heron, or small like a sandpiper? If one of the latter, does it probe the mud or pick at things? Does it teeter or bob? See also "Waders" (sandpipers, etc.), pp. 128, 129.

What Are Its Field Marks?

Some birds can be identified by color alone, but most birds are not that easy. The most important aids are what we call *field marks*, which are, in effect, the "trademarks of nature." Note whether the breast is spotted as in a thrush (1), streaked as in the Brown Thrasher (2), or plain as in a cuckoo (3). In this guide, important field marks are indicated by arrows.

Tail Patterns

Does the tail have a "flash pattern"—a white tip as in the Eastern Kingbird (1), white patches in the outer corners as in a Towhee (2), or white sides as in a junco (3)?

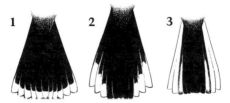

Rump Patches

Does it have a light rump like a Cliff Swallow (1) or Flicker (2)? The Harrier, Yellow-rumped Warbler, and many of the shorebirds also have distinctive rump patches.

Eyestripes and Eye-rings

Does the bird have a stripe above, through, or below the eye, or a combination of these stripes? Does it have a striped crown? A ring around the eye, or "spectacles"? A "mustache" stripe? These details are diagnostic in many small songbirds.

Wing Bars

Do the wings have light wing bars or not? Their presence or absence is important in sorting out many warblers, vireos, and flycatchers. Wing bars may be single or double, bold or obscure.

Wing Patterns

The basic wing patterns of ducks (shown below), shorebirds, and other water birds are very important. Notice whether the wings have patches (1) or stripes (2), are solidly colored (3), or have contrasting black tips (Snow Goose, etc.).

Caution in Sight Records: Fifty or sixty years ago, prior to the *Field Guide* era, most ornithologists would not accept sight records of unusual birds unless they were made along the barrel of a shotgun. Today it is difficult to secure a collecting permit unless one is an academic or a student training to be one. Moreover, rarities may show up in parks, refuges, or on other lands where collecting is out of the question. There is no reason why we should not trust our increasingly educated eyes.

To validate the sight record of a very rare or accidental bird—a state "first," for example—the rule has been that at least two competent observers should see the bird and document it in detail in their notes. A 35 mm camera equipped with a 400 mm lens or longer is becoming an increasingly useful tool for substantiating such sightings. Rarities are sometimes caught in mist nets by bird banders and can be photographed hand-held, and even videotaped for the record. For photographing birds in the hand, a 50 mm close-up lens, such as a Micro-Nikkor, is best and may be used with or without flash equipment.

There are some species—or plumages—where even the expert will hedge. And it is the mark of an expert to occasionally put a question mark after certain birds on his list: for example, accipiter, sp.?, or *Empidonax*, sp.?, or "peep," sp.?, or immature gull, sp.? Do not be embarrassed if you cannot name *every* bird you see. Not so long ago, Allan Phillips argued convincingly in *American Birds* that practically all of the Semipalmated Sandpipers so freely reported in winter on the southern coasts of the U.S. were really Western Sandpipers. It is quite impossible to identify many individuals of these two species correctly unless they are caught or collected for critical examination—or unless their distinctive call notes are heard.

Once at an A.B.A. gathering, my friend Jim Tucker, then editor of *Birding*, asked us; "How would you define a 'good' birder or a 'great' birder? Is it the guy with a Questar who is unhappy if he cannot put a name to every bird he sees?" After thinking about it, Kenn Kaufman, who had wrestled with the fine points of identification as much as anyone we know, then gave his views: "Let's face it—some birds are really tough to tell apart in the field. If you don't enjoy the challenge it is perfectly acceptable to call such birds 'unknown flycatchers' or 'unidentified gulls' . . . nobody can name them all. In fact, I would say that if you enjoy birding a lot you are a great birder. And as a great birder you should never allow those tricky identification problems to keep you from having a good time."

Suggestions for Further Reading: See p. 416.

■ **LOONS. Family Gaviidae.** Shown in flight on p. 31. Large, long-bodied swimmers with daggerlike bills; may dive from the surface or sink. Thrash along water on take-off. Seldom on land except at nest. Sexes alike. Immatures are more scaly above than winter adults. **Food:** Small fish, crustaceans, other aquatic life. **Range:** Northern parts of N. Hemisphere. **No. of species:** World 5; West 5.

RED-THROATED LOON *Gavia stellata* See also p. 30.   **M1**
25″ (63 cm). Note the sharp thin bill, distinctly *upturned. Summer:* Plain back, gray head, striped nape, *rufous throat patch. Winter:* Similar to other loons but smaller, slimmer; profile snakier; back, head, and neck paler, with less contrast or pattern.
Voice: When flying, a repeated *kwuk.* In Arctic, falsetto wails.
Range: Arctic, circumpolar. Winters southward mainly along coasts to Mediterranean, China, Florida, n. Mexico. **West:** Map 1. **Habitat:** Coastal waters, bays, estuaries; in summer, tundra lakes.

PACIFIC LOON *Gavia pacifica* See also p. 30.   **M2**
25″ (63 cm). Smaller than Common Loon, with a thinner, straight bill. *Summer:* Crown and nape rounded, *pale gray.* Back divided into four checkered patches. *Winter:* Note sharp separation of black and white neck pattern. Bill slender, *straight* (not upturned). Often has trace of a chin strap. Gregarious, often traveling in large flocks.
Voice: A deep, barking *kwow.* Falsetto wails, rising in pitch.
Range: E. Siberia, nw. N. America. Winters along coasts to Japan, nw. Mexico. **West:** Map 2. **Habitat:** Ocean, open water; in summer, tundra lakes.

ARCTIC LOON *Gavia arctica*
27″ (68 cm). Formerly regarded as conspecific with Pacific Loon. A bit larger; in breeding plumage throat may be glossed more with *green* than purple (hard to see). In winter, said to show a whitish flank patch. Has bred in Alaska; accidental, British Columbia.

COMMON LOON *Gavia immer* See also p. 30.   **M3**
28–36″ (70–90 cm). Large, long-bodied, low-swimming; bill stout, daggerlike. *Breeding:* Black head and bill. *Checkered back,* broken white necklace. *Winter:* Dark above, whitish below. Note the *stout, straight* bill and irregular or *broken neck pattern.*
Voice: In summer, falsetto wails, weird yodeling, maniacal quavering laughter; at night, a tremulous *ha-oo-oo.* In flight, a barking *kwuk.* Usually silent in winter.
Range: Alaska, Canada, n. U.S., Greenland, Iceland. In winter, chiefly coastwise to n. Mexico, w. Europe. **West:** Map 3. **Habitat:** Conifer lakes, tundra ponds (summer); open lakes, bays, sea.

YELLOW-BILLED LOON *Gavia adamsii*   **M4**
33–38″ (83–95 cm). Similar to Common Loon, but bill *pale ivory* or *straw-colored,* distinctly upturned; straight above, slightly angled below. In winter *paler* about head and neck than Common Loon; usually shows a *dark ear patch;* smaller eye. *Caution:* Bill shape is not always reliable. Bills of most winter Common Loons are pale but the culmen (upper ridge) is *dark to the tip.*
Range: Arctic, from n. U.S.S.R. to nw. Canada. Winters along coasts of n. Eurasia, nw. N. America. **West:** Map 4. **Habitat:** Tundra lakes in summer; coastal waters in winter.

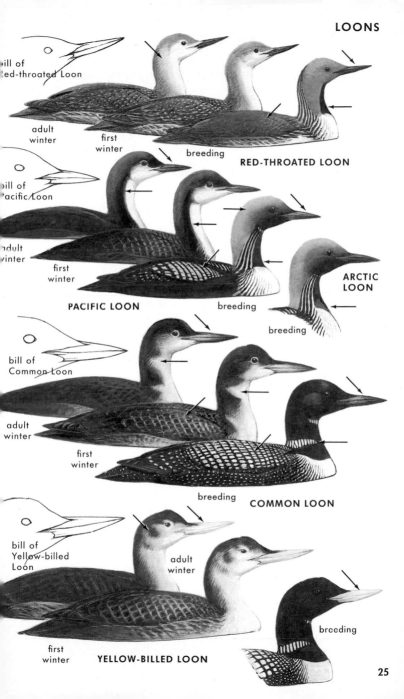

LOONS

bill of
Red-throated Loon

adult
winter

first
winter

breeding

RED-THROATED LOON

bill of
Pacific Loon

adult
winter

first
winter

breeding

PACIFIC LOON

ARCTIC LOON

breeding

breeding

bill of
Common Loon

adult
winter

first
winter

breeding

COMMON LOON

bill of
Yellow-billed
Loon

adult
winter

first
winter

breeding

YELLOW-BILLED LOON

25

■ **GREBES. Family Podicipedidae.** Ducklike divers with flat lobed toes, thin neck, tailless look. All but the Pied-bill have white wing patches, pointed bills. Sexes alike. Most young have striped heads. Grebes may dive from the surface or sink. Flight labored (with a sagging neck). **Food:** Small fish, other aquatic life. **Range:** Cosmopolitan. **No. of species:** World 20; West 7.

PIED-BILLED GREBE *Podilymbus podiceps*   **M5**
13″ (33 cm). Note the thick, ungrebe-like "chicken bill" and puffy white stern. No wing patch. *Breeding: Black throat patch* and *ring around pale bill. Winter:* Throat patch and bill ring *absent. Juvenile:* Striped on head. A small brown diver of ponds, marshes.
  Voice: *Kuk-kuk-cow-cow-cow-cowp-cowp;* also whinnying.
  Range: S. Canada to Argentina. Migratory in North. **West:** Map 5.
  Habitat: Ponds, lakes, marshes; in winter, also salt bays.

HORNED GREBE *Podiceps auritus*   **M6**
12–15″ (30–38 cm). *Breeding:* Combination of *golden ear tufts* and *chestnut neck. Winter:* Dark above, white below, with its black cap clean-cut to eye level; white foreneck, thin straight bill.
  Range: Northern parts of N. Hemisphere. Winters to s. U.S., s. Eurasia. **West:** Map 6. **Habitat:** Lakes, ponds; coastal waters.

EARED GREBE *Podiceps nigricollis*   **M7**
12–14″ (30–35 cm). *Breeding: Crested* black head, golden ear tufts, thin *black* neck. *Winter:* Similar to Horned Grebe, but neck thinner; bill slightly tilted; cap ill defined. The gray cheek sets off the white throat, *white ear patch.* The rump is raised well above the water. Very gregarious.
  Range: Eurasia, Africa, w. N. America. **West:** Map 7. **Habitat:** Prairie lakes, ponds; in winter, open lakes, salt bays, ocean.

RED-NECKED GREBE *Podiceps grisegena*   **M7**
18″ (45 cm). A largish grebe. *Breeding:* Long *rufous* neck, *light cheek,* black cap, long bill with yellow base. *Winter:* Grayish (including neck); *white crescent* on face. In flight, *double* wing patch.
  Range: Eurasia, n. N. America. Winters to n. Africa, s. U.S. **West:** Map 7. **Habitat:** Lakes, ponds; in winter, salt water.

LEAST GREBE *Tachybaptus dominicus*
9½″ (24 cm). A very small *slaty grebe,* smaller than the Pied-bill, with *white wing patches* (often concealed), puffy undertail coverts, a slender *black* pointed bill, *golden or red eyes.* In winter, throat white. **Range:** Ponds in tropical America. **West:** Resident, s. Texas; casual, se. California (has bred), s. Arizona.

WESTERN GREBE *Aechmophorus occidentalis*   **M9**
25″ (63 cm). A large, slate and white grebe with a *long, swanlike neck.* Bill long, *greenish yellow* with a *dark ridge.*
  Range: Western N. America. Winters to Mexico. **West:** Map 9. **Habitat:** Rushy lakes, sloughs; in winter, bays, ocean.

CLARK'S GREBE *Aechmophorus clarkii*
Formerly regarded as a pale morph of the Western Grebe. Intermediates are known. *White around eye; bill is orange-yellow.* Downy young are white, not gray. Voices are said to differ: Clark's, a one-note *creet* or *criik;* Western, two-noted *crik-crick.*
  Range: Imperfectly known; overlaps that of Western Grebe.

lobed foot of grebe

GREBES

juvenile

adult winter

breeding

downy young

PIED-BILLED GREBE

winter variant

winter

bill (Horned)

HORNED GREBE

breeding

winter variant

winter

breeding

bill (Eared)

EARED GREBE

imm.

winter

breeding

RED-NECKED GREBE

winter

breeding

LEAST GREBE

display

WESTERN GREBE

CLARK'S GREBE

27

■ **CORMORANTS. Family Phalacrocoracidae.** Shown in flight on p. 31. Large, blackish water birds that often stand erect on rocks or posts with the neck in an S; may strike a "spread-eagle" pose, with wings spread out to dry. Adults may have colorful face skin, throat pouch, and eyes. Bill slender, hook-tipped. Sexes alike. Cormorants swim low like loons, but with bill tilted up at an angle. Cormorants are silent except for occasional low grunts in nesting colonies. **Food:** Fish, crustaceans. **Range:** Nearly cosmopolitan. **No. of species:** World 29; West 5.

DOUBLE-CRESTED CORMORANT *Phalacrocorax auritus* **M16**
30–36" (75–90 cm). Any cormorant found well inland can be called this species except some birds near the Mexican border (see Olivaceous Cormorant). Coastally, it may be told from the others by its *orange-yellow* throat pouch. Crest seldom evident.
Range: Much of N. America, coast to coast. Winters south to Belize. **West:** Map 16. **Habitat:** Coasts, bays, lakes, rivers; nests colonially on sea cliffs, or in trees on lake margins.

OLIVACEOUS CORMORANT *Phalacrocorax olivaceus*
25" (63 cm). Similar to the Double-crest but smaller, slimmer, and *longer-tailed.* Note the duller (less orange) chin pouch and, in summer, the *narrow white border* outlining the throat pouch. At very close range, note that the feathers of the back and scapulars are pointed, not rounded. Also called Neotropic Cormorant.
Range: Gulf of Mexico to Argentina. **West:** Rare or local visitor in Mexican border states.

BRANDT'S CORMORANT *Phalacrocorax penicillatus* **M17**
33–35" (83–88 cm). Size of Double-crest, but with a dark throat pouch (*blue* when breeding). *Buffy brown band across throat* behind pouch. If a young cormorant has a whitish breast it is a Double-crest; if the breast is buffy or pale brown with a pale Y it is most likely a Brandt's. If deep rich brown below, it is a Pelagic.
Range: Pacific Coast of N. America. Map 17. **Habitat:** Ocean, coast, littoral; nests colonially on sea cliffs.

PELAGIC CORMORANT *Phalacrocorax pelagicus* **M18**
25½–30" (64–76 cm). Noticeably smaller and more iridescent than other coastal cormorants, with a more slender neck, small head, and much *thinner bill.* When breeding (Feb.–June) it has a double crest and a *white patch* on each flank. Throat pouch and part of face dull red (obvious only at close range). *Immature:* Deep brown all over, darkest on back. Note the thin bill.
Range: From Bering Sea to Japan and south along our West Coast. **West:** Map 18. **Habitat:** Coast, bays, sounds.

RED-FACED CORMORANT *Phalacrocorax urile*
28–30" (70–75 cm). Note the *bright red* of the adult's face (extending to forehead and behind eye). Throat pouch *bluish;* bill pale. Otherwise, similar to Pelagic Cormorant, which has a dull red pouch, restricted dull red on face; thinner bill. *Immature:* Differs from Pelagic in having a thicker pale bill.
Range: Alaska, ne. Asia. **West:** Resident in Pribilofs and Aleutians; east locally to Kodiak I., Prince William Sound.

CORMORANTS

Cormorants spread wings to dry.

imm.

adult

DOUBLE-CRESTED CORMORANT
adult breeding

OLIVACEOUS CORMORANT
adult breeding

Cormorants swim with bills uptilted.

imm.

adult

BRANDT'S CORMORANT
adult breeding

PELAGIC CORMORANT

imm.

pelagic adult

adult

imm.

RED-FACED CORMORANT

29

LOONS IN FLIGHT

Airborne, loons are slower than most ducks; their outline is hunch-backed, with a sagging look. The large webbed feet project rudder-like beyond the stubby tail.

Text and
color plate

COMMON LOON *Gavia immer* **pp. 24, 25**
More heavily built than the next two species. Look for the espe-cially large trailing feet and the stout straight bill. In winter plum-age note the *irregular* (half-collared) neck pattern.

RED-THROATED LOON *Gavia stellata* **pp. 24, 25**
Has a slimmer look than the other loons; paler, with a slim, up-turned bill. In winter there is *no strong demarcation* between the gray and white of the head and neck. May be sociable in winter.

PACIFIC LOON *Gavia pacifica* **pp. 24, 25**
Darker and more contrasty than Red-throated Loon; bill straight, not upturned. In winter plumage note the *well-defined, straight sep-aration* of the blackish and white on the neck. Pacific Loons often travel in sizable flocks in offshore waters.

CORMORANTS IN FLIGHT

Cormorants often fly in lines or wedges, somewhat in the manner of geese, but are silent.

Text and
color plate

DOUBLE-CRESTED CORMORANT **pp. 28, 29**
Phalacrocorax auritus
Note the *kink in the neck* and the *yellow or orange* gular (throat) pouch; tail longer than that of Brandt's Cormorant. Young birds tend to have lighter or whiter breasts than Brandt's Cormorant.

BRANDT'S CORMORANT *Phalacrocorax penicillatus* **pp. 28, 29**
Heavily built; no marked kink in the neck. Tail shorter than Double-crest's. Young birds are browner than young Double-crests. Throat pouch edged with buff. May have a pale Y on breast.

PELAGIC CORMORANT *Phalacrocorax pelagicus* **pp. 28, 29**
Note the slender neck (with no kink) and the *much thinner* bill. Tail longish. Breeding adults (Feb. to June) have a *white flank patch*. Immature birds are deep brown.

winter

LOONS IN FLIGHT

winter

COMMON LOON

breeding

RED-THROATED LOON

breeding

Loons in flight have a sagging, hunch-backed look, with the big feet projecting beyond the stubby tail.

winter

PACIFIC LOON

breeding

CORMORANTS IN FLIGHT

adult

adult

DOUBLE-CRESTED CORMORANT

imm.

imm.

adult breeding

BRANDT'S CORMORANT

imm.

PELAGIC CORMORANT

Cormorants have longer tails than loons and the feet do not project.

31

■ **AUKS, etc. Family Alcidae.** The northern counterparts of the penguins, but auks fly, beating their small narrow wings in a whir, often veering. They have short necks and pointed, stubby, or deep and laterally compressed bills. Auks swim and dive expertly. Most species nest on sea cliffs in crowded colonies. Sexes alike. **Food:** Fish, crustaceans, mollusks. **Range:** N. Atlantic, N. Pacific, Arctic oceans. **No. of species:** World 22; West 18 (+1 vagrant).

COMMON MURRE *Uria aalge*   M176
16–17" (40–43 cm). Size of a small duck, with a slender pointed bill. *Breeding:* Head, neck, back, and wings dark; underparts, wing linings, and line on rear edge of wing white. *Non-breeding:* Similar, but throat and cheeks white. A *black mark extends from eye onto cheek.* Murres often raft on water, fly in lines; stand erect on sea cliffs. Chicks at sea may be mistaken for Xantus' Murrelet.
Range: Northern parts of N. Pacific, N. Atlantic. **West:** Map 176. **Habitat:** Ocean, large bays; colonies on sea cliffs.

THICK-BILLED MURRE *Uria lomvia*   M177
17–19" (43–48 cm). Similar to Common Murre, but a bit larger and blacker above. Bill shorter, thicker, with a *whitish line along gape.* White of foreneck forms an inverted V. In winter, head darker than Common Murre's, black crown extending *well below eye;* no dark line through white ear coverts. White bill mark less evident.
Range: Cold oceans of N. Hemisphere. **West:** Map 177. **Habitat:** Ocean, nesting colonially on ledges of sea cliffs.

TUFTED PUFFIN *Fratercula cirrhata*   M183
15" (38 cm). A stocky, dark seabird with a massive bill. *Breeding:* Blackish, with a *large, triangular, orange-red* bill; white face; and *long, curved, ivory-yellow ear tufts.* Feet orange. *Winter adult:* White face and ear tufts gone (a gray trace); a blackish bird with an orange-red bill (not as triangular as in summer). *Immature:* Light grayish below; bill smaller; no red.
Range: N. Pacific (both sides). **West:** Map 183. **Habitat:** Oceanic; nests colonially in burrows on sea cliffs.

HORNED PUFFIN *Fratercula corniculata*   M184
14½" (36 cm). A puffin with *clear white underparts* and a broad black collar. Feet bright orange. *Summer:* Cheeks *white,* with a small, dark erectile horn above each eye. Bill massive, *triangular,* laterally flat; *yellow with a red tip. Winter:* Cheeks dusky; bill blackish with red tip. Young birds resemble winter adults with dusky cheeks, but the bill is smaller and all dark, lacking red.
Range: N. Pacific (both sides). **West:** Map 184. **Habitat:** Ocean, nesting colonially in burrows or crevices on sea cliffs.

RHINOCEROS AUKLET *Cerorhinca monocerata*   M182
14–15½" (35–39 cm). A dark stubby seabird. *Breeding plumage* (acquired in late winter): *White "mustaches,"* narrow *white plume* behind eye, *short erect horn* at base of yellowish bill. *Non-breeding:* Note the size and *uniform dark color.* The white plumes are shorter, the horn absent. Immature is similar, with smaller, darker bill.
Range: N. Pacific (both sides). **West:** Map 182. **Habitat:** Ocean, tide-rips; nests colonially in burrows on islands.

AUKS

COMMON
MURRE

Tufted
Puffin

Horned
Puffin

winter

winter

THICK-
BILLED
MURRE

imm.

winter

imm.

winter

TUFTED PUFFIN

imm.

winter

summer

HORNED
PUFFIN

summer

Common
Murre

summer

Thick-
billed
Murre

RHINOCEROS
AUKLET

Tufted
Puffin

Horned
Puffin

summer

TUFTED
PUFFIN

summer

HORNED
PUFFIN

summer

RHINOCEROS
AUKLET

summer

33

BLACK GUILLEMOT *Cepphus grylle*   **M178**
12–14″ (30–35 cm). Very similar to Pigeon Guillemot, which it
meets in n. Alaskan waters. White wing patch *(lacks the black bar)*.
Underwing linings *white* (dusky in Pigeon Guillemot). Winter and
juvenile birds are paler than Pigeon Guillemot.
Range: Arctic coasts and n. coasts of Atlantic. **West:** Map 178.

PIGEON GUILLEMOT *Cepphus columba*   **M178**
12–14″ (30–35 cm). *Breeding:* A small, black, pigeon-like water bird,
with large *white wing patches* (subdivided by a black bar or wedge),
red feet, a pointed black bill, and orange-red inside the open mouth.
Non-breeding: Pale with white underparts and blackish wings with
large white patches as in summer (mottled in juvenile).
Voice: A feeble, wheezy or hissing whistle, *peeeeee.*
Range: Bering Sea to Japan, s. California. **West:** Map 178. **Habitat:**
Rocky coasts, inshore waters; less pelagic than other auks. Breeds
in small groups or in solitary pairs among rocks.

CRESTED AUKLET *Aethia cristatella*
9½″ (24 cm). A droll auklet of the Bering Sea. Completely slate-gray,
darker on back; a thin white plume behind the eye. In summer,
develops a fleshy gape on its stubby *bright orange bill* and a curious
crest that *curls forward* over the bill. In winter, the orange gape on
the bill is lost and the crest is shorter.
Range: Bering Sea, ne. Asia, w. Alaska. **West:** Breeds in Bering Sea
south to Pribilofs; in Aleutians east to Shumagin and Semidi Is.
Winters in s. Bering Sea and Aleutians. Accidental, California. **Habitat:** Open sea; nests in colonies on sea cliffs.

WHISKERED AUKLET *Aethia pygmaea*
7″ (18 cm). Similar to the larger Crested Auklet, but in addition to
the curled black plume on the forehead this bird has three thin
white plumes on each side of the face. In winter the plumes are
shorter.
Range: Bering Sea. Resident in Komandorskiye Is., s. Kuriles; locally in cen. Aleutians. **Habitat:** Ocean, tide-rips, rocky coasts.

PARAKEET AUKLET *Cyclorrhynchus psittacula*
10″ (25 cm). A small auk with a *stubby, upturned red bill* and white
underparts. In summer the whole head is black, with a thin white
plume behind the eye. In winter the bill shows less red and the
throat is largely white.
Range: Breeds in ne. Siberia, islands in Bering Sea and Aleutians.
Winters from Bering Sea south to Japan and California, but rare
vagrant south of Alaska. **Habitat:** Ocean; nests in scattered pairs or
in colonies on sea cliffs.

ANCIENT MURRELET *Synthliboramphus antiquus*   **M180**
9½–10½″ (24–26 cm). *Breeding:* Note the sharply cut *black throat
patch* and *white stripe over eye.* Bill yellow. *Winter:* Similar to Marbled Murrelet (p. 37), but *without* white stripe on scapulars. *Back
paler, contrasting with black cap.* Throat may be dusky.
Range: Bering Sea and northern parts of N. Pacific (both coasts).
West: Map 180. **Habitat:** Open ocean, sounds, rarely salt bays.

AUKS

Black Guillemot

BLACK GUILLEMOT

Pigeon Guillemot

Pigeon G.

PIGEON GUILLEMOT

CRESTED AUKLET

WHISKERED AUKLET

PARAKEET AUKLET

ANCIENT MURRELET

35

MARBLED MURRELET *Brachyramphus marmoratus* **M179**
9½" (24 cm). *Breeding: Dark brown; heavily barred* on underparts.
The only alcid south of Alaska so colored (but from Glacier Bay
north, see Kittlitz's Murrelet). *Winter:* A small, chubby, neckless-
looking seabird, dark above and white below. May be known from
all similar small alcids (except Kittlitz's) by the *strip of white* between the back and wings.
Voice: A sharp *keer, keer* or a lower *kee.*
Range: Kamchatka to Japan, n. Alaska to California. **West:** Map 179.
Habitat: Coastal waters, bays. Breeds inland on mountains near
coast, mainly high on limbs of mossy conifers.

KITTLITZ'S MURRELET *Brachyramphus brevirostris*
9" (23 cm). In summer, *scaled below* (as in Marbled Murrelet) but
freckled with white above, giving a paler look. White outer tail
feathers. In winter (not likely to be seen) similar to Marbled
Murrelet, but *white on face surrounds eyes.*
Range: Summers locally along coast of Alaska from Pt. Barrow
south at least to Glacier Bay. Winters in nw. Pacific (Kamchatka to
Japan). **Habitat:** Ocean, glacier waters; nests presumably on barren
slopes above timberline in coastal mountains.

XANTUS' MURRELET *Synthliboramphus hypoleucus*
7½–10½" (19–26 cm). A small, black and white alcid, with a solid
black back and thin black bill. Suggests a miniature murre. Very
similar to Craveri's (next), but with white wing linings in flight.
The *hypoleucus* race (inset) of Baja California, a rare fall visitor to
California, has white around the eye.
Range: Breeds s. California (Anacapa and Santa Barbara Is.) to cen.
Baja. Some winter north to Monterey; casually to Washington.

CRAVERI'S MURRELET *Synthliboramphus craveri*
Very similar to Xantus' Murrelet, but with a *black half collar* on
breast and *dusky* (not white) underwing linings.
Range: Breeds on islands off Baja California; wanders north to Monterey Bay, California; casual, Oregon.

CASSIN'S AUKLET *Ptychoramphus aleuticus* **M181**
8½" (21 cm). A small, stubby seabird; all dark except for the white
belly; note the pale spot on lower mandible. In winter, all other
small alcids in its range show much more white.
Range: Map 181. **Habitat:** Ocean; colonizes sea islands.

LEAST AUKLET *Aethia pusilla*
6" (15 cm). The tiniest auk; chubby, neckless. Black above, white
below. In summer, a wide dark band across the upper breast. The
tiny size and very stubby bill separate it from other wintering alcids
of the Aleutians.
Range: Breeds in swarms on islands of Bering Sea south to Aleutians and Shumagins. Winters from Aleutians to n. Japan.

DOVEKIE *Alle alle*
7½–9" (19–23 cm). Small size and distinctive pattern (opposite)
identify this straggler from the Atlantic. **West:** Casual along Arctic
coast to n. Bering Sea, where it may breed.

MARBLED MURRELET

AUKS

KITTLITZ'S MURRELET

inset
above left,
hypoleucus
form

scrippsi
form

XANTUS' MURRELET

CRAVERI'S MURRELET

CASSIN'S AUKLET

LEAST AUKLET

DOVEKIE

37

■ **SWANS, GEESE, DUCKS. Family Anatidae.** Web-footed waterfowl; tribes discussed separately. **Range:** Worldwide. **No. of species:** World 157; West 41 (+9 casual or accidental).

■ **SWANS. Tribe Cygnini.** Huge, all-white swimmers; larger and longer-necked than geese. Young pale gray-brown. Sexes alike. Swans migrate in lines or V's. Feed by immersing head and neck, or by "tipping up." **Food:** Aquatic plants, seeds.

TUNDRA SWAN *Cygnus columbianus*   **M28**
(Whistling Swan). 53″ (133 cm); spread 6–7 ft. Our common native swan. Often heard long before the ribbonlike flock can be spotted. Bill *black*, usually with a *small yellow basal spot. Immature:* Dingy, with pinkish bill. Eurasian form ("Bewick's Swan"), casual or accidental from Alaska to California, has *much yellow on the bill* above the nostrils. **Voice:** A mellow, high-pitched cooing: *woo-ho, woo-woo, woo-ho.* **Range:** Breeds from arctic coast south to Alaska Peninsula and barren grounds of Canada. Winters to seaboards of e. and w. U.S. **West:** Map 28. **Habitat:** Tundra (summer), lakes, large rivers, bays, estuaries.

TRUMPETER SWAN *Cygnus buccinator*   **M29**
58½–72″ (147–180 cm). Larger than Tundra Swan, with a flatter head and a heavier, *all-black* bill. Black on lores wider, embracing the eyes and lacking the yellow basal spot (some Tundra Swans may also lack this spot). Trumpeters have *louder, deeper voices.*
Range: Nw. N. America. Map 29. **Habitat:** Lakes, ponds, large rivers; in winter, also bays.

SNOW GOOSE *Chen caerulescens* Tribe Anserini   **M31**
25–38″ (63–95 cm). *White* with *black primaries.* Head often rust-stained. Bill, feet pink. *Immature:* Pale gray; dark bill, dark legs.
Voice: A loud, nasal, double-noted *houck-houck,* in chorus.
Range: Ne. Siberia, arctic America. Winters to Japan, n. Mexico, Gulf Coast. **West:** Map 31. **Habitat:** Marshes, grain fields, ponds, bays; when breeding, tundra.

ROSS'S GOOSE *Chen rossii* Tribe Anserini   **M32**
23″ (58 cm). Like a miniature Snow Goose, but neck shorter, head rounder. Bill stubbier, dark and warty at base, *lacking the "grinning black lips."* Young bird whiter than young Snow. "Blue" morphs are known; hybrids with Snow Goose occur. **Voice:** No loud notes; sounds like "Cackling" Goose (p. 40), not like Snow Goose. **Range:** Arctic Canada; winters mainly in sw. U.S. Map 32.

WHOOPER SWAN *Cygnus cygnus*
56–70″ (140–175 cm). This Asian swan is a regular winter visitor to the Aleutians and rarely to the Pribilofs. Resembles Trumpeter Swan, but adult Whooper has extensive yellow base on its large bill. Compare with "Bewick's" race (Eurasian) of Tundra Swan.

MUTE SWAN *Cygnus olor*
60″ (150 cm). The graceful ornamental park swan often swims with an S-curve in the neck; wings often arched over back. The *black-knobbed orange bill* tilts downward. Dingy young have pinkish bills.
Range: Eurasia; introduced e. N. America, elsewhere. **West:** Kept locally in parks; escapes not yet established.

SWANS, GEESE

imm.

adult

adult

TUNDRA SWAN

TRUMPETER SWAN

rust-stained

juv.

adult

ROSS'S GOOSE

SNOW GOOSE adult

ROSS'S GOOSE

SNOW GOOSE

ROSS'S GOOSE

SNOW GOOSE

Asian Strays

WHOOPER SWAN

TUNDRA SWAN
("Bewick's" race)

MUTE SWAN
(an escape)

39

■ **GEESE. Tribe Anserini.** Large, gregarious waterfowl; heavier-bodied, longer-necked than ducks; bills thick at base. Noisy in flight; some fly in lines or V formations. Sexes alike. Geese are more terrestrial than ducks, often grazing (except Brant and Emperor Goose). **Food:** Grasses, seeds, aquatic plants; eelgrass (Brant); shellfish (Emperor Goose).

GREATER WHITE-FRONTED GOOSE *Anser albifrons* **M30**
30″ (75 cm). Gray-brown with a *pink* bill, *white patch on front of face,* and variable *black bars* on belly. The only other American goose with yellow or orange feet is the Emperor. *Immature:* Dusky with a pale bill, yellow or orange feet.
Voice: High-pitched tootling, *kah-lah-a-luk,* in chorus.
Range: Arctic; circumpolar. Winters to Mexico, Gulf states, n. Africa, India. **West:** Map 30. **Habitat:** Marshes, prairies, fields, lakes, bays; in summer, tundra.

EMPEROR GOOSE *Chen canagica* **M33**
26–28″ (65–70 cm). Alaskan. *Adult:* A small, blue-gray goose, *scaled* with black and white; identified by its *white head and hind-neck.* Throat *black* (not white as in "Blue" Goose, a stray). Golden legs.
Range: Ne. Siberia, w. Alaska. **West:** Map 33. **Habitat:** In summer, tundra; in winter, rocky shores, mudflats, seaweed.

BEAN GOOSE *Anser fabalis* See p. 62.
This Eurasian species is a vagrant in North America.

CANADA GOOSE *Branta canadensis* **M35**
25–43″ (63–108 cm). The most widespread goose. Note the black head and neck or "stocking" that contrasts with the pale breast, and the *white chin strap.* Flocks travel in strings or in V's, "honking" loudly. Great variation in size and neck length between populations, from short-necked, Mallard-size "Cackling" Geese, to long-necked, almost swan-size birds.
Voice: A deep, musical honking or barking, *ka-ronk* or *ka-lunk.*
Range: Alaska, Canada, n. U.S. Winters to n. Mexico. **West:** Map 35. **Habitat:** Lakes, ponds, bays, marshes, fields.

BRANT *Branta bernicla* **M34**
22–26″ (55–65 cm). A small, black-necked goose, near the size of a Mallard. Has a white stern, conspicuous when it up-ends, and a fleck of white on the neck (absent in immature). Travels in large irregular flocks. Whereas Canada Goose's breast shows light above water, foreparts of Brant are *entirely black.* Brant is more strictly coastal. The eastern race (also shown), rare on the Pacific side, has a *light belly.*
Voice: A throaty *cr-r-r-ruk* or *krr-onk, krrr-onk.*
Range: Coasts of n. Eurasia, N. America. **West:** Map 34. **Habitat:** Salt bays, estuaries; in summer, tundra.

SNOW GOOSE (dark morph— **"BLUE GOOSE"**) *Chen caerulescens*
25–30″ (63–75 cm). This dark morph of the Snow Goose (p. 38) with a *white head,* suggests the Emperor, but has a *white throat.* Intermediates with white form of Snow are frequent. *Immature:* Similar to young White-front, but feet and bill *dark.* Most "Blue Geese" migrate through the prairies; rare in Pacific states.

GEESE

GREATER WHITE-FRONTED GOOSE

imm.

adult

adult

EMPEROR GOOSE

juv.

adult

adult

BEAN GOOSE

"lesser" race

dusky race

typical

"cackling" race

CANADA GOOSE

juv.

variant

BRANT

light-bellied race

BRANT

SNOW GOOSE

gray phase ("Blue" Goose)

dark-bellied race

GEESE AND SWANS IN FLIGHT

Many **geese** and **swans** fly in line or wedge formation.

Text and
color plate

CANADA GOOSE *Branta canadensis* **pp. 40, 41**
Light chest, black neck "stocking," white chin strap. Size and neck length vary greatly between populations.

BRANT *Branta bernicla* **pp. 40, 41**
Small; black underparts, black head and neck, white stern.

GREATER WHITE-FRONTED GOOSE *Anser albifrons* **pp. 40, 41**
Adult: Gray neck, black splotches on belly.
Immature: Dusky, light bill, light feet.

EMPEROR GOOSE *Chen canagica* **pp. 40, 41**
Gray with white head, black throat.

TUNDRA SWAN *Cygnus columbianus* **pp. 38, 39**
Very long neck; plumage entirely white.

SNOW GOOSE *Chen caerulescens* **pp. 38, 39**
Adult: White with black primaries.

ROSS'S GOOSE *Chen rossii* **pp. 38, 39**
Smaller, shorter-necked than Snow Goose.

■ **WHISTLING-DUCKS. Tribe Dendrocygnini.** Shown on p. 45.
Formerly called "Tree-Ducks," these rather goose-like ducks with their long legs and erect necks are indeed more closely related to the geese (same subfamily) than they are to the other ducks, which taxonomists place in a different subfamily.

FULVOUS WHISTLING-DUCK *Dendrocygna bicolor*
20" (50 cm). Long-legged, goose-like. Note the *tawny* body, dark back, *pale side stripe.* Flies with neck slightly drooped and feet trailing, showing *black* underwings, *white* ring on rump. See also p. 69.
Voice: A squealing slurred whistle, *ka-whee-oo.*
Range: Southern U.S. to Argentina; also s. Asia, subsaharan Africa.
West: Breeds s. California (Imperial Valley); wanderers may turn up rarely elsewhere in w. U.S. **Habitat:** Fresh marshes, irrigated land. Seldom perches in trees.

BLACK-BELLIED WHISTLING-DUCK *Dendrocygna autumnalis*
21" (53 cm). A goose-like duck with long pink legs. Rusty with *black belly,* bright *coral-red* bill. Very broad *white patch* along forewing. Immature has gray bill and legs. Thrusts head and feet down when landing. Frequently perches in trees.
Range: S. Texas to n. Argentina. **West:** Resident, se. Arizona (breeds); casual, se. California, s. New Mexico, Colorado, w. Texas. **Habitat:** Ponds, fresh marshes.

GEESE, SWANS

CANADA GOOSE

BRANT

below

above

imm.

GREATER
WHITE-
FRONTED
GOOSE

adult

EMPEROR
GOOSE

below

above

TUNDRA
SWAN

SNOW
GOOSE

ROSS'S
GOOSE

43

■ **WHISTLING-DUCKS. Tribe Dendrocygnini.** Text on p. 42.

FULVOUS WHISTLING-DUCK
BLACK-BELLIED WHISTLING-DUCK

■ **MARSH OR DABBLING DUCKS. Tribe Anatini.** Surface-feeders of wetlands. Feed by dabbling and upending; sometimes feed on land. Take flight directly into the air. Most species have an iridescent speculum on the rear edge of the wing. Sexes not alike; in late summer, males molt into drab "eclipse" plumage. **Food:** Aquatic plants, seeds, grass, small aquatic life, insects.

"MEXICAN DUCK"
(Mallard, in part) 20–22″ (50–55 cm). This race of the Mallard was formerly regarded as a distinct species. Hybrids are frequent. Both sexes are very similar to the female Mallard but with a *grayish brown* instead of whitish tail. Bill of male like bill of male Mallard (unmarked yellowish green). Yellow-orange bill of female has a dark ridge. Not as dark overall as Black Duck; has a white border *on both sides* of metallic wing patch, as in female Mallard.
Range: Rare summer resident from n. New Mexico south in Rio Grande Valley to w. Texas; very local from sw. New Mexico to cen. Mexico. Accidental, Colorado, Nebraska.

AMERICAN BLACK DUCK *Anas rubripes* See also p. 68.
21–25″ (53–63 cm). A dusky duck, much darker than female Mallard. In flight, shows flashing *white wing linings.* Sooty brown, with a paler head and violet wing patch; feet red or brown. Sexes similar, except for bills (yellow in male, dull green in female).
Range: Ne. N. America. Winters to Gulf Coast. **West:** Breeds in Saskatchewan. Straggler west of 100°, but recorded from most western states.

GADWALL *Anas strepera* See also p. 66.   **M43**
19–23″ (48–58 cm). *Male:* Gray with a *black rump, white speculum* on the rear edge of wing, and a dull ruddy patch on the forewing. When swimming, wing patches may be concealed; then note the *black stern.* Belly white, feet yellow, bill dark. *Female:* Brown, mottled, with a *white speculum,* yellow feet, yellow on bill.
Voice: Male has a low *bek;* a whistling call. Female quacks.
Range: Northern N. America, n. Eurasia. Winters to Mexico, Africa, India. **West:** Map 43. **Habitat:** Lakes, ponds, marshes.

MALLARD *Anas platyrhynchos* See also p. 68.   **M38**
20–28″ (50–70 cm). *Male:* Note the uncrested *glossy green head* and *white neck-ring;* chestnut chest, white tail, yellowish bill, orange feet, blue speculum. *Female:* Mottled brown with a *whitish tail.* Bill patched with orange, feet orange. In flight, shows a white bar *on both sides* of the speculum.
Voice: Male, *yeeb;* a low *kwek.* Female, boisterous quacking.
Range: Northern parts of N. Hemisphere. Winters to Mexico, n. Africa, India. **West:** Map 38. **Habitat:** Marshes, wooded swamps, grain fields, ponds, rivers, lakes, bays, city parks.

Fulvous
Whistling-
Duck

Black-
bellied
Whistling-
Duck

**FULVOUS
WH.-DUCK**

**BLACK-
BELLIED
WH.-DUCK**

"MEXICAN
DUCK"

♂

♀

AMERICAN BLACK DUCK

marsh ducks
tip up

♀

♂

GADWALL

marsh ducks
spring directly
from the water

♀

♂

MALLARD

45

NORTHERN PINTAIL *Anas acuta* See also p. 66. **M39**
Male 28″ (70 cm); female 21″ (53 cm). *Male:* Slender, slim-necked,
white-breasted, with a long, *needle-pointed tail.* A conspicuous
white point runs onto the side of the dark head. *Female:* Mottled
brown; note the rather pointed tail, slender neck, gray bill. In flight
both sexes show a *single light border* on the rear edge of the brown
speculum.
Voice: Male, a double-toned whistle: *prrip, prrip;* wheezy notes. Female, a low *quack.*
Range: Northern parts of N. Hemisphere. Winters to n. S. America,
Africa, India. **West:** Map 39. **Habitat:** Marshes, prairies, ponds, lakes,
salt bays.

AMERICAN WIGEON *Anas americana* See also p. 66. **M44**
18–23″ (45–58 cm). In flight, recognized by the *large white patch
on the forewing.* (Similarly placed blue patches of Shoveler and
Blue-winged Teal may often appear whitish). When swimming, it
rides high, picking at water like a Coot. Often grazes on land. *Male:*
Brownish; head gray with a deep green patch. Note the *shining
white crown* (nicknamed "Baldpate"). *Female:* Brown; gray head and
neck; belly and forewing whitish.
Similar species: Female easily confused with females of Gadwall
and Pintail; note whitish patch on forewing, blue bill.
Voice: Male, a whistled *whee whee whew.* Female, *qua-ack.*
Range: Alaska, w. Canada, n. U.S. Winters to n. S. America, W.
Indies. **West:** Map 44. **Habitat:** Marshes, lakes, bays, fields.

EURASIAN WIGEON *Anas penelope*
18–20″ (45–50 cm). *Male:* Note the *red-brown* head, *buff* crown. A
gray wigeon with a vinaceous breast. *Female:* Very similar to female
American Wigeon, but in some females the head is tinged with *rust;*
in others it is not. The surest point when this duck is held in the
hand is the dusky (not white) axillars, or "wingpits."
Range: Breeds in n. Eurasia. Winters to s. Eurasia, n. Africa. **West:**
Common transient in Aleutians. Most often recorded among flocks
of American Wigeon from Alaska to California; less often in interior
states.

WOOD DUCK *Aix sponsa* Tribe Cairinini See also p. 66. **M36**
17–20½″ (43–51 cm). Highly colored; often perches in trees. In
flight, the white belly contrasts with the dark breast and wings.
Note also the long, square, dark tail; the short neck; and the angle
at which the bill points downward. *Male:* The bizarre face pattern,
swept-back crest, and rainbow iridescence are unique. *Female:* Dull-
colored; note the dark crested head and *white eye patch.*
Voice: Male, a loud, distressed *whoo-eek;* also a finch-like *jeee,*
with rising inflection. Female, *crrek, crrek.*
Range: S. Canada, nw. and e. U.S., Cuba. Winters to Mexico, Cuba.
West: Map 36. **Habitat:** Wooded swamps, rivers, ponds.

MARSH DUCKS
(Dabblers)

♀

♂

NORTHERN PINTAIL

♂ ♀

AMERICAN WIGEON

♂ ♀

EURASIAN WIGEON

♀

♂ in eclipse
(autumn)

♂

WOOD DUCK

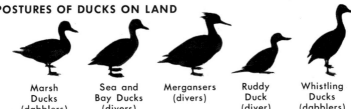

POSTURES OF DUCKS ON LAND

| Marsh Ducks (dabblers) | Sea and Bay Ducks (divers) | Mergansers (divers) | Ruddy Duck (diver) | Whistling Ducks (dabblers) |

47

NORTHERN SHOVELER *Anas clypeata* See also p. 66. **M42**
17–20″ (43–50 cm). The long, *spoon-shaped bill* gives this small duck a front-heavy look. When swimming, it sits low, with the bill angled toward the water. *Male:* Belly and sides *rufous;* pale blue patch on forewing, orange feet. *Female:* Note the big bill, blue wing patch, orange feet. Bill color variable.
Range: N. Hemisphere. Winters to n. S. America, s. Eurasia, e. Africa. **West:** Map 42. **Habitat:** Marshes, ponds; in winter, also salt bays.

BLUE-WINGED TEAL *Anas discors* See also p. 66. **M40**
15–16″ (38–40 cm). A half-sized marsh duck. *Male:* Note the *white facial crescent* and large, *chalky blue* patch on the *forewing.* Molting males hold eclipse plumage late in the year, may resemble females. *Female:* Brown, mottled; blue on the forewing.
Range: Canada to s. U.S. Winters to Argentina. **West:** Map 40. **Habitat:** Fresh ponds, marshes.

GREEN-WINGED TEAL *Anas crecca* See also p. 66. **M37**
14″ (35 cm). Teal are small, fly in tight flocks. Green-wings lack light wing patches (speculum *deep green*). *Male:* Small, compact, gray with a brown head (a green head patch shows in sunlight). When swimming, note the *vertical white mark* near the shoulder. *Female:* A small speckled duck with a *green* speculum.
Similar species: Blue-winged Teal has light blue wing patches. In flight, males show dark bellies; Green-wings, white bellies. Females of Blue-wing and Cinnamon Teal are larger, longer-billed.
Range: Northern parts of N. America. Winters to Cen. America, W. Indies. **West:** Map 37. **Habitat:** Marshes, rivers, bays.

GREEN-WINGED TEAL (Aleutian race) *Anas crecca* (in part)
Male: Longitudinal (not vertical) white stripe above wing. Resident in Aleutians from Akutan westward. Casual, Pribilofs. This or similar Eurasian race is accidental elsewhere in w. U.S.

CINNAMON TEAL *Anas cyanoptera* **M41**
15–17″ (38–43 cm). *Male:* A small, *dark chestnut* duck with a large, chalky blue patch on the fore edge of the wing. In flight, resembles Blue-winged Teal. *Female:* Very similar to female Blue-wing, but tawnier; bill a wee bit longer, line through eye less distinct.
Range: Sw. Canada, w. U.S., Mexico; S. America. **West:** Map 41. **Habitat:** Marshes, fresh ponds.

■ ALASKAN STRAYS FROM ASIA. (See also heads on p. 63.)
GARGANEY *Anas querquedula*
15½″ (39 cm). *Male:* Broad white eyebrow stripe. *Female:* Paler than female Blue-wing, less blue on wing. Rare visitor to Aleutians; accidental vagrant elsewhere in N. America.

BAIKAL TEAL *Anas formosa*
17″ (43 cm). *Male:* Creamy cheek with circular pattern. *Female:* White spot near bill; broken supercilium (eyebrow stripe). Rare vagrant to Attu, Pribilofs, w. Alaska.

FALCATED TEAL *Anas falcata*
19″ (48 cm). *Male:* Large crested head, banded white throat. Note the high-rumped look. Both sexes have a dark speculum bordered with white. Rare stray to w. Aleutians, Pribilofs.

MARSH DUCKS

NORTHERN SHOVELER ♂ ♀

BLUE-WINGED TEAL ♂ ♀

GREEN-WINGED TEAL
American race ♂ ♀

GREEN-WINGED TEAL
Eurasian race ♂

CINNAMON TEAL ♂ ♀

RARE TEAL FROM ASIA

GARGANEY ♂ ♀

BAIKAL TEAL ♂ ♀

FALCATED TEAL ♂ ♀

49

■ **SCOTERS. Tribe Mergini** (in part). Scoters are the heavy, blackish ducks seen in large flocks along the coast. They are usually in companies of their own kind, but occasionally mix, so look them over carefully. The scoters, eiders, and their allies are collectively called "sea ducks," but some may also be found at times on bays and inland waters. All dive; dabbling ducks rarely do. In taking wing, scoters patter while getting under way. Sexes not alike. Scoters are usually silent, but during mating may utter low whistles, croaks, or grunting noises. **Food:** Mainly mollusks, crustaceans.

WHITE-WINGED SCOTER *Melanitta fusca* See also p. 70. **M58**
21″ (53 cm). The White-wing, the largest of the three scoters, usually flies in lines or stringy formations. On the water, the white wing patch is often concealed (wait for the bird to flap or fly). *Male:* Black, with a tick of white near the eye; bill orange with a black basal knob. *Female:* Sooty, with a white wing patch and two light patches on the face (sometimes obscure; more pronounced on young birds).
Range: N. Eurasia, Alaska, w. Canada; winters to w. Europe, Japan, s. U.S. (both coasts). **West:** Map 58. **Habitat:** Salt bays, ocean; in summer, lakes.

SURF SCOTER *Melanitta perspicillata* See also p. 70. **M57**
19″ (48 cm). The "Skunk-duck." *Male:* Black, with one or two *white patches* on crown and nape. Bill patterned with orange, black, and white. *Female:* Dusky brown, with two light spots on side of head (sometimes obscure; more evident on young birds).
Similar species: Female White-wing has a similar head pattern, but note the wing patch (may not show until bird flaps).
Range: Alaska, n. Canada. Winters to s. U.S. (both coasts), Gulf of Mexico, Baja California. **West:** Map 57. **Habitat:** Ocean surf, salt bays, marinas; in summer, fresh arctic lakes, tundra.

BLACK SCOTER *Melanitta nigra* See also p. 70. **M56**
(Common Scoter) 18½″ (46 cm). *Male:* A sea duck with entirely black plumage. The bright *orange-yellow knob* on the bill ("butternose") is diagnostic. In flight, the underwing shows a two-toned effect (silvery gray and black), more pronounced than in the other two scoters. *Female:* Sooty; the *light cheeks* contrasting with the *dark cap.*
Similar species: (1) Coot is blackish, but has a white bill, white patch under the tail. Gunners often call scoters "coots." (2) Some young male Surf Scoters may lack head patches and thus appear all-black, but look for a round black area at the base of the bill. (3) Female and immature scoters of the other two species have light spots on side of head. (4) Female Black Scoter may suggest winter Ruddy Duck (p. 59).
Range: Alaska, ne. Canada, Iceland, n. Eurasia. Winters to s. U.S., Mediterranean, Japan. **West:** Map 56. **Habitat:** Seacoasts; in summer, coastal tundra.

Scoters fly in
line or V formation

Surf

White-winged

Black

imm.

♂

♀

imm.

WHITE-WINGED SCOTER

♂

♀

imm.

SURF SCOTER

♂

♀

1st winter

♂

BLACK SCOTER

Diving ducks (sea ducks and bay ducks)
raft on water, skitter when taking wing.

■ **EIDERS. Tribe Mergini** (in part). Eiders, like the scoters, are "sea ducks," seldom seen ashore except in summer when breeding. They usually mass in flocks off shoals and rocky coasts and often fly in stringy formations. In flight males show white shoulders.

KING EIDER *Somateria spectabilis* See also pp. 70, 71.   **M51**
21–24" (53–60 cm). *Male:* A stocky sea duck; on the water the foreparts appear white, the rear parts black. Note the protruding *orange bill shield*. In flight, the wings show large white patches. *Female:* Stocky; warm brown, heavily barred. Note the facial profile as shown. *Immature male:* Dusky, with a light breast, dark brown head; may have a pinkish bill.
Similar species: (1) Male Common Eider has a *white* back. (2) Female Common has flatter profile, longer lobe before eye.
Voice: The courting male utters a low crooning phrase; the female makes grunting croaks.
Range: Arctic regions of N. Hemisphere. **West:** Map 51. **Habitat:** Rocky coasts, ocean.

COMMON EIDER *Somateria mollissima* See also pp. 70, 71.   **M50**
23–27" (58–68 cm). These bulky, thick-necked ducks are oceanic, living in flocks about shoals. Flight sluggish and low; flocks usually in a line. *Male:* This and the Spectacled Eider are the only ducks in our area with *black bellies and white backs*. Forewing white; head white, with a black crown, greenish nape. *Female:* Large, brown, *closely barred*; long flat profile. *Immature male:* At first grayish brown; later dusky with a white collar; may develop chocolate head or breast; white areas come in irregularly.
Similar species: (1) Male King Eider has a largely *black* back; female has a different facial profile than other female eiders, as shown. (2) Female scoters are duskier, lack the heavy black barring of the female eiders.
Voice: Male, a moaning *ow-ooo-urr.* Female, a grating *kor-r-r.*
Range: Northern parts of N. Hemisphere. **West:** Map 50. **Habitat:** Rocky coasts, shoals; in summer, also islands, tundra.

SPECTACLED EIDER *Somateria fischeri*   **M52**
20½–22½" (51–57 cm). Note the white "spectacles." *Male:* Grotesque; black below, white above, suggesting a male Common Eider, but head largely pale green, with large *white "goggles"* narrowly trimmed with black. *Female:* Brown and barred like the other female eiders, but with a pale *ghost image of the goggles.* The feathering at the base of the bill extends over the nostril.
Range: Ne. Siberia, n. Alaska. **West:** Map 52. Breeds on Arctic coasts of nw. Alaska from Pt. Barrow south to Yukon–Kuskoquim Delta. Probably winters mainly at the edge of the pack ice in the Bering Sea, but to be looked for off the Pribilofs and Aleutians at that season. Casual or accidental elsewhere along Alaskan coast and in British Columbia.

SEA DUCKS (EIDERS)
(Divers)

♀ ♂ imm. ♂

KING EIDER

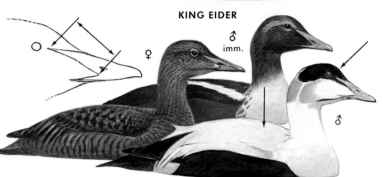

♀ ♂ imm. ♂

COMMON EIDER

♀ ♂ in eclipse ♂

SPECTACLED EIDER

Common Eider King Eider Spectacled Eider

53

■ MORE SEA DUCKS. Tribe Mergini.

STELLER'S EIDER *Polysticta stelleri*   **M53**
   17–18½" (43–47 cm). *Male:* Black and white, with *yellow-buff un-derparts; white head,* black throat, and green bump on the back of the head. Note the *round black spot* on the side of the breast. As in other eiders, the white forewing is conspicuous in flight. *Female:* Dark brown, mottled; distinguished from the other eiders by its much smaller size and the *shape of its small head and bill.* The white wing bar and purple speculum, visible at short range, suggest a female Mallard.
   Voice: Male's crooning note resembles Common Eider's, but is quieter. Female has a low growl.
   Range: Coasts of arctic Siberia, n. Alaska. **West:** Map 53. Breeds from arctic coast of Alaska south to the Yukon–Kuskokwim Delta. Winters in Pribilofs and Aleutians; east to Kodiak Island and base of the Alaskan Peninsula. Casual, British Columbia; accidental, California. **Habitat:** Coasts, ocean.

HARLEQUIN DUCK *Histrionicus histrionicus* See also p. 70.   **M54**
   18" (45 cm). Dark and bizarre. *Male:* A smallish, slaty duck with chestnut sides and odd white patches and spots. In flight, it has the stubby shape of a Goldeneye, but appears uniformly dark. *Female:* A small dusky duck with three round white spots on the side of the head; no wing patch.
   Similar species: (1) Female Bufflehead has a white wing patch and only one face spot. (2) Female scoters are larger, with larger bills.
   Voice: Male, a squeak; also *gwa gwa gwa.* Female, *ek-ek-ek-ek.*
   Range: Ne. Asia, Alaska, Canada, w. U.S., Greenland, Iceland. **West:** Map 54. **Habitat:** Turbulent mountain streams in summer; rocky coastal waters in winter.

OLDSQUAW *Clangula hyemalis* See also p. 70.   **M55**
   Male 21" (53 cm); female 16" (40 cm). This is the only sea duck combining much *white on the body and unpatterned dark wings.* It flies in bunched, irregular flocks. *Male, winter:* Note the needle-like tail, pied pattern, dark cheek; *summer:* dark, with white flanks and belly. Note the white eye patch. *Female, winter:* Dark unpat-terned wings, white face with dark cheek spot; *summer:* similar, but darker. Immatures lack the long tail feathers.
   Voice: Talkative; a musical *ow-owdle-ow,* or *owl-omelet.*
   Range: Arctic, circumpolar. Winters to s. U.S., cen. Europe, cen. Asia. **West:** Map 55. **Habitat:** Ocean, large lakes; in summer, tundra pools and lakes.

SEA DUCKS
(Divers)

♂ in eclipse

♀

♂

STELLER'S EIDER

♂

♀

HARLEQUIN DUCK

♀ summer

♀ winter

OLDSQUAW

♂ winter

♂ summer

■ **BAY DUCKS. Tribe Aythyini.** Scaups and Allies.

CANVASBACK *Aythya valisineria* See also pp. 72, 73. **M45**
20–24" (50–60 cm). *Male:* Very white-looking, with a *chestnut red* head sloping into the *long blackish* bill. Red eye, rufous neck, black chest. *Female:* Grayish, with a brown chest; pale rust on head and neck. Both sexes have the *long, sloping profile.* Flocks travel in lines or V formations.
Voice: Male, in courtship, cooing notes. Female, *quacks,* etc.
Range: Alaska, w. Canada, nw. U.S. Winters to Mexico, Atlantic and Gulf coasts. **West:** Map 45. **Habitat:** Lakes, salt bays, estuaries; in summer, fresh marshes.

REDHEAD *Aythya americana* See also pp. 72, 73. **M46**
18–23" (45–58 cm). *Male:* Gray; black chest and *round rufous head;* bill bluish with a black tip. *Female:* Brown; *suffused light patch* near bill. Both sexes have a *gray* wing stripe.
Similar species: Male Canvasback is much whiter, with a sloping forehead and black bill. See female Ring-necked Duck.
Voice: Male, a harsh catlike *meow;* a deep purr. Female, *quacks.*
Range: W. Canada, w. and n.-cen. U.S. Winters to Mexico, W. Indies. **West:** Map 46. **Habitat:** Lakes, saltwater bays, estuaries; in summer, fresh marshes.

RING-NECKED DUCK *Aythya collaris* See also pp. 72, 73. **M47**
15–18" (38–45 cm). *Male:* Like a scaup with a *black back.* Note the *vertical white mark* before the wing; bill crossed by a white ring. In flight, a broad *gray* (not white) wing stripe. *Female:* Shaped somewhat like female Lesser Scaup, but with an *indistinct* light face patch, dark eye, *white eye-ring,* and *ring on bill.* Wing stripe is *gray.*
Range: Canada, n. U.S. Winters to Panama. **West:** Map 47. **Habitat:** Wooded lakes, ponds, in winter, also rivers, bays.

TUFTED DUCK, *A. fuligula,* is a stray from Asia. See pp. 62, 63.

GREATER SCAUP *Aythya marila* See also pp. 72, 73. **M48**
16–20" (40–50 cm). Very similar to Lesser Scaup, but male is whiter; head rounder, less domed, glossed mainly with *dull green* rather than *dull purple.* Black tip on bill larger (apparent only at close range). Greater's *white wing stripe is longer,* extending onto primaries. **Range:** Alaska, Canada, n. Eurasia. Winters to California, se. U.S., Mediterranean, China. **West:** Map 48. **Habitat:** Lakes, rivers, salt bays, estuaries; in summer, tundra ponds.

LESSER SCAUP *Aythya affinis* See also pp. 72, 73. **M49**
15–18" (38–45 cm). Scaups (both species) have a broad white stripe on the trailing edge of wing; it is shorter in the Lesser. *Male:* On water, black at both ends, whitish in the middle. Bill *blue;* both glossed with *dull purple.* Flanks and back finely barred. *Female:* Dark brown, with a clean-cut white mask near bill. May also have a pale crescent on ear coverts. See Greater Scaup.
Voice: A loud *scaup;* also purring notes. Male, a low whistle.
Range: Alaska, w. Canada, nw. U.S. Winters to n. S. America. **West:** Map 49. **Habitat:** Lakes, bays, estuaries; in summer, marsh ponds.

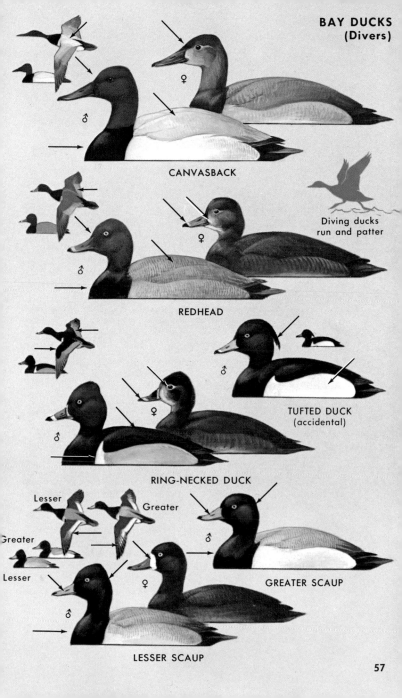

CANVASBACK

♂ ♀

Diving ducks
run and patter

REDHEAD

♂ ♀

♂

TUFTED DUCK
(accidental)

RING-NECKED DUCK

♂ ♀

Lesser

Greater

Greater

Lesser

♂ ♀

GREATER SCAUP

♂

LESSER SCAUP

57

COMMON GOLDENEYE *Bucephala clangula* See also p. 72. **M59**
20″ (50 cm). *Male:* Note the large *round white spot* before the eye.
White-looking, with a black back and puffy, green-glossed head that
appears black at a distance. In flight, short-necked; wings whistle
or "sing," show large white patches. *Female:* Gray, with a white
collar and dark brown head; wings with large square white patches
that may show on the closed wing.
Similar species: See (1) Barrow's Goldeneye; (2) male scaups have
black chests; (3) male Common Merganser is long, low.
Voice: Wings "whistle" in flight. Courting male has a harsh nasal
double note, suggesting *pee-ik* of Nighthawk. Female, a *quack.*
Range: Northern parts of N. Hemisphere. Winters to Gulf Coast,
cen. Eurasia. **West:** Map 59. **Habitat:** Forested lakes, rivers; in winter,
also salt bays, seacoasts.

BARROW'S GOLDENEYE *Bucephala islandica* **M60**
21″ (53 cm). *Male:* Note the *white face crescent.* Similar to Common Goldeneye, but blacker above; head glossed with *purple* (not
green); nape more puffy. *Female:* Similar to female Goldeneye;
darker, bill shorter and more triangular, forehead more abrupt; less
white in wing. In spring the bill may become all *yellow,* often a
good field mark but subject to seasonal change. (Female Common
Goldeneye may rarely have an all-yellow bill.)
Range: Alaska, Canada, nw. U.S., sw. Greenland, Iceland. **West:** Map
60. **Habitat:** Wooded lakes, beaver ponds. In winter, coastal waters;
a few on inland rivers.

BUFFLEHEAD *Bucephala albeola* See also pp. 72, 73. **M61**
13–15″ (33–38 cm). Small. *Male:* Mostly white, with a black back;
puffy head with a *large, bonnetlike white patch.* In flight, shows a
large white wing patch. *Female:* Dark and compact, with a *white
cheek spot,* small bill, smaller wing patch.
Similar species: (1) Male Hooded Merganser has a spikelike bill,
dark sides. (2) See winter Ruddy Duck (below).
Voice: Male, a hoarse rolling note; female, a harsh *quack.*
Range: Alaska, Canada. Winters to Mexico, Gulf Coast. **West:** Map
61. **Habitat:** Lakes, ponds, rivers; in winter, salt bays.

■ **STIFF-TAILED DUCKS. Tribe Oxyurini.** Small, chunky divers;
nearly helpless on land. Spiky tail has 18 or 20 feathers. Sexes not
alike. **Food:** Aquatic life, water plants.

RUDDY DUCK *Oxyura jamaicensis* See also pp. 72, 73. **M65**
15–16″ (38–40 cm). Small, chubby; note the *white cheek* and dark
cap. Often cocks tail vertically. Flight "buzzy." Cannot walk on
land. *Male, summer:* Rusty red with white cheek, black cap, large
blue bill. *Male, winter:* Gray with *white cheek,* dull blue or gray
bill. *Female:* Similar to winter male but cheek crossed by a dark
line.
Voice: Courting male, a sputtering *chick-ik-ik-ik-k-k-kurrrr.*
Range: Canada south, locally to Grenada and Chile. **West:** Map 65.
Habitat: Fresh marshes, ponds, lakes; in winter, salt bays.

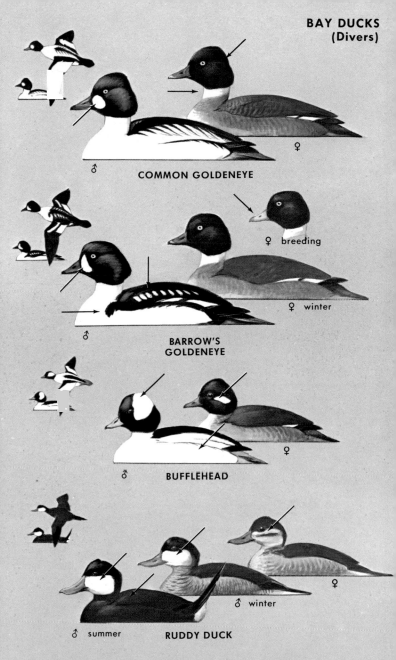

BAY DUCKS
(Divers)

♂

♀

COMMON GOLDENEYE

♀ breeding

♀ winter

♂

BARROW'S GOLDENEYE

♂

♀

BUFFLEHEAD

♀

♂ winter

♂ summer

RUDDY DUCK

■ **MERGANSERS. Tribe Mergini** (in part). Diving fish ducks with spikelike bills, saw-edged mandibles. Most species have crests and are long-lined, slender-bodied. In flight, the bill, head, neck, and body are held on a horizontal axis. Sexes not alike. **Food:** Chiefly small fish.

COMMON MERGANSER *Mergus merganser* See also p. 68.   **M63**
22–27" (55–68 cm). *Male:* Note the long whitish body, black back, green-black head. Feet and spikelike bill red; breast tinged delicate peach. *Female:* Gray, with a crested rufous head, clean white chest, and a large square white wing patch. Bill and feet red. (See female Red-breasted Merganser.) In flight, lines of these slender ducks follow the winding courses of streams. The whiteness of the males and the merganser shape (bill, neck, head, and body held horizontally) identify this species.
Similar species: (1) Female mergansers (rusty-headed) suggest male Canvasbacks or Redheads, which have black chests and no crests. (2) Male Goldeneye has a white face spot, is stockier, shorter-necked, and puffy-headed.
Voice: Male, low staccato croaks; female, a guttural *karrr.*
Range: Northern parts of N. Hemisphere. Winters to Mexico, Turkey, s. China. **West:** Map 63. **Habitat:** Wooded lakes, ponds, rivers; in winter, open lakes and rivers, rarely coastal bays.

RED-BREASTED MERGANSER *Mergus serrator* See also p. 68.   **M64**
20–26" (50–65 cm). *Male:* Rakish; black head glossed with green and *conspicuously crested;* breast at waterline dark rusty, separated from the head by a *wide white* collar; bill and feet red. *Female:* Gray, with a crested rusty head, large white wing patch, red bill and feet.
Similar species: Male Common Merganser is whiter, without collar and breastband effect; lacks crest. In female Common, white chin and chest are *sharply defined.* In Red-breast, rufous of head is paler, *blending* into whitish chin and neck; bill is less thick at base.
Voice: Usually silent. Male, a hoarse croak; female, *karrr.*
Range: Northern parts of N. Hemisphere. Winters to Gulfs of Mexico and California; Mexico, n. Africa, s. China. **West:** Map 64. **Habitat:** Lakes, open water; in winter, coastal bays, sea.

HOODED MERGANSER *Lophodytes cucullatus* See also p. 68.   **M62**
16–19" (40–48 cm). *Male:* Note the vertical *fan-shaped white crest,* which may be raised or lowered. Breast white, with two black bars on each side. Wing with a white patch; *flanks brown.* *Female:* Recognized as a merganser by its silhouette and spikelike bill; known as this species by its small size, dusky look, and *dark head, bill, and chest.* Note the loose *tawny crest.*
Similar species: (1) Male Bufflehead is chubbier, with *white* sides. (2) Other female mergansers are larger and *grayer,* with rufous heads, red bills. (3) In flight, the wing patch and silhouette separate female Hooded Merganser from female Wood Duck.
Voice: Low grunting or croaking notes.
Range: Se. Alaska, s. Canada, ne. U.S. Winters to n. Mexico, Gulf of Mexico. **West:** Map 62. **Habitat:** Wooded lakes, ponds, rivers.

Mergansers fly with bill, head, body, and tail on the same horizontal axis

MERGANSERS
(Divers)

saw-edged mandibles of merganser

♂ ♀

COMMON MERGANSER

♂ ♀

RED-BREASTED MERGANSER

♂ crest up ♂ crest down ♀ imm. ♂

HOODED MERGANSER

Common   Red-breasted   Hooded

■ MISCELLANEOUS WATERFOWL (STRAYS FROM ASIA).

COMMON POCHARD *Aythya ferina*
18″ (45 cm). This Eurasian species looks somewhat intermediate between the Redhead and the Canvasback. Head not as rounded as Redhead's; back paler. The clinching mark in both sexes is the broad *blue band* across the bill, set off by a *black band* at the base of the bill (absent in Redhead).
Range: Eurasia. Rare migrant in outer Aleutians, Pribilofs. Casual or accidental elsewhere in coastal Alaska.

TUFTED DUCK *Aythya fuligula*
15–18″ (38–45 cm). The Eurasian counterpart of our Ring-necked Duck. Male differs from male Ring-neck in having a thin wispy crest, entirely *white* (not gray) sides, and a *white* (not gray) wing stripe. The female resembles female Ring-neck but is darker, lacking eye-ring and ring on bill. It has a faint trace of a crest and may or may not have white at the base of the bill.
Range: Eurasia. **West:** Regular but uncommon migrant and winter visitor to the outer Aleutians; rare winter visitor elsewhere in Alaska; casual vagrant southward along coast from British Columbia to California. Accidental, Wyoming.

SMEW *Mergellus albellus*
16″ (40 cm). This Eurasian species is smaller and shorter-billed than the other mergansers. The male looks *very white*, with a *black eye patch* and a slight drooping black and white crest behind the eye. In flight, it shows conspicuous black and white wings. The female is small and gray, with *white cheeks* and a *chestnut cap.*
Range: Eurasia. Rare migrant and winter visitor in w. Aleutians (west of Adak). Casual vagrant elsewhere in s. Alaska. Accidental, British Columbia, Manitoba, Washington, California.

SPOT-BILLED DUCK *Anas poecilorhyncha*
22″ (55 cm). This Asian dabbler has the look of a Black Duck or female Mallard, but note the *black bill* tipped with *yellow.* The name refers to red spots at the base of the bill, absent in the subspecies that has occurred in Alaska.
Range: Asia. Accidental in Alaska (Adak, Kodiak I.).

GARGANEY, BAIKAL TEAL, FALCATED TEAL. See p. 48.

BEAN GOOSE *Anser fabalis*
28–35″ (70–88 cm). A large gray-brown goose with a *dark head and neck;* bill black with a yellow midsection, but variable.
Range: Eurasia. Rare spring transient in western Aleutians. Casual elsewhere in Bering Sea area. Accidental, Nebraska.

GRAYLAG GOOSE *Anser anser* (not shown)
Eurasia. Reported from Attu. See European *Field Guide.*

EURASIAN COOT *Fulica atra* Family Rallidae
16″ (40 cm). Very similar to the American Coot, but its bill and frontal shield (forehead) are *entirely white.* The undertail coverts are *all dark*, showing no white.
Range: Eurasia. Has occurred accidentally in the Pribilofs.

♂

♀

**COMMON
POCHARD**

♂

♀

**TUFTED
DUCK**

♂

♀

SMEW

**SPOT-BILLED
DUCK**

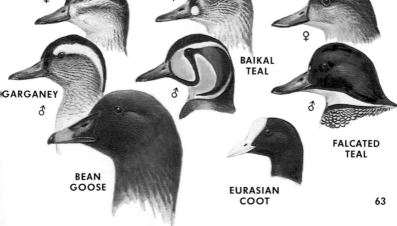

♀

♀

♀

♂

**BAIKAL
TEAL**

GARGANEY

♂

♂

**FALCATED
TEAL**

**BEAN
GOOSE**

**EURASIAN
COOT**

63

■ DUCKLIKE SWIMMERS (COOTS, GALLINULES). Family

Rallidae (in part). Coots and gallinules belong to the same family as the rails (see further family discussion on p. 118). Whereas the rails are more henlike and are basically secretive wading birds of the marshes, coots and gallinules (moorhens) are superficially more ducklike except for their smaller heads, forehead shields, and rather henlike bills. They spend most of their time swimming, although they may also feed on shores, lawns, and golf courses.

AMERICAN COOT *Fulica americana* M111

13–16″ (33–40 cm). A slaty, ducklike bird, with a blackish head and neck, *white bill,* and divided white patch under the tail. Its big feet are lobed ("scallops" on toes). Gregarious. When swimming, it pumps its head back and forth; it dabbles but also dives from the surface. Taking off, it skitters; flight labored; the big feet trail beyond the short tail; a narrow white border shows on rear of wing. Aberrant birds may show some white on the forehead above the bill. *Immature:* Paler, with a duller bill. Downy young has hairy, *orange-red* head and shoulders.
Similar species: Common Moorhen is smaller and has a red bill (with a yellow tip). Coots are more ducklike than moorhens, more widespread, and flock more on open water.
Voice: A grating *kuk-kuk-kuk-kuk; kakakakakaka,* etc.; also a measured *ka-ha, ha-ha;* various cackles, croaks.
Range: Canada to Argentina. **West:** Map 111. **Habitat:** Ponds, lakes, marshes; in winter, also fields, park ponds, salt bays.

COMMON MOORHEN *Gallinula chloropus* M110

(Common Gallinule) 13″ (33 cm). Note the rather henlike red bill, *red forehead shield,* and white band on the flanks. When walking, it flirts its white undertail coverts; while swimming, it pumps its head like a coot. The latter is stockier and shorter-necked; it has a gray back and white bill.
Voice: A croaking *kr-r-ruk,* repeated; a froglike *kup;* also *kek, kek, kek* and loud, complaining, henlike notes.
Range: S. Canada to Argentina; also Eurasia, Africa. **West:** Map 110.
Habitat: Fresh marshes, reedy ponds.

PURPLE GALLINULE *Porphyrula martinica*

13″ (33 cm). Very colorful; swims, wades, and climbs bushes. Size of Moorhen, but head and underparts *deep violet-purple,* back bronzy green. Shield on forehead *pale blue;* bill red with a yellow tip. Legs *yellow,* conspicuous in flight. *Immature:* Drab; dark above, pale below; *no side stripe;* bill dark.
Similar species: (1) Common Moorhen has a *red* frontal shield, greenish legs, and white side stripe; young Moorhen also has a similar whitish side stripe. (2) Young Coot has a pale bill; black divides the white patch under the tail.
Voice: A henlike cackling, *kek, kek, kek;* also guttural notes.
Range: Se. U.S. to n. Argentina. Winters mainly south of U.S. **West:** Casual in sw. states. **Habitat:** Fresh swamps, marshes, ponds.

DUCKLIKE SWIMMERS

Coots skitter on takeoff

lobed foot of Coot

imm.

Coot chick

adult

adult

AMERICAN COOT

Moorhen chick

imm.

adult

COMMON MOORHEN

COMMON MOORHEN

imm.

adult

PURPLE GALLINULE

PURPLE GALLINULE

FLIGHT PATTERNS OF DABBLING DUCKS

Only males are diagnosed below. Although females are unlike the males, their wing patterns are quite similar. The names in parentheses are common nicknames used by gunners.

	Text and color plate

NORTHERN PINTAIL (Sprig) *Anas acuta*   **pp. 46, 47**
    Overhead: Needle tail, white breast, thin neck.
    Topside: Needle tail, neck stripe, single white border on speculum (rear edge of wing).

WOOD DUCK *Aix sponsa*   **pp. 46, 47**
    Overhead: White belly, dusky wings, long square tail.
    Topside: Stocky; long dark tail, white border on dark wing.

AMERICAN WIGEON (Baldpate) *Anas americana*   **pp. 46, 47**
    Overhead: White belly, dark pointed tail.
    Topside: Large white shoulder patch.

NORTHERN SHOVELER (Spoonbill) *Anas clypeata*   **pp. 48, 49**
    Overhead: Dark belly, white chest, spoon bill.
    Topside: Large pale bluish shoulder patch, spoon bill.

GADWALL *Anas strepera*   **pp. 44, 45**
    Overhead: White belly, square white patch (speculum) on rear edge of wing.
    Topside: White patch (speculum) on rear edge of wing.

GREEN-WINGED TEAL *Anas crecca*   **pp. 48, 49**
    Overhead: Small (teal-sized); light belly, dark head.
    Topside: Small, dark-winged; green speculum.

BLUE-WINGED TEAL *Anas discors*   **pp. 48, 49**
    Overhead: Small (teal-sized); dark belly.
    Topside: Small; large pale bluish shoulder patch.

Wing of a dabbling duck, showing the iridescent speculum.

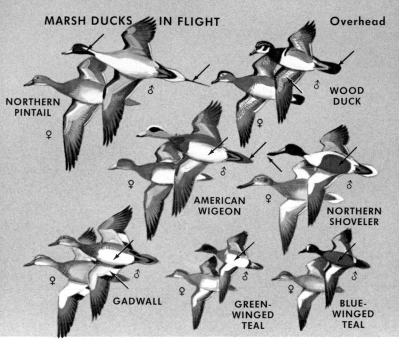

MARSH DUCKS IN FLIGHT

Overhead

NORTHERN PINTAIL ♀

♂

WOOD DUCK ♂

♀

AMERICAN WIGEON ♀ ♂

♀

NORTHERN SHOVELER ♂

GADWALL ♀ ♂

GREEN-WINGED TEAL ♀ ♂

BLUE-WINGED TEAL ♀ ♂

Topside

NORTHERN PINTAIL ♀

♂

WOOD DUCK ♂

♀

AMERICAN WIGEON ♀ ♂

NORTHERN SHOVELER ♂ ♀

GADWALL ♀ ♂

GREEN-WINGED TEAL ♀ ♂

BLUE-WINGED TEAL ♂ ♀

FLIGHT PATTERNS OF MARSH DUCKS AND MERGANSERS

Only males are diagnosed below. Although most females are unlike the males, their wing patterns are quite similar. Mergansers have a distinctive flight silhouette, with the bill, head, neck, body, and tail all on a horizontal axis. Duck hunters often call mergansers "sheldrakes" or "sawbills."

Text and
color plate

MALLARD *Anas platyrhynchos*   pp. 44, 45
Overhead: Dark chest, light belly, white neck-ring.
Topside: Dark head, neck-ring, two white borders on speculum.

AMERICAN BLACK DUCK *Anas rubripes*   pp. 44, 45
Overhead: Dusky body, white wing linings.
Topside: Dusky body, paler head.

FULVOUS WHISTLING-DUCK *Dendrocygna bicolor*   pp. 44, 45
Overhead: Tawny, with blackish wing linings.
Topside: Dark, unpatterned wings; white ring on rump.

COMMON MERGANSER *Mergus merganser*   pp. 60, 61
Overhead: Merganser shape; black head, white body, white wing linings.
Topside: Merganser shape; white chest, large wing patches.

RED-BREASTED MERGANSER *Mergus serrator*   pp. 60, 61
Overhead: Merganser shape; dark chest band, wide white collar.
Topside: Merganser shape; dark chest, large wing patches.

HOODED MERGANSER *Lophodytes cucullatus*   pp. 60, 61
Overhead: Merganser shape; dusky wing linings.
Topside: Merganser shape; small wing patches.

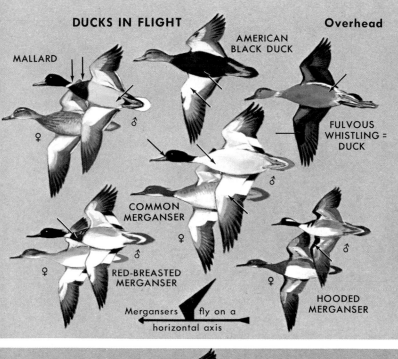

DUCKS IN FLIGHT

Overhead

MALLARD

♂

♀

AMERICAN BLACK DUCK

♂

FULVOUS WHISTLING = DUCK

COMMON MERGANSER

♀

♂

RED-BREASTED MERGANSER

♀

♂

HOODED MERGANSER

♀

Mergansers fly on a horizontal axis

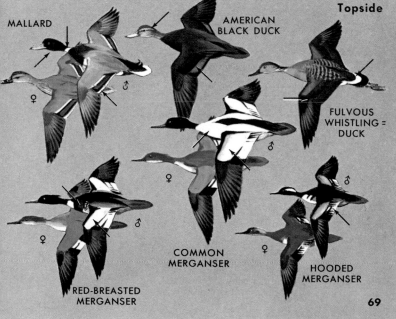

Topside

MALLARD

♀

♂

AMERICAN BLACK DUCK

FULVOUS WHISTLING = DUCK

♂

♀

COMMON MERGANSER

RED-BREASTED MERGANSER

♀

♂

♂

♀

HOODED MERGANSER

FLIGHT PATTERNS OF SEA DUCKS

Note: Only males are diagnosed below.

Text and
color plate

OLDSQUAW *Clangula hyemalis* pp. 54, 55
Overhead: Dark unpatterned wings, white belly.
Topside: Dark unpatterned wings, much white on body.

HARLEQUIN DUCK *Histrionicus histrionicus* pp. 54, 55
Overhead: Solid dark below, white head spots, small
bill.
Topside: Stocky, dark with white marks, small bill.

SURF SCOTER *Melanitta perspicillata* pp. 50, 51
Overhead: Black body, white head patches
(not readily visible from below).
Topside: Black body, white head patches.

BLACK SCOTER *Melanitta nigra* pp. 50, 51
Overhead: Black plumage, paler flight feathers.
Topside: All-black plumage.

WHITE-WINGED SCOTER *Melanitta fusca* pp. 50, 51
Overhead: Black body, white wing patches.
Topside: Black body, white wing patches.

COMMON EIDER *Somateria mollissima* pp. 52, 53
Topside: White back, white forewing, black belly.

KING EIDER *Somateria spectabilis* pp. 52, 53
Topside: Whitish foreparts, black rear parts.

SEA DUCKS IN FLIGHT

Overhead

OLDSQUAW

♂

♀

HARLEQUIN DUCK

♂

♀

♂

♀

BLACK SCOTER

♀

♂

SURF SCOTER

WHITE-WINGED SCOTER

♀

♂

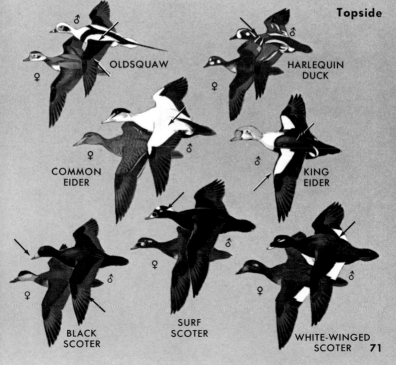

Topside

OLDSQUAW

♂

♀

HARLEQUIN DUCK

♂

♀

COMMON EIDER

♀

♂

KING EIDER

♂

BLACK SCOTER

♀

♂

SURF SCOTER

♂

WHITE-WINGED SCOTER

♀

♂

71

FLIGHT PATTERNS OF BAY DUCKS, etc.

Only males are diagnosed below. The first five all have black chests. The names in parentheses are common gunners' nicknames.

Text and
color plate

CANVASBACK *Aythya valisineria*   **pp. 56, 57**
  Overhead: Black chest, long profile.
  Topside: White back, long profile. Lacks contrasty wing
    stripe of next four species.

REDHEAD *Aythya americana*   **pp. 56, 57**
  Overhead: Black chest, roundish rufous head.
  Topside: Gray back, broad gray wing stripe.

RING-NECKED DUCK *Aythya collaris*   **pp. 56, 57**
  Overhead: Not safe to tell from Scaup overhead.
  Topside: Black back, broad gray wing stripe.

GREATER SCAUP (Bluebill) *Aythya marila*   **pp. 56, 57**
  Overhead: Black chest, white stripe showing through wing.
  Topside: Broad white wing stripe (extending onto primaries).

LESSER SCAUP (Bluebill) *Aythya affinis*   **pp. 56, 57**
  Topside: Wing stripe shorter than that of Greater Scaup.

COMMON GOLDENEYE (Whistler) *Bucephala clangula*   **pp. 58, 59**
  Overhead: Blackish wing linings, white wing patches.
  Topside: Large white wing square, short neck, black head.

RUDDY DUCK *Oxyura jamaicensis*   **pp. 58, 59**
  Overhead: Stubby; white face, dark chest.
  Topside: Small; dark with white cheeks.

BUFFLEHEAD (Butterball) *Bucephala albeola*   **pp. 58, 59**
  Overhead: Like a small Goldeneye; note head patch.
  Topside: Small; large wing patches; white head patch.

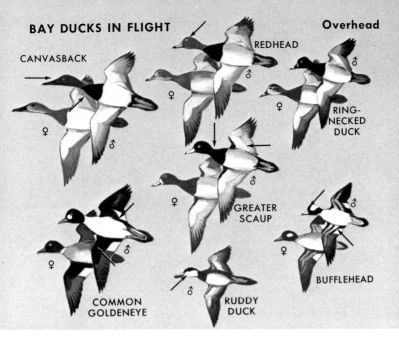

BAY DUCKS IN FLIGHT

Overhead

CANVASBACK

REDHEAD

RING-NECKED DUCK

GREATER SCAUP

COMMON GOLDENEYE

RUDDY DUCK

BUFFLEHEAD

Topside

CANVASBACK

REDHEAD

RING-NECKED DUCK

GREATER SCAUP

below: wing of Lesser Scaup

COMMON GOLDENEYE

RUDDY DUCK

BUFFLEHEAD

■ **ALBATROSSES. Family Diomedeidae.** Birds of the open ocean, with rigid gliding and banking flight. Much larger than gulls; wings proportionately longer. "Tube-nosed" (nostrils in two tubes); bill large, hooked, covered with horny plates. Sexes alike. **Food:** Cuttlefish, fish, other small marine life; some feeding at night. **Range:** Mainly cold oceans of S. Hemisphere; three species nest north of equator in Pacific. **No. of species:** World 13; West 3 (+2 accidentals).

BLACK-FOOTED ALBATROSS *Diomedea nigripes*
28–36" (70–80 cm); spread 7 ft. The great size, *sooty color,* tremendously long, saberlike wings, and rigid, shearwater-like gliding identify this species, the albatross found most regularly off our Pacific Coast. Seldom seen from shore. At close range this albatross shows a whitish face and pale areas toward the tips of wings. Bill and feet *dark.* Some birds, presumably adults, show white patches at the base of the tail.
Similar species: Immature Short-tailed Albatross is dark, but has a *pinkish bill and pinkish feet.*
Range: Breeds on islands in cen. and w. Pacific (chiefly nw. Hawaiian chain). **West:** Ranges well offshore from Bering Sea and Aleutians to Baja California. **Habitat:** Open ocean.

LAYSAN ALBATROSS *Diomedea immutabilis*
32" (80 cm); spread 6½ ft. White-bodied, with a *dark back and wings,* suggesting a huge, dark-backed gull with extra-long wings. Bill and feet dull flesh color or pale flesh-gray. Immature similar.
Range: Breeds on nw. islands of Hawaiian chain. Ranges from Hawaii to N. Pacific. **West:** Ranges regularly to Aleutians and Gulf of Alaska. Rare but regular far off coasts of British Columbia, Washington, Oregon, California.

SHORT-TAILED ALBATROSS *Diomedea albatrus*
30–37" (73–83 cm); spread 7½ ft. Note the white back, pink bill, and yellowish nape on this oceanic rarity. A white albatross with black wings and black on tip of tail. The immature is very dark brown and resembles a Black-footed Albatross, but its bill and feet are pink or flesh-colored (not black); no strong white face patch.
Range: Breeds on Bonin Is. off Japan. Near extinction in 1956 (only 14 pairs on Toroshima), now over 250 birds. Formerly ranged from Bering Sea to Baja California; may again do so.

Note: The following two albatrosses, not shown, have been recorded accidentally off our West Coast. To learn more about them or other Pacific albatrosses, consult *Seabirds, An Identification Guide* by Peter Harrison (Houghton Mifflin).

SHY ("WHITE-CAPPED") ALBATROSS *Diomedea cauta* (not shown)
Similar to Laysan Albatross (white body, dark back), but head pale gray, with a whiter crown. Underwing whiter, feet gray.
Range: Seas off Australia. Accidental, Washington.

WANDERING ALBATROSS *Diomedea exulans* (not shown)
Similar to Short-tailed Albatross, but larger, head entirely white.
Range: S. Hemisphere. Accidental in California.

ALBATROSSES

Black-foot

variant

below

Laysan

below

BLACK-FOOTED ALBATROSS

Laysan

below

Laysan

LAYSAN ALBATROSS

juv. Short-tail

Short-tail

below

SHORT-TAILED ALBATROSS

■ SHEARWATERS, PETRELS, AND FULMARS, etc. Family

Procellariidae. Gull-like birds of the *open sea* that glide low over the waves (usually with wings more stiffly extended than shown here). Wings narrower than those of gulls, tail smaller. Bills with tubelike external nostrils on top of bill. **Food:** Fish, squid, crustaceans, ship refuse. **Range:** Oceans of world. **No. of species:** World 61; West 8 (+ 6 casual or accidental).

SOOTY SHEARWATER *Puffinus griseus*

17″ (43 cm). A somewhat gull-like seabird, often seen in massive flocks offshore. Looks all dark at a distance and scales over the waves on narrow rigid wings. In good light, note the *whitish linings* on the undersurface of the wings. Mainly a summer visitor.

Range: Breeds off s. Australia, New Zealand, s. S. America; ranges to N. Atlantic, N. Pacific. **West:** Offshore, Bering Sea to Baja California.

FLESH-FOOTED SHEARWATER *Puffinus carneipes*

19½″ (43 cm). A dark-bodied shearwater, *larger* than the Sooty; flight more sluggish. Distinguished by *pale flesh or whitish bill* (with dark tip), *flesh-colored feet*, dark wing linings.

Range: Breeds on islands off Australia, New Zealand. **West:** A rather rare visitor offshore, from Alaska to California.

SHORT-TAILED SHEARWATER *Puffinus tenuirostris*

13–14″ (33–35 cm). Distinguished from the Sooty by smaller size, more rapid wingbeat, *shorter bill and tail*, and *smoky gray* wing linings. May have a whitish throat. Sooty has whiter wing linings.

Range: Breeds on islands off s. Australia. **West:** Ranges north to Aleutians and Bering Sea and thence south off coast to Baja California. Best looked for in late fall or early winter.

PINK-FOOTED SHEARWATER *Puffinus creatopus*

19½″ (49 cm). Two common *white-bellied* shearwaters often associate with the abundant Sootys: Pink-foot is *larger*, with a black-tipped pink bill, slower wingbeats; Black-vented is smaller, blacker above, whiter on underwing, with a black bill. It has faster wingbeats.

Range: Breeds on islands off Chile. **West:** Spring, summer, and fall off California, Oregon; a few to British Columbia, se. Alaska.

BULLER'S SHEARWATER *Puffinus bulleri*

(New Zealand Shearwater) 16½″ (91 cm). A rather rare white-bellied shearwater; separated from the two other white-bellied species by a broad *M or W* formed by the contrasting pattern on back and wings. Tail wedge-shaped. Feet pale, but variable.

Range: Breeds n. New Zealand. **West:** Fall visitor off California (mainly off Monterey in Oct.); casual, Oregon, Washington.

BLACK-VENTED SHEARWATER *Puffinus opisthomelas*

13″ (33 cm). A small shearwater, black above and white below; dark cap extends below the eye. The contrasting *black and white* pattern and gliding, bounding flight are distinctive.

Range: Breeds on sea islands off Pacific Coast of Baja California. **West:** Ranges north, mainly in fall and winter, along inshore waters of s. and cen. California, rarely or casually to Washington and Vancouver I.

SHEARWATERS

SOOTY SHEARWATER

SOOTY SHEARWATER

FLESH-FOOTED SHEARWATER

SHORT-TAILED SHEARWATER

PINK-FOOTED SHEARWATER

BULLER'S SHEARWATER

BLACK-VENTED SHEARWATER

77

NORTHERN FULMAR *Fulmarus glacialis* M10

18″ (45 cm). A stiff-winged oceanic glider, stockier than a shear-water; swims buoyantly. Note the bull neck, rounded forehead, *stubby yellow bill*, large dark eye, short tail. The primaries may show a *pale flash or patch.* Legs variable. *Dark phase:* Smoky gray, wing tips darker; bill yellowish. Intermediates are frequent.
Voice: A hoarse, grunting *ag-ag-ag-arrr* or *ek-ek-ek-ek-ek.*
Range: Northern oceans of N. Hemisphere. **West:** Map 10. **Habitat:** Open ocean; breeds colonially on open sea cliffs.

■ MOSTLY RARE, CASUAL, OR ACCIDENTAL PETRELS.

Some of these species, though rarely recorded in the past, may prove to be of regular occurrence far offshore due to the growing popularity of pelagic birding.

STREAKED SHEARWATER *Calonectris leucomelas*
19″ (48 cm). The *pale, lightly streaked head* may look all white at a distance, suggesting that of a Fulmar. Forehead white, nape dark.
Range: Western Pacific Ocean; casual or accidental off our coast in fall, mainly off Monterey Bay.

MURPHY'S PETREL *Pterodroma ultima*
16″ (40 cm). A dark petrel with wholly dark underwing linings, a somewhat wedge-shaped tail, and pale legs.
Range: South Pacific. **West:** Rare offshore vagrant; recorded in California, Oregon.

SOLANDER'S PETREL *Pterodoma solandri*
16″ (40 cm). A dark petrel. Head darker than body; white skua-like flash under primaries.
Range: Southwest Pacific (breeds Lord Howe I., e. Australia). **West:** Reported far offshore from California, Washington.

COOK'S PETREL *Pterodroma cookii*
10½″ (26 cm). The *black M* across the upper wings suggests the much larger Buller's Shearwater, but note the paler head with a black ear patch and the light sides of the tail.
Range: Nests on islands off New Zealand and ranges across the Pacific, rarely as far as the Aleutians and California waters.

STEJNEGER'S PETREL *Pterodroma longirostris*
10″ (25 cm). Very similar to Cook's Petrel, but darker; the cap is *black*, not gray. This petrel, which breeds off Chile and New Zealand, has been sighted off California.

MOTTLED PETREL *Pterodroma inexpectata*
(Scaled Petrel) 14″ (35 cm). *Dark M* across upper wings suggests Buller's Shearwater or Cook's Petrel, but note contrasting *dark belly* and *heavy diagonal black bar* across underwing. This New Zealand species ranges regularly to the Gulf of Alaska and Bering Sea; rarely south to California.

Note: WEDGE-TAILED SHEARWATER, *Puffinus pacificus* (not shown), of Hawaii, etc., has been sighted as an accidental in California. Size of Sooty; white-bellied (rarely dark-bellied), with a longish *wedge-shaped* tail and *flesh-colored* feet.

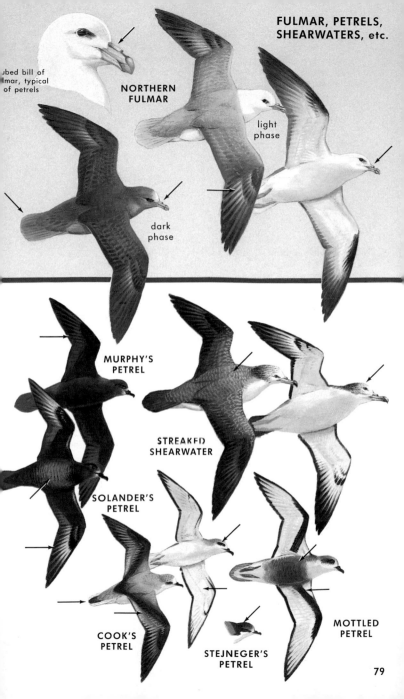

FULMAR, PETRELS, SHEARWATERS, etc.

ubed bill of
lmar, typical
of petrels

NORTHERN FULMAR

light phase

dark phase

MURPHY'S PETREL

STREAKED SHEARWATER

SOLANDER'S PETREL

COOK'S PETREL

STEJNEGER'S PETREL

MOTTLED PETREL

79

■ **STORM-PETRELS. Family Hydrobatidae.** Little dark birds that flit over the ocean; they nest colonially on islands, returning to burrows at night. Nostrils in a fused tube over top of bill. **Food:** Plankton, crustaceans, small fish. **Range:** All oceans except Arctic. **No. of species:** World 20; West 6 (+ 2 casual).

ASHY STORM-PETREL *Oceanodroma homochroa* **M13**
7½" (19 cm). Separated from Black Storm-Petrel by smaller size, shorter wings, more fluttery flight. At very close range, head looks ashy, wings show light mottling underneath.
Range: At sea from n. California (Pt. Reyes) to Baja California. Map 13. Breeds on Farallon, Channel, and Coronados Is.

BLACK STORM-PETREL *Oceanodroma melania*
9" (23 cm). The most common all-black petrel found off California. Larger than Ashy, with longer wings and *more languid flight.*
Voice: At night, in colony, *puck-apoo-puck-puck-a-poo.*
Range: Breeds on Coronados and other islands off Baja California. Ranges north along California coast to Pt. Reyes.

FORK-TAILED STORM-PETREL *Oceanodroma furcata* **M11**
8–9" (20–23 cm). Gray; paler below, unlike all our other storm-petrels, which are blackish.
Range: N. Pacific. **West:** Map 11.

LEAST STORM-PETREL *Oceanodroma microsoma*
5½–6" (14–15 cm); very small. Only storm-petrel with a *rounded or wedge-shaped* tail. Flight erratic, batlike, close to water.
Range: Breeds on islands off Baja California. A few range north in late summer and early fall to San Diego and south to Ecuador.

WILSON'S STORM-PETREL *Oceanites oceanicus*
7" (18 cm). A small storm-petrel with a *white rump patch; tail even at end.* Feet yellow-webbed (hard to see), may show beyond tail. Skims like a swallow, pausing to flutter over water. Follows ships.
Range: Breeds in the Antarctic. Ranges chiefly north to N. Atlantic.
West: Rare but regular north to Monterey Bay, California.

LEACH'S STORM-PETREL *Oceanodroma leucorhoa* **M12**
8" (20 cm). Note the obscurely divided *white rump patch* and forked tail. In flight it bounds about erratically, changing speed and direction (suggesting a Nighthawk). Does not follow ships. Baja California race is all dark, lacking white rump. There are intermediates.
Voice: At night, in flight on breeding grounds, rhythmic falsetto hooting notes. From burrows, long, crooning trills.
Range: N. Atlantic, N. Pacific. **West:** Map 12. **Habitat:** Open ocean; nests colonially in turf on offshore islands.

WEDGE-RUMPED STORM-PETREL *Oceanodroma tethys*
6½" (16 cm). Very small, with a long, *wedge-shaped, white rump* that restricts the amount of black at end of tail.
Range: Breeds Galápagos Islands, Peru. **West:** Rare or casual visitor to California (Aug. to Jan.).

BAND-RUMPED STORM-PETREL *Oceanodroma castro*
9" (23 cm). A white-rumped storm-petrel, larger than Wilson's. Its feet do not project beyond the squarish tail. A stiff-winged flier.
Range: Tropical oceans. **West:** Accidental, s. California.

STORM-PETRELS

ASHY

BLACK

FORK-TAILED

LEAST

WILSON'S

LEACH'S

WEDGE-RUMPED

BAND-RUMPED

Leach's

Wilson's

Wedge-rumped

Band-rumped

WHITE-RUMPED STORM-PETRELS

■ **BOOBIES. Family Sulidae.** Seabirds with large, tapering bills and pointed tails. Larger than most gulls; neck longer. Sexes alike. Boobies sit on buoys; they fish by plunging from the air like Brown Pelicans. **Food:** Fish, squid. **Range:** Tropical seas. **No. of species:** World 6; West 2 (+2 casual or accidental).

BROWN BOOBY *Sula leucogaster*
28–30″ (70–75 cm). A sooty brown booby, with a *white belly in clean-cut contrast* to its dark breast. Bill and feet yellowish. Males of the west Mexican race are pale around the head. *Immature:* Similar, but white of underparts smudged with dusky.
Range: Tropical oceans. **West:** A post-breeding wanderer from Gulf of California, mostly to Salton Sea, Imperial Valley, and lower Colorado R.; mainly immatures.

BLUE-FOOTED BOOBY *Sula nebouxii*
32–34″ (80–85 cm). This booby, the one most frequent in our area, has a white body, whitish head, dark mottled back and wings, and *big blue feet.* Young birds have a brownish head; note the white patches on nape and rump.
Range: Breeds w. Mexico to Peru. **West:** Post-breeding wanderer to Salton Sea in California; also Lower Colorado R. in se. California and sw. Arizona. Accidental, Washington.

RED-FOOTED BOOBY *Sula sula*
26–30″ (65–75 cm). Adults have *bright red feet* and may be white with black in wings, *white tail,* or light brown with a white tail. *Immature:* Tan with pink base of bill, dull pink feet.
Range: Tropical oceans. **West:** Accidental off California.

MASKED BOOBY *Sula dactylatra* (not shown)
27″ (68 cm). A *white* booby with black in the wings and *tail;* accidental off s. California. See illustration in eastern *Field Guide.*

■ **TROPICBIRDS. Family Phaethontidae.** These seabirds resemble large terns with two greatly elongated *central* tail feathers and stouter, slightly decurved bills. Tern-like, they dive headfirst, and swim with the tail held clear of the water. Sexes alike. **Food:** Squid, crustaceans. **Range:** Tropical oceans. **No. of species:** World 3; West 1 (+2 accidental).

RED-BILLED TROPICBIRD *Phaethon aethereus*
24–40″ (60–100 cm). A slender white seabird with *two extremely long central tail feathers* (1–2 ft.), a *heavy red bill,* a black patch through the cheek, black primaries, and a *finely barred back.* Young lack the long tail, have an orange-yellow bill.
Range: Tropical oceans worldwide. **West:** Rare but regular stray off s. California. Accidental, Arizona, Washington.

RED-TAILED TROPICBIRD *Phaethon rubricauda*
24″ (60 cm), including 16″ tail streamers. Whiter above than the other two tropicbirds; has *red* streamers.
Range: Tropical Pacific. **West:** Accidental well off California.

WHITE-TAILED TROPICBIRD *Phaethon lepturus*
32″ (80 cm), including 16″ streamers. This accidental tropicbird may be known from the others by the *diagonal black bar* across each wing. The single bird recorded in our area at Malibu Beach, California tried to mate with a toy glider!

BOOBIES

♂

♀

BROWN BOOBY

♀

♂

imm.

adult

imm.

BLUE-FOOTED BOOBY

adult

brown phase

adult

RED-FOOTED BOOBY

TROPICBIRDS

RED-BILLED TROPICBIRD

RED-TAILED TROPICBIRD

Red-billed

Red-tailed

White-tailed

■ **PELICANS. Family Pelecanidae.** Huge water birds with long flat bills and great throat pouches (flat when deflated). Neck long, body robust. Sexes alike. Flocks fly in lines, alternating several flaps with a glide. In flight, the head is hunched back on the shoulders, the long bill resting on the breast. Pelicans swim buoyantly. **Food:** Mainly fish, crustaceans. **Range:** N. and S. America, Africa, s. Eurasia, E. Indies, Australia. **No. of species:** World 8; West 2.

AMERICAN WHITE PELICAN *Pelecanus erythrorhynchos*   **M14**
62" (155 cm). Huge (wingspread 8–9½ ft.). White, with black primaries and a great orange-yellow bill. Adults in breeding plumage have a "centerboard" on the ridge of the bill. Immatures have a dusky bill. This pelican does not plunge from the air like the Brown Pelican but scoops up fish while swimming, often working in groups. Flocks fly in lines, may circle high on thermals.
Similar species: (1) Swans have no black in wings. (2) Wood Ibis and (3) Whooping Crane fly with necks extended, long legs aft. (4) Snow Goose is much smaller, with a small bill; noisy.
Range: W. and cen. N. America; winters to se. U.S. and Cen. America. **West:** Map 14. **Habitat:** Lakes, marshes, salt bays, beaches.

BROWN PELICAN *Pelecanus occidentalis*   **M15**
50" (125 cm); spread 6½ ft. A ponderous *dark* water bird; adult has much *white* about the head and neck. Immature has a dark head, whitish underparts. Size, shape, and flight (a few flaps and a glide) indicate a pelican; the dark color and habit of *plunging bill-first* proclaim it as this species. Lines of pelicans scale close to the water.
Voice: Adults silent (rarely a low croak). Nestlings squeal.
Range: Coasts; s. U.S. to n. Brazil and Chile. **West:** Map 15. **Habitat:** Salt bays, beaches, ocean. Perches on posts, buoys.

■ **FRIGATEBIRDS. Family Fregatidae.** Dark tropical seabirds with extremely long wings (greater span in relation to weight than that of any other birds). Bill long, hooked; tail deeply forked. Frigatebirds normally do not swim. **Food:** Fish, jellyfish, squid, young seabirds. Food snatched from water in flight, scavenged, or taken from other seabirds. **Range:** Pantropical oceans. **No. of species:** World 5; West 1.

MAGNIFICENT FRIGATEBIRD *Fregata magnificens*
38–41" (95–103 cm); spread 7–8 ft. A large *black* seabird with extremely long, angled wings and a *scissorlike* tail (often folded in a *point*). Soars with extreme ease. Bill long, hooked. *Male:* All black, with a *red throat pouch* (inflated like a balloon when in display). *Female:* White breast, dark head. *Immature:* Head and breast white.
Similar species: GREAT FRIGATEBIRD, *Fregata minor* of Hawaii (not shown), is a remote possibility. Adult male retains light brown wing coverts; female has a whitish throat, red eye-ring.
Voice: Silent at sea. A gargling whinny during display.
Range: Gulf of Mexico to s. Brazil; Cape Verde Is; Baja California to Peru, tropical Atlantic, e. Pacific. **West:** Wanders irregularly along coast north to n. California. Casual, Oregon. Accidental, Arizona, New Mexico, Nevada.

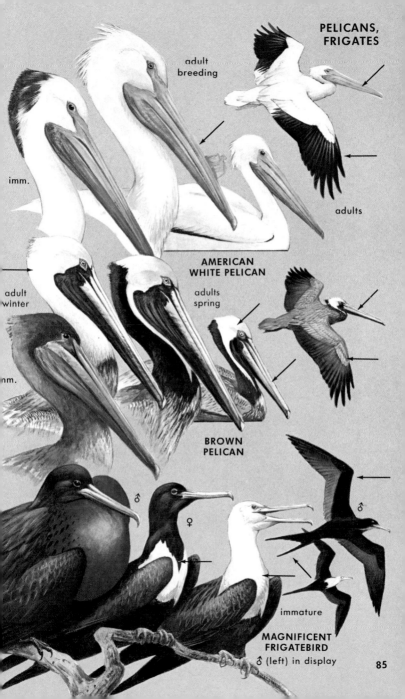

adult
breeding

imm.

adults

AMERICAN
WHITE PELICAN

adult
winter

adults
spring

imm.

BROWN
PELICAN

♂

♀

♂

immature

MAGNIFICENT
FRIGATEBIRD
♂ (left) in display

■ SKUAS, GULLS, TERNS, SKIMMERS. Family Laridae.

■ SKUAS, JAEGERS. Subfamily Stercorariinae. Dark, hawk-like or falcon-like seabirds that harass gulls and terns, forcing them to disgorge. Light, intermediate, and dark phases; all have a *flash of white in the primaries.* Jaegers have two projecting central tail feathers, which are sometimes broken or missing. They are lacking in juveniles and immatures, which may be identified (tentatively) by relative size. Skuas lack tail points and are broader-winged. Sexes alike. **Food:** In the Arctic, lemmings, eggs, young birds. At sea, food taken from other birds or from water. **Range:** Seas of world, breeding in subpolar regions. **No. of species:** World 5 (or 7?); West 4.

SOUTH POLAR SKUA *Catharacta maccormicki*
21" (53 cm). Near size of Western Gull, but stockier, with a deep-chested, hunch-shouldered look. Dark, with a short, slightly wedge-shaped tail and *conspicuous white wing patch.* "Blond" phase is much paler on head and underparts than dark phase. Flight strong and swift; harasses other seabirds. Dark jaegers may lack tail points, but skuas' wings are wider, with more striking white patches.
Range: Antarctic. Wanders into N. Atlantic as far as Greenland and in N. Pacific as far as Aleutians.

PARASITIC JAEGER *Stercorarius parasiticus*   M155
18" (45 cm). In the adult, the sharp tail points project ½–3½ in. Like other jaegers, it shows a white wing flash. It is the jaeger most frequently seen from shore. Varies from light to dark phases.
Range: Arctic, circumpolar. Winters at sea from s. U.S. to Tierra del Fuego. **West:** Map 155. **Habitat:** Ocean, coastal bays, lakes (rarely); tundra (summer).

POMARINE JAEGER *Stercorarius pomarinus*   M154
22" (55 cm). *Broad and twisted* central tail feathers project 2–7 in. Heavier than other jaegers; often heavily barred below, with a broad breastband and more white in primaries. Immature lacks the projections, is larger than other young jaegers, and has a heavier bill. Separating jaegers in obscure plumage can be difficult; then use size, proportions, and manner of flight.
Range: Arctic; circumpolar. Winters at sea from s. U.S. to S. Hemisphere. **West:** Map 154. **Habitat:** Open sea, coasts (offshore); tundra (summer).

LONG-TAILED JAEGER *Stercorarius longicaudus*   M156
20–23" (50–58 cm). The long tail streamers of adults may project 9–10 in. (usually 3–6 in.). More slender than other jaegers; whiter below, with *no breastband.* The black cap on its small head is separated by a broad white collar from the pale gray back. Bill short; legs blue-gray (black in Parasitic). Immature more slender than the others, with smaller head and bill, grayer upperparts, lighter flight.
Range: Arctic, circumpolar. Winters in S. Hemisphere. **West:** Map 156. **Habitat:** Open sea; tundra (summer). Most pelagic of the jaegers.

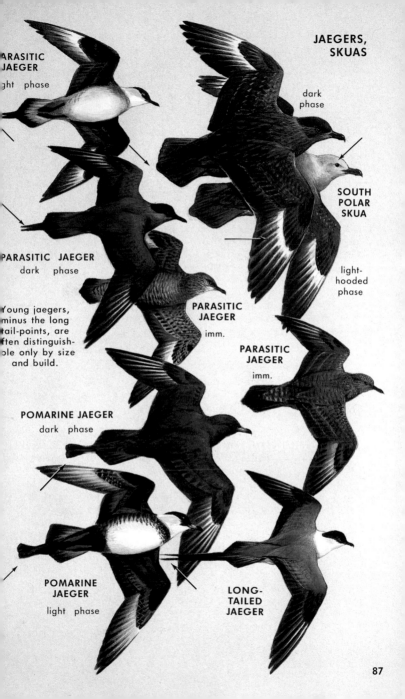

PARASITIC
JAEGER

light phase

PARASITIC JAEGER

dark phase

Young jaegers,
minus the long
tail-points, are
often distinguish-
able only by size
and build.

POMARINE JAEGER

dark phase

POMARINE
JAEGER

light phase

JAEGERS,
SKUAS

dark
phase

SOUTH
POLAR
SKUA

light-
hooded
phase

PARASITIC
JAEGER

imm.

PARASITIC
JAEGER

imm.

LONG-
TAILED
JAEGER

87

■ **GULLS. Subfamily Larinae.** Long-winged swimming birds with superb flight. More robust, wider-winged, and longer-legged than terns. Bills slightly hooked. Tails square or rounded (terns usually have forked tails). Gulls seldom dive (terns hover, then plunge head-first). **Food:** Omnivorous; marine life, plant and animal food, refuse, carrion. **No. of species:** World 46; West 21 (+3 accidentals).

SEQUENCE OF PLUMAGES: On the page opposite, the well-known **WESTERN GULL,** a coastal species, has been chosen to illustrate the transition of plumages from juvenile to adult. The Western Gull is a four-year gull—it does not attain full breeding plumage until its fourth year. However, if you know what a gull looks like in its first-winter plumage (which in some species is not too much unlike that of the juvenile), you should be able to identify the bird as to species in any of its intermediate stages.

In this field guide, intended for identification on the *species level,* I have not given similar full-page treatment to any of the other gulls. That is the province of a handbook or technical manual. But should you wish this kind of in-depth analysis, I recommend Peter J. Grant's *Gulls: A Guide to Identification,* which often devotes from 10 to 20 pages per species. Study also Kenn Kaufman's *Field Guide to Advanced Birding.*

In summary:

Four-year gulls: This category includes most of the larger species, including the Western Gull, Glaucous-winged Gull, Glaucous Gull, Herring Gull, Thayer's Gull, California Gull, and Slaty-backed Gull.

Three-year gulls: Mostly medium-sized species, including the Ring-billed Gull, Mew Gull, Heermann's Gull, Laughing Gull, and Yellow-legged Gull.

Two-year gulls: Mostly smaller species, including Franklin's Gull, Bonaparte's Gull, Black-headed Gull, Little Gull, Ross's Gull, Black-legged Kittiwake, Red-legged Kittiwake, Sabine's Gull, and Ivory Gull.

Note: Three other gulls that have been reported as accidentals in the western states are not treated in the following pages. Two, the **GREATER BLACK-BACKED GULL** and the **LESSER BLACK-BACKED GULL,** are described and illustrated in the eastern book—*A Field Guide to the Birds.* The third is an Asian vagrant, the **BLACK-TAILED GULL;** it has been reported off Alaska and California (see p. 358).

Caution: Do not feel defeated if you cannot name *every* gull you see. There is considerable variation due to age, season, molt, wear, some hybridization, and even occasional albinism. Even the experts will put question marks after some of their observations if they are not sure.

WESTERN GULL

Plumage Transition of 4-year Gull

juvenile

1st winter

2nd winter

3rd winter

A gull that attains adult plumage in its 4th year

adult breeding

89

WESTERN GULL *Larus occidentalis*   **M165**
24–27″ (60–63 cm). Note the *very dark back and wings,* contrasting with the snowy underparts. Feet dull pinkish. The northern race, *occidentalis* (cen. California to Washington) has a paler mantle, which, however, is still noticeably darker than that of the California Gull. The southern race, *wymani,* is blacker-backed. See the presentation of plumage sequences on pp. 88 and 89. *Immature:* See pp. 98, 99.
Note: There is some hybridization with the Glaucous-winged Gull where its breeding range overlaps with the Western's.
Voice: A guttural *kuk kuk kuk:* also *whee whee whee* and *ki-aa.*
Range: Resident along coast from Baja California to nw. Washington. Map 165. **Habitat:** Coastal waters, estuaries, beaches, piers, city waterfronts, lower reaches of tidal rivers.

SLATY-BACKED GULL *Larus schistisagus*
27″ (68 cm). Any large, dark-backed gull in the Bering Sea would most likely be this species. Adult is similar to Western Gull, but with more pinkish feet. Note how the broad white trailing edge of the wing invades the outer wing, forming a *white bar* crossing the black on the primaries. The primaries are *gray* beneath. **Caution:** Siberian race of Herring Gull occurs off w. Alaska.
Range: Kamchatka to Japan. **West:** Rare visitor to Alaska. Recorded at a number of points in the Pribilofs and Aleutians and along the coast of w. Alaska. Casual, British Columbia. Accidental, Missouri.

YELLOW-FOOTED GULL *Larus livens*
27″ (69 cm). This large gull closely resembles the Western Gull, but the adult has *yellow* (not pinkish) feet. It matures in its third year, not the fourth, as the Western Gull does. The brown juvenile bird has a whitish belly and by the first winter already has some black on the back. The yellow feet are attained by the second winter.
Range: Breeding in w. Mexico, this gull occurs in our area as a postbreeding visitor only at Salton Sea. It would be casual or accidental anywhere else in California. Formerly regarded as a subspecies of Western Gull.

HEERMANN'S GULL *Larus heermanni*   **M159**
18–21″ (45–53 cm). The easiest gull in the West to identify. *Adult:* Dark gray, with a black tail, *whitish head, red bill.* In winter the white head becomes gray. *Immature:* All dark, lacking the white head; bill brown or tipped with varying amounts of red. See p. 99.
Voice: A whining *whee-ee;* also a repeated *cow-auk.*
Range: Breeds mainly on islands off coasts of nw. Mexico. **West:** Map 159. **Habitat:** Coast and nearby open ocean.

ROSS'S GULL *Rhodostethia rosea*
12½–14″ (31–35 cm). A rare gull of the drift ice. Note the *wedge-shaped tail* and blue-gray wing linings. *Breeding: Rosy* blush on underparts, *fine black collar. Winter:* Loses rosy blush and black collar. *Immature:* See pp. 102, 103.
Range: Breeds mainly in ne. Siberia; a few around Hudson Bay. **West:** Arctic coast of Alaska in migration, casual, Pribilofs. Accidental, British Columbia, Colorado.

GULLS Adults
Mostly dark-backed species

southern form

WESTERN GULL

northern form

SLATY-BACKED GULL

YELLOW-FOOTED GULL

breeding

winter adult

breeding

HEERMANN'S GULL

breeding

winter

ROSS'S GULL

91

HERRING GULL *Larus argentatus* **M163**
23–26″ (58–65 cm). *Adult:* A common, widespread, large, gray-mantled gull with dull, *flesh-pink* legs. The outer primaries are *black* with white spots or "mirrors." Heavy yellow bill with a red spot on lower mandible. *Immature:* See pp. 100, 101.
Voice: A loud *hiyak. . .hiyah. . . .hyiah-hyak* or *yuk-yuk-yuk-yuk-yuckle-yuckle.* Mewing squeals. Anxiety note: *gah-gah-gah.*
Range: Northern parts of N. Hemisphere. **West:** Map 163. **Habitat:** Coasts, bays, beaches, lakes, piers, farmlands, dumps.

THAYER'S GULL *Larus thayeri* **M164**
23–25″ (58–63 cm). Thayer's Gull, formerly thought to be a race of the Herring Gull and later designated as a full species, is regarded by some as a subspecies of the Iceland Gull. Very similar in appearance to Herring Gull. Typical adult has (1) *pale to dark brown* (not pale yellow) eyes, (2) *little or no black* on underside of primaries, (3) slightly darker mantle, (4) darker pink legs, (5) slighter bill. Overhead, the *gray* (not black) on the underside of the wing tips is distinctive. Some paler birds may have slate-gray rather than black in the outer primaries above (see immature, pp. 100, 101).
Range: Arctic Canada. Winters mainly on Pacific Coast. **West:** Map 164.

CALIFORNIA GULL *Larus californicus* **M162**
20–23″ (50–58 cm). *Adult:* This abundant gull resembles the smaller Ring-billed Gull (both may have yellowish green legs or not), but note the darker mantle, *darker eye,* and *red and black spot* on the lower mandible (not a black ring). Shows more white in wing tips than the Ring-bill does. *Immature:* pp. 100, 101.
Range: Mainly w. N. America, east to cen. N. Dakota. **West:** Map 162. **Habitat:** Seacoasts, lakes, farms, urban centers.

RING-BILLED GULL *Larus delawarensis* **M161**
19″ (48 cm). *Adult:* Similar to California Gull but smaller, with a lighter gray mantle; legs may be brighter *yellowish green* (but may also be quite gray in winter). Note the complete *black ring* encircling the bill. *Immature:* See pp. 92, 93.
Voice: Higher-pitched than Herring Gull's.
Range: Canada, n. U.S. Winters to Mexico, Virgin Islands. **West:** Map 161. **Habitat:** Lakes, bays, coasts, piers, dumps, plowed fields.

MEW GULL *Larus canus* **M160**
16–18″ (40–45 cm). *Adult:* Smaller than the Ring-billed Gull, with greenish legs, but with a small, short, *unmarked greenish yellow bill.* Back darker. Mew Gull shows larger white "mirrors" in its black wingtips than either California or Ring-billed gulls. *Immature:* See pp. 100, 101.
Similar species: Young Ring-billed Gull is larger and usually has the black of the tail confined to a narrow *clean-cut* band.
Voice: A low mewing (which gives the name), *quee'u* or *mee'u.* Also *hiyah-hiyah-hiyah,* etc., higher than voice of other gulls.
Range: N. Eurasia, w. N. America. Winters to coastal s. China, California, Mediterranean. **West:** Map 160. **Habitat:** Coastal waters, tidal rivers (winter); lakes (summer).

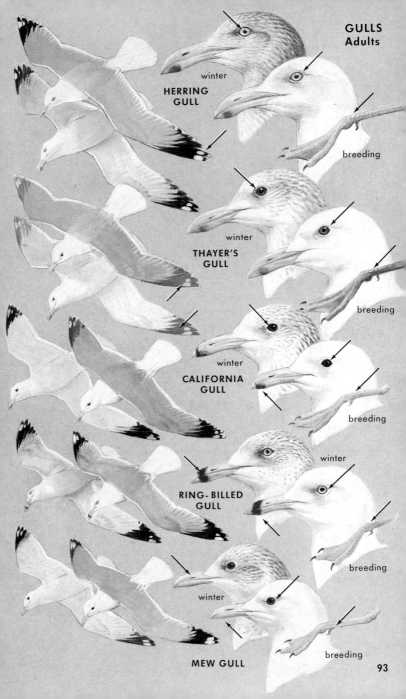

**GULLS
Adults**

**HERRING
GULL**

winter

breeding

**THAYER'S
GULL**

winter

breeding

**CALIFORNIA
GULL**

winter

breeding

**RING-
BILLED
GULL**

winter

breeding

MEW GULL

winter

breeding

93

GLAUCOUS-WINGED GULL Larus glaucescens M166
24–27″ (60–68 cm). *Adult:* A *pink-footed* gull, with a pale gray mantle and *gray* pattern on the primaries (Herring Gull has *black* pattern in primaries). *Immature:* See pp. 98, 99. Hybridizes with Western Gull where their ranges overlap in Washington and British Columbia; also may hybridize with Herring Gull in Alaska.
Similar species: See Thayer's Gull, pp. 92, 93.
Voice: A low *kak-kak-kak;* a low *wow;* a high *keer, keer.*
Range: Komandorskie Is. to nw. Oregon. Winters to w. Mexico. Map 166.

GLAUCOUS GULL Larus hyperboreus M167
26–32″ (65–80 cm). A large, chalky white gull, a bit larger than the Glaucous-winged Gull or Western Gull. Note the "frosty" wing tips. Adults have a pale gray mantle and *unmarked white outer primaries. Immature:* See pp. 98, 99.
Similar species: Glaucous-winged Gull is a bit smaller, with a smaller bill; the wing tips have various amounts of gray spotting. Adult may have a narrow *dull red* ring around eye (Glaucous has a *yellow* ring), but this is unreliable and hard to see.
Range: Arctic; circumpolar. Winters to U.S., Britain, n. China. **West:** Map 167. **Habitat:** Mainly coastal; some inland.

IVORY GULL Pagophila eburnea
15–17″ (38–43 cm). The only *all-white* gull with *black* legs. Pigeon-sized; wings long, flight tern-like. Bill black, with a yellow tip. *Immature:* See pp. 102, 103.
Similar species: Glaucous Gull is much larger, with pale legs.
Voice: Harsh, shrill, ternlike cries: *keeeer,* etc.
Range: High Arctic; circumpolar. **West:** Not known to breed in our area. Arctic ice pack and drift ice of Alaska in migration and winter; accidental elsewhere (British Columbia, Alberta, Saskatchewan, Washington, Montana, Colorado).

BLACK-LEGGED KITTIWAKE Rissa tridactyla M168
17″ (43 cm). A small, buoyant oceanic gull. In adults the wing tips lack white spots and are *solid black,* almost *straight across,* as if dipped in ink. Bill small, pale, yellow, unmarked. Legs *black. Immature:* See pp. 102, 103.
Voice: At nesting colony, a raucous *kaka-week* or *kitti-waak.*
Range: Oceans in northern parts of N. Hemisphere. Winters to both coasts of U.S., Japan, Mediterranean, n. Africa. **West:** Map 168. **Habitat:** Chiefly oceanic; rarely on beaches.

RED-LEGGED KITTIWAKE Rissa brevirostris
14–15¾″ (35–40 cm). *Adult:* Similar to Black-legged Kittiwake, but smaller; legs *bright red* (Bonaparte's Gull also has red legs). Has a similar wing pattern above, but darker; *darkish gray underwing. Immature:* Similar to young Black-leg, but darker-backed; tail lacks black terminal band; wing lacks dark diagonal bar.
Range: Bering Sea (Komandorskies, Pribilofs), w. Aleutians. Winters mainly in Bering Sea. Accidental, Yukon, nw. Oregon, Nevada.

GULLS
Adults

GLAUCOUS-WINGED GULL

winter

breeding

GLAUCOUS GULL

winter

breeding

IVORY GULL

breeding

BLACK-LEGGED KITTIWAKE

winter

breeding

RED-LEGGED KITTIWAKE

winter

breeding

95

LAUGHING GULL *Larus atricilla*

16–17″ (40–43 cm). A small coastal gull. The *dark mantle blends into the black wing tips.* A bold white trailing edge on dark wing. Head *black* in summer; white in winter, with a dark smudge across eye and nape. Bill may have red tip. *Immature:* See pp. 102, 103.

Voice: A strident laugh, *ha-ha-ha-ha-ha-haah-haah-haah,* etc.

Range: East Coast: Nova Scotia to Venezuela. Local, s. California, w. Mexico. Winters from s. U.S. south to Peru. **West:** Common post-breeding visitor to Salton Sea; has bred there. Casual, coastal California. Accidental north to Washington, Montana, Saskatchewan.

FRANKLIN'S GULL *Larus pipixcan*　　　　　　　　　　**M157**

14½″ (37 cm). Note the *white band* on the wing, separating the black from the gray. In summer, the head is black and the breast has a rosy bloom. In fall, the head is white with dark cheeks and a dark nape. *Immature:* See pp. 102, 103.

Voice: A shrill *kuk-kuk-kuk;* also mewing, laughing cries.

Range: Breeds in w. Canada and nw. and n.-cen. U.S. Winters in Pacific from Guatemala to Chile. **West:** Map 157. **Habitat:** Prairies, inland marshes, lakes; in winter, coasts, ocean.

SABINE'S GULL *Xema sabini*　　　　　　　　　　　　**M169**

13–14″ (33–35 cm). Our only gull with a *well-forked tail.* Note the black outer primaries and *triangular white wing patch.* Bill black, with a *yellow tip;* feet black. This gull has a slaty hood in summer, lacking in winter. *Immature:* See pp. 102, 103.

Range: Arctic; circumpolar. Winters in Pacific to Chile; local in Atlantic. **West:** Map 169. **Habitat:** Ocean; nests on tundra.

COMMON BLACK-HEADED GULL *Larus ridibundus*

14–15″ (35–38 cm). Similar in pattern to Bonaparte's Gull and associates with it; slightly larger. Shows much *blackish on underside of primaries;* bill *dark red,* not black. In winter loses its dark brown hood and has a black earspot. *Immature:* See pp. 102, 103.

Range: Eurasia, Iceland; increasingly frequent in e. N. America. **West:** Regular spring visitor to Aleutians, Pribilofs; rare elsewhere in Alaska. Casual stray to British Columbia, Pacific states.

BONAPARTE'S GULL *Larus philadelphia*　　　　　　　**M158**

13″ (33 cm). A petite, almost tern-like gull. Note the *wedge of white* on the *fore edge* of the wing. Legs red; bill small, black. Adult in summer has a blackish head. Winter adult has a white head with a *black earspot. Immature:* See pp. 102, 103.

Voice: A nasal *cheeer* or *cherr.* Some notes tern-like.

Range: Alaska, w. and cen. Canada. Winters from n. U.S. to Mexico, Puerto Rico. **West:** Map 158. **Habitat:** Ocean bays, lakes, muskeg.

LITTLE GULL *Larus minutus*

11″ (28 cm). The smallest gull; usually associates with Bonaparte's. Note the *blackish undersurface* of the *rather rounded wing* and absence of black above. Legs red. In summer the head is black, bill dark red, breast may be pinkish. In winter, head is *dark-capped,* bill is black. *Immature:* See pp. 102, 103.

Range: Eurasia, wintering to n. Africa, Japan. A small population breeds in n.-cen. N. America. **West:** Casual or accidental, Alaska, nw. Canada, Pacific states, Nevada, Colorado, etc.

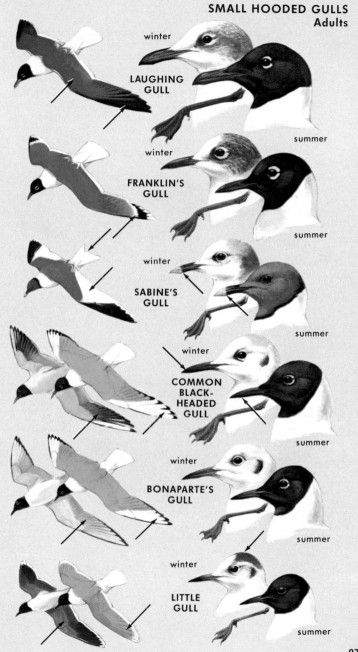

SMALL HOODED GULLS
Adults

LAUGHING GULL
winter
summer

FRANKLIN'S GULL
winter
summer

SABINE'S GULL
winter
summer

COMMON BLACK-HEADED GULL
winter
summer

BONAPARTE'S GULL
winter
summer

LITTLE GULL
winter
summer

- **IMMATURE GULLS.** *Immatures* are more difficult to identify than adults. They are usually darkest the first year and lighter the second; in the larger species they may not develop their full adult plumage until the third or fourth year. See pp. 88, 89. Leg colors of most immatures are not as diagnostic as those of adults. However, in some cases bill colors may be helpful. Go mainly by pattern and size. The most typical plumages are shown in the following pages; intermediate and successive stages can be expected, but do not feel you must identify *every* immature gull. Because of variables such as the stage of molt, wear, age, individual variation, frequent hybridization, and even occasional albinism, some birds may remain a mystery even to the expert unless the specimen is in the hand. See also pp. 100–103.

GLAUCOUS GULL *Larus hyperboreus*   Adult, pp. 94, 95.
A four-year gull. *First winter:* Recognized by its large size (a bit larger than Glaucous-winged or Western Gull), pale tan coloration, and unmarked *frosty primaries*, a shade lighter than the rest of the wing. Bill *pale flesh pink* with a dark tip. The pale gray mantle is acquired later, with approaching adulthood. *Second year:* Paler buff; occasional worn or faded birds may appear to be pure white throughout with only a hint of mottling.

GLAUCOUS-WINGED GULL *Larus glaucescens*   Adult, pp. 94, 95.
A four-year gull; variable. Size of Western Gull, and with a similar sequence of plumages (see p. 89), but primaries are much the same tone as the rest of the wing, not darker as in Western or Herring gulls, or paler, frosty, or translucent as in Glaucous Gull.

WESTERN GULL *Larus occidentalis*
A four-year gull; see sequences of plumages on pp. 88, 89. First-year birds are larger and less brown than first-year Herring Gulls.

HEERMANN'S GULL *Larus heermanni*   Adult, pp. 90, 91.
A three-year gull. Readily told by its size and all-dark, sooty or slaty color. Note the bicolored bill.

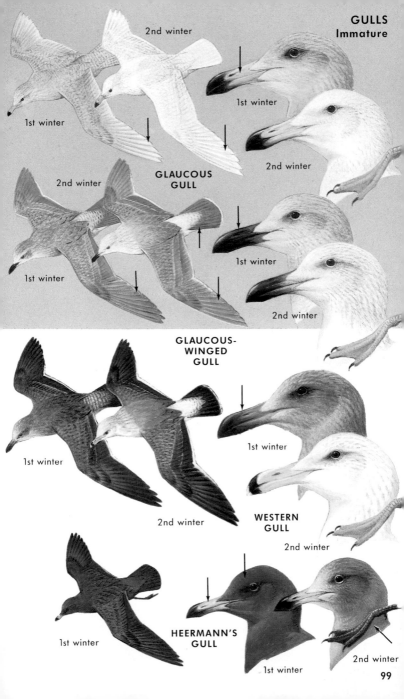

GULLS
Immature

2nd winter

1st winter

1st winter

GLAUCOUS GULL

2nd winter

1st winter

1st winter

2nd winter

1st winter

2nd winter

GLAUCOUS-WINGED GULL

1st winter

1st winter

2nd winter

WESTERN GULL

2nd winter

1st winter

HEERMANN'S GULL

1st winter

2nd winter

■ IMMATURE GULLS, continued.

HERRING GULL *Larus argentatus* **Adult, pp. 92, 93.**
  A four-year gull. *Juvenile:* Relatively uniform dusky brown. *First winter:* Much like juvenile but not quite as dark. Bill all dark at first, becoming paler at base later. *Second and third winter:* Paler. Head and underparts whiter; tail feathers dark-tipped, contrasting with white rump; bill pale, dark-tipped. The gray mantle is acquired with approaching adulthood.

THAYER'S GULL *Larus thayeri* **Adult, pp. 92, 93.**
  A four-year gull. *First winter:* Gray-brown throughout; similar to first-winter Western and Herring gulls, but lighter; primaries usually *the same gray-brown as the rest of the wing* (not darker or blackish, as in Western or most other gulls). *Second winter:* Paler and grayer; primaries gray-brown. *In any plumage, gray or pale gray-brown wing tips* from below.
  Similar species: See immature Glaucous-winged Gull, p. 98.

CALIFORNIA GULL *Larus californicus* **Adult, pp. 92, 93.**
  A four-year gull. *Juvenile:* As *dark* as the somewhat larger juvenile Herring Gull, but with a smaller, *bicolored bill. First winter:* Similar but with paler mottling. *Second winter:* Much like first-winter Ring-bill (gray on back) but tail mostly all dark, not with a well-defined subterminal band.

RING-BILLED GULL *Larus delawarensis* **Adult, pp. 92, 93.**
  A three-year gull. Juveniles are much smaller, paler, and more speckled than juvenile Herring Gulls, but first-winter immatures may be confused with second- and third-winter Herring Gulls, which have a semblance of a ring near the tip of the longer bill. In the Herring Gull and California Gull the tail is mostly dark, terminating in a very *broad*, ill-defined band. The subterminal band in young Ring-bills is much narrower (a little over 1 in. wide) and usually (but not always) well defined. The leg color is not useful, as young Ring-bills have dull flesh-pink, flesh-gray, or grayish legs, not unlike those of certain other young gulls.

MEW GULL *Larus canus* **Adult, pp. 92, 93.**
  A three-year gull. *Juvenile:* Very dark; might suggest a young Heermann's Gull, but has a smaller, shorter bill and pale legs. *First winter:* More like a second-winter California Gull, but considerably smaller, with a rounder head and smaller, thinner bill.

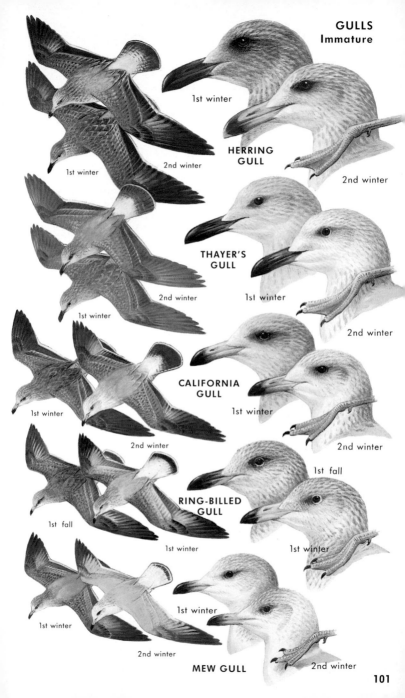

GULLS
Immature

1st winter

2nd winter

1st winter

HERRING GULL

2nd winter

2nd winter

1st winter

THAYER'S GULL

1st winter

2nd winter

1st winter

2nd winter

1st winter

CALIFORNIA GULL

1st winter

2nd winter

1st fall

2nd winter

RING-BILLED GULL

1st fall

1st winter

1st winter

1st winter

1st winter

2nd winter

1st winter

MEW GULL

2nd winter

IMMATURE GULLS: SMALLER SPECIES

LAUGHING GULL *Larus atricilla* **Adult, pp. 96, 97.**
A three-year gull. *Juvenile:* Very *dark,* with a *white rump* and a *broad white border* on the trailing edge of the dark wing. *First winter:* Paler or whiter on the chest and forehead; not easy to separate from young Franklin's Gull. *Second winter:* Similar to winter adult, but with a trace of black in the tail.

FRANKLIN'S GULL *Larus pipixcan* **Adult, pp. 96, 97.**
A two-year gull. *First winter:* Very similar to first-winter Laughing Gull, but smaller-billed and more petite. It perhaps may best be distinguished by the incomplete tail band. Note also the *darker cheek* and *more distinctly hooded* effect. Outer tail feathers *white.* Juvenile Laughing Gull is separated from Franklin's by its brown breast and brown forehead, which become whiter as fall progresses.

SABINE'S GULL *Xema sabini* **Adult, pp. 96, 97.**
A two-year gull. *Juvenile and first winter:* Dark grayish brown on the back, but with the adult's bold *triangular wing pattern.* Note the scaly pattern and also the *forked* tail. Young Kittiwake is similar, but has a dark bar on the nape, a diagonal bar across the wing, and only a slight tail notch.

BLACK-LEGGED KITTIWAKE *Rissa tridactyla* **Adult, pp. 94, 95.**
A two-year gull. *First winter:* Note the *dark bar on the nape,* the black outer primaries, and the dark bar across the inner wing. The tail may seem notched.

BONAPARTE'S GULL *Larus philadelphia* **Adult, pp. 96, 97.**
A two-year gull. Petite, tern-like. *First winter:* Note the cheek spot, narrow black tail band, and pattern of black and white in the outer primaries.

COMMON BLACK-HEADED GULL *Larus ridibundus* **Adult, pp. 96, 97.**
A two-year gull. *First winter:* Similar in pattern to immature Bonaparte's Gull, with which it associates, but slightly larger and less tern-like; the bill is longer, ochre at the base, black at the tip. Underwing as in adult Black-head, but not as dark.

IVORY GULL *Pagophila eburnea* **Adult, pp. 94, 95.**
A two-year gull. *First winter:* A tern-like white gull, with irregular gray smudges on the face, a *sprinkling of black spots* above, and a narrow black border on the rear edge of its white wings.

LITTLE GULL *Larus minutus* **Adult, pp. 96, 97.**
A two-year gull. *First winter:* Smaller than young Bonaparte's, with rounder wings and a *blacker M pattern* formed by the outer primaries and the dark band across the wing. Note especially the *dusky cap.*

ROSS'S GULL *Rhodostethia rosea* **Adult, pp. 90, 91.**
A two-year gull. *First winter:* Similar in pattern to immature Black-legged Kittiwake, but note the *wedge-shaped* tail (not square or notched) and the *blue-gray* linings of the underwing. It lacks the dark nape of the immature Kittiwake.

SMALL GULLS
Immature

juvenile

1st winter

juvenile

LAUGHING

1st winter

LAUGHING

1st winter

1st winter

FRANKLIN'S

FRANKLIN'S

SABINE'S

BLACK-LEGGED
KITTIWAKE

BONAPARTE'S

COMMON
BLACK-HEADED

IVORY

LITTLE

ROSS'S

103

■ **TERNS. Subfamily Sterninae.** Graceful water birds, more streamlined than gulls; wings more pointed, tail usually forked. Bill sharp-pointed, often tilted toward the water. Most terns are whitish with black caps; in winter, black of forehead replaced by white. Sexes alike. Terns often hover and plunge headfirst for fish. Normally they do not swim (gulls do). **Food:** Small fish, marine life, large insects. **Range:** Almost worldwide. **No. of species:** World 42; West 11.

GULL-BILLED TERN *Sterna nilotica*
14″ (35 cm). Note the stout, almost *gull-like black* bill. Stockier and paler than Common Tern; tail much less forked; feet *black*. In winter the head is white with a dark ear patch, pale dusky on nape; suggests a small gull with a notched tail. *Immature:* Similar to nonbreeding adult. This tern often hawks for insects.
Voice: A throaty, rasping *za-za-za*; also *kay-week, kay-week*.
Range: Breeds locally, wanders widely in many parts of world. **West:** Summer resident Salton Sea, California. Casual, sw. Arizona. **Habitat:** Salt marshes, fields, coastal bays.

ELEGANT TERN *Sterna elegans*
16–17″ (40–43 cm). This Mexican species should be looked for in fall along the coast. In size, midway between Royal and Forster's terns. Bill orange-yellow, with no black tip (Forster's has black tip), and proportionately more slender than the more orange bill of the Royal. Its black crest is longer. In winter, it has a blacker crown than Royal Tern. **Voice:** A nasal *karreek*, or *ka-zeek.*
Range: Breeds on islands off Baja California. Winters Peru to Chile. **West:** Wanders irregularly (mainly Aug.–Oct.) north to San Francisco Bay; recently even to Washington. Breeds near San Diego.

ROYAL TERN *Sterna maxima*
18–21″ (45–53 cm). A large tern, slimmer than Caspian, with a large *orange* bill (Caspian's bill is redder). Tail deeply forked. Although some Royal Terns in spring show a solid cap, they usually have much white on the forehead, the black feathers forming a crest. Whiter under primaries than Caspian.
Voice: *Keer*, higher than Caspian's note; also *kaak* or *kak.*
Range: Coasts of se. U.S. to Argentina; s. California to Peru; also w. Africa. Winters s. U.S. to Argentina; w. Africa. **West:** Irregular visitor (Sept.–Mar.) along coast north to Morro Bay, rarely to San Francisco. Has bred near San Diego. **Habitat:** Coasts, beaches, salt bays.

CASPIAN TERN *Sterna caspia*   M170
19–23″ (48–58 cm). Large size and *large red bill* set the Caspian apart from all other terns except the slimmer Royal. Caspian ranges inland, Royal does not. Tail of Caspian is shorter; bill is thicker, *red* rather than orange, with a *touch of dark* at the tip. Royal has a more *crested* look; its forehead is usually *clear white* (in this plumage, Caspian has a *streaked* forehead). Caspian shows *much more black under the primaries.*
Voice: A hoarse, low *kraa-uh* or *karr*; also repeated *kaks.*
Range: Breeds locally, wanders widely around the world. **West:** Map 170. **Habitat:** Large lakes, coastal waters, beaches, bays.

Gull-billed

winter

breeding

GULL-BILLED TERN

Elegant

winter

breeding

ELEGANT TERN

Royal

most of year

early
summer

ROYAL TERN

Caspian

winter

CASPIAN TERN   105
breeding

FORSTER'S TERN *Sterna forsteri* **M173**

14–15″ (35–38 cm). A slim, graceful, gull-like bird with a *black cap*; long, pointed wings; and a *deeply forked tail*. This, the most widespread of the three similar medium-sized terns in the West, is readily separated from the other two by its *frosty wing tips*. Very similar to the Common Tern, but paler; primaries lighter than the rest of the wing (darker in Common). Tail grayer; bill more orange. In fall and winter, adult and immature Forster's have a *black mask or patch through the eye and ear* (not around the nape). *Immature:* Lacks the dusky forewing (dark shoulder) of Common Tern.
Voice: A harsh, nasal *za-a-ap* and a nasal *kyarr.*
Range: W. Canada, w. U.S., and cen. Atlantic Coast to Tamaulipas. Winters s. U.S. to Guatemala. **West:** Map 173. The most widespread tern in the West. **Habitat:** Marshes (fresh, salt), lakes, bays, beaches, ocean. Nests in marshes.

ARCTIC TERN *Sterna paradisaea* **M172**

14–17″ (35–43 cm). Very similar to Common or Forster's terns, but *grayer*; the *white cheeks* contrast with the grayish throat and breast. The shorter bill is usually *blood-red* to the tip. Legs shorter. Overhead, note the *translucent* effect of the primaries and the *narrow* black trailing edge. In the fall the bill and feet of adults become dark. The most pelagic (sea-going) tern.
Voice: *Kee-yah,* similar to Common Tern's cry; less slurred, higher. A high *keer-keer* is characteristic.
Range: Northern parts of N. Hemisphere; circumpolar. Winters in sub-Antarctic seas. **West:** Map 172. **Habitat:** Open ocean, rocky coasts, islands; in summer, also tundra lakes.

COMMON TERN *Sterna hirundo* **M171**

13–16″ (33–40 cm). *Summer:* White, with a pearl gray mantle and black cap; bill red-orange with a black tip; feet orange-red. Very similar to Forster's Tern, but the five outer primaries form a *dark wedge*, contrasting with the light inner primaries. *Winter adult:* The black cap is incomplete, the bill blackish. The Siberian race (*longipennis*) is a rare visitor in the w. Aleutians and other islands in the Bering Sea. It is darker, with a *black bill* in breeding plumage and *black feet. Immature:* Similar to winter adult but shoulder and leading edge of wing darker than those of imm. Arctic Tern.
Similar species: (1) See Forster's Tern, the most widespread tern in the West. (2) Arctic Tern is more widespread at sea.
Voice: A drawling *kee-arr* (downward inflection); also *kik-kik-kik*; a quick *kirri-kirri.*
Range: Temperate zone of N. Hemisphere. Winters to S. Hemisphere. **West:** Map 171. **Habitat:** Lakes, ocean, bays, beaches; nests colonially on sandy beaches and small islands.

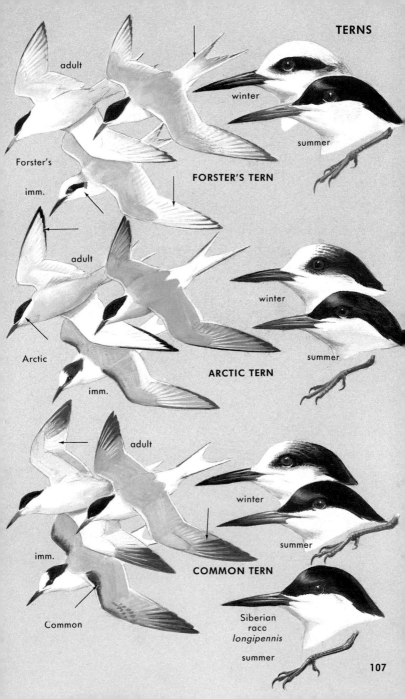

TERNS

adult

Forster's

winter

summer

FORSTER'S TERN

imm.

adult

Arctic

winter

summer

imm.

ARCTIC TERN

adult

winter

summer

imm.

COMMON TERN

Common

Siberian
race
longipennis

summer

107

LEAST TERN *Sterna antillarum*   **M174**
9″ (23 cm). A *very small*, pale tern, with a *yellow bill, yellow feet*, and a *white forehead*. Flight more fluttery than that of other terns. *Immature:* Dark bill, dark nape, much dark on forewing. In the fall, all birds may have dark bills, but feet still show yellow.
Voice: A sharp, repeated *kit;* a harsh, squealing *zree-eek* or *zeek;* also a rapid *kitti-kitti-kitti.*
Range: Temperate and tropical oceans. Winters south of U.S. **West:** Map 174. **Habitat:** Sea beaches, bays; large rivers, bars.

ALEUTIAN TERN *Sterna aleutica*
15″ (38 cm). A lead-colored tern of Alaskan coastal waters. Known from Arctic Tern by its much grayer color, blackish primaries, *blackish or dark bill and feet, clean-cut white forehead.* The gray body and mantle contrast with the white tail.
Voice: A three-syllable whistle, suggesting a shorebird.
Range: Breeds on Sakhalin I., Kamchatka, and locally in s. and w. Alaska north to Bering Straits and west sparsely through Aleutians. Winters in nw. Pacific.

BLACK TERN *Chlidonias niger*   **M175**
9–10″ (23–25 cm). A *black-bodied* tern. *Breeding:* Head and underparts black; back, wings, and tail dark gray; wing linings white. By midsummer, molting birds are mottled, with the black largely replaced by white. Note the pied head, smudge on side of the breast. *Immature:* Similar to non-breeding adult.
Voice: A sharp *kik, keek,* or *klea.*
Range: Temperate N. America, w. Eurasia. Winters mainly in S. America, w. Africa. **West:** Map 175. **Habitat:** Fresh marshes, lakes; in migration, also coastal waters.

Note: WHITE-WINGED TERN, *Chlidonias leucopterus* of Eurasia, has occurred as a stray in extreme w. Aleutians (Nizki I.). In breeding plumage it differs from the Black Tern in having a largely *white* upperwing and *black* wing linings. In winter, paler than Black Tern, lacking the dark shoulder spot.

■ **SKIMMERS. Subfamily Rynchopinae.** Slim, short-legged relatives of gulls and terns. Scissorlike red bill; lower mandible longer than upper. **Food:** Small fish, crustaceans. **Range:** Coasts, large rivers of warmer parts of world. **No. of species:** World 3; West 1.

BLACK SKIMMER *Rhynchops niger*
16–20″ (40–50 cm). More slender than a gull, with extremely long wings. Black above, white below. Note the unequal scissorlike bill. The bright red bill (tipped with black) is long and flat vertically; lower mandible juts a third beyond upper. *Immature:* Brownish, speckled, smaller-billed. Primarily coastal; skims low, dipping knifelike lower mandible in water.
Voice: Soft, short, barking notes. Also *kaup, kaup.*
Range: Cape Cod, s. California, south to s. S. America. **West:** A recently established resident of s. California, nesting at Salton Sea and near San Diego. Occasional elsewhere on California coast; casual, Arizona, New Mexico.

TERNS, SKIMMER

imm.

winter

LEAST TERN

breeding

below

breeding

ALEUTIAN TERN

breeding

winter

winter

below

BLACK TERN

breeding

winter

winter

WHITE-WINGED TERN

below

breeding

juvenile

adult

BLACK SKIMMER

109

■ **HERONS, BITTERNS. Family Ardeidae.** Medium to large wading birds with long necks, spearlike bills. They stand with the neck erect or the head back on the shoulders. In flight, the neck is folded in an S; legs trail. Some herons may have plumes when breeding. Sexes similar. **Food:** Fish, frogs, crawfish, other aquatic life; mice, insects. **Range:** Worldwide except colder regions, some deserts and islands. **No. of species:** World 67; West 13 (+ 1 accidental).

GREAT BLUE HERON *Ardea herodias*   **M21**
42–52″ (105–130 cm). A lean gray bird, often miscalled a "crane" (pp. 116, 117); may stand 4 ft. tall. Its long legs, long neck, dagger-like bill, and, in flight, its folded neck indicate a heron. Great size and blue-gray color, white about the head (in adults), mark it as this species.
Voice: Deep harsh croaks: *Frahnk, frahnk, frahnk.*
Range: S. Canada to Mexico. Winters to n. S. America. **West:** Map 21. **Habitat:** Marshes, swamps, shores, tideflats.

LITTLE BLUE HERON *Egretta caerulea*
24″ (60 cm). A slender, rather small, dark heron. *Adult:* Bluish slate with a deep maroon-brown neck; legs dark, bill pale bluish with a dark tip. *Immature:* See pp. 112, 113. All white with grayish wing tips. Legs *dull olive;* bill pale *bluish,* tipped with black. Birds in transition are boldly pied white and dark.
Similar species: Adults may be mistaken for Reddish Egret.
Range: Eastern U.S. to Peru, Argentina. **West:** A rare visitor to the sw. states; most frequent in California (has bred there). Accidental, Washington, British Columbia.

GREEN-BACKED HERON *Butorides striatus*   **M25**
(Green Heron) 16–22″ (40–55 cm). A small dark heron that in flight looks crow-like (but flies with bowed wingbeats). When alarmed it stretches its neck, elevates a shaggy crest, and jerks its tail. The comparatively *short* legs are *greenish yellow* or *orange* (when breeding). Back with a blue-green gloss; neck deep chestnut. The immature has a streaked neck and breast.
Voice: A series of *kuck's;* a loud *skyow* or *skewk.*
Range: Nw. U.S., se. Canada to Argentina; se. Asia, Africa, Australia. **West:** Map 25. **Habitat:** Lakes, ponds, marshes, streams.

TRICOLORED HERON *Egretta tricolor*
(Louisiana Heron) 26″ (65 cm). A very slender, dark heron with a contrasting *white belly* and white rump.
Range: Eastern U.S. to Brazil. **West:** A rare but regular visitor to s. California. Casual, other sw. states; accidental, Oregon, Alberta.

REDDISH EGRET *Egretta rufescens*
29″ (73 cm). Note the pinkish, black-tipped bill. Neutral gray, with a rusty head and neck; paler than Little Blue Heron, which has pale bluish at base of bill. Loose-feathered, neck shaggy (adult). When feeding, lurches about, wings half spread; acts drunk. The white morph presumably does not occur in the West.
Range: Gulf states, W. Indies to n. Venezuela; Baja California to El Salvador. **West:** A rare visitor to s. California (especially the coast); accidental, Arizona, Colorado.

DARK HERONS

immature

Herons fly with necks pulled in.

Herons necks may stretch or be looped in.

adult

adult

GREAT BLUE HERON

adult

LITTLE BLUE HERON

adult

immature

adult

immature

GREEN-BACKED HERON

adult

REDDISH EGRET

TRICOLORED HERON

Reddish Egret "dancing"

111

GREAT EGRET *Casmerodius albus*   **M22**
(Common Egret) 38″ (95 cm). A tall, stately, slender white heron with a largely *yellow bill*. Legs and feet *black*. When breeding, *straight plumes* on the back extend beyond the tail; bill may have a dark ridge. When feeding, the bird assumes an eager, forward-leaning pose, with its neck extended.
Voice: A low, hoarse croak. Also, *cuk, cuk, cuk*.
Range: U.S. to s. S. America; warmer parts of Old World. **West:** Map 22. **Habitat:** Marshes, ponds, shores, mudflats.

SNOWY EGRET *Egretta thula*   **M23**
20–27″ (50–68 cm). Note the *"golden slippers."* A rather small white heron, with a *slender black bill*, black legs, and *yellow feet*. *Recurved plumes* on the back during breeding season. A yellow loral spot is before the eye (red when bird is breeding). When feeding, this heron rushes about, shuffling its feet to stir up food. Young birds may show yellowish or greenish on much of rear side of legs.
Voice: A low croak; in colony, a bubbling *wulla-wulla-wulla*.
Range: Northern U.S. to Argentina. **West:** Map 23. **Habitat:** Marshes, swamps, ponds, shores, tideflats.

LITTLE BLUE HERON *Egretta caerulea*   **Adult, pp. 110, 111.**
Immature: White, with a touch of gray in the wing tips. Lores gray, legs dull greenish. May be confused with immature Snowy Egret.

CHINESE EGRET *Egretta eulophotes*
This endangered Asiatic bird has occurred once in the w. Aleutians (Aggatu I.). When breeding it resembles a Snowy Egret (black legs, yellow feet), but the bill is *yellow*, the lores *dark*.

CATTLE EGRET *Bubulcus ibis*   **M24**
20″ (50 cm). A recent invader. Slightly smaller, stockier than Snowy Egret. Breeding plumage shows a wash of *buff* on crown, breast, and back; little or none at other times. Bill relatively short, *yellow* (orange-pink on nesting birds). Legs may be yellow, greenish, or coral-pink (on nesting birds), or dusky (immature).
Range: S. Eurasia, Africa; recent immigrant to N. and S. America, Australia. Introduced Hawaii. **West:** Map 24. **Habitat:** Farms, marshes, highway edges; often associates with cattle.

■ **IBISES AND SPOONBILLS. Family Threskiornithidae.** Ibises are long-legged, heron-like marsh waders with slender, *decurved* bills. Spoonbills have *spatulate* bills. Both fly in V's or lines and, unlike herons, fly with necks *outstretched*. **Food:** Small crustaceans, small fish, insects, etc. **Range:** Tropical and warm temperate regions. **No. of species:** World 30; West 3.

WHITE IBIS *Eudocimus albus*
22–27″ (55–68 cm). Note the *red face*, long *decurved red bill*, and restricted black wing tips. Immature is dark brownish; note the *white belly*, *white rump*, curved *red* bill. Immature Glossy Ibis differs in being uniformly dark with a dark bill.
Range: Se. U.S. to n. S. America. **West:** A casual stray to California, Arizona, New Mexico; accidental, Wyoming, Idaho, Dakotas.

ROSEATE SPOONBILL *Ajaia ajaja*   **Adult shown on pp. 114, 115.**
Immature: Spatulate bill; pale pink plumage.

112

WHITE HERONS
etc.

immature

adult

breeding

GREAT EGRET

in molt

SNOWY EGRET

CHINESE
EGRET

immature

LITTLE
BLUE
HERON

accidental
Alaska

imm.

breeding

CATTLE EGRET

in molt
1st spring

adult

WHITE
IBIS

ROSEATE
SPOONBILL

immature
1st fall

113

BLACK-CROWNED NIGHT-HERON *Nycticorax nycticorax* **M26**
23–28″ (58–70 cm). This stocky, thick-billed, short-legged heron is usually hunched and inactive; flies to feed at dusk. *Adult: Black back and cap* contrast with pale gray or whitish underparts. Eyes red; legs yellowish or greenish (pink when breeding). Breeding birds have two long white head plumes. *Immature:* Warm brown, streaked and spotted with buff and white.
Voice: A flat *quok!* or *quark!* Most often heard at dusk.
Range: S. Canada to Falklands; Eurasia, Africa, Pacific Is. **West:** Map 26. **Habitat:** Marshes, shores; roosts in trees.

YELLOW-CROWNED NIGHT-HERON *Nyctanassa violacea*
22–28″ (55–70 cm). A chunky *gray* heron; head black, with a *white cheek patch and crown. Immature:* Similar to young Black-crown; duskier, *more finely streaked and spotted.* Bill thicker, legs *longer.* In flight, the entire foot extends beyond the tail.
Voice: *Quark,* higher pitched than note of Black-crown.
Range: Eastern U.S. to n. Peru and s. Brazil. **West:** Casual or accidental straggler west of 100° to Saskatchewan, Montana, Wyoming, Colorado, New Mexico, Arizona, and California.

AMERICAN BITTERN *Botaurus lentiginosus* **M19**
23″ (58 cm). Stocky; size of a young Night-Heron, but warmer brown; *black stripe* on neck. In flight, outer wing *blackish,* bill held more horizontal. At rest, it may stand rigid, bill pointed up.
Voice: "Pumping," or song, a slow, deep *oong-ka' choonk, oong-ka' choonk, oong-ka' choonk,* etc. Flushing note, *kok-kok-kok.*
Range: Canada to Gulf states; winters to Panama. **West:** Map 19.
Habitat: Marshes, reedy lakes. Seldom sits in trees.

LEAST BITTERN *Ixobrychus exilis* **M20**
11–14″ (28–35 cm). Very small, thin, furtive; straddles reeds. Note the large *buff wing patch* (lacking in rails).
Voice: Song, a low, muted *coo-coo-coo,* heard in the marsh.
Range: Se. Canada, U.S. to ne. Argentina. **West:** Map 20. **Habitat:** Fresh marshes, reedy ponds; not easy to flush.

ROSEATE SPOONBILL *Ajaia ajaja* (family on p. 112)
32″ (80 cm). A *bright pink* wading bird with a long, flat, spoonlike bill. Adults are *shell-pink,* with a blood-red "drip" on the shoulders; tail orange. Head naked, greenish gray. *Immature:* See pp. 112, 113. When feeding, the bill is swept from side to side. In flight, the neck is extended.
Range: Gulf states to Argentina, Chile. **West:** Irregular post-breeding visitor to s. California (Salton Sea, lower Colorado R.). Accidental, Nevada, Utah, Colorado, Arizona, New Mexico, w. Texas.

WHITE-FACED IBIS *Plegadis chihi* (family on p. 112) **M27**
22–25″ (55–63 cm). A long-legged marsh wader with a *long, decurved bill.* Deep purplish chestnut; suggests a large, blackish curlew. Flies in lines with its neck outstretched, alternately flapping and gliding. Breeding birds show a *white border* at the base of the bill; also red legs and red lores. Immatures and non-breeding adults lack the white on the face and the red legs.
Range: Western U.S. to Argentina. **West:** Map 27. **Habitat:** Fresh marshes, irrigated land, tules.

LONG-LEGGED WADERS

imm.

breeding

imm.

breeding

BLACK-CROWNED NIGHT HERON

YELLOW-CROWNED NIGHT HERON

AMERICAN BITTERN

"freezing"

breeding

ROSEATE SPOONBILL

♂ adult

LEAST BITTERN

imm.

breeding

WHITE-FACED IBIS

breeding

White Ibis
imm. (1st fall),
for comparison

115

■ **STORKS. Family Ciconiidae.** Large, long-legged, and heron-like, with straight, recurved or decurved bills. Some have naked heads. Sexes alike. Walk is sedate; flight deliberate, neck and legs extended. **Food:** Frogs, crustaceans, lizards, rodents. **Range:** Southern U.S. to S. America; Africa, Eurasia, E. Indies, Australia. **No. of species:** World 18; West 1.

WOOD STORK *Mycteria americana*
34–47″ (85–118 cm). Very large (spread 5½ ft.). White, with a *dark naked head* and *much black* in the wing; black tail. Bill long, *thick, decurved.* Immature has a yellow bill. When feeding, keeps its head down and walks. In flight, it alternately flaps and glides.
Voice: A hoarse croak; usually silent.
Range: Southern U.S. to Argentina. **West:** Regular visitor in late summer and fall to s. California (especially Salton Sea), sw. and cen. Arizona, s. Nevada; casual or accidental to ne. California, British Columbia, Utah, Idaho, s. Montana, Wyoming, Colorado, New Mexico, and eastward. **Habitat:** Marshes, ponds, lagoons.

■ **CRANES. Family Gruidae.** Stately birds, more robust than herons, often with *red facial skin.* Note the *tufted appearance* over the rump. In flight, neck extended; migrate in V's or lines like geese. Large herons are sometimes wrongly referred to as "cranes." **Food:** Omnivorous. **Range:** Nearly cosmopolitan except Cen. and S. America and Oceania. **No. of species:** World 15; West 2 (+1 accidental).

WHOOPING CRANE *Grus americana*
50″ (125 cm); spread 7½ ft. The tallest North American bird and one of the rarest. A large *white* crane with a *red face.* Primary wing feathers *black.* Young birds are washed with rust color, especially about the head.
Voice: A shrill, buglelike trumpeting, *ker-loo! ker-lee-oo!*
Range: Breeds in Wood Buffalo Park border of n. Alberta and N.W.T.; migrates through Great Plains to coastal Texas. Reintroduced at Gray's Lake, Idaho (migrating via Colorado to Bosque Del Apache Refuge in New Mexico). *Endangered* but slowly increasing.

SANDHILL CRANE *Grus canadensis*   **M112**
40–48″ (100–120 cm); spread 6–7 ft. Note the *bald red crown,* bustlelike rear. A long-legged, long-necked, gray bird, often stained with rust. The immature is brown. In flight, the neck is extended and the wings beat with an upward flick.
Voice: A shrill, rolling *garoo-a-a-a;* repeated.
Range: Ne. Siberia, N. America, Cuba. Winters to Mexico. **West:** Map 112. **Habitat:** Prairies, fields, marshes; tundra.

COMMON CRANE *Grus grus*
41″ (103 cm). Eurasian. Note the *black neck* (left). May occur as a very rare vagrant in flocks of Sandhill Cranes. **West:** Has been recorded in Alaska, Alberta, New Mexico, Nebraska, and Texas.

STORKS, CRANES

Below, for comparison:
left, White Ibis
right, Wood Stork

adult

WOOD STORK

imm.

Storks, ibises, and
cranes fly with
necks outstretched.

adult

WHOOPING CRANE

imm.

adult

imm.

SANDHILL CRANE

■ **RAILS, GALLINULES, AND COOTS. Family Rallidae** (in part). Rails are rather hen-shaped marsh birds of secretive habits and mysterious voices, more often heard than seen. Their flight is brief and reluctant, with legs dangling. Gallinules and coots swim; they resemble ducks except for their smaller heads, forehead shields, and chicken-like bills. See them on pp. 64, 65; heads only are shown here. **Food:** Aquatic plants, seeds, insects, frogs, crustaceans, mollusks. **Range:** Nearly worldwide. **No. of species:** World 128; West 8 (+2 accidental).

SORA *Porzana carolina* **M109**
8–9¾" (20–24 cm). Note the *short yellow* bill. The adult is a small, plump, gray-brown rail, with a *black patch* on the face and throat. The short, cocked tail reveals white or buff undertail coverts. Immature lacks the throat patch and is browner.
Voice: A descending whinny. In spring, a plaintive whistled *kerwee!* When hands are clapped, startled birds utter a sharp *keek*.
Range: Canada; w., n.-cen., and ne. U.S. Winters from s. U.S. to Peru. **West:** Map 109. **Habitat:** Fresh marshes, wet meadows; in winter, also salt marshes.

BLACK RAIL *Laterallus jamaicensis* **M106**
5–6" (13–15 cm). A tiny blackish rail with a small *black* bill; about the size of a young sparrow. Nape deep chestnut. Very difficult to glimpse, but may respond at night to a tape recording. *Caution:* All young rails in downy plumage are black.
Voice: Male at night, *kiki-doo* or *kiki-krrr* (or "*kitty go*").
Range: Ne. and cen. U.S. and cen. California south locally to W. Indies, Chile. **West:** Map 106. **Habitat:** Tidal marshes, (coast); grassy marshes, stubble fields (inland).

YELLOW RAIL *Coturnicops noveboracensis* **M105**
7" (18 cm). Note the *white wing patch* (in flight). A small buffy rail, suggesting a week-old chick. Bill very short, greenish. Back dark, striped and checkered with buff and black. Mouse-like; difficult to see or flush.
Voice: Nocturnal ticking notes, often in long series: *tic-tic, tic-tic-tic, tic-tic, tic-tic-tic,* etc., in groups of 2 and 3.
Range: Mainly Canada, n. U.S. east of Rockies. Winters se. U.S. **West:** Map 105. **Habitat:** Grassy marshes, meadows; rarely salt marshes.

VIRGINIA RAIL *Rallus limicola* **M108**
9" (23 cm). A small rusty rail with gray cheeks, black bars on the flanks, and a long, slightly decurved, reddish bill. Near the size of a meadowlark; the only small rail with a *long, slender* bill. Grown young in late summer show much black.
Voice: *Wak-wak-wak,* etc., descending; also *kidick, kidick,* etc. and various "kicking" and grunting sounds.
Range: S. Canada to s. S. America. **West:** Map 108. **Habitat:** Fresh and brackish marshes; in winter, also salt marshes.

CLAPPER RAIL *Rallus longirostris* **M107**
14–16" (35–40 cm). The large tan and gray "marsh hen" of California coastal marshes. Note the henlike appearance; strong legs; long, slightly decurved bill; barred flanks; and white patch under the short cocked tail, which it flirts nervously. *(continued on p. 120)*

breeding **SORA**

juvenile

chick

BLACK RAIL

YELLOW RAIL

adult

juvenile

VIRGINIA RAIL

CLAPPER RAIL

chick

Moorhen

Coot

See pp. 64, 65.

119

CLAPPER RAIL (continued). See illustration on previous page.
Voice: A clattering *kek-kek-kek-kek*, etc., or *cha-cha-cha*, etc.
Range: Coasts of e. U.S. and California to n. S. America. **West:** Map 107. **Habitat:** Salt marshes and brackish marshes.
Note: The similar and closely related **KING RAIL** *(Rallus elegans)*, a large rusty rail of marshes east of our area, has strayed west to Colorado. See illustration in eastern *Field Guide.*

■ **OYSTERCATCHERS. Family Haematopodidae.** Large waders with long, laterally flattened, chisel-tipped, red bills. Sexes alike. **Food:** Mollusks, crabs, marine worms. **Range:** Widespread on the coasts of the world; inland in some areas of Europe and Asia. **No. of species:** World 7; West 2.

BLACK OYSTERCATCHER *Haematopus bachmani* **M119**
17–17½″ (43–44 cm). A large, heavily built, blackish shorebird, with a straight *red bill*, flattened laterally. Legs a pale flesh color. Immature may have a black tip on the bill.
Voice: A piercing, sharply repeated, whistled *wheep!* or *kleep!*
Range: Resident from w. Aleutians (Attu), east and south along coast to Morro Bay, California; on offshore islands to Baja California. **West:** Map 119. **Habitat:** Rocky coasts, sea islets.

AMERICAN OYSTERCATCHER *Haematopus palliatus*
17–21″ (43–53 cm). Differs from Black Oystercatcher in having a *white belly* and large *white wing and tail patches*. Its red bill and pale legs are like those of the Black Oystercatcher.
Range: Shores of Cape Cod south to Argentina; w. Mexico to Chile. **West:** Casual stray to California coast, Channel Islands, Salton Sea.

■ **AVOCETS, STILTS. Family Recurvirostridae.** Slim waders with very long legs and very slender bills (bent upward in avocets). Sexes similar. **Food:** Insects, crustaceans, other aquatic life. **Range:** U.S., Cen. and S. America, Africa, s. Eurasia, Australia, Pacific region. **No. of species:** World 9; West 2.

BLACK-NECKED STILT *Himantopus mexicanus* **M120**
13–17″ (33–43 cm). A large, extremely slim wader; black above, white below. Note the *grotesquely long red legs* and needle-like bill. In flight, the black *unpatterned* wings contrast strikingly with the white rump, tail, and underparts.
Voice: A sharp yipping: *kyip, kyip, kyip.* **Range:** W. and se. U.S. to Argentina. Winters mainly south of U.S. **West:** Map 120. **Habitat:** Grassy marshes, mudflats, pools, shallow lakes (fresh and alkaline).

AMERICAN AVOCET *Recurvirostra americana* **M121**
16–20″ (40–50 cm). A large, slim shorebird with a very slender, *upturned*, somewhat godwit-like bill, more upturned in the female. This and the striking white and black pattern make this bird unique. In breeding plumage, the head and neck are pinkish tan; in winter this is replaced with pale gray. Avocets feed with a scythe-like sweep of the head and bill.
Voice: A sharp *wheek* or *kleet*, excitedly repeated. **Range:** Breeds sw. Canada, w. U.S. Winters from s. U.S. to Guatemala. **West:** Map 121. **Habitat:** Beaches, flats, shallow lakes, prairie ponds.

Black
Oystercatcher

American
Oystercatcher

BLACK
OYSTERCATCHER

BLACK-NECKED
STILT

summer

winter

AMERICAN AVOCET

121

■ **PLOVERS. Family Charadriidae.** Wading birds, more compactly built and thicker-necked than most sandpipers, with shorter, pigeon-like bills and larger eyes. Call notes assist identification. Unlike most sandpipers, plovers run in short starts and stops. Sexes alike. *Note:* The turnstones (pp. 142, 143) until recently were assigned to the plover family, but are now regarded as more closely allied to the sandpipers, *Scolopacidae.* **Food:** Small marine life, insects, some vegetable matter. **Range:** Nearly worldwide. **No. of species:** World 67; West 12 (+ 1 accidental).

BLACK-BELLIED PLOVER *Pluvialis squatarola* **M113**
10½–13½" (26–34 cm). A large plover. In breeding plumage adults have a *black breast* and pale speckled back. Winter birds and immatures are gray-looking, but can be recognized as plovers by their stocky shape; hunched posture; and short, pigeon-like bill. In flight, in any plumage, note the *black axillars* ("wingpits") and the white rump and tail.
Similar species: American Golden-Plover and Pacific Golden-Plover are browner and lack the pattern of white in the wings and tail. Their axillars are gray, not black.
Voice: A plaintive slurred whistle, *tlee-oo-eee* or *whee-er-ee* (middle note lower).
Range: Arctic; circumpolar. Winters from coastal U.S. and s. Eurasia to S. Hemisphere. **West:** Map 113. **Habitat:** Mudflats, open marshes, beaches; in summer, tundra.

AMERICAN GOLDEN-PLOVER *Pluvialis dominica* **M114**
(Lesser Golden-Plover) 9½–11" (24–28 cm). Size of Killdeer. Breeding adults are dark, spangled above with *whitish and pale yellow spots;* underparts black. A *broad white stripe* runs over the eye and down the sides of the neck and breast. Young birds and winter adults are brown, darker above than below. In flight, they can be recognized from Black-bellied Plovers by their browner look and *lack of pattern* in wings and tail.
Similar species: Formerly this bird was lumped as one species with the Pacific Golden-Plover; collectively they were known as the "Lesser Golden-Plover."
Voice: A whistled *queedle* or *que-e-a* (dropping at end).
Range: Breeds in arctic America; migrates mainly east of Rockies to s. S. America. **West:** Map 114. **Habitat:** Prairies, mudflats, shores; tundra (summer).

PACIFIC GOLDEN-PLOVER *Pluvialis fulva* **M114**
Very similar to the American Golden-Plover, overlapping in summer only in nw. mainland Alaska. It is the species most likely to be seen in the Pacific states. The white neck stripe *extends along the flank* (but molting American Golden-Plovers may have this look). The golden spangles on the back are brighter. Winter and juvenile birds are also *more golden* than the other species.
Range: Breeds across n. Siberia and in nw. Alaska. Winters in se. Asia, Australia, Pacific islands. **West:** A few migrate along the Pacific Coast to winter in California. Map 114.

PLOVERS

winter

breeding

juvenile

BLACK-BELLIED PLOVER

winter

juv.

breeding

AMERICAN GOLDEN-PLOVER

juvenile

breeding

PACIFIC GOLDEN-PLOVER

123

SEMIPALMATED PLOVER *Charadrius semipalmatus* **M116**
6½–7½″ (16–19 cm). A small, plump, brown-backed plover, half the size of a Killdeer, with a *single dark breastband*. Bill deep yellow with a black tip, or (in winter) nearly all dark. Legs bright orange or yellow. Whereas the Piping and Snowy plovers are pale—the color of dry sand—the Semipalmated is darker, like wet sand or mud.
Voice: A plaintive, upward-slurred *chi-we* or *too-li*.
Range: Arctic and subarctic America. Winters to S. America. **West:** Map 116. **Habitat:** Shores, tideflats, tundra.

PIPING PLOVER *Charadrius melodus* **M115**
6–7½″ (15–19 cm). As pallid as a beach flea or sand crab—the color of dry sand. A complete or incomplete dark ring around the neck. Legs yellow or orange; bill yellow with a black tip. In non-breeding plumage the black on the collar is indistinct or lacking and the bill is black. Note the tail pattern.
Voice: A plaintive whistle; *peep-lo* (first note higher).
Range: Breeds s. Canada to ne. and cen. U.S. Winters s. Atlantic and Gulf coasts. **West:** Map 115. **Habitat:** Sandy beaches.

SNOWY PLOVER *Charadrius alexandrinus* **M115**
6½″ (16 cm). A pale plover of the beaches. Similar to the Piping Plover, which replaces it to the east and north (see map), but male Snowy has a *slim black bill*, dark (sometimes pale) legs, and a *dark ear patch*. Females and juveniles may lack the black in their plumage. Juvenile and winter Piping Plovers may also have dark bills, but they have *white on the rump*, visible in flight.
Voice: A musical whistle; *pe-wee-ah* or *o-wee-ah*.
Range: Southern U.S., cen. and S. America, s. Eurasia, Africa, Australia. **West:** Map 115. **Habitat:** Beaches, sandy flats.

COMMON RINGED PLOVER *Charadrius hiaticula*
7¼″ (19 cm). A Eurasian stray, very similar to the Semipalmated Plover; distinguished in the hand by the presence of a basal web between only two toes. The breastband may be wider. Best recognized from Semipalmated by voice, a softer, more minor *poo-eep* or *too-li*.
Range: N. Eurasia, Greenland, arctic Canada. **West:** Casual visitor to w. Aleutians and St. Lawrence I., where it has bred.

LITTLE RINGED PLOVER *Charadrius dubius*
6″ (15 cm). Resembles Common Ringed Plover, but decidedly smaller. Best distinguished by a *bright yellow eye-ring* and, in flight, *lack of a white wing bar*. Legs *flesh-colored* (not orange), but color not reliable when legs are muddy. Different voice.
Voice: A high, piping *tee-u*.
Range: Eurasia, n. Africa, New Guinea. **West:** Accidental, w. Aleutians.

WILSON'S PLOVER *Charadrius wilsonia*
7–8″ (18–20 cm). A "ringed" plover of the Mexican beaches, larger than the Semipalmated, with a much longer *heavy black bill*. Legs *flesh-gray*. Tends to have a heavier breastband.
Voice: An emphatic whistled *whit!* or *wheet!*
Range: New Jersey, and w. Mexico to n. S. America. **West:** Casual, s. California.

Semipalmated

SMALL "BELTED"
PLOVERS

winter

summer

SEMIPALMATED
PLOVER

Piping

Variant

summer

winter

Snowy

PIPING PLOVER

imm.

summer

SNOWY PLOVER

HEADS OF "BELTED" PLOVERS

SEMIPALMATED   **PIPING**   **SNOWY**

RARE STRAYS

COMMON RINGED   **LITTLE RINGED**   **WILSON'S**

125

KILLDEER *Charadrius vociferus* M117

9–11″ (23–28 cm). The common noisy breeding plover of the farm country. Note the *two black breastbands* (the chick has only one band). In flight, or distraction display near the nest, shows a *golden-tawny rump;* longish tail, white wing stripe.

Voice: Noisy; a loud, insistent *kill-deeah*, repeated; a plaintive *dee-ee* (rising), *dee-dee-dee*, etc. Also a low trill.

Range: S. Alaska, Canada to cen. Mexico, W. Indies; also coastal Peru. **West:** Map 117. **Habitat:** Fields, airports, lawns, river banks, mudflats, shores.

MOUNTAIN PLOVER *Charadrius montanus* M118

8–9½″ (20–24 cm). Somewhat like a small Killdeer, but with *no breast-rings*. In breeding season, has a *white forehead and line over the eye*, contrasting with a *dark crown*. In nondescript winter plumage, it may be told from winter Golden-Plovers by its grayer back (devoid of mottling), *pale legs*, light wing stripe, and dark tail band.

Voice: A low whistle; variable.

Range: Western Great Plains. Map 118. **Habitat:** Semi-arid plains, grasslands, plateaus.

EURASIAN DOTTEREL *Charadrius morinellus*

8½″ (21 cm). In breeding plumage the narrow white stripe crossing mid-breast identifies this dark plover. Belly *russet orange*. The broad *white eyebrow stripes* join in a broad "V" on the nape. Throat white. Non-breeding adults and juveniles are paler, but show enough of the basic pattern to be recognized.

Voice: A repeated piping: *titi-ri-titi-ri*, running into a trill.

Range: Eurasia. **West:** Breeds locally on the high tundra of nw. Alaska and St. Lawrence I. It has been recorded in fall in the w. Aleutians and as an accidental in Washington and California.

MONGOLIAN PLOVER *Charadrius mongolus*

7½″ (19 cm). This Asian plover is very distinctive in breeding plumage, with its *broad cinnamon breastband* separating its white throat from its white belly. The female is duller. The rufous band is absent in non-breeding or juvenile birds.

Range: Asia, migrating to e. Africa, India, Australia. **West:** Rare migrant in the western Aleutian Islands. Occasional on the northern and western mainland of Alaska (has bred there). Accidental in Oregon and California.

PLOVERS

KILLDEER

chick

♂ breeding   winter

MOUNTAIN PLOVER

Alaskan Rarities

juvenile   breeding   ♀

winter   **EURASIAN DOTTEREL**

winter   **MONGOLIAN PLOVER**   ♂   breeding   ♀

127

SHOREBIRDS

The shorebirds (or "waders," as they are often called) are real puzzlers to the novice. There are a dozen plovers in our area and nearly 60 sandpipers and their allies, not to mention the very obvious oystercatchers, stilts, and avocets. To start with, here are a few things to look for:

Plovers vs. Sandpipers

Plovers are usually more compact and thicker-necked than most sandpipers, with pigeon-like bills and larger eyes. They run in short starts and stops.

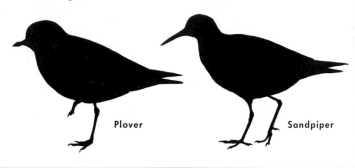

Plover   Sandpiper

BILL SHAPES OF SHOREBIRDS

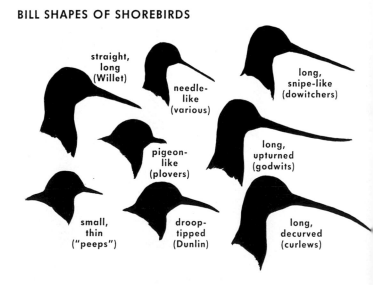

straight, long (Willet)

needle-like (various)

long, snipe-like (dowitchers)

pigeon-like (plovers)

long, upturned (godwits)

small, thin ("peeps")

droop-tipped (Dunlin)

long, decurved (curlews)

SANDPIPERS, PHALAROPES. Family Scolopacidae.

Small to medium-sized waders. Bills more slender than those of plovers. Sexes similar, except in phalaropes (swimmers that were formerly regarded as a separate family). **Food:** Insects, crustaceans, mollusks, worms, etc. **Range:** Cosmopolitan. **No. of species:** World 129; West 51 (+ 7 accidental).

SOME BASIC BODY SHAPES AND ACTIONS OF SANDPIPERS

Sanderlings run.

If it swims, it is a phalarope.

Does it teeter like a "Spotty?'

Or does it nod like a Solitary?

Is it slim like a yellowlegs?

Or is it squat like a turnstone?

Does it probe with a sewing-machine motion?

(dowitcher)

HUDSONIAN GODWIT *Limosa haemastica*

13–16″ (33–40 cm). Note the flight pattern (p. 133). The rather large size and long, straight or *slightly upturned* bill mark this wader as a godwit; the black tail is *ringed broadly with white*. The *blackish* wing linings proclaim it as this species. In spring the male is ruddy-breasted; the female duller. In fall, both sexes are gray-backed, pale-breasted.

Similar species: The Black-tailed Godwit, a stray from Asia, is shown on p. 153.

Voice: *Tawit!* (or *godwit!*); higher-pitched than Marbled Godwit's.

Range: Mainly arctic Canada; winters in S. America. **West:** Breeds locally in s. Alaska (Cook Inlet), probably w. Alaska (Kotzebue and Norton Bay), Mackenzie and nw. British Columbia. Migrates in spring through Great Plains; very rare west to Pacific states. **Habitat:** Beaches, prairie pools; in summer, tundra.

MARBLED GODWIT *Limosa fedoa* **M132**

16–20″ (40–50 cm). Godwits are large shorebirds with long, straight or slightly *upturned* bills. The rich, mottled *buff-brown* color identifies this species. The linings of the underwing are *cinnamon*.

Voice: An accented *kerwhit! (godwit!)*; also *raddica, raddica*.

Range: N. Great Plains; locally sw. Alaska. Winters s. U.S. to n. S. America. **West:** Map 132. **Habitat:** Prairies, pools, shores, tideflats.

LONG-BILLED CURLEW *Numenius americanus* **M130**

20–26″ (50–65 cm). Note the *very long, sickle-shaped bill* (4–8½″). Much larger than the Whimbrel and more buffy; lacks the bold crown stripes. Overhead, shows *cinnamon wing linings*. In young birds the bill may be scarcely longer than that of the Whimbrel (see inset).

Voice: A loud *cur-lee* (rising inflection); a rapid, whistled *kli-li-li-li*. "Song," a trilled, liquid *curleeeeeeeeuuu*.

Range: Sw. Canada, w. U.S. Winters s. U.S. to Guatemala. **West:** Map 130. **Habitat:** High plains, rangeland. In winter, also cultivated land, tideflats, beaches, salt marshes.

WHIMBREL *Numenius phaeopus* **M129**

15–19″ (38–48 cm). A large, gray-brown wader with a long, *decurved bill*. Grayer than the Long-billed Curlew; bill shorter (2¾–4 in.), crown *striped*. Whimbrels fly in lines. The pale-rumped Eurasian race (not shown) is a rare migrant in the Bering Sea area of Alaska.

Voice: Five to seven short, rapid whistles: *ti-ti-ti-ti-ti-ti*.

Range: Arctic, circumpolar. Winters to s. S. America. **West:** Map 129. **Habitat:** Shores, mudflats, marshes, prairies, tundra.

ESKIMO CURLEW *Numenius borealis*

12–14″ (30–35 cm). Much smaller than the Whimbrel. Bill shorter (1¾–2½″) and thinner, *only slightly curved*. More patterned above than the Whimbrel. Linings of raised wing *cinnamon*. Legs slate-gray. Note the unbarred primaries. See Little Curlew (p. 152).

Voice: *Tee-dee-dee*, or a repeated *tee-dee*.

Range: Near extinction. Formerly arctic America, wintering in s. S. America. Migrated down East Coast in fall, through Great Plains in spring. **West:** Bred formerly in nw. Canada, perhaps Alaska. A very few pairs apparently still breed in nw. Canada.

LARGE
SANDPIPERS

summer

winter

HUDSONIAN
GODWIT

winter

♂ summer

MARBLED
GODWIT

LONG-
BILLED
CURLEW

underwing

ESKIMO
CURLEW

WHIMBREL

LARGE SHOREBIRDS IN FLIGHT

Learn to know their flight calls, which are quite diagnostic.

	Text and color plate

HUDSONIAN GODWIT *Limosa haemastica*   pp. 130, 131
Upturned bill, white wing stripe, ringed tail. Overhead,
shows blackish wing linings.
Flight call, tawit!, higher-pitched than Marbled's.

WILLET *Catoptrophorus semipalmatus*   pp. 134, 135
Contrasty black, gray, and white wing pattern.
Overhead, the wing pattern is even more striking.
Flight call, a whistled *whee-wee-wee.*

MARBLED GODWIT *Limosa fedoa*   pp. 130, 131
Long upturned bill, tawny brown color. Overhead, shows
cinnamon wing linings.
Flight call, an accented *kerwhit!* (or *godwit!*).

WHIMBREL *Numenius phaeopus*   pp. 130, 131
Decurved bill, gray-brown color, striped crown.
Overhead, grayer than next species, lacks cinnamon
wing linings.
Flight call, 5–7 short rapid whistles: *ti-ti-ti-ti-ti-ti.*

LONG-BILLED CURLEW *Numenius americanus*   pp. 130, 131
Very long, sickle-like bill; no head striping. Overhead,
shows bright cinnamon wing linings.
Flight call, a rapid, whistled *kli-li-li-li.*

BAR-TAILED GODWIT   pp. 152, 153
Limosa lapponica (shown below)
Upturned bill, barred tail, a mottled rump.

BRISTLE-THIGHED CURLEW   pp. 152, 153
Numenius tahitensis (shown below)
Decurved bill, tawny-buff rump.

BRISTLE-
THIGHED
CURLEW

BAR-
TAILED
GODWIT

WADERS IN FLIGHT

HUDSONIAN GODWIT
summer

HUDSONIAN GODWIT
winter

WILLET
winter

WHIMBREL

MARBLED GODWIT

bill of
juvenile
Long-bill

LONG-BILLED CURLEW

WILLET *Catoptrophorus semipalmatus* **M125**

14–17″ (35–43 cm). When standing, stockier than the Greater Yellowlegs; has a grayer look, heavier bill, bluish legs. In flight, note the *striking black and white wing pattern.* At rest, when the banded wings cannot be seen, this large wader is rather nondescript: gray above, somewhat scaled below in summer, unmarked below in fall and winter; legs bluish gray.

Voice: A musical, repetitious *pill-will-willet* (in breeding season); a loud *kay-ee* (second note lower). Also a rapidly repeated *kip-kip-kip,* etc. In flight, *whee-wee-wee.*

Range: Cen.-s. Canada to Gulf of Mexico, W. Indies. Winters s. U.S. to Brazil and Peru. **West:** Map 125. **Habitat:** Marshes, wet meadows, mudflats, beaches.

GREATER YELLOWLEGS *Tringa melanoleuca* **M122**

14″ (35 cm). Note the *bright yellow legs* (shared with the next species, but leg joints thicker). A slim gray sandpiper; back checkered with gray, black, and white. In flight, it appears *dark-winged* (no stripe), with a *whitish rump and tail.* Bill long, slightly upturned, paler at base.

Voice: Three-noted whistle, *whew-whew-whew,* or *dear! dear! dear!*

Range: Alaska, Canada. Winters U.S. to Tierra del Fuego. **West:** Map 122. **Habitat:** Open marshes, mudflats, streams, ponds; in summer, wooded muskegs, spruce bogs.

LESSER YELLOWLEGS *Tringa flavipes* **M123**

10–11″ (25–28 cm). Like the Greater Yellowlegs, but noticeably smaller. Its shorter, slimmer, all-black bill is quite straight; that of Greater appears slightly uptilted. Readily separated by voice.

Similar species: (1) Stilt Sandpiper and (2) Wilson's Phalarope in the fall have flight patterns similar to that of Yellowlegs.

Voice: *Yew* or *yu-yu* (usually one or two notes); lower, less forceful than the clear, three-syllabled whistle of Greater Yellowlegs.

Range: Alaska, Canada. Winters from s. U.S. to Argentina. **West:** Map 123. **Habitat:** Marshes, mudflats, shores, pond edges; in summer, open boreal woods.

SOLITARY SANDPIPER *Tringa solitaria* **M124**

8–9″ (20–23 cm). Note the dark wings and conspicuous *white sides of the tail* (crossed by bold black bars). A dark-backed sandpiper, whitish below, with a *light eye-ring* and greenish legs. Nods like a yellowlegs. Usually alone, seldom in groups.

Similar species: (1) Lesser Yellowlegs has bright yellow (not greenish) legs, white (not dark) rump. (2) Spotted Sandpiper teeters more and has a white wing stripe; it has a stiff, shallow wing arc. (Solitary has a darting, almost swallow-like wing stroke.)

Voice: *Peet!* or *peet-weet-weet!* (higher than Spotted's).

Range: Alaska, Canada. Winters Gulf of Mexico to Argentina. **West:** Map 124. **Habitat:** Streamsides, wooded swamps and ponds, fresh marshes.

STILT SANDPIPER *Calidris himantopus* See pp. 144, 145.

Fall: Long, yellow-green legs; white rump; light eyebrow.

WILSON'S PHALAROPE *Phalaropus tricolor* See pp. 136, 137.

Fall: Needle bill, clear white underparts; dull yellow legs.

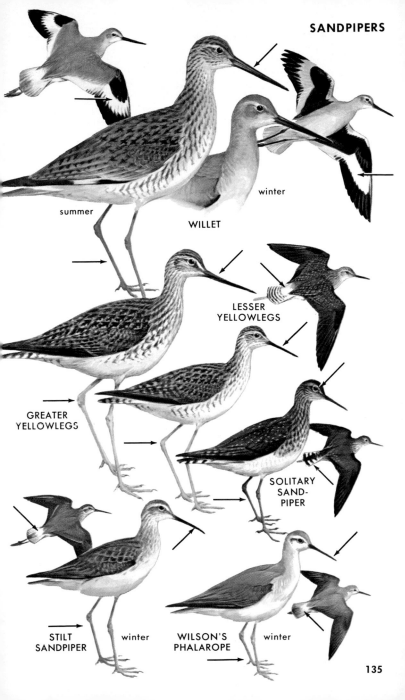

WILLET

summer

winter

LESSER
YELLOWLEGS

GREATER
YELLOWLEGS

SOLITARY
SAND-
PIPER

STILT
SANDPIPER   winter

WILSON'S
PHALAROPE   winter

■ **PHALAROPES. Subfamily Phalaropodinae.** Sandpiper-like birds with lobed toes; equally at home wading or swimming. Placed by some taxonomists in a family of their own, *Phalaropodidae*. When feeding, phalaropes often spin like tops, rapidly dabbling at the disturbed water for plankton, brine shrimp and other marine invertebrates, mosquito larvae, and insects. Females are larger and more colorful than males. Two of the three species are circumpolar, wintering at sea; the other species breeds on the N. American plains and winters in S. America.

WILSON'S PHALAROPE *Phalaropus tricolor*   **M151**
9″ (23 cm). This trim phalarope is dark-winged (no stripe), with a white rump. The breeding female is unique, with a *broad black face and neck stripe blending into cinnamon.* Males are duller, with just a wash of cinnamon on the sides of the neck and a white spot on the hind-neck. *Fall:* Suggests a Lesser Yellowlegs (dark wings, white rump), but whiter below, with no breast streaking; bill *needle-like;* legs greenish or straw-colored (not canary yellow). The other two phalaropes show white wing stripes.
Voice: A low nasal *wurk;* also *check, check, check.*
Range: Sw. Canada, w. U.S. and Great Lakes. Winters in s. S. America. **West:** Map 151. **Habitat:** Shallow prairie lakes, fresh marshes, pools, shores, mudflats; in migration, also salt marshes.

RED-NECKED PHALAROPE *Phalaropus lobatus*   **M152**
(Northern Phalarope) 7–8″ (18–20 cm). A sanderling-like bird at sea is most likely to be a phalarope. This is the commonest of the two "sea snipes" and the one most likely to occur inland. In the fall, both sexes are gray above (strongly streaked) and white below. Note the dark "phalarope patch" through the eye and the needle-like black bill. Breeding females are gray above, with a patch of *rufous on the neck* and a white throat. Males are browner, but similar in pattern.
Voice: A sharp *kit* or *whit,* similar to note of Sanderling.
Range: Circumpolar. Winters at sea, to S. Hemisphere. **West:** Map 152. **Habitat:** Ocean, bays, lakes, ponds; tundra (summer).

RED PHALAROPE *Phalaropus fulicaria*   **M153**
8–9″ (20–23 cm). The sea-going habits (swimming buoyantly like a tiny gull) distinguish this as a phalarope; in breeding plumage, the deep *reddish underparts* and *white face* and yellow bill designate it as this species. Male duller than female. In fall and winter, both sexes are gray above, white below; in flight suggests a Sanderling, but with a *dark patch* through the eye.
Similar species: Fall Red-necked Phalarope is darker, with a strongly striped back, blacker crown. Its wing stripe contrasts more; its bill is more needle-like. Thicker bill of fall Red Phalarope may be yellowish at base (usually not). Immature has a black bill.
Voice: Similar to Red-necked Phalarope's *whit* or *prip.*
Range: Arctic; circumpolar. Winter range at sea poorly known; from s. U.S. to S. Hemisphere. **West:** Map 153. **Habitat:** More strictly pelagic than Northern. In summer, tundra.

PHALAROPES

breeding ♀

winter

juv.

winter

WILSON'S PHALAROPE

winter

♂ breeding

♀ breeding

juv.

winter

RED-NECKED PHALAROPE

winter

♂ breeding

♀ breeding

juv.

winter

RED PHALAROPE

winter

♂ breeding

lobed foot of phalarope

breeding

137

COMMON SNIPE *Gallinago gallinago* **M150**
11″ (28 cm). A tight-sitting bog-prober; note the *extremely long bill.*
Brown, with *buff stripes on the back* and a *striped head.* When
flushed, flies off in a *zigzag,* showing a *short orange tail* and uttering
a rasping note.
Voice: A rasping *scaip.* Song, a measured *chip-a, chip-a, chip-a,* etc.
In high aerial display, a winnowing *huhuhuhuhuhuhu.*
Range: Northern N. America, n. Eurasia. Winters to Brazil, cen.
Africa. **West:** Map 150. **Habitat:** Marshes, bogs, wet meadows.
Note: The **AMERICAN WOODCOCK,** *Scolopax minor,* has been
recorded casually or accidentally west of 100° as far as Saskatche-
wan, Montana, Wyoming, Colorado, and New Mexico. See eastern
Field Guide.

SHORT-BILLED DOWITCHER *Limnodromus griseus* **M148**
10½–12″ (26–30 cm). A snipe-like bird of the open *mudflats.* Note
the very long bill, and in flight, the *long white wedge up the back.*
In breeding plumage the underparts are rich rusty with some barring
on the flanks; by fall, the bird is gray. Dowitchers feed with a
sewing-machine motion. The Short-bill is very similar to the Long-
billed Dowitcher, but the bill averages shorter. The race most likely
to be seen in the West *(caurinus)* has wider white bars on the tail
than the Long-bill; this gives the tail a paler look. The two are more
easily separated by voice, providing they speak up.
Voice: A staccato *tu-tu-tu;* pitch of Lesser Yellowlegs'.
Range: S. Alaska, Canada. Winters s. U.S. to Brazil. **West:** Map 148.
Habitat: Mudflats, tidal marshes, pond edges. More frequent on saltwater margins than the Long-billed Dowitcher.

LONG-BILLED DOWITCHER *Limnodromus scolopaceus* **M149**
11–12½″ (28–31 cm). Bill lengths of the two dowitchers overlap,
but birds of this species with very long bills (3″), usually females,
may be recognized with a fair degree of certainty in any plumage;
many other individuals can be rather indeterminate unless they call.
In breeding plumage the underparts are *rusty to the lower belly*
(may be whitish in Short-bill). The dark bars on the tail are denser,
giving the tail a darker look. In fall the bird is gray; then the best
clue is voice.
Voice: A single thin *keek* is distinctive. Occasionally the notes are
doubled or trebled, but thinner than the Short-bill's.
Range: Breeds ne. Siberia to nw. Canada. Winters s. U.S. to Guatemala. **West:** Map 149. **Habitat:** Mudflats, shallow pools, margins.
More addicted to fresh water than other dowitcher.

RED KNOT *Calidris canutus* **M136**
10–11″ (25–28 cm). Larger than the Sanderling (p. 140). Stocky, with
a moderately short bill and short legs. *Spring:* Face and underparts
pale robin-red; back mottled with black, gray, and russet. *Fall:* A
dumpy wader with a washed-out gray look; short bill, pale rump,
greenish legs. At close range shows *scaly feather edgings,* especially
in juvenile birds.
Voice: A low *knut;* also a low, mellow *tooit-wit* or *wah-quoit.*
Range: Arctic; circumpolar. Winters to S. Hemisphere. **West:** Map
136. **Habitat:** Tidal flats, shores; tundra when breeding.

SNIPELIKE SHOREBIRDS and KNOT

COMMON SNIPE

juvenile

winter

breeding

SHORT-BILLED DOWITCHER

juvenile

winter

LONG-BILLED DOWITCHER

breeding

juvenile

winter

breeding

RED KNOT

SPOTTED SANDPIPER *Actitis macularia* **M127**

7½" (19 cm). The most widespread sandpiper along the shores of small lakes and streams. Teeters up and down as if a bit too delicately balanced. In summer, note the *round breast spots.* In fall and winter, no spots; olive-brown above, with a white line over the eye. A dusky smudge enclosing a white wedge near the shoulder is a good aid. The flight is distinctive: the wings beat in a *shallow arc,* giving a stiff, bowed appearance. The underwing is strongly striped.
Voice: A clear *peet* or *peet-weet!* or *peet-weet-weet-weet-weet.*
Range: Alaska, Canada to cen. U.S. Winters s. U.S. to n. Argentina.
West: Map 127. **Habitat:** Pebbly lake shores, ponds, streamsides; in winter, also seashores.

DUNLIN *Calidris alpina* **M145**

8–9" (20–23 cm). Slightly larger than the Sanderling, with a *downward droop* toward the tip of its rather long, stout bill. When feeding, the bird's posture is hunched. *Summer: Rusty red above,* with a *black patch across the belly. Winter:* Unpatterned gray-brown above, with a grayish wash across the breast (not clean white as in the Sanderling). Juvenile is rusty above, with a buffy breast and streaked flanks. In all plumages note the longish, droop-tipped bill.
Voice: A nasal, rasping *cheezp* or *treezp.*
Range: Arctic; circumpolar. Winters from coasts of U.S., s. Eurasia to Mexico, n. Africa, India. **West:** Map 145. **Habitat:** Tidal flats, beaches, muddy pools; in summer, wet tundra.

SANDERLING *Calidris alba* **M137**

7–8" (18–20 cm). A plump, active sandpiper of the outer beaches, where it chases the retreating waves like a clockwork toy. Note the bold *white wing stripe* on birds in flight. *Breeding plumage:* Bright rusty about the head, back, and breast. *Winter plumage:* The palest sandpiper; snowy white below, plain pale gray back, *black shoulders.* Juvenile birds differ from winter adults by having a pattern of black on the back.
Voice: A short *twick* or *quit* is distinctive.
Range: Arctic; circumpolar. Winters from U.S., Britain, China to S. Hemisphere. **West:** Map 137. **Habitat:** Outer beaches, tideflats, lake shores; when nesting, stony tundra.

BASIC FLIGHT PATTERNS
OF SANDPIPERS

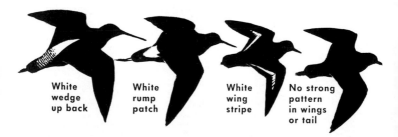

White wedge up back   White rump patch   White wing stripe   No strong pattern in wings or tail

SANDPIPERS

winter

breeding

SPOTTED SANDPIPER

winter

juvenile

DUNLIN

breeding

immature
winter

adult
winter

breeding

SANDERLING

WANDERING TATTLER *Heteroscelus incanus* **M126**
10½–11½" (26–29 cm). Recognized at any time from the other shorebirds that inhabit similar rocks by its *lack of pattern in flight.* Solid grayish above; light line over the eye, dark line through it. Legs yellowish. In breeding plumage, underparts narrowly *barred.* In fall and winter, gray-chested, with no barring. Bobs and teeters like the Spotted Sandpiper.
Voice: A clear *whee-we-we-we*, less sharp than Greater Yellowlegs; or *tweet-tweet-tweet*, similar to Spotted Sandpiper's call.
Range: Breeds nw. N. America; winters coastally south to Ecuador and on many Pacific islands. **West:** Map 126. **Habitat:** Rock coasts, pebbly beaches. Nests near mountain streams above timberline.

SURFBIRD *Aphriza virgata* **M135**
10" (25 cm). A stocky dark sandpiper of wave-washed rocks. Note the conspicuous *white tail tipped with a broad black band.* *Breeding:* Heavily streaked and spotted with blackish above and below; golden scapulars. *Winter:* Solid gray above and across breast. Bill short, yellow at base; legs *yellowish.*
Voice: A sharp *pee-weet* or *key-a-weet.*
Range: Breeds in Alaska, Yukon. Winters on coast to s. S. America.
West: Map 135. **Habitat:** Rocky coasts; nests on mountain tundra.

ROCK SANDPIPER *Calidris ptilocnemis* **M144**
8–9" (20–23 cm). In breeding plumage suggests a Dunlin, with rusty back, black splotch on breast (but the Dunlin is redder, with black splotch lower down, black legs; see p. 141). In winter, similar to the Purple Sandpiper of the Atlantic, but paler. Stocky and slaty, with a white belly, white wing stripe. Legs dull yellow or greenish. Its rock-feeding associates, the Black Turnstone and the Surfbird, both show a broad *white band* across the base of the tail.
Voice: A flicker-like *du-du-du.* When breeding, a trill.
Range: Ne. Siberia, w. Alaska; winters along coast to California Map 144. **Habitat:** Rocky shores; nests on mossy tundra.

BLACK TURNSTONE *Arenaria melanocephala* **M134**
9" (23 cm). A squat, blackish shorebird with a blackish chest and white belly. In spring, a round white spot before the eye, and white speckling. Flight pattern similar to Ruddy Turnstone's. Legs dark.
Voice: A rattling note, higher than note of Ruddy Turnstone.
Range: Breeds in Alaska. Winters along coast to w. Mexico. Map 134. **Habitat:** Strictly coastal. Rocky shores, breakwaters, bay shores, surf-pounded islets; nests on coastal tundra.

RUDDY TURNSTONE *Arenaria interpres* **M133**
8–10" (20–25 cm). A squat, robust, *orange-legged* shorebird, with a *harlequin pattern.* In breeding plumage, with its russet back and curious face and breast pattern, the bird is unique, but in flight it is even more striking. Winter adults and young birds are duller, but retain enough of the basic pattern to be recognized.
Voice: A staccato *tuk-a-tuk* or *kut-a-kut;* also a single *kewk.*
Range: Arctic, sub-Arctic; circumpolar. Winters coastal U.S., Hawaii, s. Eurasia to S. Hemisphere. **West:** Map 133. **Habitat:** Beaches, mudflats, jetties, rocky shores; in summer, tundra.

ROCK-LOVING SHOREBIRDS

WANDERING TATTLER

winter

breeding

SURFBIRD

winter

breeding

breeding

winter

ROCK SANDPIPER

BLACK TURNSTONE

breeding

winter

winter

breeding

RUDDY TURNSTONE

breeding

STILT SANDPIPER *Calidris himantopus* **M146**
8″ (20 cm). In spring, heavily marked below with *transverse bars*.
Note *rusty cheek patch*. In fall, yellowlegs-like; gray above, white
below; dark-winged and *white-rumped;* note the *greenish legs* and
white eyebrow. Bill long, with a slight droop at tip. Feeds like a
Dowitcher (sewing-machine motion).
Voice: A single *whu* (like Lesser Yellowlegs but lower, hoarser).
Range: American Arctic. Winters s. U.S. to Argentina. **West:** Map
146. **Habitat:** Shallow pools, mudflats, marshes; tundra (summer).

BUFF-BREASTED SANDPIPER *Tryngites subruficollis* **M147**
7½″ (19 cm). No other small shorebird is as *buff below* (paling to
whitish on undertail coverts). A tame buffy wader, with an erect
stance, small head, short bill, and yellowish legs. The dark eye
stands out on a plain face. In flight or in "display," the buff body
contrasts with the underwing (white with a marbled tip). Juveniles
are very scaly above, paler on the belly (most Pacific Coast birds
are in this plumage).
Voice: A low, trilled *pr-r-r-reet*. A sharp *tik.*
Range: Breeds in nw. Arctic. Winters in Argentina. **West:** Map 147.
Habitat: Shortgrass prairies; in summer, tundra ridges.

UPLAND SANDPIPER *Bartramia longicauda* **M128**
(Upland Plover) 11½″ (29 cm). A "pigeon-headed" brown sandpiper;
larger than a Killdeer. The short bill, *small head,* shoe-button eye,
thin neck, and *long tail* are helpful points. Often perches on
fenceposts and poles; upon alighting, holds wings elevated.
Voice: A mellow, whistled *kip-ip-ip-ip,* often heard at night. Song,
weird windy whistles: *whooooleeeeee, wheelooooooooooo.*
Range: Mainly Canada, n. U.S. Winters on pampas of Argentina.
West: Map 128. **Habitat:** Grassy prairies, open meadows, fields.

RUFF *Philomachus pugnax*
Male 12″ (30 cm); female 9″ (23 cm). *Male* ("Ruff"), *summer:*
Unique, with erectile *ruffs* and *ear tufts* that may be black, brown,
rufous, buff, white, or barred, in various combinations. Legs may
be greenish, yellow, orange, or pink. Bill also variable. *Male, winter:*
Rather plain, a small-headed, thick-necked shorebird with a scaly
gray-brown back, whitish underparts with a mottling of gray across
the breast, and a whitish area on the lower face. Note the *erect
stance* and (in flight) the *oval white patch* on each side of the dark
tail. *Female* ("Reeve"): Smaller than the male; when breeding lacks
ruffs, breast *heavily blotched* with dark. Juvenile birds are buffy
below and very scaly on the back. See Sharp-tailed Sandpiper.
Voice: Flight note, a low *too-i* or *tu-whit.*
Range: N. Eurasia; winters in s. Eurasia, Africa. Rare visitor to N.
America. **West:** Rare but regular spring and fall migrant in outer
Aleutians and Bering Sea area (has bred in Alaska). Rare fall migrant
along coast south to s. California, where it may winter. Accidental
inland in West.

SANDPIPERS

juvenile

winter

breeding

**STILT
SANDPIPER**

**UPLAND
SANDPIPER**

juvenile

**BUFF-BREASTED
SANDPIPER**

winter ♀
("Reeve")

breeding
dress of ♂
variable

winter ♂
("Ruff")

RUFF

♀ ("Reeve")

WHITE-RUMPED SANDPIPER *Calidris fuscicollis*   M141
7–8″ (18–20 cm). Larger than the Semipalmated Sandpiper, smaller than the Pectoral. The only *small* streaked sandpiper with a completely *white rump*, conspicuous in flight. At rest, the bird has an attenuated look, with wing tips extending well beyond the tail; sides show *streaks below the wings*, a good point. Bill yellow at base of lower mandible. In spring, adults are quite rusty; in fall, adults are grayer than the other "peeps," but juveniles have rusty edges on the crown and back.
Voice: A mouselike *jeet*, like two flint pebbles scraping.
Range: Arctic N. America. Winters in s. S. America. **West:** Map 141.
Habitat: Prairies, shores, mudflats; in summer, tundra.

BAIRD'S SANDPIPER *Calidris bairdii*   M142
7–7½″ (18–19 cm). Larger than the Semipalmated or Western Sandpiper, with a more *pointy look* (wings extend ½″ beyond tail tip). Browner, *buffier* across the breast. Suggests a large Least Sandpiper with black legs. Back of juvenile has a more *scaled* look.
Similar species: (1) Buff-breasted Sandpiper is buffier below, without streaks, and has *yellowish* (not *blackish*) legs. See also (2) breeding Sanderling; (3) Pectoral Sandpiper.
Voice: Note, *kreep* or *kree;* a rolling trill.
Range: Ne. Siberia and N. American Arctic. Winters from Andean Ecuador to Tierra del Fuego. **West:** Map 142. **Habitat:** Rainpools, pond margins, mudflats, shores.

PECTORAL SANDPIPER *Calidris melanotos*   M143
8–9″ (20–23 cm). Medium-sized (but variable); neck longer than in smaller "peeps." Note that the heavy breast streaks end rather *abruptly*, like a bib. The dark back is *lined* (snipe-like) with white; the wing stripe is faint or lacking; the crown is rusty. The legs usually are dull yellowish green. Bill may be pale yellow-brown at base.
Voice: A reedy *churrt* or *trrip, trrip.*
Range: Siberian and American Arctic. Winters in S. America, se. Australia. **West:** Map 143. **Habitat:** In migration, prairie pools, muddy shores, fresh and tidal marshes; in summer, tundra.

SHARP-TAILED SANDPIPER *Calidris acuminata*
8½″ (21 cm). Similar to the Pectoral Sandpiper, but in fall the breast is rich buffy (juvenile) or pale gray-buff (adult), spotted lightly on the sides only. Crissum is streaked. In no plumage is there the sharp contrast between the white belly and streaked breast, as in the Pectoral. The juvenile is especially distinctive, with its rich orange-buff breast and rufous cap.
Voice: A low, trilled *prreeet* or *trrit-trrit,* sometimes twittered.
Range: Breeds in n. Siberia. Winters in Australian region. **West:** Fall migrant along coasts of Alaska, British Columbia; rarely south to California (usually juveniles). Accidental in interior. **Habitat:** Grassy borders of salt marshes.

SANDPIPERS

fall

breeding

WHITE-RUMPED
SANDPIPER

juvenile

breeding

BAIRD'S
SANDPIPER

♂
breeding

juvenile

PECTORAL
SANDPIPER

juvenile

breeding

SHARP-TAILED
SANDPIPER

147

■ **"PEEPS."** Collectively, the three common, streaked, sparrow-sized sandpipers resident in North America are nicknamed "peeps." The British call their similar ones "stints."

LEAST SANDPIPER *Calidris minutilla* M140

5–6½" (13–16 cm). The Least may be known from the other two common peeps by its smaller size, *browner* look, *yellowish or greenish* (not blackish) legs, and *slighter bill.*

Voice: A thin *krreet, kree-eet.* More drawn out than the *jeet* of the Western. Very unlike the *chit* or *chet* of the Semipalmated.

Range: Alaska, Canada. Winters s. U.S. to Brazil. **West:** Map 140.

Habitat: Mudflats, grassy marshes, rainpools, shores. More addicted to marshy areas than the other "peeps."

SEMIPALMATED SANDPIPER *Calidris pusilla* M138

5½–6½" (14–16 cm). Compared to the Western Sandpiper (which also has blackish legs), the "Semi" is a trifle smaller, grayer in spring, and usually has a shorter, straighter bill. In fall it lacks the rusty on the scapulars often shown by the Western.

Similar species: (1) Typical Western Sandpiper (especially the female) has a *longer bill,* thicker at the base, *slightly drooped* at the tip. Some males in fall or winter may not be safely separable in the field except by voice. (2) Least Sandpiper is smaller, browner, and thinner-billed; it has *yellowish or greenish* legs and in the fall has a more streaked breast.

Voice: Note *chit* or *cheh* (lacks *ee* sound of Least, Western).

Range: Breeds in N. American Arctic. Migrates mainly east of the Rockies (scarcer on West Coast) to S. America. **West:** Map 138. **Habitat:** Beaches, mudflats; in summer, tundra.

WESTERN SANDPIPER *Calidris mauri* M139

6–7" (15–18 cm). This and the Least Sandpiper are the two common small "peeps" in most of the West (west of the Plains). The Western is the larger bird; its bill is *very noticeably longer* (especially in females), *thicker at the base,* and droops slightly at the tip. Legs *black.* Breeding adults are *heavily streaked* on the breast. They show *rusty on the scapulars* and have a *rusty crown and ear patch.* (A trace of rusty may persist on the scapulars in fall, giving a two-toned effect.) In winter, gray or gray-brown; perhaps the palest "peep."

Similar species: Because of their shorter bills, many males in fall or winter plumage are almost impossible to separate from Semipalmateds except by voice. The latter species does not winter on the West Coast, but the Western does. If the birds do not call, it is fairly safe to assume they are Westerns.

Voice: A thin *jeet,* not as drawn out as note of Least.

Range: Breeds in Alaska. Winters from s. U.S. to Peru. **West:** Map 139. **Habitat:** Shores, beaches, mudflats; in summer, dry tundra.

SMALL "PEEP" SANDPIPERS

winter

juvenile

breeding

LEAST SANDPIPER

winter

juvenile

breeding

♂ immature winter

♀ winter

juvenile

SEMIPALMATED SANDPIPER

♀ breeding

WESTERN SANDPIPER

HEADS AND BILLS OF "PEEPS"

LEAST   SEMIPALMATED   WESTERN

■ **"STINTS." Alaskan Strays from Asia.** Whereas we may affectionately refer to our small, sparrow-sized sandpipers as "peeps," the British usually call the Eurasian species "stints." Within our geographic limits, stray "stints" from Asia occur as overshoots in migration most frequently in the outer Aleutians (Attu, etc.), but might turn up casually or accidentally elsewhere. Identification can be tricky; for further analysis and color plates of subtle plumage variations, see Viet and Jonsson in *American Birds* (Sept.–Oct. 1984).

LITTLE STINT *Calidris minuta*
6″ (15 cm). Size of the Least Sandpiper but rustier above, with *black* legs. Toes lack webbing (unlike those of the larger Semipalmated and Western sandpipers). Similar to some Rufous-necked Stints but body less elongated, stance more erect; tarsi longer. Call, a sanderling-like *tit*. **West:** Accidental, w. Aleutians, Bering Sea area.

TEMMINCK'S STINT *Calidris temminckii*
6″ (15 cm). A distinctive stint; gray, with *irregular black spots* on the scapulars. Has an elongated, crouching look; *short, dull yellow legs.* In flight, shows *white outer tail feathers.* Call in flight, a high ringing *trree*, often repeated in a cricketlike trill. **West:** A very rare overshoot in migration to outer Aleutians and other Bering Sea islands.

LONG-TOED STINT *Calidris subminuta*
6¼″ (16 cm). Much like the Least Sandpiper (which is unlikely to occur in the outer Aleutians), but *brighter* in color, with more erect stance, longer legs, more *spindly toes*, and an even thinner bill. Call, a purring *prrp*. **West:** Regular migrant in outer Aleutians (may breed); vagrant Pribilofs, St. Lawrence I., etc. Prefers marshes.

SPOONBILL SANDPIPER *Eurynorhynchus pygmeus*
6½″ (16 cm). A stint-sized sandpiper, with a curious *spoonlike tip on the bill.* In spring, it has a bright rusty head and breast and could be mistaken for a Rufous-necked Stint until it turns head-on. **West:** Accidental, n. Alaska, outer Aleutians, British Columbia.

RUFOUS-NECKED STINT *Calidris ruficollis*
6½″ (16 cm.) This rare stray is recognized in breeding plumage by its *bright rusty head and upper breast.* In non-breeding plumage it is very much like Western and Semipalmated sandpipers (black legs, clear breast, but bill is slighter, forehead whiter, and (at close range) toes unwebbed. Call, a short, clipped *chit*, or *chit chit*, suggesting Semipalmated. Also a squeak, lower in pitch than Western's call. Basically Eurasian, but breeds n. and w. Alaska (Pt. Barrow, Seward Peninsula, etc.). Migrant in Aleutians, Pribilofs, Bering Sea coasts, and casually (perhaps regularly) south along coast to s. California.

BROAD-BILLED SANDPIPER *Limicola fulcinellus*
6¾″ (17 cm). The key mark is the *forked white eyebrow stripe.* Its *long bill*, drooped at tip, suggests a small Dunlin, but its back is dark, striped like a Snipe's. **West:** Vagrants (juveniles) have occurred in fall in the outer Aleutians.

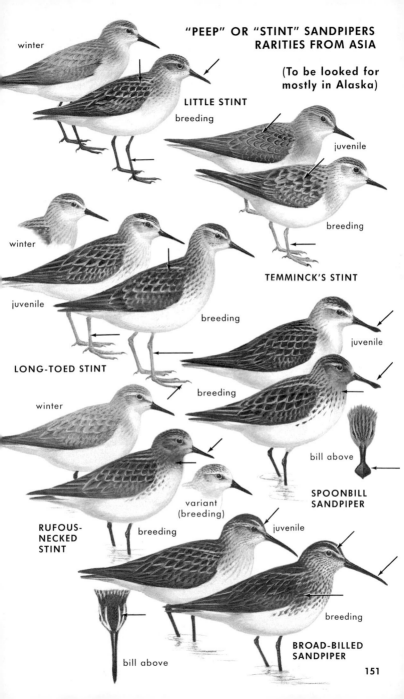

"PEEP" OR "STINT" SANDPIPERS
RARITIES FROM ASIA

(To be looked for mostly in Alaska)

winter

LITTLE STINT

breeding

juvenile

breeding

TEMMINCK'S STINT

winter

juvenile

breeding

LONG-TOED STINT

juvenile

breeding

winter

bill above

SPOONBILL SANDPIPER

RUFOUS-
NECKED
STINT

variant
(breeding)

breeding

juvenile

breeding

bill above

BROAD-BILLED
SANDPIPER

151

BAR-TAILED GODWIT *Limosa lapponica* M131

15–18″ (38–45 cm). This Alaskan godwit is near the size of the Whimbrel. In summer, male is rich *reddish chestnut*, particularly on head and underparts; female duller. In non-breeding plumage both are grayish above, white below. Alaskan birds have a *mottled rump* and *whitish tail* crossed by narrow dark bars. See also p. 132 for additional illustration of bird in flight.

Voice: Flight note, a harsh *kirrick*; alarm, a shrill *krick.*

Range: N. Eurasia, Alaska. Winters cen. Eurasia to n. Africa, Australia. **West:** Map 131. **Habitat:** Mudflats, shores, tundra.

BLACK-TAILED GODWIT *Limosa limosa*

15¾″ (40 cm). The small Asian race of this elegant godwit resembles the Hudsonian Godwit (white rump, white wing stripe, black tail), but the bill is straighter. In breeding plumage it has chestnut head and neck, black-and-white barred belly. The best field distinction is this: the underwing linings are *white* in the Black-tail, *black* in the Hudsonian. This holds for all plumages.

Voice: The flight call is a clear *reeka-reeka-reeka.*

Range: Eurasia, migrating to Africa, Australia. A rare spring migrant in the outer Aleutians; casual on other Bering Sea islands.

BRISTLE-THIGHED CURLEW *Numenius tahitiensis*

17″ (43 cm). Very similar to the Whimbrel, but tawnier, especially about tail; *tawny, unbarred rump.* Breast less streaked, bill paler. See additional illustration of bird in flight on p. 132.

Voice: A slurred *chi-u-it* (Inuit name); suggests the call of the Black-bellied Plover. Also like a "wolf whistle," *whee-wheeo* (A. A. Allen).

Range: Breeds in w. Alaska (near mouth of Yukon). Recorded elsewhere in w. Alaska. Winters on islands in cen. and s. Pacific. **Habitat:** Tundra (Alaska); reefs and beaches.

FAR EASTERN CURLEW *Numenius madagascariensis*

25″ (63 cm). The largest curlew; resembles the Long-billed Curlew (pp. 130–133), but lacks the cinnamon tones. Length of bill variable. The surest point is the heavily barred *whitish underwing* (deep cinnamon in Long-billed Curlew).

Range: Ne. Asia. Very rare spring vagrant to outer Aleutians, Pribilofs, nw. Alaska.

LITTLE CURLEW *Numenius minutus*

12″ (30 cm). The tiniest curlew, even smaller than the nearly extinct Eskimo Curlew. Bill *very short.* Breast washed with buff, finely streaked. At rest, wing tips are even with the tail tip (they extend beyond tail in Eskimo Curlew). Note difference in underwing pattern (pale buff, not cinnamon).

Range: N. Siberia. Accidental, California.

ESKIMO CURLEW *Numenius borealis* See pp. 130, 131.

LONG-BILLED ALASKAN SHOREBIRDS
(Including strays from Asia)

winter

juv.

winter

breeding

BAR-TAILED GODWIT

winter

BLACK-TAILED GODWIT

winter

breeding

BRISTLE-THIGHED CURLEW

FAR EASTERN CURLEW

LITTLE CURLEW

Little

Eskimo

underwings

ESKIMO CURLEW

153

COMMON SANDPIPER *Actitis hypoleucos*
8″ (20 cm). At all seasons resembles the Spotted Sandpiper in non-breeding plumage (no spots). Best feature is the *longer tail.* At rest, wing tips of Common reach only halfway to the tip of the tail, whereas those of Spotted reach closer to the tip. The dusky wedge on the side of the breast is more diffuse. Legs grayer. Less contrast between base of bill and tip. Flight note, *twee-see-see,* similar to Spotted's call but thinner. Rare but regular, mostly in spring, in the outer Aleutians; casual elsewhere in the Bering Sea area.

GREEN SANDPIPER *Tringa ochrophus*
8¾″ (22 cm). Similar to the Solitary Sandpiper, but a bit stockier, with a *white rump* (not dark). Underwings *dark,* as in Solitary. Call, when flushed, a thin, high-pitched *weet weet weet.* Accidental in extreme w. Aleutians (Attu).

TEREK SANDPIPER *Xenus cinereus*
9¼″ (23 cm). Note the *upturned bill* and short, *orange-yellow legs.* In breeding plumage this bird has a *jagged black stripe* along the scapulars that is nearly lacking in fall adults. Juveniles are brown, with a trace of this stripe. Often bobs like a "Spotty." In flight, a broad *white band* at rear edge of wing. Voice a fluty *dudududu* or a sharp piping, *twita-wit-wit-wit.* Vagrants occur regularly in outer Aleutians, casually on Bering Sea islands. Accidental on mainland Alaska.

WOOD SANDPIPER *Tringa glareola*
7¾″ (19 cm). Shape of Solitary Sandpiper, but has whitish (not dark) underwings. Upperparts paler and browner, *heavily spotted* with pale buff. Rump patch *white* (Solitary has a dark rump). Legs dull yellow. Voice, a sharp, high *chew-chew-chew* or *chiff-chiff-chiff.* Regular migrant in outer Aleutians (rare breeder); also Pribilofs, St. Lawrence I.; rarely on mainland of nw. Alaska.

CURLEW SANDPIPER *Calidris ferruginea*
7–9″ (18–23 cm). In spring, *dark russet* on head and underparts (do not mistake for Red Knot). In fall, resembles a fall Dunlin but longer-legged, less streaked on breast; bill *curved slightly throughout.* Main distinction is the *whitish rump.* Most birds seen in fall are juveniles, which have *buff edges* on feathers of back that give a very scaly look. Breast tinged with buff. Call, a liquid *chirrip,* less grating than Dunlin's note. Vagrant in Alaska (w. Aleutians, St. Lawrence I.), w. and n. coasts (has bred Pt. Barrow); accidental, British Columbia, Alberta, Montana, Washington, Oregon, California.

GREAT KNOT *Calidris tenuirostris*
10½″ (26 cm). Shaped somewhat like the Red Knot, but larger. In spring, when this species is most likely to occur, it lacks the Red Knot's brick red underparts. *Breast heavily blotched* with dark, which extends down the sides as bold, *chevronlike spots. Scapulars bright rusty.* In flight, shows more contrast between rump and tail than Red Knot. *Very rare* spring vagrant in w. Aleutians, Pribilofs, St. Lawrence I., Seward Peninsula.

STRAY SANDPIPERS FROM ASIA

breeding

above

Solitary
Sandpiper,
for comparison

below

**COMMON
SANDPIPER**

non-breeding
Spotted Sandpiper,
for comparison

**GREEN
SANDPIPER**

juvenile

**TEREK
SANDPIPER**

breeding

**WOOD
SANDPIPER**

breeding

**CURLEW
SANDPIPER**

breeding

GREAT KNOT

155

MARSH SANDPIPER *Tringa stagnatilis*
9¼" (23 cm). A bit smaller than the Lesser Yellowlegs, this slim *Tringa* can be told from that bird by its more needle-like bill and long, spindly *olive-green* legs. The white rump patch *extends up the back in a wedge,* like that of a Dowitcher (or a Greenshank). Thus, the Marsh Sandpiper might be compared to the Greenshank in the way the Lesser Yellowlegs might be compared to the Greater. Accidental, w. Aleutians.

GRAY-TAILED TATTLER *Heteroscelus brevipes*
(Polynesian Tattler) 10" (25 cm). Very similar to Wandering Tattler (pp. 142, 143), but in breeding plumage the underparts are not as strongly barred. At rest, the wing tips of the Wandering extend further beyond the tail. In fall migration the two are more difficult to separate. Best distinguished by voice, a sharp, upslurred whistle—*too-weet'* or *tu-whip',* with the accent on the second syllable. Rare, but regular migrant in outer Aleutians and Bering Sea islands; casual, n. Alaska. Also called Siberian Tattler.

SPOTTED REDSHANK *Tringa erythropus*
12" (30 cm). A slender, long-legged, long-billed wader; in breeding plumage it is *sooty black,* with minute white speckles on back and wings, making the bird appear a trifle paler above. The long legs are *dark red;* the long black bill is red basally. In non-breeding plumage this bird is gray and somewhat yellowlegs-like, but legs *deep red,* bill *orange-red* basally. In flight, a long white wedge shows on the back, as in Greenshank or Dowitcher. Note, a sharp, whistled *tcheet',* with rising inflection. Casual migrant (spring and fall) in outer Aleutians, Pribilofs. Accidental, British Columbia, Oregon, Nevada, California.

COMMON GREENSHANK *Tringa nebularia*
12½" (31 cm). Size and shape of the Greater Yellowlegs, but legs *dull greenish* (not bright yellow). The wedgelike white rump patch runs farther up the back, as in the Dowitcher. Call, a ringing, whistled *tew tew tew,* similar to Greater Yellowlegs'. Rare but regular migrant, mainly in spring, in the outer Aleutians, Pribilofs.

ORIENTAL PRATINCOLE *Glareola maldivarum* Family Glareolidae
9¼" (23 cm). Pratincoles are long-winged, fork-tailed shorebirds that look somewhat like terns or giant swallows. This species is dark-winged, with a white rump and a creamy throat outlined with black. The wing linings are chestnut. Accidental, in outer Aleutians (Attu).

JACK SNIPE *Lymnocryptes minimus*
7" (18 cm). A small Old World snipe, the size of a Dunlin. It has a *shorter bill than Common Snipe, no white or orange* on its wedge-shaped tail, and lacks bars on its flanks. *Usually silent when flushed;* does not zig-zag. Accidental, Pribilofs, California. See Broad-billed Sandpiper (pp. 150, 151).

Look for these species mostly in Alaska

STRAY SANDPIPERS FROM ASIA

Wandering Tattler, for comparison

winter

fall

breeding

MARSH SANDPIPER

breeding

GRAY-TAILED TATTLER

winter

breeding

SPOTTED REDSHANK

breeding

GREENSHANK

ORIENTAL PRATINCOLE

JACK SNIPE

157

■ GALLINACEOUS OR FOWL-LIKE BIRDS (Turkeys, Pheasants, Grouse, Partridges, and Quail) Family Phasianidae.

Turkeys are very large, with wattles and fanlike tails. Pheasants (introduced) have long, pointed, sweeping tails. Grouse are plump, chicken-like birds, without long tails. Partridges (of Old World origin) are intermediate in size between grouse and quail. Quail are the smallest. **Food:** Insects, seeds, buds, berries. **Range:** Nearly cosmopolitan. **No. of species:** World 207; West 17 (+3–4 introduced successfully; others have failed). Often called "upland game birds."

WILD TURKEY *Meleagris gallopavo*   M99
Male 48″ (120 cm); female 36″ (90 cm). A streamlined version of the barnyard Turkey, with buffy white tips on the tail feathers in most southwestern birds (but tail feathers may have rusty tips in some other populations). Head naked; bluish with red wattles, intensified in male's display. Tail of male is erected like a fan during display. Bronzy iridescent body; barred wings (primaries and secondaries); "beard" on breast. The female is smaller, with a smaller head; less iridescent, and less likely to have a beard.
Voice: "Gobbling" of male like domestic Turkey's. Alarm, *pit!* or *put-put!* Flock call, *keow-keow.* Hen clucks to brood.
Range: E. and sw. U.S. to cen. Mexico. Introduced widely elsewhere. **West:** Map 99. **Habitat:** Woods, mountain forests, wooded swamps.

SAGE GROUSE *Centrocercus urophasianus*   M96
Male 26–30″ (65–75 cm); female 22–23″ (56–58 cm). A large, grayish grouse of open sage country, as large as a small Turkey; identified by its contrasting *black belly patch* and spikelike tail feathers. The male is considerably larger than the female, has a black throat, and, in communal dancing display, puffs out its white chest, exposing two yellow air sacs on the neck, at the same time erecting and spreading its pointed tail feathers in a spiky fan.
Voice: Flushing note, *kuk kuk kuk.* In courtship display the male makes a popping sound.
Range: Western N. America. Map 96. **Habitat:** Sagebrush plains; also foothills and mountain slopes where sagebrush grows.

RING-NECKED PHEASANT *Phasianus colchicus*   M89
Male 30–36″ (75–90 cm); female 21–25″ (53–63 cm). A large, chicken-like or gamecock-like bird. Note the long, sweeping, pointed tail. Runs swiftly; flight strong, take-off noisy. Male highly colored and *iridescent*, with *scarlet wattles* on its face and a *white neck-ring* (not always present). The female is mottled brown, with a moderately *long, pointed tail.*
Voice: Male when crowing has a loud double squawk, *kork-kok,* followed by a brief whir of wings. When flushed, utters harsh croaks. The roosting call is a two-syllabled *kutuck-kutuck,* etc.
Range: Eurasia. Introduced widely in N. America and elsewhere. **West:** Map 89. **Habitat:** Farms, fields, marsh edges, brush.

MISC. FOWL-LIKE BIRDS

display

♂

♂

♀

WILD TURKEY

♀

♂

cock in display

SAGE GROUSE

♂

♀

♀

RING-NECKED PHEASANT

159

■ **GROUSE. Subfamily Tetraoninae.** Ground-dwelling, chicken-like birds; larger than quail and lacking the long tails of pheasants. **Food:** Insects, seeds, buds, berries. **Range:** N. America, Europe, Asia. **No. of species:** World 17; West 10.

RUFFED GROUSE *Bonasa umbellus*   **M95**
16–19″ (40–48 cm). Note the fan-shaped tail, with a broad *black band* near the tip. A large, *red-brown* or *gray-brown*, chicken-like bird of brushy woodlands, usually not seen until it flushes with a startling whir. Two color morphs: "Red" birds with rufous tails, and "gray" birds with gray tails. Red birds are more common in southern parts of range, gray birds northward or at higher altitudes.
Voice: Drumming of male suggests a distant motor starting up. Muffled thumping starts slowly, accelerating into a whir: *Bup . . . bup . . . bup . . . bup . . bup,bup,up,r-rrrrrr.*
Range: Alaska, Canada, n. U.S. **West:** Map 95. **Habitat:** Ground and understory of deciduous or mixed woodlands.

SHARP-TAILED GROUSE *Tympanuchus phasianellus*   **M98**
15–20″ (38–50 cm). A pale, speckled brown grouse of prairie brush. Note the *short pointed tail*, which in flight shows *white* at the sides. Displaying male inflates *purplish* neck sacs.
Similar species: (1) Prairie-chickens have *short, rounded, dark* tails. (2) Female Pheasant (p. 159) has a *long, pointed* tail. (3) Ruffed Grouse has a large, banded, *fan-shaped* tail, and black neck ruff.
Voice: A cackling *cac-cac-cac*, etc. Courting note, a single low *coo-oo*, accompanied by quill-rattling, foot-shuffling.
Range: Alaska, Canada, nw. and n.-cen. U.S. **West:** Map 98. **Habitat:** Prairie, brushy groves, open thickets, forest edges, clearings, coulees, open burns in coniferous forests, etc.

GREATER PRAIRIE-CHICKEN *Tympanuchus cupido*   **M97**
17–18″ (43–45 cm). A henlike bird of prairies. Brown, heavily barred. Note the short, *rounded dark tail* (black in males, barred in females). Courting males in communal "dance" inflate orange neck sacs and erect black, hornlike neck feathers.
Similar species: (1) See Lesser Prairie-Chicken. (2) Sharp-tailed Grouse, often called "Prairie-Chicken," has a whitish tail. (3) Female Pheasant (p. 159) has a long, pointed tail.
Voice: "Booming" male in dance makes a hollow *oo-loo-woo*, suggesting the sound made by blowing across the mouth of a bottle.
Range: Canadian prairies (where it is now extirpated, or nearly so) to coastal Texas. **West:** Map 97. **Habitat:** Native tallgrass prairie, now very limited; some agricultural land.

LESSER PRAIRIE-CHICKEN *Tympanuchus pallidicinctus*   **M97**
16″ (40 cm). A small, pale prairie-chicken; best identified by range (see Map 97). The gular sacs of the male are dull *purplish* or *plum-colored* (not yellow-orange as in Greater Prairie-Chicken).
Voice: Courtship "booming" not as rolling nor as loud as Greater Prairie-Chicken's. Both have clucking, cackling notes.
Range: Resident southwest of the range of the Greater Prairie-Chicken, as shown on the map. **Habitat:** Sandhill country (sage and bluestem grass, oak shinnery).

GROUSE

gray phase

red phase

♂

display

RUFFED GROUSE

♂ display

SHARP-TAILED GROUSE

♂ display

GREATER PRAIRIE-CHICKEN

♂ display

LESSER PRAIRIE-CHICKEN

♀

♂ display

■ **PTARMIGANS.** These hardy arctic and alpine grouse with feathered feet molt three times a year, camouflaging themselves to match the seasons; they change from dark plumage in summer to white in winter. During the spring and fall molts they have a patchy look. A red comb above the eye may be erected or concealed.

WILLOW PTARMIGAN *Lagopus lagopus* M92

16″ (40 cm). The Willow and Rock Ptarmigan are similar; in summer variable, brown or gray, with white wings and a white belly; in winter, white with black tails. In breeding plumage the male Willow Ptarmigan is more deeply chestnut about the head and body than the Rock. There is much variation between various molts.

Similar species: Some races of the Rock Ptarmigan are decidedly gray, finely barred. The bill is always smaller and more slender. In winter, male Rocks have a *black mark* between the eye and bill, lacking in both sexes of Willow Ptarmigan. Habitats differ; the Rock prefers higher, more barren hills.

Voice: Deep raucous calls, *go-out, go-out.* Male, a staccato crow, *kwow, kwow, tobacco, tobacco,* etc., or *go-back, go-back.*

Range: Arctic regions; circumpolar. **West:** Map 92. **Habitat:** Tundra, willow scrub, muskeg; in winter, sheltered valleys at lower altitudes.

ROCK PTARMIGAN *Lagopus mutus* M93

13″ (33 cm). The most hardy ptarmigan. The male in summer is usually grayer than the Willow, lacking the rich chestnut around the head and neck, but populations vary greatly. Some may be even paler than shown here or like the dark bird from Attu figured opposite. Females of the two species are similar but the Rock has a smaller bill. In winter, the white males have a *black mark* between the eye and the bill. This is absent in most females, which may be told from female Willows by their smaller bills.

Voice: Croaks, growls, cackles; usually silent.

Range: Arctic and alpine regions of N. Hemisphere. **West:** Map 93. **Habitat:** Above timberline in mountains (to lower levels in winter); also near sea level in bleak tundra of northern coasts.

WHITE-TAILED PTARMIGAN *Lagopus leucurus* M94

12–13″ (30–33 cm). The only ptarmigan normally found south of Canada. Note the *white tail.* In summer, this ptarmigan is brown, with a white belly and white wings and tail. In winter, it is pure white except for the black eyes and bill. The other two ptarmigan are larger and have *black* tails.

Voice: Cackling notes; clucks, soft hoots.

Range: Western N. America. Map 94. **Habitat:** Rocky alpine tundra; mountains above timberline.

PTARMIGANS

winter ♂
♀
summer
spring

winter
breeding

WILLOW PTARMIGAN

winter
♂
♀
♂
summer

winter
breeding

ROCK PTARMIGAN

winter
♂
♀
♂
molting
summer

winter
breeding

WHITE-TAILED PTARMIGAN

163

SPRUCE GROUSE *Dendragapus canadensis*   **M90**

15–17″ (38–43 cm). Look for this *very tame,* dusky grouse in the deep, wet conifer forests of the North. The male has a sharply defined *black breast,* with some white spots or bars on the sides and a *chestnut band* on the tip of the tail. A comb of erectile red skin above the eye is visible at close range. Birds of the n. Rockies and Cascades, known as "Franklin's Grouse," lack the chestnut tip and have large white spots on the upper tail coverts. Female is dark rusty or grayish brown, thickly barred; tail short and dark, with a rusty tip (except in "Franklin's" form).
Range: Alaska, Canada, n. U.S. **West:** Map 90. **Habitat:** Conifer forests, jack pines, muskeg, blueberry patches, etc.

BLUE GROUSE *Dendragapus obscurus*   **M91**

15½–21″ (39–53 cm). The male is a dusky or sooty grouse. At the tip of its blackish tail is a *broad pale band* (absent in populations in the n. Rockies). Above each eye is a *yellow or orange comb,* erectile in display. In courtship display, coastal birds have *yellow* neck sacs; in birds of the Rockies, the neck sacs are *purplish.* Females are brown, mottled with black, and pale-bellied; their dark tails are somewhat like those of the males. Ruffed Grouse may be confused with female Blue Grouse, but both sexes of that bird have a lighter tail, with a bold *black band* near the tip.
Voice: Male in courtship gives a series of 5–7 low, muffled, booming or hooting notes, ventriloquial.
Range: Western N. America. Map 91. **Habitat:** Deciduous and mixed forests in mountains in summer; in conifer forests at higher elevations in winter.

GRAY PARTRIDGE *Perdix perdix*   **M87**

12–14″ (30–35 cm). A rotund grayish partridge, larger than a quail; when flushed, note the short *rufous* tail, *rusty face,* chestnut bars on sides. Male has a dark, U-shaped splotch on the belly.
Similar species: Chukar (which also has a rufous tail) has a red bill and feet, and a black "necklace."
Voice: A loud, hoarse *kar-wit, kar-wit.*
Range: Eurasia. Introduced in N. America. **West:** Map 87. **Habitat:** Cultivated land, hedgerows, bushy pastures, meadows.

CHUKAR *Alectoris chukar*   **M88**

13″ (33 cm). Like a large, sandy-colored quail; gray-brown with *bright red legs and bill;* light throat bordered by a clean-cut black "necklace." Sides *boldly barred.* Tail *rufous.*
Similar species: (1) Gray Partridge lacks the black necklace, has a dark gray bill and dark feet. (2) Mountain Quail is darker, with a long head plume. (3) The related **RED-LEGGED PARTRIDGE,** *A. rufa,* introduced into ne. Colorado, is darker; its necklace breaks into short streaks.
Voice: A series of *chuck's;* a sharp *wheet-u.*
Range: Asia, e. Europe. **West:** Introduced and established in w. N. America. Map 88. **Habitat:** Rocky, grassy, or brushy slopes; arid mountains, canyons.

164

GROUSE

SPRUCE GROUSE

♂

♂

typical

♀

"Franklin's" form ♂

♂

♀

♂ Rockies

♂ in display;

♂ in display

coastal

BLUE GROUSE

PARTRIDGES

♂

GRAY PARTRIDGE

♂

CHUKAR

♂

Red-legged Partridge

CALIFORNIA QUAIL *Callipepla californica* **M104**
9½–11″ (24–28 cm). A small, plump, grayish, chicken-like bird, with a *short black plume* curving forward from the crown. Males have a *black and white face* and throat pattern. Females are duller.
Voice: A three-syllabled *qua-quer'go*, or *Chi-ca'go*. Also light clucking notes. Male on territory, a loud *kurr*.
Range: Resident, British Columbia to Baja California; see Map 104. On western edge of Mojave and Colorado deserts where ranges of California and Gambel's quail overlap, hybrids occur. **Habitat:** Broken chaparral, woodland edges, coastal scrub, parks, estates, farms.

GAMBEL'S QUAIL *Callipepla gambelii* **M103**
10–11½″ (25–29 cm). Replaces the California Quail in the deserts. Similar to that bird, but male has a *black patch* on a light, *unscaled belly*; flanks and crown more russet (a local name is "Redhead"). Female also *lacks* scaly pattern on belly.
Range: Resident sw. U.S., nw. Mexico. Map 103.

MOUNTAIN QUAIL *Oreortyx pictus* **M100**
10½–11½″ (26–29 cm). A gray and brown quail of the mountains. Distinguished from California Quail by a long *straight* head plume and *chestnut* (not black) *throat*. Note the chestnut and white side pattern. Female similar to male but duller, with a shorter plume.
Voice: A mellow *wook!* or *to-wook!*, repeated at intervals by male.
Range: Western U.S. to n. Baja California. Map 100.

SCALED QUAIL *Callipepla squamata* **M102**
10–12″ (25–30 cm). Note the *bushy white crest* or "cotton top." A pale grayish quail ("Blue Quail") of arid country, with scaly markings on breast and back. Runs; often reluctant to fly.
Voice: A guinea-hen-like *chekar'* (also interpreted as *pay-cos*).
Range: Sw. U.S. to cen. Mexico. Map 102. **Habitat:** Grasslands, brush, arid country.

NORTHERN BOBWHITE *Colinus virginianus* **M101**
(Common Bobwhite) 8½–10½″ (21–26 cm). A small, rotund fowl, near the size of a Meadowlark. Ruddy, barred and striped, with a short, dark tail. Male has a conspicuous white throat and white eyebrow stripe; in the female these are buff. A dark Mexican form, **"MASKED BOBWHITE,"** with a *black throat* and *rusty underparts* once lived in s. Arizona, where it has been reintroduced.
Voice: A clearly whistled *Bob-white!* or *poor, Bob-whoit!* Covey call, *ko-loi-kee!*, answered by *whoil-kee!*
Range: Cen. and e. U.S. to Guatemala, Cuba. **West:** Map 101. **Habitat:** Farms, brushy open country, roadsides, wood edges.

MONTEZUMA QUAIL *Cyrtonyx montezumae* **M100**
(Harlequin Quail) 8–9½″ (20–24 cm). A rotund quail of Mexican mountains. Note the male's oddly striped *clown's face*, bushy crest on the nape, and *spotted body*. Females are brown, with less obvious facial stripings. Tame (called "Fool's Quail").
Voice: A soft, whinnying or quavering cry; ventriloquial.
Range: Resident sw. U.S. to s. Mexico. Map 100. **Habitat:** Grassy oak canyons, wooded mountain slopes with bunch grass.

QUAIL

♀

CALIFORNIA QUAIL

♂

♀

♂

GAMBEL'S QUAIL

MOUNTAIN QUAIL

♂

♂

SCALED QUAIL

♂

"Masked" Bobwhite

♀

♂

♂

NORTHERN BOBWHITE

MONTEZUMA QUAIL

♀

BIRDS OF PREY. We tend to lump all the diurnal (day-flying) raptors with hooked beaks and hooked claws as "birds of prey." Actually, they fall into two quite separate families:

(1) The **hawk group** (*Accipitridae*)—kites, eagles, buteos, accipiters, and harriers—of which there are 217 species in the world, 20 in the West + 3 or 4 accidentals.

(2) The **falcon group** (*Falconidae*)—falcons and caracaras. These are shown on pp. 184–187. There are 52 species in the world, 7 in the West + 2 accidentals.

The illustrations in the following pages present the obvious "field marks." For a more in-depth treatment of variable plumages, see *A Field Guide to the Hawks* (No. 35 in the Field Guide series) by Clark and Wheeler. For the subtleties of "jizz" (general impression and shape) at a distance, study *Hawks In Flight* by Dunne, Sutton, and Sibley.

The various groups of raptors can be sorted out by their basic shapes and flight style. When not flapping they may alternate between *soaring*, with wings fully extended and tails fanned, and *gliding*, with wings slightly pulled back and tails folded. These two pages show some basic silhouettes.

BUTEOS (buzzard hawks) are stocky, with broad wings and wide rounded tails. They soar and wheel high in the open sky.

full soar   glide

ACCIPITERS (true hawks) have small heads, *short rounded wings*, and longish tails. They fly with several rapid beats and a glide.

full soar   glide

HARRIERS are slim, with slim, round-tipped wings and long tails. They fly in open country and glide low, with a vulture-like dihedral.

glide

full soar

KITES (western species) are falcon-shaped, but unlike falcons, they are buoyant gliders, not power-fliers.

full soar

glide

FALCONS have long, pointed wings and long tails. Their wing strokes are strong and rapid.

full soar

glide

■ **KITES.** Graceful birds of prey, of southern distribution. U.S. species (except Snail Kite of Florida) are falcon-shaped, with pointed wings. **Food:** Large insects, reptiles, rodents.

BLACK-SHOULDERED KITE *Elanus caeruleus* **M68**
(White-tailed Kite) 15–17″ (38–43 cm). This whitish kite is falcon-shaped, with long, pointed wings and a *long white tail.* Soars and glides like a small gull; *often hovers. Adult:* Pale gray with a white head, underparts, and tail. A *large black patch* on the fore edge of the upperwing is obvious in perched birds. Overhead, shows an oval black patch at the carpal joint ("wrist") of the underwing. *Immature:* Recognizable as this kite, but has a *rusty breast,* a brown back, and a narrow dark band near the tip of its pale grayish tail.
Voice: A whistled *kee kee kee,* abrupt or drawn out.
Range: W. Oregon and s. Texas to Chile, Argentina. **West:** Map 68.
Habitat: Open groves, river valleys, marshes, grasslands.

MISSISSIPPI KITE *Ictinia mississippiensis* **M69**
14″ (35 cm). Falcon-shaped, graceful and gray. Gregarious; spends much time soaring. Adult is dark above, lighter below; head *pale gray;* tail and underwing blackish. No other falcon-like bird has a *black unbarred tail.* A broad *pale patch* shows on the rear edge of the wing (not visible when the bird is overhead). The immature is heavily streaked on its rusty underparts; the tail shows white bars when seen overhead.
Voice: Usually silent; about nest, a two-syllabled *phee-phew.*
Range: Mainly s. U.S.; winters Cen. and n. S. America. **West:** Map 69. **Habitat:** Wooded streams; groves, shelterbelts.

AMERICAN SWALLOW-TAILED KITE *Elanoides forficatus*
This raptor of the se. U.S. (not shown) has been recorded as an accidental in New Mexico, Arizona, and Colorado. See eastern *Field Guide to the Birds.*

■ **HARRIERS.** Slim raptors with slim wings, long tails. Flight low, languid, gliding, with wings in a shallow V. Sexes not alike. Harriers hunt in open country. We have only one species in N. America.

NORTHERN HARRIER *Circus cyaneus* **M71**
(Marsh Hawk) 17½–24″ (44–60 cm). A slim, long-winged, long-tailed raptor of the open country. In all plumages shows a *white rump patch.* Males are pale gray, whitish beneath with a gray hood; females are brown with heavy streaks; immatures are russet or orangy below. Glides and flies buoyantly and unsteadily low over the ground, with wings slightly above the horizontal, suggesting the Turkey Vulture's dihedral. Overhead, the wing tips of the pale male have a "dipped-in-ink" look, and there is a black border on the trailing edge of each wing.
Voice: A weak, nasal whistle, *pee, pee, pee.*
Range: Alaska, Canada to s. U.S.; n. Eurasia. Winters to n. S. America, n. Africa. **West:** Map 71. **Habitat:** Marshes, fields, prairies.

imm.

adult

adult

adult

imm.

BLACK-SHOULDERED KITE

m.

adult

adult

imm.

MISSISSIPPI KITE

imm.

♂

♀

NORTHERN HARRIER

■ **ACCIPITERS, or "BIRD HAWKS."** Long-tailed woodland raptors with rounded wings, adapted for hunting among the trees. Typical flight consists of several quick beats and a glide. Sexes similar; female larger. Size not always reliable in separating the three species; they may almost overlap, but not quite. **Food:** Chiefly birds, some small mammals.

SHARP-SHINNED HAWK *Accipiter striatus*   **M72**
10–14″ (25–35 cm). Near the size of a jay; a small, slim-bodied woodland hawk, with a slim tail and *short, rounded wings*. Flies with several quick beats and a glide. Adult has a dark back, *rusty-barred* breast. Folded tail of male is *slightly notched* or *square* (may seem a bit rounded when spread). Head and neck proportionately smaller than Cooper's. Immature is dark brown above, *streaked* with rusty on underparts.
Similar species: Female Cooper's Hawk is obviously larger, with a *well-rounded* tail; but male Cooper's and female Sharp-shin may approach each other so closely in size and tail shape that some cannot be safely identified in the field. See *A Field Guide to Birds of Prey* (Clark and Wheeler) and *Hawks in Flight* (Dunne, Sibley, and Sutton) for further discussion.
Voice: Like Cooper's Hawk's, but shriller; a high *kik, kik, kik.*
Range: Tree limit in Alaska, Canada to n. Argentina. Winters from n. U.S. south. **West:** Map 72. **Habitat:** Open deciduous woodlands, mixed or coniferous forests, thickets, edges.

COOPER'S HAWK *Accipiter cooperii*   **M73**
14–20″ (35–50 cm). A short-winged, long-tailed hawk, very similar to the Sharp-shinned Hawk but larger; female usually is not quite as long as a Crow. The tail of the female is *well rounded*, even when folded; male's less so. Adult has a proportionately larger head and neck than the Sharp-shin, with more contrast between blackish crown and gray nape. When the bird is gliding the head projects well beyond the wrists of the wing. The white tip on the tail is broader than in the "Sharpie." The immature is brown, streaked on breast, white on belly. No strong white eyestripe as in the Goshawk.
Voice: About nest, a rapid *kek, kek, kek;* suggests a Flicker.
Range: S. Canada to n. Mexico. **West:** Map 73. **Habitat:** Mature forest, open woodlands, wood edges, river groves.

NORTHERN GOSHAWK *Accipiter gentilis*   **M74**
20–26″ (50–65 cm). *Adult:* A large, robust hawk with a longish tail, rounded wings. Crown and cheek blackish; *broad white stripe over the eye.* Underparts *pale gray, finely barred;* back paler and grayer than in Cooper's or Sharp-shin; tail broader. More buteo-like when soaring. *Immature:* Like an immature Cooper's; usually larger; note pale stripe over the eye, and irregular tail-banding. Striping on underparts covers both breast and belly.
Voice: *Kak, kak, kak,* or *kuk, kuk, kuk,* heavier than Cooper's.
Range: Eurasia, northern N. America. **West:** Map 74. **Habitat:** Coniferous and deciduous forests, especially in mountains; forest edges; winters in lowlands.

ACCIPITERS

Accipiters (true hawks) have small heads, short rounded wings, long tails.

imm.

adult

SHARP-SHINNED HAWK

imm.

adult

COOPER'S HAWK

imm.

adult

NORTHERN GOSHAWK

glide (tail folded)

full soar (tail spread)

Accipiter Flight Silhouettes (Cooper's Hawk)

■ **BUTEOS, or BUZZARD HAWKS.** Large, thick-set hawks, with broad wings and wide, rounded tails. Buteos habitually soar high in wide circles. Much variation; sexes similar, females larger. Young birds are usually *streaked* below. Black morphs often occur. For an in-depth discussion of variant plumages, see *A Field Guide to Hawks of North America* (Clark and Wheeler). **Food:** Rodents, rabbits, sometimes small birds, reptiles, grasshoppers.

RED-TAILED HAWK *Buteo jamaicensis* M78

19–25″ (48–63 cm). When this large, broad-winged, wide-tailed hawk veers while soaring, the *rufous* on the topside of the tail is evident (on adults). From below the tail is pale, but it may transmit a hint of red. Overhead, a dependable mark on all but blackish birds is a *black or dark patagial bar* on the fore edge of the wing. Immature birds have grayish tails that may or may not show narrow banding. They also show the patagial bar. Underparts of typical Red-tails east of the Rockies are "zoned" (light breast, broad *band of streaks across the belly*), except in some birds of sw. Texas ("Fuertes" Red-tail). On the Great Plains, the pale *kriderii* form is found. There is much variation further west; these Red-tails tend to be darker. One might encounter the blackish *harlani*, as well as deep rusty and melanistic birds. The latter usually have the tell tale rust on their tails. Red-tails usually perch conspicuously.

Voice: An asthmatic squeal, *keeer-r-r* (slurring downward).

Range: Alaska, Canada, to Panama. **West:** Map 78. **Habitat:** Open country, woodlands, prairie groves, mountains, plains, roadsides.

"HARLAN'S" RED-TAILED HAWK *Buteo jamaicensis harlani*

A variable blackish race of the Red-tail; regarded by some as a distinct species. Similar to other melanistic Red-tails, but tail never solid red; usually dirty white, with a *longitudinal* mottling and freckling of black merging into a dark terminal band, giving a *white-rumped look*. Some may have a mottling of red on the tail.

Range: Breeds in e. Alaska and nw. Canada. Winters southeastward to Texas and the lower Mississippi Valley.

"KRIDER'S" RED-TAILED HAWK *Buteo jamaicensis kriderii*

A pale prairie race or form of the Red-tail, with a whitish tail that may be tinged with pale rufous.

Range: Prairies and plains of Canada and north-central U.S. Winters south through the southern plains to Texas, Louisiana.

SWAINSON'S HAWK *Buteo swainsoni* M77

19–22″ (48–55 cm). A buteo of the plains, proportioned like a Red-tail but wings a bit more pointed. When gliding, wings are held slightly above horizontal. Typical adults have a *dark breastband*. Overhead, *buffy wing linings* contrast with *dark flight feathers*. Tail gray above, often becoming white at the base. There are confusing individuals with light breasts, and dark melanistic birds; note the underwing with its dark flight feathers.

Voice: A shrill, plaintive whistle, *kreeeeeeer.*

Range: Nw. N. America to n. Mexico; winters to Argentina. **West:** Map 77. **Habitat:** Plains, range, open hills, sparse trees.

BUTEOS

Overhead patterns on pp. 191, 193.

rufous morph

imm.

dark morph

typical

from above

RED-TAILED HAWK

typical western form

"Harlan's"

from above

"KRIDER'S" RED-TAILED HAWK

"HARLAN'S" RED-TAILED HAWK

typical

from below

imm.

dark morph

dark morph

from below

typical adult

SWAINSON'S HAWK

ROUGH-LEGGED HAWK *Buteo lagopus* **M80**

19–24″ (48–60 cm). This big hawk of open country habitually *hovers* on beating wings. A buteo by shape; larger and with somewhat longer wings and tail than the others (except Ferruginous Hawk). Typical birds (but not all adults) show a *dark or blotched belly* and a *black patch* at the "wrist" (carpal joint) of the underwing. Tail *white*, with a *broad black band or bands* toward the tip. Black morph may lack extensive white on tail, but the broad terminal band and extensive white on the underwing are good points.
Similar species: See (1) Northern Harrier; (2) Golden Eagle.
Range: Arctic; circumpolar. Winters to s. U.S., cen. Eurasia. **West:** Map 80. **Habitat:** Tundra escarpments, arctic coasts; in winter, open fields, plains, marshes.

RED-SHOULDERED HAWK *Buteo lineatus* **M75**

17–24″ (43–60 cm). *Adult:* Recognized as a buteo by the ample tail and broad wings; as this species by the heavy dark bands across both sides of the tail. Adults have dark *rufous shoulders* (not always easy to see) and robin-red underparts. In flight, note the *translucent patch*, or "window," at the base of the primaries. *Immature:* Streaked; recognized by proportions, tail bands, and, in flight overhead, by the wing "windows."
Similar species: See other reddish-breasted hawks: (1) Adult Broadwing has paler wing linings, broader white bands on tail. See also immature Broad-wing; (2) Cooper's Hawk; (3) Red-tail.
Voice: A two-syllabled scream, *kee-yer* (dropping inflection).
Range: Se. Canada, e. U.S., California, Mexico. **West:** Map 75. **Habitat:** Bottomland woods, wooded rivers.

BROAD-WINGED HAWK *Buteo platypterus* **M76**

14–19″ (35–48 cm). A small, chunky buteo, the size of a crow. Note tail banding of adult—white bands *about as wide* as the black ones. Wing linings white. The rare dark morph, which breeds in Alberta, has dark wing linings, but shows the usual Broad-wing tail pattern. *Immature:* Tail bands more numerous, restricting the white.
Similar species: Young Red-shouldered Hawk is similar to immature Broad-wing, but the latter is chunkier, with a stubbier tail and shorter wings; the underwing is usually whiter.
Voice: A shrill, high-pitched *pweeeeeee* (diminuendo).
Range: S. Canada, e. U.S. Winters mainly in Cen. and S. America. **West:** Map 76. **Habitat:** Woods, groves.

FERRUGINOUS HAWK *Buteo regalis* **M79**

23–25″ (58–63 cm). A large, narrow-winged buteo of the plains. *Rufous above*, whitish below, with a *whitish or pale rufous tail* and light patch on upper surface of primaries. Head often quite pale. Overhead, typical adults show a *dark V* formed by the *rufous thighs*. Immatures lack this and also the rusty patches on the underwing. They show a *white rump* and a gray tail. Dark morphs (adults) overhead have dark wing linings, contrasting with white flight feathers and white tails.
Range: Sw. Canada, w. U.S. Winters sw. U.S., n. Mexico. Map 79.
Habitat: Plains, prairies.

BUTEOS

Overhead patterns on pp. 191, 193, 195.

dark morph

imm.

ROUGH-LEGGED HAWK

adult ♂

adult

imm.

adult

RED-SHOULDERED HAWK

adult

imm.

dark morph

adult

BROAD-WINGED HAWK

typical

dark morph

typical adult

FERRUGINOUS HAWK

typical

dark morph

177

HARRIS'S HAWK *Parabuteo unicinctus*

28″ (70 cm); spread 3½–3¾ ft. A black hawk of the *Buteo* type, with a flashing *white rump* and *white band* at the tip of the tail. Shows *chestnut areas* on thighs and shoulders—a mark of distinction from other black or melanistic buteos or the much chunkier Black-Hawk. Immature has light, streaked underparts and *rusty shoulders;* might be confused with Red-shouldered Hawk except for the conspicuous *white* at the base of the tail. Also known as Bay-winged Hawk.

Range: Sw. U.S. south to Argentina. **West:** Resident, s. and cen. Arizona, se. New Mexico, w. Texas. Also se. California (Colorado R.), where it formerly bred and has been reintroduced. Casual, s. Nevada, Utah. **Habitat:** River woods, mesquite, brush, cactus deserts.

ZONE-TAILED HAWK *Buteo albonotatus*

18½–21½″ (47–54 cm); spread 4 ft. A dull *black* hawk, with more slender wings than most other buteos. Might be mistaken for Turkey Vulture because of its proportions and two-toned underwing, but the hawk head and *white tail bands* (pale gray on topside) identify the adult. The immature has narrower tail bands and a scattering of *small white spots* on its black body.

Range: Breeds locally in nw., cen., and se. Arizona, s. and ne. New Mexico, w. Texas (Trans-Pecos) to n. S. America. Casual visitor to s. California (has bred). Accidental, Nevada, Utah. **Habitat:** River woodlands, desert mountains, canyons.

COMMON BLACK-HAWK *Buteogallus anthracinus*

20–23″ (50–58 cm); spread 4 ft. A black, buteonine hawk with exceptionally wide wings and *long,* chicken-like yellow legs. Identified by its chunky shape and the broad white *band* crossing the middle of the tail. In flight, a whitish spot shows near the tip of the wing at the base of the primaries. *Immature:* Dark-backed with a heavily striped *buffy* head and underparts; the tail is narrowly banded with five or six dark bands.

Similar species: Whereas the slimmer-winged Zone-tailed Hawk bears a superficial resemblance to a Turkey Vulture, the broader-winged Black-Hawk suggests a Black Vulture.

Range: Sw. U.S. to Ecuador. **West:** Breeds locally in cen. and s. Arizona. Has bred in s. New Mexico. Casual, w. Texas (Trans-Pecos), Utah. **Habitat:** Wooded stream bottoms.

GRAY HAWK *Buteo nitidus*

16–18″ (40–45 cm); spread 3 ft. A small *Buteo.* Adults are distinguished by their buteo-like proportions, gray back, and *thickly barred gray* underparts, white band on rump, and *widely banded* tail (similar to Broad-winged Hawk's). Immature has a narrowly barred tail, striped buffy underparts. Note the relatively short wing, barred thighs, strongly marked buffy face, *white bar* across rump.

Range: Sw. U.S. to Brazil. **West:** Breeds locally in se. Arizona, sw. New Mexico; casual, w. Texas. **Habitat:** Wooded lowland streams.

WHITE-TAILED HAWK *Buteo albicaudatus* (not shown)

A resident of s. Texas which has occurred accidentally in s. Arizona and New Mexico. See *A Field Guide to the Birds of Texas.*

Southwestern Specialties

BUTEOS

imm.

adult

HARRIS'S HAWK

imm.

adult

ZONE-TAILED HAWK

imm.

adult

COMMON BLACK-HAWK

imm.

GRAY HAWK

adult

179

■ **EAGLES. Subfamily Accipitrinae** (in part); shown in flight on p. 189. Eagles are distinguished from buteos, to which they are related, by their much greater size and proportionately longer wings. The powerful bill is nearly as long as the head. **Food:** Golden Eagle eats chiefly rabbits and large rodents; Bald Eagle, chiefly dead or dying fish.

BALD EAGLE *Haliaeetus leucocephalus* **M70**
30–43″ (75–108 cm); spread 7–8 ft. The national bird of the U.S. The adult, with its *white head* and *white tail*, is "all field mark." Bill yellow, massive. The dark immature has a dusky head and tail and a dark bill. It shows considerable whitish in the wing linings and often on the breast (see overhead pattern, p. 189). Variable, depending on age.
Voice: A harsh creaking cackle, *kleek-kik-ik-ik-ik*, or a lower *kak-kak-kak.*
Range: Alaska, Canada, to s. U.S. **West:** Map 70. **Habitat:** Coasts, rivers, large lakes; in migration, also mountains, open country.

GOLDEN EAGLE *Aquila chrysaetos* **M81**
30–40″ (75–100 cm). Majestic, the Golden Eagle glides and soars flat-winged with occasional wingbeats. Its greater size and longer wings (spread about 7 ft.) set it apart from the large buteos. *Adult:* Uniformly dark below, or with a slight lightening at the base of the obscurely banded tail. On the hind-neck, a *wash of gold. Immature:* In flight, more readily identified than the adult; shows a *white flash in the wings* at the base of the primaries, and a *white tail* with a *broad dark terminal band.*
Similar species: (1) Immature Bald Eagle usually has white in the wing linings and often on the body. Tail may be mottled with white at the base, but is not definitely banded. (2) Black morph of Rough-legged Hawk is smaller and has more white on the underwing.
Voice: Seldom heard, a yelping bark, *kya;* also whistled notes.
Range: Mainly mountain regions of N. Hemisphere. **West:** Map 81. **Habitat:** Open mountains, foothills, plains, open country.

WHITE-TAILED EAGLE *Haliaeetus albicilla*
(Gray Sea Eagle) 30–36″ (75–90 cm); spread 7½–8 ft. This Eurasian eagle is like a pale Bald Eagle, but *only the tail is white.* The tail is somewhat wedge-shaped. A bird that looks like a Bald Eagle with a *light brown* head and a *yellow bill* would be this straggler to the Aleutians of Alaska. It breeds on Attu. Also recorded on Kodiak I.

STELLER'S SEA-EAGLE *Haliaeetus pelagicus*
33–41″ (83–103 cm); spread 8–8½ ft. This accidental stray from Asia has extensive *white shoulders*, a *massive* yellow-orange beak and a deeply *wedge-shaped* white tail. Immature birds lack the white shoulders, but the massive bill and tail contours would be diagnostic. Casual or accidental in Alaska (Attu, Unalaska, St. Paul, Kodiak I.).

EAGLES

Overhead patterns on p. 191

BALD EAGLE adult

BALD EAGLE imm.

GOLDEN EAGLE adult

GOLDEN EAGLE imm.

ASIAN STRAYS TO ALASKA

White-tailed

Steller's

WHITE-TAILED EAGLE

STELLER'S SEA EAGLE

181

■ **AMERICAN VULTURES. Family Cathartidae.** Blackish, eagle-like birds, often seen soaring high in wide circles. Their naked heads are relatively smaller than those of hawks and eagles. Vultures are often incorrectly called "buzzards." **Food:** Carrion. **Range:** S. Canada to Cape Horn. **No. of species:** World 7; West 2 (+1 no longer in the wild but held in captivity).

TURKEY VULTURE *Cathartes aura*   M66
26–32" (65–80 cm). Nearly eagle-sized (spread 6 ft.). Overhead, note the great two-toned blackish wings (flight feathers paler). Soars with wings in a dihedral (a shallow V); rocks and tilts unsteadily. At close range the small naked *red head* of the adult is evident; immature birds have blackish heads.
Similar species: See (1) Zone-tailed Hawk, which "mimics" the Turkey Vulture; (2) the Black Vulture; and (3) eagles, which have larger heads, shorter tails, and soar in a flat plane.
Range: S. Canada to Cape Horn. Migratory in North. **West:** Map 66.
Habitat: Usually seen soaring in the sky or perched on dead trees, posts, carrion, or on the ground.

BLACK VULTURE *Coragyps atratus*
23–27" (58–68 cm); wingspan less than 5 ft. This big black scavenger is readily identified by the short square tail that barely projects beyond the rear edge of the wings, and by the *whitish patch* toward the wing tip. Legs longer and whiter than Turkey Vulture's. Note the quick labored flapping, alternating with short glides.
Similar species: Turkey Vulture has a longer tail; flaps less, soars more (with a noticeable dihedral). Black Vulture is blacker than Turkey; tail stubby; wings shorter, wider, with a white patch. *Caution:* Young Turkey Vulture has a blackish head.
Range: Ohio, Pennsylvania to n. Chile, n. Argentina. **West:** Uncommon local resident in s. Arizona, w. Texas (Big Bend). **Habitat:** Similar to Turkey Vulture's; avoids higher mountains.

CALIFORNIA CONDOR *Gymnogyps californianus*
45–55" (113–138 cm); spread 8½–9½ ft. Much larger than the Turkey Vulture; adults have extensive *white underwing linings* toward the fore edge of the wing. Head yellowish or orange. Young birds are dusky-headed and lack the white wing linings, but are twice the size of the Turkey Vulture and have much broader proportions. The Condor has a *flatter wing plane* when soaring; it does not rock or tilt. Many Golden Eagles show some white under the wing, but it is placed differently (see p. 189); the shape is also different.
Range: California. Formerly resident mainly in s. Coast Range from se. Monterey Co. to n. Los Angeles Co.; also mountains at s. end of San Joaquin Valley. Now gone in the wild due to capture. All surviving birds are now in zoos in Los Angeles and San Diego. Hopefully, through captive breeding, they may eventually be returned to the wild. *Caution:* Wild Andean Condors have been released as part of this rehabilitation program.

VULTURES

adult

imm.

TURKEY
VULTURE

BLACK
VULTURE

adult

adult

imm.

CALIFORNIA
CONDOR

183

■ **OSPREYS. Subfamily Pandioninae.** Formerly considered a mono-typic family comprising a single large bird of prey that hovers above the water and plunges feet-first for fish. Sexes alike. **Range:** All continents except Antarctica. **No. of species:** World 1; West 1.

OSPREY *Pandion haliaetus* M67

21–24½″ (53–61 cm). Large (spread 4½–6 ft.). Our only raptor that hovers over the water and plunges into it feet-first for fish (Bald Eagle may pick up fish from the surface). Blackish above, *white below*; head largely white, suggesting a Bald Eagle, but with a *broad black cheek patch.* Often flies with a kink or crook in the wing, showing a black "wrist" patch below. Immature has a scaly pattern on the back.

Voice: A series of sharp, annoyed whistles, *cheep, cheep,* or *yewk, yewk,* etc. Near nest, a frenzied *cheereek!*

Range: Almost cosmopolitan. **West:** Map 67. **Habitat:** Rivers, lakes, coasts.

■ **CARACARAS AND FALCONS. Family Falconidae.** Caracaras are large, long-legged birds of prey, some with naked faces. Sexes alike. **Food:** Our one U.S. species feeds mostly on carrion. **Range:** S. U.S. to Tierra del Fuego, Falklands. **No. of species:** World 10; West 1. Falcons suggest kites; they are streamlined birds of prey with pointed wings and longish tails. **Food:** Birds, rodents, insects. **Range:** Almost cosmopolitan. **No. of species:** World 52; West 7 (+2 accidental).

CRESTED CARACARA *Polyborus plancus*

20–25″ (50–63 cm). A large, long-legged, long-necked, dark bird of prey, often seen feeding with vultures; its *black crest* and *red face* are distinctive. In flight, its underbody presents alternating areas of light and dark: a white chest, a black belly, and a whitish, dark-tipped tail. Note the combination of the *pale wing patches* and *pale chest.* Young birds are browner, streaked on the breast.

Range: Sw. U.S., Texas, Florida to Tierra del Fuego. **West:** Uncommon resident of s. Arizona; casual or accidental, New Mexico. **Habitat:** Prairies, rangeland.

GYRFALCON *Falco rusticolus* M85

20–25″ (50–63 cm). A very large arctic falcon, larger and more robust and buteo-like than the Peregrine; slightly broader-tailed. Wingbeats deceptively slower. More uniformly colored than the Peregrine, with thinner sideburns. In the Arctic there are black, gray, and white forms; these are color morphs, not races.

Similar species: Peregrine is smaller and more contrastingly patterned, with a dark hood and broad black sideburns. It is slimmer with a more tapered tail.

Range: Arctic regions; circumpolar. **West:** Map 85. **Habitat:** Arctic barrens, seacoasts, open mountains.

OSPREY
CARACARA
GYRFALCON

immature

OSPREY

immature

CRESTED CARACARA

white phase

gray phase

gray phase

dark phase

dark phase

GYRFALCON

MERLIN *Falco columbarius* **M83**
(Pigeon Hawk) 10–13½" (25–34 cm). A small compact falcon, the length of a jay; suggests a miniature Peregrine. *Male:* Blue-gray above, with broad black bands on a *gray tail. Female and young:* Dusky brown, with banded tails. Both adults and young are boldly striped below. The prairie form is paler, lacking mustaches. Coastal Northwest form is dusky, lacking the light eyebrow stripe.
Range: Northern parts of N. Hemisphere. Winters to n. S. America, n. Africa. **West:** Map 83. **Habitat:** Open woods, cliffs, adjacent to grassland, tundra; in migration also foothills, marshes, open country coasts.

AMERICAN KESTREL *Falco sparverius* **M82**
(Sparrow Hawk) 9–12" (23–30 cm). A swallow-like falcon, the size of a jay. No other *small* hawk has a *rufous back or tail.* Males have blue-gray wings. Both sexes have a black and white face with a double mustache. *Hovers* for prey on rapidly beating wings; king-fisher-like. Sits fairly erect, occasionally lifting its tail.
Similar species: Sharp-shinned Hawk has rounded wings. Both Sharp-shin and Merlin have gray or brown backs and tails.
Voice: A rapid, high *klee klee klee* or *killy killy killy.*
Range: Most of N. and S. America. **West:** Map 82. **Habitat:** Open country, farmland, cities, wood edges, dead trees, wires, highways.

PEREGRINE FALCON *Falco peregrinus* **M84**
15–20" (38–50 cm); near the size of a crow. Note the *wide black "sideburns."* Known as a falcon by its pointed wings, narrow tail, and quick wingbeats, not unlike flight of a pigeon. Size and strong face pattern indicate this species. Adults slaty-backed, light-chested, barred and spotted below. Immatures are brown, heavily streaked. The northwestern population *pealei,* breeding on humid islands off Alaska and British Columbia, is *darker* and more heavily spotted on the breast.
Voice: At eyrie, a repeated *we'chew;* a rapid *kek kek kek kek.*
Range: Nearly worldwide. **West:** Map 84. **Habitat:** Open country, cliffs (mountains to coast); sometimes cities. *Endangered.*

PRAIRIE FALCON *Falco mexicanus* **M86**
17" (43 cm). Like a sandy Peregrine, with a *white eyebrow stripe* and a *narrower mustache.* In flight overhead this bird shows *black-ish patches* in the wingpits (see p. 197).
Similar species: Peregrine has a slaty back, more black on the face.
Range: Sw. Canada, w. U.S. to s. Mexico. **West:** Map 86. **Habitat:** Mountainous grasslands, open hills, plains, prairies.

APLOMADO FALCON *Falco femoralis*
15–18" (38–45 cm). A medium-sized falcon, a little smaller than the Peregrine. Note the *dark underwing* and *black belly,* contrast-ing with the white or pale cinnamon breast. Thighs and undertail coverts orange-brown.
Range: U.S.–Mexican border to Patagonia. **West:** Formerly a very rare local summer resident in s. Arizona, sw. New Mexico, and w. Texas (Big Bend). Recently there has been an attempt to reintroduce it through releases. **Habitat:** Arid brushy prairie, yucca flats.

FALCONS

Merlin

Kestrel

MERLIN

♀

♂

♂

♂

columbarius
richardsonii

suckleyi

AMERICAN
KESTREL

♀

♂

imm.

Peregrine

pealei

typical

PEREGRINE
FALCON

Prairie
Falcon

Aplomado
Falcon

PRAIRIE
FALCON

APLOMADO
FALCON

187

EAGLES AND OSPREY OVERHEAD

	Text and color plate
BALD EAGLE *Haliaeetus leucocephalus*	**pp. 180, 181**

  Adult: White head and white tail.
  Immature: Some white in wing linings; variable.

GOLDEN EAGLE *Aquila chrysaetos* **pp. 180, 181**
  Adult: Almost uniformly dark; wing linings dark.
  Immature: "Ringed" tail; white patches at base of primaries.

OSPREY *Pandion haliaetus* **pp. 184, 185**
  Clear white belly; black wrist patches.

Where the Bald Eagle, Turkey Vulture, and Osprey all are found, they can be separated at a great distance by their manner of soaring: the Bald Eagle with flat wings; the Turkey Vulture with a dihedral; the Osprey often with a kink or crook in the wings.

BALD EAGLE adult

BALD EAGLE immature

GOLDEN EAGLE adult

GOLDEN EAGLE immature

OSPREY

BLACKISH BIRDS OF PREY OVERHEAD

Text and
color plate

CRESTED CARACARA *Polyborus plancus* **pp. 184, 185**
Whitish chest, black belly, large *pale patches* in primaries.

ROUGH-LEGGED HAWK *Buteo lagopus* (dark morph) **pp. 176, 177**
Dark body and wing linings; *whitish flight feathers;* tail light from below, with one broad, *black terminal band* in female; additional bands in male.

FERRUGINOUS HAWK *Buteo regalis* (dark morph) **pp. 176, 177**
Similar to dark morph of Rough-leg, but tail whitish, without the dark banding. Note also the white wrist marks, or "commas," as they have been called.

SWAINSON'S HAWK *Buteo swainsoni* (dark morph) **pp. 174, 175**
In the dark morph, the wings are usually dark throughout, *including the flight feathers,* tail narrowly banded. Rufous morph may be rustier, with lighter rufous wing linings.

RED-TAILED HAWK *Buteo jamaicensis* (dark morph) **pp. 174, 175**
Chunky; tail reddish above, pale tinged with rusty below; variable. May not always be safely distinguishable underneath from "Harlan's" form of Red-tail.

"HARLAN'S" HAWK *Buteo jamaicensis* (in part) **pp. 174, 175**
Similar to dark morph of Red-tail, but tends to be mottled with gray or whitish at the base of the tail.

BROAD-WINGED HAWK **pp. 192, 193**
Buteo platypterus (dark morph)
Distinctive tail pattern and flight feathers as in the light morph, but body and wing linings dark. Rare; breeds in Alberta.

ZONE-TAILED HAWK *Buteo albonotatus* (immature) **pp. 178, 179**
Longish, *two-toned wings* (suggesting a Turkey Vulture). Three white tail bands (only one visible on folded tail).

HARRIS'S HAWK *Parabuteo unicinctus* **pp. 178, 179**
Chestnut wing linings. A very broad white band at the base of the black tail, and a narrow white terminal band.

COMMON BLACK-HAWK *Buteogallus anthracinus* **pp. 178, 179**
Thick-set black wings; light patches near wing tips. A broad white band at *mid-tail* and a very broad, black subterminal band. Whereas the Zone-tailed Hawk seems to mimic the Turkey Vulture, a deceptive ploy when it is hunting, the chunkier Black-Hawk may be compared to the Black Vulture.

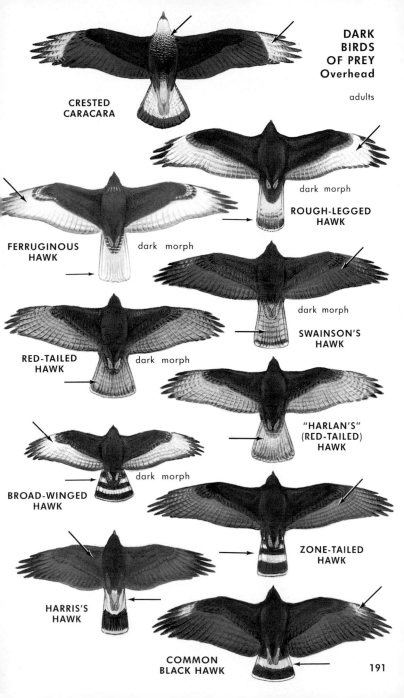

**DARK
BIRDS
OF PREY
Overhead**

adults

CRESTED
CARACARA

ROUGH-LEGGED
HAWK

dark morph

FERRUGINOUS
HAWK

dark morph

SWAINSON'S
HAWK

dark morph

RED-TAILED
HAWK

dark morph

"HARLAN'S"
(RED-TAILED)
HAWK

BROAD-WINGED
HAWK

dark morph

ZONE-TAILED
HAWK

HARRIS'S
HAWK

COMMON
BLACK HAWK

191

BUTEOS OVERHEAD

Buteos, or "buzzard hawks," are chunky, with broad wings and broad, rounded tails. They soar and wheel high in the air.

Text and color plate

RED-TAILED HAWK *Buteo jamaicensis*   **pp. 174, 175**
(Typical western form)
The *dark patagial bar* at the fore edge of the wing is the best mark from below. Light chest, streaked belly; tail plain, with little or no banding. Immature birds are streaked below and have tail banding. Note always the *patagial bar.*

SWAINSON'S HAWK *Buteo swainsoni*   **pp. 174, 175**
Adult has a dark chest band. Note also the contrast between the light wing linings and dark flight feathers. The immature has a similar look, but has streaks on the underbody.

RED-SHOULDERED HAWK *Buteo lineatus*   **pp. 176, 177**
The tail is strongly banded (white bands *narrower* than the dark ones). The adult is *strongly barred with rusty* on the body and wing linings. The immature has a striped body. There is a *light "window"* on the outer wing of adults as well as immatures.

BROAD-WINGED HAWK *Buteo platypterus*   **pp. 176, 177**
Smaller and chunkier, with a widely banded tail (*white bands wide*); underwing pale. *Immature:* Body striped, tail narrowly banded. The pale underwings may show lighter "windows" near the wing tips.

ROUGH-LEGGED HAWK *Buteo lagopus*   **pp. 176, 177**
Note the *black carpal patch* contrasting with the *white* flight feathers. A *broad, blackish band* or cummerbund across the belly is distinctive in most but not all birds. Tail light, with a broad, dark terminal band. Adult males may be darker-chested and have more bands on the tail.

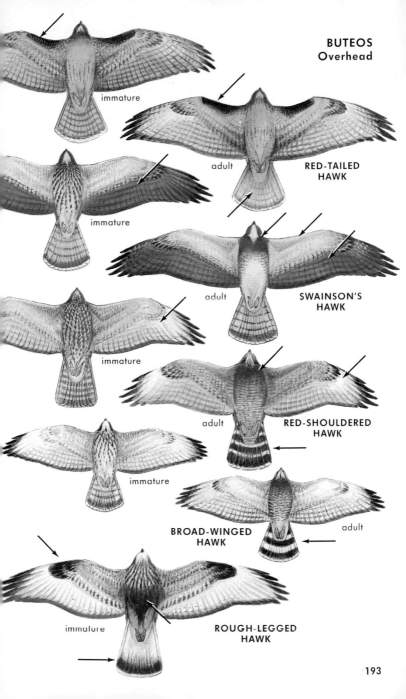

BUTEOS
Overhead

immature

adult

**RED-TAILED
HAWK**

immature

adult

**SWAINSON'S
HAWK**

immature

adult

**RED-SHOULDERED
HAWK**

immature

**BROAD-WINGED
HAWK**

adult

immature

**ROUGH-LEGGED
HAWK**

193

FERRUGINOUS HAWK *Buteo regalis*   **pp. 176, 177**
   Whitish underparts, with a *dark V formed by the legs*. Wings and
   tail longish for a buteo. A bird of arid plains, open range.

GRAY HAWK *Buteo nitidus*   **pp. 178, 179**
   Stocky. Broadly banded tail (suggestive of Broad-wing); *gray-barred
   underparts*. Very local in se. Arizona.

WHITE-TAILED HAWK *Buteo albicaudatus*
   Whitish underparts; white tail with one subterminal black band.
   Has a gray head. Soars with a marked dihedral. A bird of south
   Texas, Mexico. Would be a casual or accidental stray if seen in Ar-
   izona or New Mexico.

Kites are falcon-shaped, but are
buoyant gliders, not power-fliers.

BLACK-SHOULDERED KITE *Elanus caeruleus*   **pp. 170, 171**
   Falcon-shaped, with a *white tail*. Note also the conspicuous black
   carpal spot. *Immature:* Similar, but with a rusty wash on the chest
   and a dusky subterminal band on the tail.

MISSISSIPPI KITE *Ictinia mississippiensis*   **pp. 170, 171**
   Falcon-shaped. Dusky, with a solid *black tail.*
   Immature: Striped below, with white bands on its black tail.

Harriers are slim, with somewhat
rounded wings, long tails, and
long bodies. They fly low, with a
vulture-like dihedral and languid
flight.

NORTHERN HARRIER *Circus cyaneus*   **pp. 170, 171**
   Male: Whitish, with black wing tips and trailing edge. Gray hood.
   Female: Harrier shape. Brown; heavily streaked. From above, all
   plumages have a white rump.

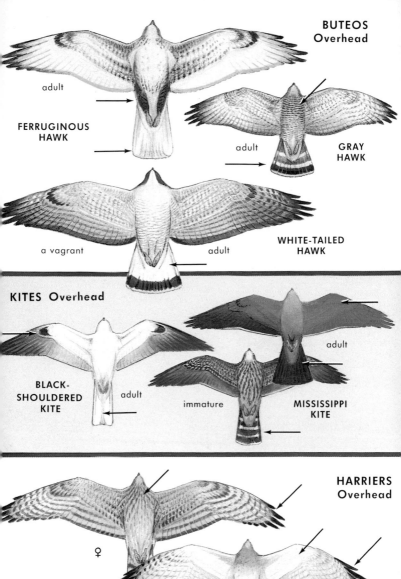

BUTEOS
Overhead

adult

FERRUGINOUS HAWK

adult

GRAY HAWK

a vagrant

adult

WHITE-TAILED HAWK

KITES Overhead

BLACK-SHOULDERED KITE

adult

immature

adult

MISSISSIPPI KITE

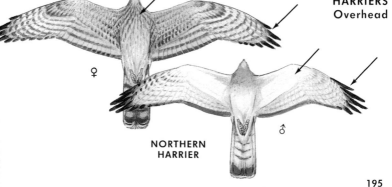

HARRIERS
Overhead

♀

NORTHERN HARRIER

♂

ACCIPITERS have short, rounded wings and long tails. They fly with several rapid beats and a short glide. They are better adapted to hunting in woodlands than most other hawks.

Text and color plate

NORTHERN GOSHAWK *Accipiter gentilis*   **pp. 172, 173**
Very large; adult (shown) with a pale, pearly gray breast. A bit more buteo-like than other accipiters. Fluffy white undertail coverts.

COOPER'S HAWK *Accipiter cooperii*   **pp. 172, 173**
Medium-sized. Near size of a crow; tail *rounded*. Head larger, more squarish than that of Sharp-shin.

SHARP-SHINNED HAWK *Accipiter striatus*   **pp. 172, 173**
Small; near size of a jay; tail *squarish* or notched, but may appear slightly rounded when spread. Head rounder and proportionately smaller than Cooper's.

FALCONS have long, pointed wings and long tails. The wing strokes are strong and rapid, but shallow.

PEREGRINE FALCON *Falco peregrinus*   **pp. 186, 187**
Falcon shape; near size of an American Crow; bold face pattern.

AMERICAN KESTREL *Falco sparverius*   **pp. 186, 187**
Small size; banded *rufous tail.*

MERLIN *Falco columbarius*   **pp. 186, 187**
Small size, near that of a jay; banded *gray tail.*

GYRFALCON *Falco rusticolus*   **pp. 184, 185**
Larger than Peregrine; grayer, without that bird's contrasting pattern. Dark and white phases or morphs also occur. Arctic.

PRAIRIE FALCON *Falco mexicanus*   **pp. 186, 187**
Size of Peregrine. *Dark axillars* ("wingpits") and inner coverts. Plains, prairies, open country.

APLOMADO FALCON *Falco femoralis*   **pp. 186, 187**
Black belly band, light chest. (A Mexican border possibility.)

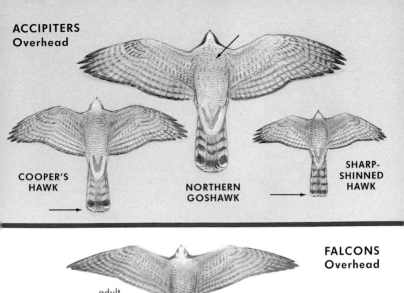

ACCIPITERS
Overhead

COOPER'S HAWK

NORTHERN GOSHAWK

SHARP-SHINNED HAWK

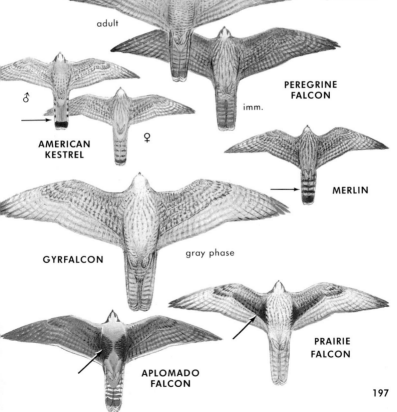

FALCONS
Overhead

adult

♂

♀

AMERICAN KESTREL

PEREGRINE FALCON

imm.

MERLIN

GYRFALCON

gray phase

APLOMADO FALCON

PRAIRIE FALCON

197

■ OWLS. Families Strigidae (Typical Owls) and Tytonidae (Barn Owls).

Chiefly nocturnal birds of prey, with large heads and flattened faces forming facial disks; large, forward-facing eyes; hooked bills and claws; usually feathered feet (outer toe reversible). Flight noiseless, mothlike. Some species have "horns" or "ears." Sexes similar; female larger. **Food:** Rodents, birds, reptiles, fish, large insects. **Range:** Nearly worldwide. **No. of species:** World 134; West 12 (+1 accidental).

BARRED OWL *Strix varia*　　　　　　　　　　　　　M203
17–24" (43–60 cm). A large, brown, puffy-headed woodland owl with big, moist *brown* eyes. Barred *across* chest and streaked *lengthwise* on belly; this combination separates it from the Spotted Owl (p. 205), which it might eventually displace in the Northwest.
Voice: Not so deep as Great Horned Owl's. Usually eight accented hoots, in two groups of four: *hoohoo-hoohoo, hoohoohoohooaw.*
Range: Canada to Honduras. **West:** Map 203. **Habitat:** Woodlands, wooded river bottoms, wooded swamps.

BARN OWL *Tyto alba*　　　　　　　　　　　　　　　M193
14–20" (35–50 cm). A long-legged, knock-kneed, pale, monkey-faced owl. *White heart-shaped face and dark eyes;* no ear tufts. Distinguished in flight as an owl by the large head and mothlike flight; as this species, by the unstreaked whitish or pale cinnamon underparts (ghostly at night) and the rusty back.
Similar species: Short-eared Owl (marshes) is streaked, has darker face and underparts, *yellow* eyes, shorter legs.
Voice: A shrill, rasping hiss or snore: *kschh* or *shiiish.*
Range: Nearly worldwide in tropical and temperate regions; in New World from s. Canada to Tierra del Fuego. **West:** Map 193. **Habitat:** Woodlands, groves, farms, barns, towns, cliffs.

GREAT GRAY OWL *Strix nebulosa*　　　　　　　　　M204
24–33" (60–83 cm). Largest owl; very tame. Dusky gray, heavily striped *lengthwise* on underparts. Round-headed, without ear tufts; the large, *strongly lined facial disks* dwarf the *yellow* eyes. Note the *black chin spot* bordered by two broad white patches like *white mustaches.* Tail long for an owl (12"). Often hunts by day.
Voice: A deep, booming *whoo-hoo-hoo.* Also deep single *whoo's.*
Range: Boreal forests of N. Hemisphere; rare. **West:** Map 204. **Habitat:** Dense conifer forests, adjacent meadows, bogs. Often hunts by day.

SNOWY OWL *Nyctea scandiaca*　　　　　　　　　　M197
20–27" (50–68 cm). A large *white* Arctic owl, flecked or barred with dusky. Round head, *yellow eyes.* Some birds (adult males) are much whiter than others. Day-flying. Perches on dunes, posts, haystacks, ground in open country. Sometimes buildings.
Similar species: (1) Barn-Owl is whitish on underparts only; has *dark* eyes. (2) All young owls are whitish when in down.
Voice: Usually silent. Flight note when breeding is a loud, repeated *krow-ow;* also a repeated *rick.*
Range: Arctic; circumpolar. Has cyclic winter irruptions southward. **West:** Map 197. **Habitat:** Prairies, fields, marshes, beaches, dunes; in summer, arctic tundra.

BARRED OWL

COMMON BARN-OWL

GREAT GRAY OWL

SNOWY OWL

199

SHORT-EARED OWL *Asio flammeus*   **M206**
13–17″ (33–43 cm). An owl of open country, often abroad by day.
Streaked tawny brown color and irregular flopping flight identify it.
Large buffy wing patches show in flight and on the underwing, along
with a black carpal ("wrist") patch. *Dark facial disks* emphasize the
yellow eyes. Long-ear has similar mothlike flight but is gray.
Voice: An emphatic, sneezy bark: *kee-yow!, wow!,* or *waow!*
Range: Nearly worldwide. **West:** Map 206. **Habitat:** Prairies,
marshes (fresh and salt), dunes, tundra.

WESTERN SCREECH-OWL *Otus kennicottii*   **M195**
7–10″ (18–25 cm). A common widespread small owl with conspicuous ear tufts. Usually *gray,* but those in n. Great Basin population
have two color morphs, *gray* and *brown.* Those in northern humid
regions are *usually* darker brown; those in arid regions paler, grayer.
Voice: A series of hollow whistles on one pitch, running into a tre-
molo (rhythm of a small ball bouncing to a standstill).
Range: Se. Alaska to cen. Mexico. Map 195. **Habitat:** Wooded canyons, farm groves, shade trees.

EASTERN SCREECH-OWL *Otus asio* (not shown)   **M195**
7–10″ (18–25 cm). Two color morphs: red-brown and gray. Like the
Western Screech-Owl, but separated by voice and range. Also differs
in having a bright *red-brown* morph.
Voice: A mournful whinny or wail; tremulous, *descending* in pitch.
Sometimes a series of notes on a single pitch.
Range: S. Canada to cen. Mexico. **West:** Map 195.

WHISKERED SCREECH-OWL *Otus trichopsis*
6½–8″ (16–20 cm). Very similar to the Western Screech-Owl. Has
large white spots on scapulars, coarser black spots on underparts,
longer facial bristles, yellow-green bill. Readily identified by voice.
Voice: *Boobooboo-boo, boobooboo-boo,* etc.; arrangement of this
"code" may vary. At times a repeated, four-syllabled *chooyoo-coo-
cooo,* vaguely suggestive of White-winged Dove.
Range: Resident from mountains of se. Arizona through Mexico to
n. Nicaragua. **Habitat:** Canyons, pine-oak woods, oaks, sycamores.

LONG-EARED OWL *Asio otus*   **M205**
13–16″ (33–40 cm). A slender, crow-sized owl with long ear tufts.
Usually seen "frozen" close to the trunk of a tree. Much smaller
than the Great Horned Owl; underparts streaked *lengthwise,* not
barred crosswise. Ears closer together, erectile.
Voice: One or two long *hooo's;* usually silent.
Range: Canada to sw. and s.-cen. U.S.; Eurasia, n. Africa. **West:** Map
205. **Habitat:** Woodlands, conifer groves. Often roosts in groups.

GREAT HORNED OWL *Bubo virginianus*   **M196**
18–25″ (45–63 cm). The "Cat Owl." A *large* owl with ear tufts or
"horns." Heavily *barred* beneath; conspicuous *white throat bib.* In
flight, as large as our largest hawks; looks neckless, large-headed.
Varies regionally from very dark to very pale.
Voice: Male usually utters five or six resonant hoots: *Hoo!, hu-hu-
hu, Hoo! Hoo!* Female's hoots are said to be higher, in shorter sequence.
Range: Tree limit in N. America to Tierra del Fuego. **West:** Map
196. **Habitat:** Forests, woodlots, streamsides, open country.

EARED OWLS

SHORT-EARED OWL

northwest coast

WESTERN SCREECH-OWL

WHISKERED SCREECH-OWL

LONG-EARED OWL

subarctic form

GREAT HORNED OWL

typical

BOREAL OWL *Aegolius funereus*   **M200**

9–10″ (23–25 cm). A small, flat-headed, earless owl. Very tame. Similar to the Saw-whet Owl, but a bit larger; facial disks pale grayish white *framed with black;* bill a pale horn color or *yellowish;* forehead *thickly spotted* with white. *Juvenile:* Similar to young Saw-whet Owl, but duskier; eyebrows dirty whitish or gray; belly obscurely blotched, not tawny ochre.

Similar species: (1) Saw-whet Owl is smaller. Adult has a blacker bill, lacks black facial frames, and has fine white streaks, not spots, on the forehead. (2) Hawk Owl is larger, grayer, and *long-tailed;* it is *barred below.*

Voice: Like a soft, high-pitched bell or dripping of water; an endlessly repeated *ting-ting-ting-ting-ting-ting,* etc.

Range: Boreal forests of N. Hemisphere. **West:** Map 200. **Habitat:** Mixed-wood and conifer forests, muskeg. Winters in valleys, lowlands.

NORTHERN SAW-WHET OWL *Aegolius acadicus*   **M207**

7–8½″ (18–21 cm). A very tame little owl; smaller than a Screech-Owl, without ear tufts. Underparts have soft blotchy brown streaks. Young birds in summer are chocolate-brown, with conspicuous white eyebrows forming a broad V over the bill; belly *tawny ochre.*

Similar species: Boreal Owl is somewhat larger, has a whitish face framed with black, and a yellowish or pale horn-colored bill.

Voice: Song, a mellow, whistled note repeated mechanically in endless succession, often 100–130 times per minute: *too, too, too, too, too, too, too, too,* etc. Much faster than Northern Pygmy-Owl's.

Range: Se. Alaska, Canada, w. and ne. U.S. to s. Mexico. **West:** Map 207. **Habitat:** Forests, conifers, groves.

BURROWING OWL *Athene cunicularia*   **M201**

9–11″ (23–28 cm). A small owl of open country, often seen by day standing erect on the ground or on posts. Note the *long legs* (for an owl). About the size of a Screech-Owl; barred and spotted, with a white chin stripe, round head, and stubby tail. Bobs and bows when agitated.

Voice: A rapid, chattering *quick-quick-quick.* At night, a mellow *co-hoo,* higher than Mourning Dove's *coo.*

Range: Sw. Canada, w. U.S., Florida to s. Argentina. Migratory in North. **West:** Map 201. **Habitat:** Open grassland, prairies, farmland, airfields. Nests in burrows in the ground, even in suburbs.

NORTHERN HAWK OWL *Surnia ulula*   **M198**

14½–17½″ (37–44 cm). A medium-sized, hawklike, day-flying owl (smaller than American Crow), with a *long, rounded tail* and *completely barred underparts.* Does not sit as erect as other owls; often perches at the tip of a tree and jerks its tail like a Kestrel. Shrikelike, it flies low, rising abruptly to its perch. Note the broad black sideburns framing the pale face.

Voice: A chattering *kikikiki,* more like a falcon than an owl. A kestrel-like *illy-illy-illy-illy.* Also a harsh scream.

Range: Boreal forests of N. Hemisphere. **West:** Map 198. **Habitat:** Open conifer forests, birch scrub, tamarack bogs, muskeg.

SMALL OWLS

BOREAL OWL

NORTHERN SAW-WHET OWL

juvenile

adult

NORTHERN SAW-WHET OWL

NORTHERN HAWK OWL

BURROWING OWL

203

SPOTTED OWL *Strix occidentalis*   **M202**
16½–19″ (41–48 cm). A large, dark-brown forest owl with a puffy round head. Large *dark eyes* (all other large N. American owls except Barn and Barred owls have yellow eyes) and *heavily spotted chest and barred belly* identify this reportedly endangered bird, which may eventually be displaced by the Barred Owl (p. 199).
Voice: High-pitched hoots, like barking of a small dog; usually in groups of three (*hoo, hoo-hoo*) or four (*hoo, who-who-whooo*). Also a longer series of rapid hoots in crescendo.
Range: Resident of old forests from sw. British Columbia to cen. Mexico; Map 202. **Habitat:** Mature old-growth forests, conifers, wooded canyons.

FLAMMULATED OWL *Otus flammeolus*   **M194**
6–7″ (15–18 cm). Smaller than a Screech-Owl. *Our only small owl with dark eyes.* Largely gray, with *tawny scapulars* and inconspicuous ear tufts. Southern birds are rustier. A little-known owl.
Voice: A mellow *hoot* (or *hoo-hoot*), low in pitch for so small an owl; repeated steadily at intervals of 2–3 seconds.
Range: Southern British Columbia, w. U.S. to Guatemala. **West:** Map 194. **Habitat:** Open pine, fir forests in mountains.

ELF OWL *Micrathene whitneyi*   **M200**
5–6″ (13–15 cm). A tiny, small-headed, short-tailed, earless owl, the size of a chunky sparrow. Underparts softly striped with rusty; "eyebrows" white. Hides by day in woodpecker holes in saguaros, telephone poles, or trees. Found at night by calls.
Voice: A rapid, high-pitched *whi-whi-whi-whi-whi-whi* or *chewk-chewk-chewk-chewk*, etc., often becoming higher and more yipping or "puppy like," and chattering in the middle of the series.
Range: Sw. U.S. to cen. Mexico. Map 200. **Habitat:** Saguaro deserts, wooded canyons.

FERRUGINOUS PYGMY-OWL *Glaucidium brasilianum*
6½–7″ (16–18 cm). Very similar to Northern Pygmy-Owl; best clue is its desert habitat along the U.S.–Mexican border. Streaking on breast *brownish* rather than black; crown has fine pale streaks (not dots). Tail rusty, barred with black.
Voice: *Chook* or *took*; sometimes repeated monotonously 2–3 times per second. Calls in daytime but more often at night.
Range: Resident from s. Arizona and lower Rio Grande Valley, Texas, to Strait of Magellan. **Habitat:** Mesquite thickets, desert riverine woods, saguaros. Hunts by day. Often mobbed by birds.

NORTHERN PYGMY-OWL *Glaucidium gnoma*   **M199**
7–7½″ (18–19 cm). *Black patches* on each side of the hind-neck suggest "eyes on back of the head." A very small, "earless" owl; brown, with *sharply streaked flanks* and a rather long barred tail. Frequently heard calling or seen flying in daytime. The spotted head is proportionately smaller than that of a Saw-whet or Screech-Owl. Tail often held at a perky angle.
Voice: A single mellow whistle, *hoo*, repeated every 2 or 3 seconds. Also a rolling series, ending with 2–3 deliberate notes: *too-too too-too-too-too-too-too-too-took-took-took.*
Range: Se. Alaska, w. Canada to Honduras. Map 199. **Habitat:** Open coniferous or mixed woods, wooded canyons.

SPOTTED OWL and SMALL OWLS

red phase

gray phase

FLAMMULATED OWL

SPOTTED OWL

comparison of
Spotted Owl (left),
Barred Owl (right)

ELF OWL

gray phase

FERRUGINOUS PYGMY-OWL

NORTHERN PYGMY-OWL

Note the
eyed pattern
on the nape.

■ **TROGONS. Family Trogonidae.** Solitary, brightly colored forest birds with a short neck, stubby bill, long tail, and very small feet. Erect when perched. Trogons flutter when plucking berries. **Food:** Small fruits, insects. **Range:** Mainly tropical parts of world. **No. of species:** World 36; West 2.

EARED TROGON *Euptilotis neoxenus*
12½" (31 cm). This Mexican trogon can be separated from the Elegant Trogon by its *black* (not yellow) bill, *lack of a white band* between the green and the red, and a greater amount of white on the underside of the blue tail. "Ears" of male inconspicuous. A very rare visitor to se. Arizona (Chiricahuas).

ELEGANT TROGON *Trogon elegans*
(Coppery-tailed Trogon) 11–12" (28–30 cm). Note the erect posture, slightly parrot-like profile, *geranium-red belly.* Male: Head, chest, and upperparts deep glossy green, separated from the red belly by a *narrow white band* across the breast. Tail square-tipped, moderately long; bill yellow. *Female:* Brown, not green; less red on underparts. Note the *white mark* on the cheek.
Voice: A series of low, coarse notes, suggesting a hen Turkey; *kowm kowm kowm kowm kowm kowm* or *koa, koa, koa,* etc.
Range: Breeds from mountains of se. Arizona south to Costa Rica. Winters south of U.S. Casual, sw. New Mexico, Texas (Big Bend).
Habitat: Mountain forests, pine-oak or sycamore canyons.

■ **KINGFISHERS. Family Alcedinidae.** Solitary birds with large heads, heron-like bills, and small syndactyl feet (two toes partially joined). Most are fish-eaters, perching above water, or hovering and plunging headfirst. **Food:** Mainly fish; some species eat insects, lizards. **Range:** Almost worldwide. **No. of species:** World 91; West 2.

GREEN KINGFISHER *Chloroceryle americana*
7–8½" (18–21 cm). Kingfisher shape, small size; flight buzzy, direct. Upperparts deep green with white spots; collar and underparts white, sides spotted. *Male* has a *rusty* breastband; *female* has one or two greenish bands. (Note the switch: In the Belted Kingfisher, the *female* has the rusty band.)
Voice: A sharp clicking, *tick tick tick;* also a sharp squeak.
Range: Texas to Argentina. **West:** Resident in s. Texas north along Rio Grande to Pecos R. Sparse straggler in Arizona (mainly Santa Cruz drainage and San Pedro Valley). **Habitat:** Rivers, streams.

BELTED KINGFISHER *Ceryle alcyon*   **M223**
13" (33 cm). Hovering on rapidly beating wings in readiness for the plunge, or flying with uneven wingbeats (as if changing gear), rattling as it goes, the Kingfisher is easily recognized. Perched, it is big-headed and big-billed, larger than a Robin; blue-gray above, with a ragged bushy crest and a broad gray breastband. The female has an additional rusty breastband.
Voice: A loud dry rattle.
Range: Alaska, Canada to s. U.S. Winters to n. S. America. **West:** Map 223. **Habitat:** Streams, lakes, bays, coasts; nests in banks, perches on wires.

TROGONS

EARED
TROGON

♀   ♂

ELEGANT
TROGON

♀   ♂

KINGFISHERS

hovering

GREEN
KINGFISHER

♀

♂

♀

♂

BELTED
KINGFISHER

plunging

207

■ **PIGEONS AND DOVES. Family Columbidae.** Plump, fast-flying birds with small heads and low, cooing voices; they nod their heads as they walk. Two types: (1) birds with fanlike tails (Rock Dove, or Domestic Pigeon); (2) smaller, brownish birds with rounded or pointed tails (Mourning Dove). Sexes similar. **Food:** Seeds, waste grain, fruits, insects. **Range:** Nearly worldwide in tropical and temperate regions. **No. of species:** World 297; West 5 (+3 accidental, 3 introduced). The Red-billed Pigeon *(Columba flavirostris)* and White-tipped Dove *(Leptotila verrauxi)* of lower Rio Grande may be vagrants in w. Texas. See *Field Guide to the Birds of Texas.*

MOURNING DOVE *Zenaida macroura* **M187**
12″ (30 cm). The common wild dove. Brown; smaller and slimmer than Rock Dove. Note the *pointed tail* with large white spots.
Voice: A hollow, mournful *coah, cooo, cooo, coo.* At a distance only the three *coo's* are audible.
Range: Se. Alaska, s. Canada to Panama. **West:** Map 187. **Habitat:** Farms, towns, open woods, scrub roadsides, grassland.

COMMON GROUND-DOVE *Columbina passerina* **M189**
6½″ (16 cm). A very small dove, *not much larger than a sparrow.* Note the *stubby black tail,* scaly breast, and rounded wings that flash *rufous* in flight. Feet yellow or pink.
Voice: A soft, monotonously repeated *woo-oo, woo-oo,* etc. May sound monosyllabic—*wooo,* with rising inflection.
Range: Southern U.S. to Costa Rica; n. S. America. **West:** Map 189.
Habitat: Farms, orchards, wood edges, roadsides.

INCA DOVE *Columbina inca* **M188**
7½″ (19 cm). A very small, slim dove with a *scaly* look. *Rufous* in the primaries (as in Ground-Dove), but has a *longer,* square-ended tail, with *white sides.* **Voice:** A monotonous *coo-hoo* or *no-hope.*
Range: Sw. U.S. to nw. Costa Rica. **West:** Map 188. **Habitat:** Towns, parks, farms.

WHITE-WINGED DOVE *Zenaida asiatica* **M186**
11–11½″ (28–29 cm). A dove of the desert, readily known by the *large white wing patches.* Otherwise similar to the Mourning Dove, but tail *rounded,* and tipped with broad white corners.
Voice: A harsh cooing, *"who cooks for you?"*; also, *ooo-uh-cuck'oo.* Sounds vaguely like the crowing of a young rooster.
Range: Sw. U.S. to n. Chile. **West:** Map 186. **Habitat:** River woods, mesquite, saguaros, desert oases, groves, towns.

BAND-TAILED PIGEON *Columba fasciata* **M185**
14–15½″ (35–39 cm). Heavily built; might be mistaken for a Rock Dove (Domestic Pigeon) except for its woodland or mountain habitat and greater tendency to alight in trees. Note the *broad pale band* across the end of the fanlike tail. At close range, shows a *white crescent* on nape. Feet *yellow.* Bill *yellow* with *dark tip.*
Voice: A hollow, owl-like *oo-whoo* or *whoo-oo-whoo,* repeated.
Range: Sw. British Columbia through Pacific states and Rockies to Argentina. Map 185. **Habitat:** Oak canyons, foothills, chaparral, mountain forests; spreads in winter.

RINGED TURTLE-DOVE, SPOTTED DOVE. See p. 210.

PIGEONS, DOVES continued on p. 210.

PIGEONS, DOVES

MOURNING DOVE

COMMON GROUND-DOVE

INCA DOVE

WHITE-WINGED DOVE

BAND-TAILED PIGEON

RINGED TURTLE-DOVE

plumages variable

ROCK DOVE (Domestic or Feral Pigeon)

SPOTTED DOVE

typical or ancestral form

RINGED TURTLE-DOVE *Streptopelia "risoria"*
12" (30 cm). Near size of Mourning Dove, but paler beige. Note the *narrow black ring on the hind-neck*. Tail *rounded*, with much white in the corners. Dark primaries contrast boldly with its pale coloration. A domestic bred variant of the African Turtle-Dove (*S. roseogrisea*). Seen very locally in city parks in Los Angeles, rarely elsewhere; not established.
Voice: A purring cooing; rising, then dropping in pitch.

SPOTTED DOVE *Streptopelia chinensis*
13" (33 cm). Note the *broad collar of black and white spots* on the hind-neck. A bit larger than the Mourning Dove; tail rounded or blunt-tipped, with much white in the corners. Juvenile birds lack the collar, but may be told by the shape of the spread tail (Mourning Dove's tail is pointed).
Voice: *Coo-who-coo*; resembles cooing of White-winged Dove.
Range: Se. Asia. **West:** Introduced in Los Angeles; has spread radially to Santa Barbara, Bakersfield, Oceanside, San Diego, s. Arizona.
Habitat: Residential areas, parks, river woods.

ROCK DOVE *Columba livia*
(Domestic Pigeon) 13" (33 cm). Typical birds are gray with a *whitish rump, two black wing bars*, and a broad, dark tail band. Domestic stock or feral birds may have many color variants.
Voice: Familiar to city dwellers; a soft, gurgling *coo-roo-coo*.
Range: Old World origin; worldwide in domestication. **West:** Sustains self in wild about cities, farms, cliffs, bridges.

■ **PARROTS, PARAKEETS. Family Psittacidae.** Noisy and gaudily colored. Compact, short-necked birds with stout, hooked bills. Parakeets are smaller, with pointed tails. Feet zygodactyl (two toes fore, two aft). **Range:** Worldwide in tropics and subtropics. **No. of species:** World 271; West 1 formerly (+ at least 6 introduced).

THICK-BILLED PARROT *Rhynchopsitta pachyrhyncha*
15–16½" (38–41 cm). A stocky green parrot with a longish tail, heavy black bill, and dark red forehead. In flight, a yellow patch under the wing. Northern and cen. Mexico. Formerly a sporadic visitor to mountains of se. Arizona, sw. New Mexico. Last recorded in the wild in 1922. Recently a small number from Mexico have been released into the Chiricahuas (Arizona) with the hope that a resident population will become established.

■ **EXOTIC PARROTS.** A number of these have been released or have escaped, especially around urban centers in California. Six are shown here.

CANARY-WINGED PARAKEET *Brotogeris versicolurus*
(S. America) Note the white and yellow wing patch. Local resident of Palo Verdes, Los Angeles; a few elsewhere.

RED-CROWNED PARROT *Amazona viridigenalis*
(Mexico) *Entire crown red* (compare Lilac-crowned). A few live in the Los Angeles area. Has nested in San Gabriel Valley.

ROSE-RINGED PARAKEET *Psittacula krameri*
(India) Narrow rose and black necklace; red bill; slender tail. A few in suburbs on coastal slopes of s. California.

EXOTIC PARROTS continued on p. 212.

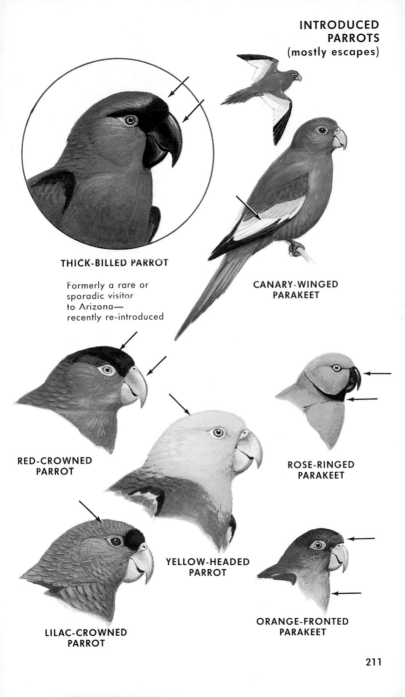

INTRODUCED PARROTS
(mostly escapes)

THICK-BILLED PARROT

Formerly a rare or sporadic visitor to Arizona—recently re-introduced

CANARY-WINGED PARAKEET

RED-CROWNED PARROT

ROSE-RINGED PARAKEET

YELLOW-HEADED PARROT

LILAC-CROWNED PARROT

ORANGE-FRONTED PARAKEET

■ **EXOTIC PARROTS** (continued). See illustrations on p. 211.

YELLOW-HEADED PARROT *Amazona ochrocephala*
(Tropical America) Distinctive; breeds locally in and around w. Los Angeles and w. San Gabriel Valley; often seen elsewhere.

LILAC-CROWNED PARROT *Amazona finschi*
(Mexico) Red forehead, *lilac* crown, green cheeks, pale bill. A few live in the Los Angeles area. Has nested in San Gabriel Valley.

ORANGE-FRONTED PARAKEET *Aratinga canicularis*
(Mexico) Orange forehead, brown breast. Local, s. California.

■ **CUCKOOS, ROADRUNNERS, ANIS. Family Cuculidae.**
Slender, long-tailed birds; feet zygodactyl (two toes forward, two aft). Sexes alike. **Food:** Cuckoos eat caterpillars, other insects; roadrunners eat reptiles; anis eat seeds, fruits. **Range:** Warm and temperate regions of the world. **No. of species:** World 132; West 4 (+2 accidental, see pp. 352, 353). Our cuckoos are not parasitic.

YELLOW-BILLED CUCKOO *Coccyzus americanus*   **M191**
11–13″ (28–33 cm). Known as a cuckoo by the slim sinuous look, brown back, and white underparts; as this species, by *rufous* in the wings, *large white* spots at tips of black undertail feathers, and *yellow* lower mandible on the slightly curved bill.
Voice: Song, a rapid throaty *ka-ka-ka-ka-ka-ka-ka-ka-ka-ka-ka-ka-kow-kow-kowlp-kowlp—kowlp—kowlp* (retarded toward end).
Range: S. Canada to Mexico, W. Indies. Winters to Argentina. **West:** Map 191. **Habitat:** Riverine woodlands, thickets, farms; declining.

BLACK-BILLED CUCKOO *Coccyzus erythropthalmus*   **M190**
11–12″ (28–30 cm). Similar to Yellow-billed Cuckoo, but bill black; narrow *red eye-ring* (in adult). No rufous in the wing; undertail spots small. The immature has a yellow eye-ring like the Yellow-billed Cuckoo's, but has an all-black bill.
Voice: A fast, rhythmic *cucucu, cucucu, cucucu,* etc. The grouped rhythm (three or four) is typical. May sing at night.
Range: S. Canada, cen. and ne. U.S. Winters to Argentina. **West:** Map 190. **Habitat:** Wood edges, groves, thickets.

GROOVE-BILLED ANI *Crotophaga sulcirostris*
13″ (33 cm). A coal-black, grackle-sized bird, with a loose-jointed tail, short wings, and a deep bill with a high, curved, puffin-like ridge. Flight weak; alternately flaps and sails.
Voice: A repeated *whee-o* or *tee-ho,* first note slurring up.
Range: Gulf of Mexico to Argentina. **West:** A very rare but regular stray to s. Arizona; casual or accidental, New Mexico, Colorado, Nevada, s. California.

GREATER ROADRUNNER *Geococcyx californianus*   **M192**
20–24″ (50–60 cm). The cuckoo that runs on the ground (tracks show two toes forward, two aft). A large, slender, streaked bird, with a long, white-edged tail; shaggy crest; and long legs. White crescent on wing (visible when spread).
Voice: Six to eight low, dove-like *coo's,* descending in pitch.
Range: Sw. U.S. to cen. Mexico. **West:** Map 192. **Habitat:** Deserts; dry, open country with scattered cover, brush.

CUCKOOS, etc.
Sexes similar

adult

YELLOW-BILLED CUCKOO

adult

Yellow-billed Cuckoo

imm.

adult

Black-billed Cuckoo

adult

BLACK-BILLED CUCKOO

GROOVE-BILLED ANI

GREATER ROADRUNNER

■ **GOATSUCKERS (NIGHTJARS). Family Caprimulgidae.** Nocturnal birds with ample tails, large eyes, tiny bills, large bristled gapes, and very short legs. By day, they rest horizontally on limbs or on the ground, camouflaged by "dead-leaf" pattern. Identified at night by voice. **Food:** Nocturnal insects. **Range:** Nearly worldwide in temperate and tropical land regions. **No. of species:** World 72; West 5 (+ 1 accidental).

COMMON NIGHTHAWK *Chordeiles minor*   **M209**
9½" (24 cm). A slim-winged, gray-brown bird, often seen high in the air; flies with easy strokes, "changing gear" to quicker erratic strokes. Note the *broad white bar* across the pointed wing. Male has a white bar across its notched tail and a white throat. Prefers dusk, but may be abroad at midday.
Voice: A nasal *peent* or *pee-ik*. In aerial display, the male dives, then zooms up sharply with a sudden deep whir of wings.
Range: Canada to Panama. Winters to Argentina. **West:** Map 209.
Habitat: Open country to mountains; open pine woods; often seen in air over cities, towns. Sits on ground, posts, rails, roofs, limbs.

LESSER NIGHTHAWK *Chordeiles acutipennis*   **M208**
8–9" (20–23 cm). Smaller than the Common Nighthawk; white bar (buffy in female) *closer to tip of wing.* Readily identified by odd calls and manner of flight—*very low*, seldom high. Does not power-dive. A bird of lowlands, not mountains.
Voice: A low *chuck chuck* and a soft purring or whinnying sound, much like the trilling of a toad.
Range: Sw. U.S. to n. Chile, Brazil. **West:** Map 208. **Habitat:** Arid scrub, dry grassland, fields, prairie, desert washes.

WHIP-POOR-WILL *Caprimulgus vociferus*   **M211**
9½" (24 cm). A voice in the night woods. When flushed by day, flits away on rounded wings, like a large brown moth. Male shows large *white tail patches;* in female these are buffy.
Voice: At night, a rolling, tiresomely repeated *whip' poor-weel'*, or *purple-rib*, etc.; accent on first and last syllables.
Range: E. Canada, sw. U.S. to Honduras. Winters from Gulf states to Honduras. **West:** Map 211. **Habitat:** Leafy woodlands.

BUFF-COLLARED NIGHTJAR *Caprimulgus ridgwayi*
8½–9" (21–23 cm). Similar to the Whip-poor-will, but with a *buff or tawny collar* across the hind-neck.
Voice: Staccato, cricketlike notes, terminating with a longer, strongly accented phrase, *cuk-cuk-cuk-cuk-cuk-cuk-cuk-cukacheea.*
Range: Mainly Mexico (Sonora to Chiapas). **West:** Guadalupe Canyon (sw. New Mexico and se. Arizona); occasionally elsewhere in se. Arizona. **Habitat:** Rocky juniper-mesquite slopes.

COMMON POORWILL *Phalaenoptilus nuttallii*   **M210**
7–8" (18–20 cm). Best known by its night cry in arid hills. It appears smaller than a Nighthawk, has more rounded wings (no white bar), and its short, rounded tail has *white corners.*
Voice: At night, a loud, repeated *poor-will* or *poor-jill.*
Range: Se. British Columbia, w. U.S. to cen. Mexico. **West:** Map 210.
Habitat: Dry hills, open brush, dirt roads.

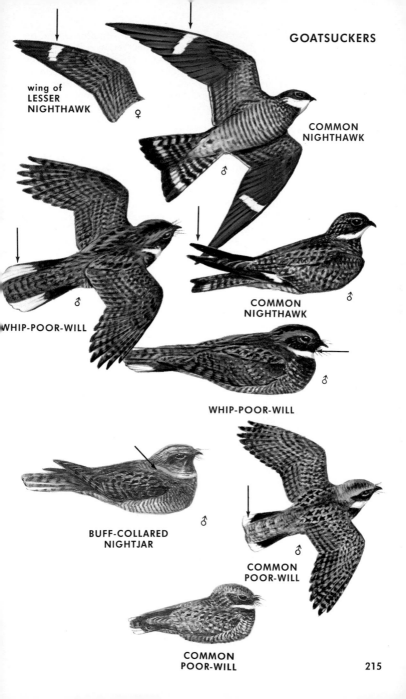

GOATSUCKERS

wing of
LESSER
NIGHTHAWK ♀

COMMON
NIGHTHAWK ♂

COMMON
NIGHTHAWK ♂

WHIP-POOR-WILL ♂

WHIP-POOR-WILL ♂

BUFF-COLLARED
NIGHTJAR ♂

COMMON
POOR-WILL ♂

COMMON
POOR-WILL

■ **HUMMINGBIRDS. Family Trochilidae.** The smallest birds. Iridescent, with needle-like bills for sipping nectar. Jewel-like gorgets (throat feathers) adorn most adult males. Hummingbirds hover when feeding; their wing motion is so rapid that the wings appear blurred. They can fly backward. Pugnacious. **Food:** Nectar (red flowers favored); small insects, spiders. **Range:** W. Hemisphere; majority in tropics. **No. of species:** World 308; West 15 (+3 accidental).

ANNA'S HUMMINGBIRD *Calypte anna*   M217
3½–4″ (9–10 cm). *Male:* The only U.S. hummer with a *red crown.* Throat red. *Female:* Similar to females of other West Coast hummers; larger, darker green above. Grayer below, with a more heavily spotted throat than female Costa's or Black-chin. Often a central patch of red spots on throat. The only hummingbird commonly found in California in midwinter.
Voice: Feeding note, *chick.* Song (from a perch), squeaking, grating notes. When diving in its aerial "pendulum display," the male makes a *sharp popping sound* at the bottom of the arc.
Range: See Map 217. **Habitat:** Gardens, chaparral, open woods.

BROAD-TAILED HUMMINGBIRD *Selasphorus platycercus*   M220
4–4½″ (10–11 cm). The male of this Rocky Mt. species may be known by the sound of its wings, a *shrill trilling. Male:* Back green; throat bright *rose-red. Female:* Larger than the female Black-chin; sides tinged with buffy; touch of rufous at basal corners of tail.
Range: Western U.S. to Guatemala. Map 220. **Habitat:** Mountains.

RUBY-THROATED HUMMINGBIRD *Archilochus colubris*   M215
3–3¾″ (8–9 cm). Male of Ruby-throat, an eastern species, has a glowing *fiery-red throat,* iridescent green back. Note the *forked tail.* Female lacks the red throat; tail blunt, with white spots.
Similar species: Male Broad-tailed Hummer lacks forked tail.
Range: S. Canada to Gulf states. Winters s. Texas, s. Florida to w. Panama. **West:** Map 215.

ALLEN'S HUMMINGBIRD *Selasphorus sasin*   M222
3½″ (9 cm). *Male:* Like the Rufous Hummingbird (*rufous* sides, rump, tail, and cheeks; fiery throat), but the back is *green. Female:* Indistinguishable in the field from the female Rufous (in the hand, Allen's has narrower outer tail feathers).
Similar species: Male Rufous has the entire back rufous.
Voice: Aerial display of male unlike that of Rufous. Starts "pendulum display" in a shallow arc and after a number of swoops goes into a steep climb and swoops back, with an air-splitting *vrrrip.* (H. Cogswell).
Range: Breeds in coastal California; winters in nw. Mexico. Map 222. **Habitat:** Wooded or brushy canyons, parks, gardens; mountain meadows.

RUFOUS HUMMINGBIRD *Selasphorus rufus*   M221
3½″ (9 cm). *Male:* No other North American hummingbird has a *rufous back.* Upperparts bright red-brown; throat flaming orange-red. Aerial display, a closed ellipse, slowing on return climb. *Female:* Green-backed; dull *rufous on sides and at base of tail.*
Range: Breeds in nw. N. America; winters in Mexico. Map 221.

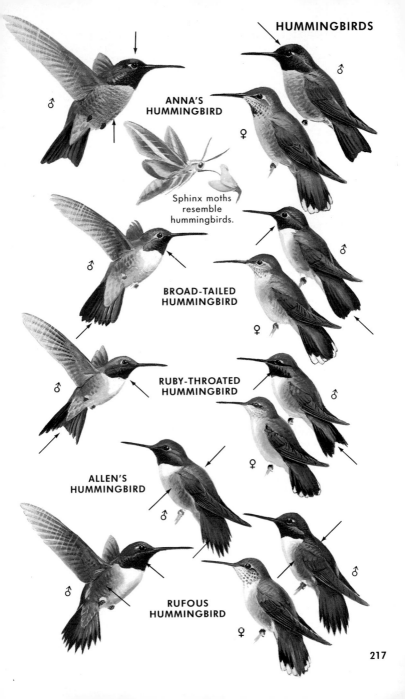

HUMMINGBIRDS

ANNA'S
HUMMINGBIRD

♂

♀

Sphinx moths
resemble
hummingbirds.

♂

BROAD-TAILED
HUMMINGBIRD

♂

♀

♂

RUBY-THROATED
HUMMINGBIRD

♂

♀

♂

ALLEN'S
HUMMINGBIRD

♂

♂

RUFOUS
HUMMINGBIRD

♀

BLUE-THROATED HUMMINGBIRD *Lampornis clemenciae*

4½–5½" (11–14 cm). Note the big tail with its *exceptionally large white patches. Male:* A very large hummingbird, with black and white streaks around the eye and a light *blue throat;* big black tail with large white patches. *Female:* Large, with *evenly gray* underparts, white marks on the face, and a big, blue-black tail with *large white corners,* as in the male.

Voice: Note, a squeaking *seek.*

Range: Sw. U.S. to s. Mexico. **West:** Mountains of se. Arizona, extreme sw. New Mexico, w. Texas (Chisos Mts.). Casual or accidental California, Nevada, Utah, Colorado. **Habitat:** Wooded streams in lower canyons of mountains.

MAGNIFICENT HUMMINGBIRD *Eugenes fulgens*

(Rivoli's Hummingbird) 4½–5" (11–13 cm). *Male:* A very large hummingbird with a *blackish belly, bright green throat,* and *purple crown.* Looks all black at a distance. Wingbeats discernible; sometimes the bird scales on set wings. *Female:* Large; greenish above, washed with greenish or dusky below. Known from female Blue-throated by more mottled underparts, spotted throat, dark greenish tail, obscure pale tail corners.

Voice: Note, a thin, sharp *chip;* distinctive.

Range: Sw. U.S. to n. Nicaragua. **West:** Breeds or summers in mountains of se. Arizona and locally in sw. New Mexico, w. Colorado, w. Texas. Casual or accidental, Nevada, California, Utah, Wyoming. **Habitat:** Mountain glades, pine-oak woods, canyons.

BROAD-BILLED HUMMINGBIRD *Cynanthus latirostris*

3¼–4" (8–10 cm). *Male:* Dark green above and below, with a *blue throat* (bird may look all black at a distance). Bill bright *red,* with a black tip. *Female:* Identified by combination of red *bill* and *unmarked, pearly gray* throat; thin white line behind eye. Females of most other hummers have some spots on the throat.

Range: Sw. U.S. to s. Mexico. **West:** Summers (rarely winters) in s. Arizona; also summers sw. New Mexico, w. Texas (sparse; Big Bend to Alpine); casual, se. California, Utah. **Habitat:** Desert canyons, mountain slopes, agaves, mesquite.

WHITE-EARED HUMMINGBIRD *Hylocharis leucotis*

3½" (9 cm). *Male: Bill red,* with a black tip; *broad white stripe behind the eye.* Underparts dark greenish, throat blue and green, crown purple. *Female:* Has the red bill and bold white stripe behind the eye. Note the small *green spots* on the throat.

Similar species: Male Broad-billed Hummingbird has a well-forked tail and only a touch of white behind the eye. *Caution:* Female Broad-bill is often mistaken for a female White-eared (red bill and pronounced white eyestripe), but if the throat and underparts are evenly gray, the bird is a female Broad-bill.

Range: Mexican border to Nicaragua. A sparse summer visitor to mountains of se. Arizona. Casual or accidental, sw. New Mexico, w. Texas (Chisos Mts.). **Habitat:** Pine-oak woods near streams.

HUMMINGBIRDS

♂

♀

♂

**BLUE-THROATED
HUMMINGBIRD**

♂

♀

♂

**MAGNIFICENT
HUMMINGBIRD**

♂

♀

**BROAD-BILLED
HUMMINGBIRD**

♂

♀

**WHITE-EARED
HUMMINGBIRD**

CALLIOPE HUMMINGBIRD *Stellula calliope* **M219**
2¾–3¼" (7–8 cm). The smallest hummer normally found in the U.S. *Male: Throat with purple-red rays on white ground* (may be folded like a dark inverted V on a white throat); the only U.S. hummingbird with this effect. *Female:* Very similar to females of Broad-tailed and Rufous hummingbirds (buffy sides, rufous base of tail), but decidedly smaller; rusty on sides paler.
Range: Sw. Canada to Baja California. Winters in Mexico. Map 219.
Habitat: Seldom away from high mountains; canyons, forest glades.

BLACK-CHINNED HUMMINGBIRD *Archilochus alexandri* **M216**
3½" (9 cm). *Male:* Note the *black throat* and conspicuous white collar. The blue-violet of lower throat shows only in certain lights. Throats of other hummers may look black until they catch the light. *Female:* Greenish above, whitish below. Cannot safely be told in field from female Costa's or Ruby-throat. Call note, *teew.*
Range: Western U.S., n. Mexico. Map 216. **Habitat:** Semi-arid country, river groves, canyons, slopes, chaparral, suburbs.

VIOLET-CROWNED HUMMINGBIRD *Amazilia violiceps*
4¼" (10 cm). A rather large hummer with *immaculate white underparts, including the throat;* bill red, with a black tip. Sexes similar, but crown violet-blue in male, dull greenish blue in female and immature. No iridescent gorget on male.
Range: Mainly Sonora to Chiapas. Breeds in Guadalupe Canyon in extreme se. Arizona, sw. New Mexico, rarely elsewhere in se. Arizona. **Habitat:** Stream groves in canyons, sycamores, agaves.

LUCIFER HUMMINGBIRD *Calothorax lucifer*
3½" (9 cm). Note the *decurved bill.* Male has a *purple throat, rusty or buffy sides. No* purple on crown (as in Costa's); tail *deeply forked,* often folded. *Female:* Decurved bill, *uniform buff breast.*
Range: W. Texas to s. Mexico. Breeds in w. Texas (Chisos Mts.), rarely se. Arizona, sw. New Mexico. **Habitat:** Arid slopes, agaves.

COSTA'S HUMMINGBIRD *Calypte costae* **M218**
3–3½" (8–9 cm). *Male:* Note the *purple* or *amethyst* throat and crown. Feathers of gorget *project* markedly at sides. *Female:* Very similar to female Black-chin, but prefers more arid conditions. Voices differ. Often *soars* from one flower clump to another.
Range: Sw. U.S., nw. Mexico. Map 218. **Habitat:** Deserts, washes, mesas, sage scrub, arid hillsides.

BUMBLEBEE HUMMINGBIRD *Atthis heloisa*
2¾" (7 cm). Tiny; resembles the Lucifer Hummingbird (elongated purple gorget) but bill short, straight; tail rounded, with a rufous base. **Range:** Mexico. Accidental, se. Arizona.

PLAIN-CAPPED STARTHROAT *Heliomaster constantii*
4½" (11 cm). A large, long-billed hummer, with a red throat, *white facial stripes, white rump.* **Range:** Mexico. Casual or accidental stray to se. Arizona (usually at feeders).

BERYLLINE HUMMINGBIRD *Amazilia beryllina*
3½" (9 cm). *Male: Glittering green* on underparts; *deep rich rufous* in wings, rump, and tail. Bill partly red. *Female:* Duller; belly gray.
Range: Mexico. **West:** Sparse visitor and rare breeder in mountains of se. Arizona.

HUMMINGBIRDS

CALLIOPE HUMMINGBIRD

♂
♀

BLACK-CHINNED HUMMINGBIRD

♂
♀

VIOLET-CROWNED HUMMINGBIRD

♂
♀

LUCIFER'S HUMMINGBIRD

♂
♀

Tail may fold in a spikelike point.

COSTA'S HUMMINGBIRD

♂
♀

Rare strays from Mexico

BUMBLEBEE HUMMINGBIRD

♀
♂

PLAIN-CAPPED STARTHROAT

BERYLLINE HUMMINGBIRD

♀
♂

221

■ **WOODPECKERS. Family Picidae.** Chisel-billed, wood-boring birds with strong zygodactyl feet (usually two toes front, two rear), remarkably long tongues, and stiff spiny tails that act as props when climbing. Flight usually undulating. Most males have some red on the head. **Food:** Tree-boring insects; some species eat ants, flying insects, berries, acorns, sap. **Range:** Mainly wooded parts of the world; absent in Australian region, Madagascar, most oceanic islands. **No. of species (including allies):** World 212; West 20 (+2 accidental).

PILEATED WOODPECKER *Dryocopus pileatus*   M238
16–19½" (40–49 cm). A spectacular black, *crow-sized* woodpecker, with a flaming red *crest.* The female has a blackish forehead, lacks red on the mustache. The great size, sweeping wingbeats, and flashing white underwing areas identify the Pileated in flight. The diggings—large *oval* or *oblong* holes—indicate its presence.
Voice: Call resembles that of Flicker, but louder, irregular: *kik-kik-kikkik-kik-kik*, etc. Also a more ringing, hurried call that may rise or fall slightly in pitch and volume.
Range: Canada to s. U.S. **West:** Map 238. **Habitat:** Conifer, mixed, and hardwood forests; woodlots.

LEWIS'S WOODPECKER *Melanerpes lewis*   M224
10½–11½" (26–29 cm). A large, dark, black-backed woodpecker, with an extensive *pinkish red belly* (the only N. American woodpecker so colored). Has a *wide gray collar* and dark red face patch. The pink underparts and wide black wings are the best marks. Sexes similar. Has straight crow-like flight; fly-catching habit.
Voice: Usually silent. Occasionally a harsh *churr* or *chee-ur.*
Range: Sw. Canada, w. U.S. Map 224. **Habitat:** Scattered or logged forest, river groves, burns, foothills.

RED-HEADED WOODPECKER *Melanerpes erythrocephalus*   M225
8½–9½" (21–24 cm). A black-backed woodpecker with a head that is *entirely red* (other woodpeckers may have a patch of red). Back *solid black*, rump white. Large, square white patches are conspicuous on the wing (making the lower back look white when the bird is on a tree). Sexes similar. Immature is dusky-headed; the large white wing patches identify it.
Similar species: Red-breasted Sapsucker also has an entirely red head but a different range (Pacific states). See p. 227.
Voice: A loud *queer* or *queeah.*
Range: East of Rockies from s. Canada to Gulf states. **West:** Map 225. **Habitat:** Groves, farm country, orchards, shade trees in towns, large scattered trees.

ACORN WOODPECKER *Melanerpes formicivorus*   M226
8–9½" (20–24 cm). Note the clownish black, white, and red head pattern. A black-backed woodpecker showing a conspicuous white rump and white wing patches in flight. Both sexes have whitish eyes, red on crown. This woodpecker stores acorns in bark.
Voice: *Whack-up, whack-up, whack-up*, or *ja-cob, ja-cob.*
Range: Resident, w. U.S. to Colombia. Map 226. **Habitat:** Oak woods, groves, mixed forest, oak-pine canyons, foothills.

WOODPECKERS

♀

♂

PILEATED WOODPECKER

juvenile

LEWIS'S WOODPECKER

juvenile

RED-HEADED WOODPECKER

♂

♀

ACORN WOODPECKER

223

WHITE-HEADED WOODPECKER *Picoides albolarvatus*　　**M234**
9″ (23 cm). Our only woodpecker with a *white head*. Male has a red patch on the nape; otherwise black, with a large white patch in the primaries. No white on the rump (as in Acorn).
Voice: A sharp *chick*, sometimes rapidly repeated, *chick-ik-ik-ik*; also a rattle similar to Downy Woodpecker's.
Range: Western N. America. Map 234. **Habitat:** Mountain pine forests.

DOWNY WOODPECKER *Picoides pubescens*　　**M232**
6½″ (16 cm). Note the *white* back and *small* bill. This industrious bird is like a small edition of the Hairy Woodpecker, which has a *large* bill. Birds of the humid Pacific Northwest have smoky gray-brown underparts. The amount of white spotting in the wings varies regionally, as it does in the next species.
Voice: A rapid whinny of notes, descending in pitch. Note, a flat *pick*, not as sharp as the Hairy's *peek!*
Range: Alaska, Canada to s. U.S. **West:** Map 232. **Habitat:** Forests, woods, river groves, willows, orchards, shade trees.

HAIRY WOODPECKER *Picoides villosus*　　**M233**
9½″ (24 cm). Note the *white* back and *large* bill. The Downy and Hairy are almost identical in pattern, checkered and spotted with black and white; *males* with a small red patch on back of the head, *females* without. The Hairy is like an exaggerated Downy, especially the bill. Hairys of the humid northwestern belt have a soiled tinge on the back and smoky underparts.
Similar species: The Downy at close range shows spots on the outer tail feathers. The small bill is the best character.
Voice: A Kingfisher-like rattle, run together more than the call of the Downy. Note, a sharp *peek!* (Downy says *pick*.)
Range: Alaska, Canada to Panama. **West:** Map 233. **Habitat:** Forests, woodlands, river groves, shade trees.

THREE-TOED WOODPECKER *Picoides tridactylus*　　**M235**
(Northern Three-toed Woodpecker) 8–9½″ (20–24 cm). Males of this and the next species are our only woodpeckers that normally have *yellow caps*. Both have *barred sides*. This species is distinguished by the irregular white patch on the back (Rockies) or *bars* (further north). The female lacks the yellow cap and suggests a Downy or Hairy Woodpecker. Note the *barred sides*.
Similar species: (1) Black-backed Three-toed Woodpecker has a *solid black* back. (2) Rarely, an immature Hairy Woodpecker has a yellowish or orange cap, but lacks bars on the flanks.
Range: Boreal forests of N. Hemisphere. **West:** Map 235. **Habitat:** Conifer forests.

BLACK-BACKED WOODPECKER *Picoides arcticus*　　**M236**
(Black-backed Three-toed Woodpecker) 9–10″ (23–25 cm). Note the combination of the *solid black back* and *barred sides*. Males have *yellow* caps. This and the preceding species (both have three toes) inhabit the colder boreal forests; their presence can be detected by patches of bark scaled from dead conifers.
Voice: A short, sharp *kik* or *chik*. Also in series.
Range: Boreal forests of n. N. America. **West:** Map 236. **Habitat:** Forests of firs and spruces.

WOODPECKERS

WHITE-HEADED
WOODPECKER

♂

♀

Northwest

♂

Rockies

♀

DOWNY
WOODPECKER

typical

♂

♂

Pacific
Northwest

♂

♂

♀

Rockies

HAIRY
WOODPECKER

Rockies

♀

♂

North

♂

THREE-TOED
WOODPECKER

♂

♀

BLACK-BACKED
WOODPECKER

225

NORTHERN FLICKER *Colaptes auratus*   **M237**
(Including "Yellow-shafted," "Red-shafted," and "Gilded" Flicker.)
12–14″ (30–35 cm). In flight, note the conspicuous *white rump*.
This and the barred *brown back* mark the bird as a Flicker. Close
up, it shows a *black patch* across the chest. Flight deeply undulating. Often hops awkwardly on the ground, feeding on ants. Three
basic types are recognized:
(1) **"YELLOW-SHAFTED" FLICKER:** The northern and eastern form.
Overhead, it flashes *golden yellow* under the wings and tail. *Red
crescent* on nape; the male has a *black* mustache.
(2) **"RED-SHAFTED" FLICKER:** The widespread western form. Similar
to "Yellow-shafted," but wing and tail linings *salmon-red*. Both
sexes lack red crescent on nape; male has *red* mustache. Where
ranges overlap (western edge of Plains) hybrids occur; these may
have orange linings or a combination of characters.
(3) **"GILDED" FLICKER:** Resident in deserts of se. California (Colorado R.), s. Arizona, Baja California. Wing and tail linings usually
yellow, but males have a *red* mustache. In essence, has head of
"Red-shafted" but body of "Yellow-shafted."
Voice: A loud *wick wick wick wick wick*, etc. Also a loud *klee-yer*
and a squeaky *flick-a, flick-a,* etc.
Range: Tree limit in Alaska, Canada, south to Nicaragua. **West:**
Map 237. **Habitat:** Open forests, woodlots, groves, farms, towns,
semi-open country. Also saguaros, deserts ("Gilded" Flicker).

WILLIAMSON'S SAPSUCKER *Sphyrapicus thyroideus*   **M230**
9½″ (24 cm). *Male:* Black crown, black back, long white shoulder
patch. Note white facial stripes, red throat, yellow belly. In flight,
black with white rump and shoulder patches. *Female:* A brownish,
"zebra-backed" woodpecker with a white rump, *barred sides,
brown head,* yellow belly. This coloration and evergreen habitat separate it from other zebra-backed woodpeckers.
Voice: A nasal *cheeer.* Drumming; several rapid thumps followed
by three or four slow, accented thumps: ———————,–,–,–.
Range: Se. British Columbia, w. U.S.: winters into n. Mexico. Map
230. **Habitat:** Higher conifer forests, burns.

RED-BREASTED SAPSUCKER *Sphyrapicus ruber*   **M229**
8–9″ (20–23 cm). This sapsucker of the Pacific region has the *entire
head and breast bright red.* Long white wing patch and other markings much like those of Red-naped and Yellow-bellied sapsuckers,
with which it was formerly lumped as a single species. East of Rockies, see Red-headed Woodpecker (p. 223).
Range: Se. Alaska to Baja California. Map 229.

RED-NAPED SAPSUCKER *Sphyrapicus nuchalis*   **M228**
8–9″ (20–23 cm). Note the longish white wing patch, red forehead
and nape. *Immature:* Brown, with the distinctive white wing patch.
Sapsuckers drill orderly rows of small holes in trees for sap.
Voice: A nasal mewing note: *cheerrrr.* Also drums: several rapid
thumps followed by several slow, rhythmic thumps.
Range: Rockies, Great Basin, etc. Winters to cen. Mexico. **West:**
Map 228. **Habitat:** Woodlands, aspen groves, orchards.

YELLOW-BELLIED SAPSUCKER See text on p. 228.

WOODPECKERS

Flickers and Sapsuckers

"Red-shafted" form

♀

♂

"Red-shafted"

"Yellow-shafted"

"Gilded"

"Yellow-shafted" form

♂

NORTHERN FLICKER

"Gilded" form ♂

♂

"Red-shafted"

immature ♂

♀

♂

WILLIAMSON'S SAPSUCKER

dagetti

ruber

juv.

RED-BREASTED SAPSUCKER

♀

♂

juv.

RED-NAPED SAPSUCKER

♂

♀

YELLOW-BELLIED SAPSUCKER

YELLOW-BELLIED SAPSUCKER *Sphyrapicus varius*   **M228**
Illus., p. 227. 8–9″ (20–23 cm). This sapsucker replaces the Red-naped Sapsucker to the north and east of the Rockies (Map 228). Differs in lacking red on the nape. Female has a white throat.

NUTTALL'S WOODPECKER *Picoides nuttallii*   **M225**
7–7½″ (18–19 cm). The only black and white, "zebra-backed" wood-pecker with a *black-and-white-striped face* normally found in California *west of the Sierra*. Males have red caps. The similar Lad-der-backed Woodpecker lives in arid country; ranges barely overlap (hybrids are known). See Downy Woodpecker.
Voice: A high-pitched whinny or rattle. Note, a low *pa-teck*.
Range: Resident, California, nw. Baja California. Map 225. **Habitat:** Wooded canyons and foothills, river woods, groves, orchards.

LADDER-BACKED WOODPECKER *Picoides scalaris*   **M231**
6–7½″ (15–19 cm). The only black and white, "zebra-backed" wood-pecker with a *black and white striped face* in the more arid country *east of the Sierra* (Map 231). Males have red caps.
Similar species: Nuttall's Woodpecker is found only in California *west* of the Sierra, not in the desert. There are minor differences in the face pattern and the amount of black on the back.
Voice: A rattling series; *chikikikikikikikikikik*; diminishing. Call note, a sharp *pick* or *chik*.
Range: Resident, sw. U.S. to ne. Nicaragua. Map 231. **Habitat:** Des-erts, canyons, river woods, groves, dry woods, arid brush.

GILA WOODPECKER *Melanerpes uropygialis*   **M227**
8–10″ (20–25 cm). *Male:* Note the *round red cap*. A "zebra-backed" woodpecker; in flight, shows a *white wing patch*. Head and under-parts gray-brown. *Female:* Similar, but without the red cap.
Similar species: The only other woodpeckers resident in the desert where this bird is found are: (1) Flicker (brown); (2) Ladder-backed (striped face). Neither has a white wing patch.
Voice: A rolling *churr* and a sharp *pit* or *yip*.
Range: Resident, sw. U.S. to cen. Mexico. Map 227. **Habitat:** Desert washes, saguaros, river groves, cottonwoods, towns.

GOLDEN-FRONTED WOODPECKER *Melanerpes aurifrons*   **M227**
8½–10½″ (21–26 cm). *Male:* Note the separated patches of bright color on the head (yellow near ,bill, poppy-red on crown, orange nape). A "zebra-backed" woodpecker with light underparts and a white rump. Shows a white wing patch in flight. *Female:* Similar, without the red crown patch; has a yellow-orange nape patch. Young bird lacks color patches on its head.
Voice: A tremulous *churrr*. A flicker-like *kek-kek-kek-kek*, etc.
Range: Sw. Oklahoma, Texas south to Nicaragua. **West:** Map 227.
Habitat: Mesquite, stream woodlands, groves.

RED-BELLIED WOODPECKER *Melanerpes carolinus*
9½–10½″ (24–26 cm). This eastern "zebra-backed" woodpecker barely crosses the 100° line into the West. Males have a *complete red cap*; females are red on the nape only.
Range: Eastern U.S., resident locally west to cen. and n. Texas, w. Oklahoma, s. Colorado.

STRICKLAND'S WOODPECKER See text on p. 230.

♂

♀

NUTTALL'S
WOODPECKER

♀

LADDER-BACKED
WOODPECKER

♂

♀

GILA
WOODPECKER

♂

♀

GOLDEN-FRONTED
WOODPECKER

♂

♀

STRICKLAND'S
WOODPECKER

♂

♀

RED-BELLIED
WOODPECKER

229

STRICKLAND'S WOODPECKER *Picoides stricklandii* (illus., p. 229)
(Arizona Woodpecker) 7–8″ (18–20 cm). A dark, *brown-backed*
woodpecker, with a *white-striped face;* spotted and barred below.
Male has a red nape patch. The only U.S. woodpecker with a *solid
brown* back (Flicker has a *barred brown back,* white rump).
Voice: A sharp *spik.* A hoarse whinny.
Range: Resident from mountains of se. Arizona and sw. New Mexico south to s.-cen. Mexico. **Habitat:** Oaks in mountains, pine-oak
canyons.

■ **TYRANT FLYCATCHERS, etc. Family Tyrannidae.** Most flycatchers perch quietly, sitting upright on exposed branches, and
sally forth to snap up insects. Bill flattened, with bristles at base.
Food: Mainly flying insects. **Range:** New World; majority in tropics.
No. of species: World 401; West 35 (+ 1 accidental).

ROSE-THROATED BECARD *Pachyramphus aglaiae*
6½″ (16 cm). Big-headed and thick-billed. *Male:* Dark gray above,
pale to dusky below, with a *blackish cap and cheeks* and a lovely
rose-colored throat. Female: Brown above, with a *dark cap* and a
light buffy collar around the nape. Underparts strong buff. The be-
cards, a subfamily of the Tyrannidae, were formerly placed in a
different family, the cotingas, Family Cotingidae.
Voice: A thin, slurred whistle, *seeoo.*
Range: Mexican border to Costa Rica. A local summer resident in
se. Arizona and lower Rio Grande Valley, Texas. **Habitat:** Wooded
canyons, river groves, sycamores.

SCISSOR-TAILED FLYCATCHER *Tyrannus forficatus*   **M257**
11–15″ (28–38 cm). A beautiful bird, pale pearly gray, with an *extremely long, scissorlike tail* that is usually folded. Sides and wing
linings salmon-pink. Young birds with shorter tails may suggest
Western Kingbird. Hybrids are known.
Voice: A harsh *keck* or *kew;* a repeated *ka-leep;* also shrill, king-
bird-like bickerings and stutterings.
Range: Breeds sw. U.S.; winters s. Mexico to Panama. Map 257.
Habitat: Semi-open country, ranches, farms, roadsides, wires.

VERMILION FLYCATCHER *Pyrocephalus rubinus*   **M251**
6″ (15 cm). *Male:* Crown (often raised in a bushy crest) and underparts *flaming vermilion;* upperparts and tail dusky to blackish. *Immature male:* Breast whitish, with some streaks; belly and undertail
coverts washed with vermilion. *Female:* Breast whitish, narrowly
streaked; belly washed with pinkish. *Immature female:* Belly
washed with yellow.
Voice: *P-p-pit-zee* or *pit-a-zee.*
Range: Sw. U.S. to Argentina. **West:** Map 251. **Habitat:** Wooded
streams in arid country, dry scrub, desert, savanna, ranches.

BECARD,
FLYCATCHERS

♀

ROSE-THROATED
BECARD

♂

♂

juvenile

SCISSOR-
TAILED
FLYCATCHER

♀
imm.

♀

♂
imm.

♂

VERMILION
FLYCATCHER

231

EASTERN KINGBIRD *Tyrannus tyrannus* M256

8″ (20 cm). The *white band* across the tail tip marks the Eastern Kingbird. Red crown mark is concealed, rarely seen. Often seems to fly quiveringly on "tips of wings." Harasses crows, hawks.

Voice: A rapid sputter of high bickering notes: *dzee-dzee-dzee*, etc., and *kit-kit-kitter-kitter*, etc. Also a nasal *dzeep*.

Range: Cen. Canada to Gulf of Mexico. Winters Colombia to n. Argentina. **West:** Map 256. **Habitat:** Wood edges, river groves, farms, shelter belts, orchards, roadsides, fencerows, wires.

WESTERN KINGBIRD *Tyrannus verticalis* M255

8″ (20 cm). The most widespread kingbird in the West. Like several similar species, it has a yellowish belly and gray head, but the black tail has a *narrow white edging* on each side.

Voice: Shrill, bickering calls; a sharp *whit* or *whit-ker-whit*.

Range: Sw. Canada to n. Mexico. Winters to Costa Rica. **West:** Map 255. **Habitat:** Farms, semi-open country, roadsides, wires.

CASSIN'S KINGBIRD *Tyrannus vociferans* M254

8–9″ (20–23 cm). Like the Western Kingbird but darker, with a darker olive-gray back; *no distinct white sides* on its black tail (which may be *lightly tipped*). Cassin's appears to have a *whiter chin* due to its *darker chest*.

Similar species: Some Western Kingbirds may lack white sides on the tail, but the paler olive-gray back and paler breast identify them. Cassin's prefers higher altitudes. Calls very different.

Voice: A low, nasal *queer* or *chi-queer* or *ki-dear*; also an excited *ki-ki-ki-dear, ki-dear, ki-dear*, etc.

Range: Western U.S. to s. Mexico, Guatemala. Map 254. **Habitat:** Semi-open high country, pine-oak mountains, ranch groves.

THICK-BILLED KINGBIRD *Tyrannus crassirostris*

9½″ (24 cm). A large kingbird with an *outsize bill*; differs from similar kingbirds in having a *dark cap* and back and *whitish* underparts. However, autumn birds may be quite yellow below.

Voice: A quick, shrill *brrr-zee* or *purr-eet*.

Range: W. Mexico, w. Guatemala. **West:** Breeds locally in se. Arizona, sw. New Mexico. Casual in fall and winter in sw. Arizona, se. California. Accidental, British Columbia.

TROPICAL KINGBIRD *Tyrannus melancholicus*

8–9½″ (20–24 cm). Very similar to Western and Cassin's kingbirds, but tail *notched* and *dusky brown, without white edgings*. Back olive or olive-gray; head gray, with a dark mask through the eye; belly *bright yellow*. Little or no gray across the breast. Cassin's Kingbirds and also some Western Kingbirds in worn plumage lack white tail sides; but their tails are *blacker*, without the strong notch.

Voice: A nasal *queer* or *chi-queer*, resembling notes of Cassin's Kingbird.

Range: S. Arizona to Argentina. **West:** Breeds locally and irregularly in se. Arizona. Rare to casual vagrant elsewhere in Southwest and in fall, from coastal California north to British Columbia. Accidental, Alaska. **Habitat:** River groves, scattered trees.

KINGBIRDS

EASTERN
KINGBIRD

WESTERN
KINGBIRD

CASSIN'S
KINGBIRD

THICK-BILLED
KINGBIRD

Thick-billed
in fall

TROPICAL
KINGBIRD

BROWN-CRESTED FLYCATCHER *Myiarchus tyrannulus*

(Wied's Crested Flycatcher) 8½–9½" (21–24 cm). Similar to the Ash-throated Flycatcher, but larger, with a noticeably larger bill. Underparts more yellow; back more olive. Tail rusty, a bit less so than in Ash-throated. These are subtle differences; to tell the two apart it is well to have a good ear.

Voice: A sharp *whit* and a rolling, throaty *purreeer*. Voice much more vigorous and raucous than Ash-throated Flycatcher's.

Range: Sw. U.S. to Argentina. **West:** Breeds s.-cen. Arizona, sw. New Mexico. Casual, se. California, s. Nevada. Winters mostly south of U.S. **Habitat:** Sycamore canyons; in Arizona, saguaros.

GREAT CRESTED FLYCATCHER *Myiarchus crinitus*   **M253**

8–9" (20–23 cm). This kingbird-sized flycatcher with cinnamon wings and tail, very similar to the preceding species, is an eastern bird that normally occurs west of the 100th meridian only in the prairie states and provinces. Note the golden lower mandible.

Voice: A loud, whistled *wheeep!* Also a rolling *prrrrrreet!*

Range: S. Canada, e. and cen. U.S. Winters e. Mexico to Colombia. **West:** Map 253. **Habitat:** Woodlands, groves.

DUSKY-CAPPED FLYCATCHER *Myiarchus tuberculifer*

(Olivaceous Flycatcher) 6½–7" (16–18 cm). Similar to the Ash-throated Flycatcher, but considerably smaller; throat a bit grayer, belly brighter yellow, and *almost no rusty* in the tail. Voice is distinctive.

Voice: A mournful, drawling whistle, slurring down, *peeur.*

Range: Breeds from mountains of se. Arizona, extreme sw. New Mexico to nw. Argentina. Winters south of U.S. Casual, w. Texas, Colorado, s. California, Nevada. **Habitat:** Oak slopes, pine-oak canyons, junipers.

ASH-THROATED FLYCATCHER *Myiarchus cinerascens*   **M252**

8" (20 cm). A medium-sized flycatcher, smaller than a kingbird, with two white wing bars, a *whitish* throat, a very *pale yellowish belly*, and a *rufous tail.* Head slightly bushy. Except for the prairie and sw. border area, this is the only flycatcher in the West with a rusty tail.

Voice: *Pwit*; also a rolling *chi-beer* or *prit-wheer.*

Range: Western U.S. to s. Mexico. **West:** Map 252. **Habitat:** Semi-arid country, deserts, brush, mesquite, pinyon, juniper, open woods.

SULPHUR-BELLIED FLYCATCHER *Myiodynastes luteiventris*

7½–8½" (19–21 cm). A large flycatcher with a *bright rufous tail* and a black patch through the eye; underparts *pale yellowish, with black streaks.* No other U.S. flycatcher is streaked *above and below.*

Voice: A high, penetrating *kee-zee'ick! kee-zee'ick!*

Range: Sw. U.S. to Costa Rica. Winters sw. Amazonia, east of Andes. **West:** Breeds in canyons in s. Arizona. Casual, s. California, sw. New Mexico, w. Texas. **Habitat:** Sycamore-walnut canyons.

FLYCATCHERS
Mostly with rusty tails
(Outer 3 feathers shown)

BROWN-CRESTED FLYCATCHER

GREAT CRESTED FLYCATCHER

DUSKY-CAPPED FLYCATCHER

SULPHUR-BELLIED FLYCATCHER

ASH-THROATED FLYCATCHER

WESTERN WOOD-PEWEE *Contopus sordidulus* **M240**
6–6½" (15–16 cm). A dusky, sparrow-sized flycatcher with two narrow wing bars but *no* eye-ring. The slightly larger size and lack of an eye-ring distinguish it from the *Empidonax* flycatchers.
Voice: A nasal *peeyee* or *peeeer.*
Range: Breeds from cen. Alaska to Cen. America; winters from Panama to Peru. Map 240. **Habitat:** Woodlands, pine-oak forests, open conifers, river groves.

EASTERN WOOD-PEWEE *Contopus virens*
Very similar to Western Wood-Pewee; not as strongly olive-gray on breast and sides. Distinguished by voice and range.
Voice: A sweet, plaintive whistle: *pee-a-wee,* slurring down, then up. Also, *pee-ur,* slurring down. Very distinctive.
Range: S. Canada, e. U.S. Winters Cen. and S. America. **West:** Breeds west of 100° only in the Edwards Plateau, Texas. Sparse migrant e. Colorado; casual west to Montana, Wyoming, Oregon, California.

EASTERN PHOEBE *Sayornis phoebe* **M249**
6½–7" (16–18 cm). Note the *tail-bobbing.* A gray-brown, sparrow-sized flycatcher without an eye-ring or strong wing bars (but may have dull ones, especially in yellowish-bellied young birds). Bill *all black.* Other small gray flycatchers have conspicuous wing bars.
Voice: Song, a well-enunciated *phoe-be,* or *fi-bree* (second note alternately higher or lower). Call note, a sharp *chip.*
Range: East of Rockies, Canada to s. U.S. Winters to s. Mexico. **West:** Map 249. **Habitat:** Streamsides, bridges, farms, roads.

GREATER PEWEE *Contopus pertinax*
(Coues' Flycatcher) 7–7¾" (18–19 cm). A large gray flycatcher of high mountains near Mexican border. Resembles Olive-sided Flycatcher, but breast more uniformly gray; *no white strip* down center.
Voice: A thin, plaintive whistle, *ho-say, re-ah,* or *ho-say, ma-re-ah* (nickname, "Jose Maria"). Note, *pip-pip* or *pil-pil.*
Range: Breeds from cen. and se. Arizona, sw. New Mexico to n. Nicaragua. Winters south of U.S. Accidental, se. California, w. Texas. **Habitat:** Pine and pine-oak forests of mountains, canyons.

OLIVE-SIDED FLYCATCHER *Contopus borealis* **M239**
7–8" (18–20 cm). A stout, large-headed flycatcher; often perches at tips of dead trees. Note the large bill and *dark chest patches* separated by a narrow strip of white (like an unbuttoned vest). A *cottony tuft* may poke from behind the wing.
Voice: Note, a trebled *pip-pip-pip.* Song, a spirited whistle, *I say' there;* middle note highest, last one sliding.
Range: Alaska, Canada, w. and ne. U.S. Winters w. S. America. **West:** Map 239. **Habitat:** Conifer forests, burns, slashings. In California also in eucalyptus trees in foothill canyons.

BLACK PHOEBE *Sayornis nigricans* **M248**
6¼–7" (16–18 cm). Our only *black* flycatcher; belly white. Has the typical phoebe tail-bobbing habit.
Voice: A thin, strident *fi-bee, fi-bee;* rising, then dropping.
Range: Sw. U.S. to n. Argentina. **West:** Map 248. **Habitat:** Shady streams, walled canyons, farmyards, towns; near water.

SAY'S PHOEBE See text on p. 238.

FLYCATCHERS
Sexes alike

EASTERN
WOOD
PEWEE

WESTERN
WOOD
PEWEE

EASTERN
PHOEBE

GREATER
PEWEE

OLIVE-SIDED
FLYCATCHER

BLACK
PHOEBE

SAY'S
PHOEBE

237

SAY'S PHOEBE *Sayornis saya* (illus., p. 237) **M250**
7–8″ (18–20 cm). A gray-brown flycatcher with a black tail and pale *rusty belly*, giving it the look of a small Robin.
Voice: A plaintive, down-slurred *pweer* or *pee-ee*.
Range: Western N. America. Map 250. **Habitat:** Scrub, canyons, ranches.

■ **THE EMPIDONAX COMPLEX.** Several small, drab flycatchers share the characters of *light eye-ring* and *two pale wing bars*. When breeding, these birds may be separated by voice, habitat, and manner of nesting. Listen to the recordings in *A Field Guide to Western Bird Songs*. See also *A Field Guide to Western Birds' Nests* by Hal Harrison. In migration these birds seldom sing or even call, so we are forced to let most of them go simply as "empids." If you wish the challenge of trying to name them in migration, study Kenn Kaufman's *Field Guide to Advanced Birding*, but first *know each one well when it is on its nesting ground, singing and calling.*

ALDER FLYCATCHER *Empidonax alnorum* **M242**
5¾″ (15 cm). Alder and Willow flycatchers, formerly lumped as Traill's, are now regarded as two species. They are almost identical, with little or no eye-ring. Alder is a shade more olive; Willow is slightly darker and browner. They are safely separated only by voice.
Voice: Song, an accented *fee-BE'-o* or *rree-BE'-o*. Note, *kep* or *pit*.
Range: Alaska, Canada, ne. U.S. Winters in South America. **West:** Map 242. **Habitat:** Willows, alders, brushy swamps, swales.

WILLOW FLYCATCHER *Empidonax traillii* **M243**
5¾″ (15 cm). Safely separated from the Alder Flycatcher (with which it was formerly lumped) only by voice and to some extent by breeding habitat. The eye-ring is very narrow or absent.
Voice: Song, a sneezy *fitz-bew*. Note, *whit* or *weet*.
Range: Alaska, Canada to sw. and e.-cen. U.S. Winters s. Mexico to Panama. **West:** Map 243. **Habitat:** Somewhat like Alder's (willow thickets, etc.); often in drier situations; more southern.

HAMMOND'S FLYCATCHER *Empidonax hammondii* **M245**
5½″ (14 cm). Both Hammond's and Dusky breed in the transition and Canadian zones of the mountains. Hammond's ranges further north and lives at higher altitudes in taller firs, while Dusky prefers chaparral or a mixture of chaparral and conifers. Hammond's is more olive; underparts more yellowish, with a grayer chest. The lower mandible of its smallish bill is mostly *dark*.
Voice: An abrupt *tse-beek*. Note, a sharp thin *pik*, or *peek*.
Range: E.-cen. Alaska, w. Canada, w. U.S. Winters se. Arizona to Nicaragua. **West:** Map 245. **Habitat:** High conifer forests; in migration through lowlands, other trees, thickets.

DUSKY FLYCATCHER *Empidonax oberholseri* **M246**
5¾″ (15 cm). Very similar to Hammond's Flycatcher (gray throat, etc.), but identified by habitat, voice, white outer tail feathers.
Voice: Three-parted song ends in a high *preet*. Note, a dry *whit*.
Range: W. Canada, w. U.S. Winters in Mexico. **West:** Map 246. **Habitat:** Breeds in mountain chaparral (Canadian-zone brush) with scattering of trees. Also open conifers in mountains of s. California.

GRAY FLYCATCHER (Text on p. 240.)

EMPIDONAX FLYCATCHERS
Sexes similar

Empidonax flycatchers have wingbars, usually eye-rings. When breeding they are best identified by habitat and voice.

ALDER FLYCATCHER

alder swamps, wet thickets; usually near water

WILLOW FLYCATCHER

wet and dry thickets, brushy pastures, old orchards, willows

HAMMOND'S FLYCATCHER

high conifer forest

DUSKY FLYCATCHER

mountain chaparral, scattering of trees

GRAY FLYCATCHER

sagebrush; pinyon, juniper

239

GRAY FLYCATCHER *Empidonax wrightii* (illus., p. 239)   **M183**
6" (15 cm). Similar to Dusky or Hammond's, but tentatively identified if the lower mandible is mostly flesh-colored, and if the back is *grayer* and the underparts whiter with no trace of yellow except in fall. It has a habit of *dipping its tail* like a phoebe (other empids may *flick* their tails). Best identified by breeding habitat and voice.
Voice: A two-syllabled *chewip* or *cheh-we*. Note a dry *whit*.
Range: Western U.S.; winters to s. Mexico. Map 183. **Habitat:** Sagebrush; also pinyon and juniper. In winter, willows, brush.

YELLOW-BELLIED FLYCATCHER *Empidonax flaviventris*   **M241**
5½" (14 cm). Yellowish underparts (including throat) separate this Canadian species from all other empids except the "Westerns," which have a different range. Other empids may have a tinge of yellow, especially in fall. Eye-ring may be yellowish in this species.
Voice: Song, a simple *chi-lek*; also a rising *per-ee*.
Range: Canada, ne. U.S. Winters Mexico to Panama. **West:** Map 241. **Habitat:** Boreal forests, muskegs, bogs.

LEAST FLYCATCHER *Empidonax minimus*   **M244**
5¼" (13 cm). An eastern species ranging to the northwest (east of the Rockies). Smaller and grayer than others in its range; whiter below, with a white throat. Actively flicks its wings and tail. Range, habitat, voice, and nest (on a horizontal branch) identify it.
Voice: An emphatic, sharply snapped *che-bek'!* Note, a dry *whit*.
Range: Canada, n. U.S., east of Rockies. Winters Mexico to Panama. **West:** Map 244. **Habitat:** Orchards, groves, poplars, aspens.

"WESTERN" FLYCATCHER *Empidonax* (two species)   **M247**
5¾" (15 cm). This, the most widely encountered type of empid in the West, has *yellowish* underparts, *including the throat*. Others in its range may have a wash of yellow, especially in fall, but their throats are gray or whitish. Eye-ring tends to be tear-shaped. Now split by the A.O.U. into two species, separated by range and call notes of males: **PACIFIC-SLOPE FLYCATCHER,** *E. difficilis* — (an upslurred *tseep*), and **CORDILLERAN FLYCATCHER,** *E. occidentalis*, of the Rocky Mt. region — (a two-noted *pit-weet*). Song of both birds a thin, squeaky *pseet-trip-seet!*; variable.
Range: Se. Alaska, w. Canada to Honduras. Map 247. **Habitat:** Moist woods, mixed or conifer forests, shady canyons, groves.

BUFF-BREASTED FLYCATCHER *Empidonax fulvifrons*
4½–5" (11–13 cm). Easily distinguished from the other more confusing empids by its small size and *rich buffy breast*.
Voice: An accented *chee-lik*. Note, a dry *pit* or *whit*.
Range: Cen. and se. Arizona, cen.-w. New Mexico to Honduras. Winters from Sonora south. **Habitat:** Canyons, oak-pines.

NORTHERN BEARDLESS-TYRANNULET *Camptostoma imberbe*
(Beardless Flycatcher) 4¼" (11 cm). A very small, nondescript flycatcher that may suggest a kinglet, Bell's Vireo, or immature Verdin. Dull brown wing bars and indistinct eye-ring. Distinguished from "empids" by its smaller size, head, and bill; also by its behavior.
Voice: A thin *peeee-yuk*. A gentle *ee, ee, ee, ee, ee*.
Range: Resident from se. Arizona, sw. New Mexico, s. Texas to Costa Rica. **Habitat:** Low woods, mesquite, stream thickets, lower canyons. Builds a globular nest with entrance on side.

EMPIDONAX FLYCATCHERS
Sexes similar

Empidonax flycatchers have wingbars, usually eye-rings. When breeding are best identified by habitat and voice.

YELLOW-BELLIED FLYCATCHER

Canadian boreal forests, muskegs, bogs

LEAST FLYCATCHER

orchards, groves, poplars, aspens, mainly east of Rockies

"WESTERN" FLYCATCHER
(see text)
may be 2 species

moist woods, groves, shady canyons

not an Empidonax

BUFF-BREASTED FLYCATCHER

oak-pine canyons; Ariz., N.M.

NORTHERN BEARDLESS-TYRANNULET

stream thickets, mesquite, low woods; se. Ariz., sw. N. Mex.

241

■ **LARKS. Family Alaudidae.** Streaked, brown, terrestrial birds with long hind claws. Gregarious. Larks often sing in high display flight. **Food:** Seeds, insects. **Range:** Mainly Old World. **No. of species:** World 78; West 1 (+ 1 introduced).

HORNED LARK *Eremophila alpestris* M258
7–8″ (18–20 cm). A brown ground bird, with *black sideburns*, two small *black horns*, and a black breast splotch. *Walks,* does not hop. Overhead, pale with a *black* tail; folds wings after each beat. Female and immature duller. Varies from paler to darker races.
Voice: Song, tinkling, irregular, high-pitched, often prolonged; from ground or high in air. Note, a clear *tsee-titi.*
Range: Widespread in N. Hemisphere. **West:** Map 258. **Habitat:** Prairies, fields, golf courses, airports, shores, tundra.

EURASIAN SKYLARK *Alauda arvensis*
7–7½″ (18–19 cm). Slightly larger than a sparrow; brown, strongly streaked; underparts buff-white; breast streaked. Tail has conspicuous white on outer feathers. Short, rounded *crest.*
Voice: Note, a clear, liquid *chir-r-up.* Song, in hovering flight, high-pitched, with long-sustained runs and trills.
Range: Eurasia, n. Africa. **West:** Rare spring migrant outer Aleutian Is., Pribilofs. Resident, s. Vancouver I., where introduced. Accidental California. **Habitat:** Open country, fields.

■ **WAGTAILS. Family Motacillidae** (in part). Old World relatives of pipits (see pp. 224, 245). Strong patterns; slender tails are wagged.

YELLOW WAGTAIL *Motacilla flava*
6½″ (16 cm). *Very slender,* long legs; *yellow below.* Long tail is black with white sides; *constantly wagged. Immature:* Whitish below; throat outlined in black. Flight undulating.
Voice: A loud, musical *tsoueep.* Song, *tsip-tsip-tsipsi.*
Range: Eurasia, w. Alaska. In winter to Africa, India. **West:** Breeds across n. Alaska to n. Yukon; south through w. Alaska to Nunivak. **Habitat:** Willow scrub on tundra, marshy country.

BLACK-BACKED WAGTAIL *Motacilla lugens*
7¼″ (18 cm). Similar to the White Wagtail, but in breeding plumage has a *black back, more white in wings. Winter adult and immature:* Grayer back, white chest, black necklace; similar to next species.
Range: Ne. Asia. **West:** Rare but regular in spring in outer Aleutians (has bred), Nome. Casual or accidental along coast to California.

WHITE WAGTAIL *Motacilla alba*
7″ (18 cm). Black and white, with a black chest, throat, and nape; *pale gray back.* Immature much like Black-backed Wagtail. **Voice:** A lively *tchizzik.* Also an abrupt *tchik.*
Range: Eurasia. **West:** Breeds locally in w. Alaska, usually around stone buildings. **Habitat:** Open country.

GRAY WAGTAIL *Motacilla cinerea*
7″ (18 cm). In spring, combination of black throat, yellow underparts, and gray back identify this wagtail. Females and winter birds have a whitish throat and are paler below. Wing stripe in flight.
Range: Eurasia. **West:** Spring visitor in outer Aleutians; casual, Pribilofs, St. Lawrence I. **Habitat:** Pebbly streams.

242

LARKS

overhead

imm.

towering flight

SKYLARK

dark race

pale race

adults

adult

HORNED LARK

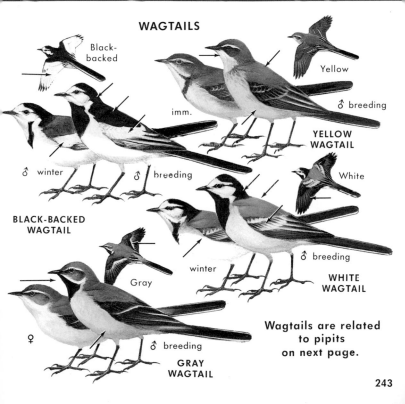

WAGTAILS

Black-backed

Yellow

imm.

♂ breeding

YELLOW WAGTAIL

♂ winter

♂ breeding

BLACK-BACKED WAGTAIL

White

winter

♂ breeding

WHITE WAGTAIL

Gray

♀

♂ breeding

GRAY WAGTAIL

Wagtails are related to pipits on next page.

■ **PIPITS. Family Motacillidae (in part).** Streaked brown ground birds with white outer tail feathers, long hind claws, thin bills. They walk briskly instead of hopping and constantly bob their tails. **Food:** Insects, seeds. **Range:** Nearly cosmopolitan. **No. of pipits in family:** World 35; West 3 (+3 casual or accidental).

AMERICAN PIPIT *Anthus rubescens* **M320**
(Water Pipit) 6–7" (15–18 cm). A slender, brown, sparrow-sized bird of open country. Bill *slender;* underparts buffy with streaks; *outer tail feathers white;* legs black. Walks, *bobbing its tail* almost constantly. In flight, dips up and down. Learn the note—Pipits are usually detected as they fly over.
Voice: Note, a thin *jeet* or *jee-eet*. In aerial flapping song flight, *chwee chwee chwee chwee chwee chwee chwee*.
Range: Colder parts of N. Hemisphere. Winters to El Salvador, n. Africa, s. Asia. **West:** Map 320. **Habitat:** Tundra, alpine slopes; in migration and winter, plains, bare fields, shores.

SPRAGUE'S PIPIT *Anthus spragueii* **M321**
6½" (16 cm). Note the *pale flesh or yellowish legs*. Buffy, with a striped back and white outer tail feathers. Suggests Vesper Sparrow or longspur, but with a *thin bill*. Back streaked *buff and black*, cheeks buffy. More solitary than the American Pipit; when flushed, often towers high, then drops.
Similar species: American Pipit has a darker (not strongly striped) back, deeper buff breast, darker cheek, dark legs.
Voice: Sings high in the air; a sweet, thin jingling series, descending in pitch: *shing-a-ring-a-ring-a-ring-a* (Salt, Wilk).
Range: Prairie provinces of Canada, northern prairie states. **West:** Map 321. **Habitat:** Plains, shortgrass prairies.

RED-THROATED PIPIT *Anthus cervinus*
6" (15 cm). Male in breeding plumage has a *rusty red face and breast*, less extensive in females and fall males. In fall, females and immatures are heavily striped; may resemble Pechora Pipit.
Voice: Call notes, a hoarse *tzeez*, and a soft *tau*.
Range: This basically Eurasian species breeds commonly on the mainland of nw. Alaska. Regular spring migrant, w. Aleutians (Attu, etc.); rare fall migrant through s. California.

PECHORA PIPIT *Anthus gustavi*
6" (15 cm). A dark, heavily streaked pipit with pink legs; *two pale streaks* on the back; *buffy* outer tail feathers (not white as in Red-throated). Call, a hard *pwit*, repeated. This Asian stray has been recorded in the outer Aleutians (Attu) and on St. Lawrence I. (Gambell).

OLIVE TREE-PIPIT *Anthus hodgsoni*
6½" (16 cm). Similar to the American Pipit, but *legs pinkish*. Olive-gray back. Note the strong face pattern; the key mark is a *white spot* behind the dark ear patch. Call, a loud *tseet*. This Asian stray is a rare visitor to the outer Aleutians and should be looked for elsewhere in the Bering Sea area.

BROWN TREE-PIPIT *Anthus trivialis* (not shown)
This Eurasian species has been collected once in nw. Alaska. See *A Field Guide to the Birds of Britain and Europe*.

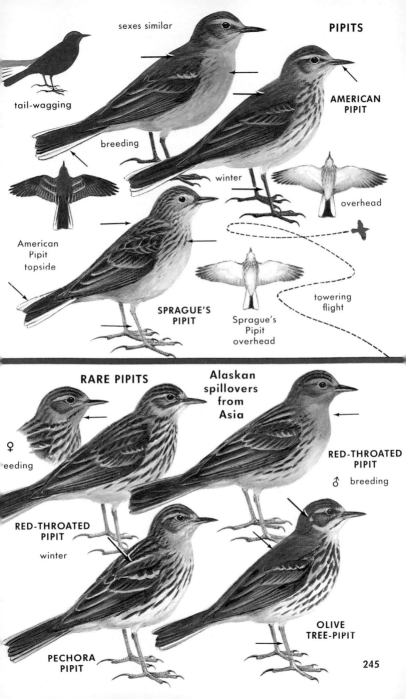

PIPITS

sexes similar

tail-wagging

breeding

AMERICAN PIPIT

American Pipit topside

winter

overhead

SPRAGUE'S PIPIT

Sprague's Pipit overhead

towering flight

RARE PIPITS

Alaskan spillovers from Asia

♀ eeding

RED-THROATED PIPIT

♂ breeding

RED-THROATED PIPIT

winter

PECHORA PIPIT

OLIVE TREE-PIPIT

245

■ **SWIFTS. Family Apodidae.** Swallow-like, but structurally distinct, with a flat skull and all four toes pointing forward. Flight very rapid, "twinkling," sailing between spurts; narrow wings often stiffly *bowed*. **Food:** Flying insects. **Range:** Nearly worldwide. **No. of species:** World 73; West 4 (+3 accidental).

VAUX'S SWIFT *Chaetura vauxi* M213
4½" (11 cm). A small, dark, swallow-like bird with no apparent tail (unless spread); "like a cigar with wings." It appears to beat its wings alternately (actually an illusion), unlike the skimming of swallows. It may glide between spurts, the wings *bowed* in a *crescent*. The twinkling flight style marks it as a swift; the range, small size, and dingy underparts as this species.
Voice: Loud, rapid, ticking or chippering notes.
Range: Western N. America to Venezuela. Map 213. **Habitat:** Open sky over woodlands, lakes, and rivers.

CHIMNEY SWIFT *Chaetura pelagica* M213
5–5½" (13–14 cm). Larger than Vaux's Swift; darker, especially on underparts and throat. Any small dark swift east of the Rockies would almost certainly be this species.
Range: Eastern N. America. Winters in Peru. **West:** Map 213. **Habitat:** Open sky, especially over cities, towns; nests in chimneys.

BLACK SWIFT *Cypseloides niger* M212
7–7½" (18–19 cm). A large *black* swift with a notched tail (sometimes fanned). At close range, a touch of white on the forehead. Flight more leisurely than that of other U.S. swifts.
Voice: A sharp *plik-plik-plik-plik-plik*, etc. (H. Cogswell).
Range: Se. Alaska to Costa Rica; W. Indies. **West:** Map 212. **Habitat:** Open sky; favors mountain country, coastal cliffs; nests in sea cliffs or wet mountain cliffs, often behind waterfalls.

WHITE-THROATED SWIFT *Aeronautes saxatalis* M214
6–7" (15–18 cm). Known from other N. American swifts by its contrasting *black and white pattern*. Underparts white, with black side patches.
Voice: A shrill, excited *jejejejejeje*, in descending scale.
Range: From s. British Columbia and w. U.S. to Honduras. **West:** Map 214. **Habitat:** Open sky; cruising widely. Breeds mainly in dry mountains, canyons; locally on sea cliffs (California).

COMMON SWIFT *Apus apus*
6½" (16 cm). This Eurasian swift, recorded as an accidental in the Pribilofs, is entirely blackish except for its white chin. Tail deeply forked. It *lacks* the white rump patch of the Fork-tailed Swift, another stray from Asia.

FORK-TAILED SWIFT *Apus pacificus*
7¼" (18 cm). A large dark swift with a white throat and *deeply forked tail*. Shows a *white rump* (see House Martin, p. 352). Breeds e. Asia; straggler in outer Aleutians and Pribilofs.

WHITE-THROATED NEEDLETAIL *Hirundapus caudacutus*
8" (21 cm). A very large, dark swift with a broad, *white U or V* on the undertail coverts. Tail *square* (not forked); throat white. A pale patch on lower back. Casual in outer Aleutians (Attu, Shemya).

SWIFTS

CHIMNEY SWIFT

VAUX'S SWIFT

BLACK SWIFT

WHITE-THROATED SWIFT

Asian strays to outer islands of Alaska

COMMON SWIFT

FORK-TAILED SWIFT

WHITE-THROATED NEEDLETAIL

247

- **SWALLOWS. Family Hirundinidae.** Slim, streamlined form and graceful flight characterize these sparrow-sized birds. Long, pointed wings; short bills with very wide gapes; tiny feet. **Food:** Mostly flying insects. **Range:** Cosmopolitan except for polar regions, some islands. **No. of species:** World 81; West 8 (+1 accidental).

TREE SWALLOW *Tachycineta bicolor*   **M260**
5–6" (13–15 cm). Steely blue-green-black above, *white below*. Immature has a dusky brown back and pale smudge across the breast; may be confused with the Rough-winged Swallow (dingy throat) or Bank Swallow (dark breastband). Tree Swallow glides in circles, ending glides with quick flaps and a short climb.
Voice: *Cheet* or *chi-veet*; a liquid twitter, *weet, trit, weet,* etc.
Range: Alaska, Canada to California, cen.-e. U.S. Winters s. U.S. to n. S. America. **West:** Map 260. **Habitat:** Open country near water, marshes, meadows, streams, lakes, wires. Roosts in reeds. Nests in holes in trees, birdhouses.

BANK SWALLOW *Riparia riparia*   **M263**
4½–5½" (11–14 cm). A small, *brown-backed* swallow. Note the distinct *dark breastband*. Flight irregular, fluttery.
Voice: A dry, trilled chitter or rattle, *brrt* or *trr-tri-tri*.
Range: Widespread in N. Hemisphere. Winters in S. America, Africa, s. Asia. **West:** Map 263. **Habitat:** Near water; fields, marshes, streams, lakes. Nests colonially in sand banks.

NORTHERN ROUGH-WINGED SWALLOW   **M262**
Stelgidopteryx serripennis
5–5¾" (13–14 cm). *Brown-backed*; lighter brown than Bank Swallow; throat dusky; no breastband. Flight more like Barn Swallow's; wings pulled back at end of stroke.
Voice: A harsh *trrit*, rougher than Bank Swallow's.
Range: S. Canada to Costa Rica. Winters Gulf Coast to Panama.
West: Map 262. **Habitat:** Near streams, lakes, river banks. Nests in banks, but not colonially as in Bank Swallow.

VIOLET-GREEN SWALLOW *Tachycineta thalassina*   **M261**
5–5½" (13–14 cm). Note the *white patches that almost meet* over the base of the tail. Dark and shiny above—adults glossed with green and purple; clear white below. Separated from the Tree Swallow by its greener back and white patches on the sides of its rump. The white of the face *partially encircles the eye*.
Voice: A twitter; a thin *chip*; rapid *chit-chit-chit wheet, wheet.*
Range: Breeds from cen. Alaska, w. Canada, south locally to mountains of Mexico. Winters California, Mexico, Cen. America. **West:** Map 261. **Habitat:** Widespread when foraging; nests in holes in trees in open forests, foothill woods, mountains, canyons, cliffs, towns.

CAVE SWALLOW *Hirundo fulva*
5–6" (13–15 cm). Similar to the Cliff Swallow (rusty rump), but face colors reversed; throat and cheeks *pale or buffy* (not dark), forehead *dark chestnut* (not pale).
Similar species: Locally, in w. Texas and se. Arizona, a race of the Cliff Swallow occurs in which young birds may be dark on *both* the forehead and throat. *(continued on p. 250)*

nests in
tree holes or
bird boxes

SWALLOWS
Sexes similar

**TREE
SWALLOW**

adult

first
fall

Bank Swallow
colony

**BANK
SWALLOW**

**NORTHERN
ROUGH-WINGED
SWALLOW**

Cliff
Southwest

**VIOLET-GREEN
SWALLOW**

**CAVE
SWALLOW**

Bank | Rough-
winged | Tree | Violet-
green | Cliff | Barn | Purple
Martin

SWALLOWS ON A WIRE

249

CAVE SWALLOW (continued). See illustration on p. 249.
>**Voice:** A clear *weet* or *cheweet*; a loud, accented *chu, chu.*
>**Range:** S. New Mexico, s.-cen. Texas, Mexico, W. Indies, to Peru. Nests in colonies in limestone caves in se. New Mexico and along s. edge of Edwards Plateau, Texas. Often builds its *cuplike* nests under bridges. Rapidly expanding range. Accidental, s. Arizona.

PURPLE MARTIN *Progne subis*   **M259**
7½–8½″ (19–21 cm). The largest North American swallow. *Male:* Uniformly blue-black *above and below;* no other swallow is dark-bellied. *Female:* Light-bellied; throat and breast grayish, often with a faint collar. Glides in circles, alternating quick flaps and glides; often spreads its tail.
>**Similar species:** Tree Swallow is much smaller than female Purple Martin; immaculate white, no gray on underparts.
>**Voice:** A throaty and rich *tchew-wew,* etc., or *pew, pew.* Song gurgling, ending in a succession of rich, low gutturals.
>**Range:** S. Canada to n. Mexico, Gulf states. Winters S. America. **West:** Map 259. **Habitat:** Towns, farms, open or semi-open country near water. Attracted to martin houses. In s. Arizona, it nests in saguaros. Local and declining.

CLIFF SWALLOW *Hirundo pyrrhonota*   **M264**
5–6″ (13–15 cm). Note the *rusty* or *buffy rump.* Overhead, appears square-tailed, with a dark throat patch. Glides in a long ellipse, ending each glide with a roller-coaster-like climb.
>**Voice:** *Zayrp;* a low *chur.* Alarm note, *keer!* Song, creaking notes and guttural gratings; harsher than Barn Swallow's song.
>**Range:** Alaska, Canada to Mexico. Winters s. Brazil to cen. Argentina. **West:** Map 264. **Habitat:** Open to semi-open land, farms, cliffs, river bluffs, lakes. Nests colonially on cliffs, barns. When nesting on a barn, the Cliff Swallow is colonial, building "mud jugs" outside, under the eaves. Barn Swallow builds a cuplike open nest, *usually* but not always *inside* the barn.

BARN SWALLOW *Hirundo rustica*   **M265**
6–7¾″ (15–19 cm). Our only swallow that is truly *swallow-tailed;* also the only one with *white tail spots.* Blue-black above; cinnamon-buff below, with a darker throat. Juvenile is whitish below. Flight direct, close to the ground; wing tips pulled back at the end of the stroke; not much gliding.
>**Similar species:** Most other N. American swallows have notched (not deeply forked) tails. (1) Cliff Swallow is colonial, building *mud jugs* under eaves or cliffs. (2) See Cave Swallow.
>**Voice:** A soft *vit* or *kvik-kvik, vit-vit.* Also *szee-szah* or *szee.* Anxiety note, a harsh, irritated *ee-tee* or *keet.* Song, a long, musical twitter interspersed with gutturals.
>**Range:** Widespread in N. Hemisphere. Winters Costa Rica to Argentina, Africa, s. Asia. **West:** Map 265. **Habitat:** Open or semi-open land; farms, fields, marshes, lakes; often perches on wires; usually near habitation. Builds its *cuplike nest inside* barns, not in tight colonies under eaves, like Cliff Swallow.

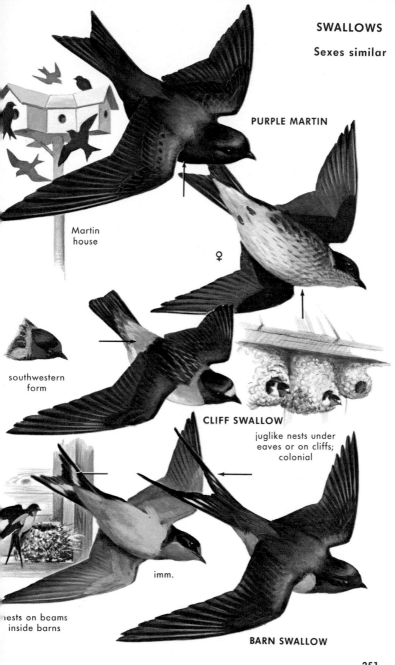

SWALLOWS

Sexes similar

PURPLE MARTIN

♀

Martin
house

southwestern
form

CLIFF SWALLOW

juglike nests under
eaves or on cliffs;
colonial

imm.

nests on beams
inside barns

BARN SWALLOW

251

■ **CROWS, JAYS, etc. Family Corvidae.** Large perching birds with strong, longish bills; nostrils covered by forward-pointing bristles. Crows and ravens are very large and black. Jays (pp. 254–257) are often colorful (usually blue). Magpies are black and white, with long tails. Sexes alike. Most immatures (not all) resemble adults. **Food:** Almost anything edible. **Range:** Worldwide except s. S. America, some islands, Antarctica. **No. of species:** World 110; West 14 (+ 1 accidental).

AMERICAN CROW *Corvus brachyrhynchos* **M274**
(Common Crow) 17–21″ (43–53 cm). A large, chunky, ebony bird. Completely black; glossed with purplish in strong sunlight. Bill and feet strong and black. Often gregarious.
Similar species: (1) Common Raven is larger, has a wedge-shaped tail. See (2) Chihuahuan Raven and (3) Northwestern Crow.
Voice: A loud *caw, caw, caw* or *cah* or *kahr*; easily imitated.
Range: Canada to s. U.S., n. Baja California. **West:** Map 274. **Habitat:** Woodlands, farms, fields, river groves, shores, towns, dumps.

NORTHWESTERN CROW *Corvus caurinus* **M275**
16–17″ (40–43 cm). This small beachcombing crow of the Northwest is smaller than the American Crow and has a quicker wingbeat. It replaces the American Crow on the narrow northwestern coast strip. There is apparently some integration with the American Crow in the Puget Sound area, hence some believe they may be conspecific.
Voice: *khaaa* or *khaaw.* Usually more resonant than Common Crow's *caw.* Also, *cowp-cowp-cowp.*
Range: Northwest coast. Map 275. **Habitat:** Near tidewater, shores.

CHIHUAHUAN RAVEN *Corvus cryptoleucus* **M276**
(White-necked Raven). 19–21″ (48–53 cm). Near the size of the American Crow; a small raven of the arid plains. Flies with the typical flat-winged glide of a raven; has a somewhat wedge-shaped tail. White feather bases on the neck and breast sometimes show when the feathers are ruffled by the wind, hence the former name "White-necked Raven."
Voice: A hoarse *kraak,* flatter and higher than Common Raven's.
Range: Sw. U.S. to cen. Mexico. **West:** Map 276. **Habitat:** Arid and semi-arid scrub and grassland, desert, yucca, mesquite.

COMMON RAVEN *Corvus corax* **M277**
22–27″ (55–68 cm). Note the *wedge-shaped tail.* Much larger than American Crow; has a heavier voice and is inclined to be not as gregarious, often solitary. Hawklike in flight, it alternates flapping and sailing, gliding on flat wings (Crow glides with a slight upward dihedral). When it is perched and not too distant, note the "goiter" look created by the shaggy throat feathers and the heavier "Roman-nose" bill.
Voice: A croaking *cr-r-ruck* or *prruk;* also a metallic *tok.*
Range: Widespread in N. America, Eurasia, Africa. **West:** Map 277.
Habitat: Boreal and mountain forests, coastal cliffs, tundra.

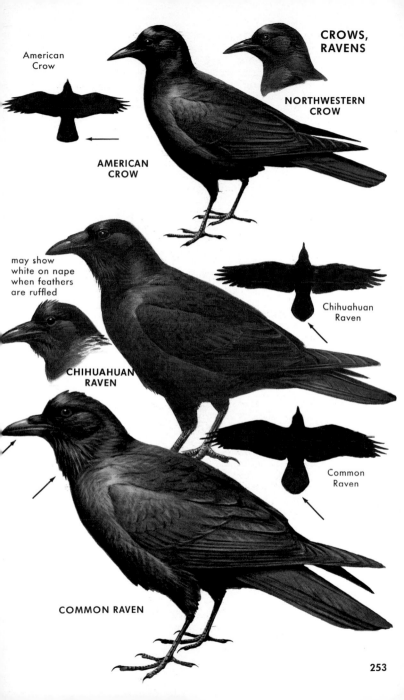

CROWS, RAVENS

American
Crow

NORTHWESTERN
CROW

AMERICAN
CROW

may show
white on nape
when feathers
are ruffled

Chihuahuan
Raven

CHIHUAHUAN
RAVEN

Common
Raven

COMMON RAVEN

253

SCRUB JAY *Aphelocoma coerulescens*   **M269**
11–13″ (28–33 cm). Look for this *crestless* jay in the oaks. Head, wings, and tail are blue; back *pale brownish*; white throat with *necklace*. Near Mexican border, see next species.
Voice: A rough, rasping *kwesh. . .kwesh.* Also a harsh *check-check-check-check* and a rasping *zhreek, zhreek.*
Range: Western U.S. to s. Mexico. Also Florida. **West:** Map 269. **Habitat:** Foothills, oaks, oak-chaparral, brush, river woods, pinyon, junipers, some suburbs.

GRAY-BREASTED JAY *Aphelocoma ultramarina*   **M270**
(Mexican Jay) 11½–13″ (29–33 cm). A blue jay without a crest. Resembles the Scrub Jay, but upperparts and underparts *more uniform*; back and breast grayer. No strong contrast between throat and breast (as in Scrub Jay, which has a whiter throat and necklace). Also lacks narrow whitish line over eye. In Arizona, juveniles may have yellow bills. Voice very different.
Voice: A rough, querulous *wink? wink?* or *zhenk?*
Range: Sw. U.S. to cen. Mexico. Map 270. **Habitat:** Open oak forests (Arizona); oak-pine woods (w. Texas).

BLUE JAY *Cyanocitta cristata*   **M268**
11–12½″ (28–31 cm). This showy, noisy, *crested* jay, widespread east of the Rockies (but expanding northwestward), is readily known from Steller's Jay by the *white spots in wings and tail*, the whitish or dull gray underparts, and the *black necklace.* Except for Steller's, other western jays lack crests. Has hybridized with Steller's Jay.
Voice: A harsh, slurring *jeeah* or *jay*; a musical *queedle, queedle*; also many other notes. Often mimics cry of Red-tailed Hawk.
Range: S. Canada, mainly east of Rockies to Gulf states. **West:** Map 268. **Habitat:** Oak and pine woods, suburban gardens, groves, towns.

STELLER'S JAY *Cyanocitta stelleri*   **M267**
12–13½″ (30–34 cm). A *large, dark, black and blue bird* with a *long crest.* Foreparts blackish; rear parts (wings, tail, belly) deep blue. In the conifer woodlands between the Rockies and Pacific, this is the resident jay with a crest.
Similar species: (1) Scrub and (2) Gray-breasted jays are paler, *lack crests*; prefer oaks, scrub. (3) Blue Jay (east of Rockies) is a crested jay but has *white spots* in the wings and tail. A few wander in winter into n. Rockies (see Map 268).
Voice: A loud *shook-shook-shook* or *shack-shack-shack* or *wheck––wek––wek––wek––wek* or *kwesh kwesh kwesh*; many other notes. Frequently mimics Red-tailed Hawk, Golden Eagle.
Range: Western N. America south; se. Alaska, sw. Canada south through conifer regions of Pacific states and Rockies to Nicaragua. Map 267. **Habitat:** Conifer and pine-oak forests.

PINYON JAY *Gymnorhinus cyanocephalus*   **M271**
9–11¾″ (23–30 cm). Looks *like a small dull blue crow*, but nearer the size of a Robin, with a long sharp bill. Readily told from Scrub Jay by its short tail, uniform blue coloration, and crow-like flight; from Steller's Jay by lack of a crest. *Text continued on p. 256.*

JAYS

Sexes alike

inland

coastal

SCRUB JAY

Ariz. juvenile

GRAY-BREASTED JAY

BLUE JAY

STELLER'S JAY

PINYON JAY

PINYON JAY (continued). See illustration on p. 255.
(*Caution:* Steller's Jay depresses crest when flying). Pinyon Jays are gregarious, often gathering in large noisy flocks and walking about like small crows.
Voice: A high nasal cawing, *kaa-eh, karn-eh* (descending inflection); has mewing effect. Also jay-like notes; chattering.
Range: Western U.S., n. Baja California. **West:** Map 271. Wanders widely. **Habitat:** Pinyon pines, junipers ("cedars"); ranges into sagebrush.

CLARK'S NUTCRACKER *Nucifraga columbiana*   M272
12–13" (30–33 cm). Built like a small crow, with a *light gray* body and large *white patches* in its black wings and tail. If these patches are seen, it should be confused with no other bird of the high mountains. Tame birds can often be fed by hand.
Similar species: Gray Jay does not have white patches.
Voice: A flat, grating caw, *khaaa* or *khraa.*
Range: Sw. Canada, w. U.S. to n. Mexico. **West:** Map 272. **Habitat:** High mountains; conifers near tree line; mountain resorts.

GRAY JAY *Perisoreus canadensis*   M266
11–13" (28–33 cm). A large, fluffy, gray bird of the cool northern forests; larger than a Robin, with a *black* patch or partial cap across the back of the head and a *white forehead* (or crown); suggests a huge overgrown chickadee. Juvenile birds in their first summer are a *dark sooty* color, almost blackish; the only distinguishing mark is a *whitish whisker.* Called "Whiskey Jack" by woodsmen.
Voice: A soft *whee-ah;* also many other notes, some harsh.
Range: Boreal forests of N. America. **West:** Map 266. **Habitat:** Spruce and fir forests. Becomes tame around mountain resorts.

YELLOW-BILLED MAGPIE *Pica nuttalli*   M273
16–18" (40–45 cm). Similar to the Black-billed Magpie, but the bill is yellow. At close range shows a crescent of bare yellow skin below the eye.
Voice: Similar to Black-billed Magpie's *maag?,* etc.
Range: California only; chiefly in Sacramento and San Joaquin valleys and adjacent low foothills; also valleys of Coast Ranges from San Francisco Bay to Santa Barbara Co. **West:** Map 273. **Habitat:** Stream groves, scattered oaks, ranches, farms.

BLACK-BILLED MAGPIE *Pica pica*   M273
17½–22" (44–55 cm); tail 9½–12" (24–30 cm). A large, slender, black and white bird, with a long, wedge-tipped tail. In flight, the iridescent greenish black tail streams behind and large white patches flash in the wings.
Voice: A harsh, rapid *queg queg queg queg* or *wah-wah-wah-wah.* Also a querulous, nasal *maag?* or *aag-aag?*
Range: Eurasia, w. N. America. **West:** Map 273. **Habitat:** Rangeland, brushy country, conifers, streamsides, forest edges, farms.

JAYS, MAGPIES

Sexes alike

CLARK'S
NUTCRACKER

flight
pattern

dark-capped
form

adult   GRAY JAY

light-capped
form

YELLOW-
BILLED
MAGPIE

GRAY JAY
immature

flight
pattern

BLACK-BILLED
MAGPIE

257

■ CHICKADEES, TITMICE. Family Paridae.

Small, plump, small-billed birds. Acrobatic when feeding. Sexes usually alike. **Food:** Insects, seeds, acorn mast, berries; at feeders, suet, sunflower seeds. **Range:** Widespread in N. America, Eurasia, Africa. **No. of species:** World 62; West 9.

MOUNTAIN CHICKADEE *Parus gambeli*   M279

5–5¾" (13–14 cm). Similar to the Black-capped Chickadee, but black of cap interrupted by a *white line over the eye.*
Voice: Song, a clear whistled *fee-bee-bee,* first note higher; also *tsick-a-zee-zee-zee,* huskier than Black-cap's.
Range: Resident, sw. Canada, w. U.S., n. Baja California. Map 279.
Habitat: Mountain forests, conifers; lower levels in winter.

BLACK-CAPPED CHICKADEE *Parus atricapillus*   M278

4¾–5¾" (12–14 cm). The small, tame Black-cap can be separated from the other widespread western chickadees by the *solid black cap* in conjunction with its *gray back* and buffy sides.
Voice: A clearly enunciated *chick-a-dee-dee-dee.* Song, a clear whistle, *fee-bee-ee* or *fee-bee,* first note higher.
Range: Alaska, Canada, northern half of U.S. **West:** Map 278. **Habitat:** Mixed and deciduous woods; willow thickets, groves, shade trees. Visits feeders, eating suet, sunflower seeds.

MEXICAN CHICKADEE *Parus sclateri*   M280

5" (13 cm). Similar to Black-capped Chickadee, but *black of throat more extensive,* spreading across upper breast. Note the *dark gray sides.* The only chickadee in its local U.S. range.
Voice: Nasal and husky for a chickadee. A low *dzay-dzeee.*
Range: Resident, Chiricahuas, se. Arizona; Animas Mts., sw. New Mexico; to Oaxaca. **West:** Map 280. **Habitat:** Conifers in mountains.

CHESTNUT-BACKED CHICKADEE *Parus rufescens*   M281

4½–5" (11–13 cm). The cap, bib, and white cheeks indicate a chickadee; the *chestnut back* this species. Sides *chestnut* (or *gray,* in the race found along the coast of cen. California).
Voice: Hoarser than Black-cap's. No whistled song.
Range: Western N. America. Map 281. **Habitat:** Moist conifer forests; adjacent oaks, shade trees.

GRAY-HEADED CHICKADEE *Parus cinctus*

(Siberian Tit, an inappropriate name.) 5½" (14 cm). This subarctic chickadee can be separated from the Boreal Chickadee by its *grayer cap* and *more extensive white cheeks.* Looks smaller-headed, longer-tailed, and not as brown on the flanks; it has a "dusty" appearance.
Voice: A peevish *dee-deer* or *chee-ee.*
Range: N. Eurasia, nw. N. America. Very local in n. Alaska from tree limit to cen. Alaska range; also n. Yukon, nw. MacKenzie. **Habitat:** Spruce forest, streamside thickets.

BOREAL CHICKADEE *Parus hudsonicus*   M280

5–5½" (13–14 cm). The small size, bib, and cap mark it as a chickadee; the *dull brown cap,* rich brown flanks, and restricted white on its *dusky cheeks* as this species.
Voice: Notes, slower, more drawling than those of Black-cap.
Range: Boreal woods of Alaska, Canada, ne. U.S. **West:** Map 280.

CHICKADEES

Sexes alike

Rockies form

MOUNTAIN CHICKADEE

BLACK-CAPPED CHICKADEE

MEXICAN CHICKADEE

CHESTNUT-BACKED CHICKADEE

cen. Calif. coast

GRAY-HEADED CHICKADEE (SIBERIAN TIT)

BOREAL CHICKADEE

TUFTED TITMOUSE *Parus bicolor* **M282**
(Black-crested Titmouse) 5–6″ (13–15 cm). A small gray bird, which in w. Texas has a *black crown and crest.* Underparts pale, sides rusty, light spot between the eye and bill. Females may have some gray in the crest. East of our area this species lacks the black on the crest. Young birds (gray-crested) are almost indistinguishable from Plain Titmouse.
Voice: Chickadee-like notes. Song, a whistled *peter peter peter peter* or *hear hear hear hear.* Varied.
Range: Eastern N. America to w. Texas, ne. Mexico. The west Texas birds are regarded by some as a distinct species *(Parus atricristatus)* known as the "Black-crested Titmouse." **West:** Map 282.
Habitat: Oak woods, canyons, cedars, groves, towns.

PLAIN TITMOUSE *Parus inornatus* **M282**
5½″ (14 cm). The birds bearing the name "titmouse" are our only *small,* gray-backed birds with pointed crests (female Phainopepla is larger). Birds of coastal California are browner. This, the sole titmouse in most of the West, is without distinctive marks. Plain Titmice reported from w. Texas (Big Bend, Edwards Plateau) may be young Tufted ("Black-crested") Titmice, which have short gray crests.
Voice: *Tchick-a-dee-dee,* similar to notes of chickadees. Song, a whistled *weety weety* or *tee-wit tee-wit tee-wit.*
Range: Resident, w. U.S. **West:** Map 282. **Habitat:** Oak woods, pinyon, juniper; locally river woods, shade trees.

BRIDLED TITMOUSE *Parus wollweberi*
4½–5″ (11–13 cm). The crest and black-and-white *"bridled" face* identify this small gray titmouse of the southwestern mountains.
Voice: Similar to that of other titmice and chickadees, but higher. Song, a repeated two-syllabled phrase.
Range: Resident from mountains of se. Arizona, sw. New Mexico to s. Mexico. **Habitat:** Oak and sycamore canyons, pine-oak woods.

BUSHTIT *Psaltriparus minimus* Family Aegithalidae **M284**
4″ (10 cm). Very small, plain birds that move from bush to tree in straggling flocks, conversing in light gentle notes. Nondescript; gray backs, pale underparts, brownish cheeks, stubby bills, longish tails. Birds in the Rockies and Great Basin have gray crowns. Males of the form known as "Black-eared Bushtit" in sw. New Mexico (San Luis Mts.) and w. Texas (Davis, Chisos Mts.) have black or black-flecked cheeks.
Voice: Insistent light *tsit's, lisp's,* and *clenk's.*
Range: Resident, sw. B.C. to Guatemala. **West:** Map 284. **Habitat:** Oak scrub, chaparral, mixed woods, pinyons, junipers.

VERDIN *Auriparus flaviceps* Family Remizidae **M283**
4–4½″ (10–11 cm). Tiny, gray, with a *yellowish head, rufous bend of wing* (often hidden). Juveniles lack these marks.
Similar species: Bushtit is longer-tailed than immature Verdin. Does not usually live in desert valleys; prefers oak slopes. See also Northern Beardless-Tyrannulet (pp. 238–239).
Voice: Insistent *see-lip.* Rapid chipping. Song, *tsee, seesee.*
Range: Resident, sw. U.S., n. and w. Mexico. Map 283. **Habitat:** Brushy desert valleys, mesquite, semi-arid plains and savannas.

TUFTED TITMOUSE

West Texas form

"Black-crested" Titmouse

PLAIN TITMOUSE

Mountain Chickadee for comparison; see previous plate

BRIDLED TITMOUSE

coastal form

adult

grayer interior form

Females have yellow eyes.

"black-eared" plumage, juvenile ♂

VERDIN

juv.

BUSHTIT

■ **NUTHATCHES. Family Sittidae.** Small, stubby tree-climbers with strong, woodpecker-like bills and strong feet. The short, square-cut tails are not braced like woodpeckers' tails during climbing. Nuthatches habitually go down trees *headfirst.* Sexes similar. **Food:** Bark insects, seeds, nuts; attracted to feeders by suet, sunflower seeds. **Range:** Most of N. Hemisphere. **No. of species:** World 22; West 3.

WHITE-BREASTED NUTHATCH *Sitta carolinensis*   **M286**
5–6″ (13–15 cm). Nuthatches climb down trees *headfirst.* This, the most familiar species, is known by its black cap and beady black eye on a white face. The undertail coverts are chestnut.
Voice: Song, a rapid series of low, nasal, whistled notes on one pitch: *whi, whi, whi, whi, whi, whi,* or *who, who, who,* etc. Note, a nasal *yank;* also a nasal *tootoo.*
Range: S. Canada to s. Mexico. **West:** Map 286. **Habitat:** Forests, woodlots, groves, shade trees; visits feeders.

RED-BREASTED NUTHATCH *Sitta canadensis*   **M285**
4½″ (11 cm). A small nuthatch with a *broad black line* through the eye and a white line above it. The underparts are washed with rusty.
Voice: Call higher, more nasal than that of White-breast; *ank* or *enk,* sounding like a baby nuthatch or a tiny tin horn.
Range: Se. Alaska, Canada, w. U.S., ne. U.S. Winters irregularly to s. U.S., nw. Mexico. **West:** Map 285. **Habitat:** Conifer forests; in winter, also other trees, may visit feeders.

PYGMY NUTHATCH *Sitta pygmaea*   **M287**
3¾–4½″ (9–11 cm). A very small, pine-loving nuthatch, with a *gray-brown cap coming down to the eye* and a whitish spot on the nape. Usually roams about in little flocks.
Voice: A piping *kit-kit——kit* or *pit-pi-dit-pi-dit.* Also a high *ki——dee;* incessant, sometimes becoming an excited chatter.
Range: Resident from s. British Columbia to cen. Mexico. Map 287. **Habitat:** Yellow pines, other pines, Douglas fir.

■ **CREEPERS. Family Certhiidae.** Small, slim, stiff-tailed birds, with slender, slightly curved bills that are used to probe the bark of trees. **Food:** Bark insects. **Range:** Cooler parts of N. Hemisphere. **No. of species:** World 7; West 1.

BROWN CREEPER *Certhia americana*   **M288**
5″ (13 cm). A very small, slim, camouflaged tree-climber. Brown above, white below, with a *slender decurved bill* and a stiff tail, which is braced during climbing. Ascends trees spirally from the base, hugging the bark closely.
Voice: Note, a single high, thin *seee,* similar to the quick trebled note (*see-see-see*) of the Golden-crowned Kinglet. Song, a thin, sibilant *see-ti-wee-tu-wee* or *"trees, trees, trees, see the trees."*
Range: S. Alaska, Canada to Nicaragua. **West:** Map 288. **Habitat:** Woodlands, groves, shade trees.

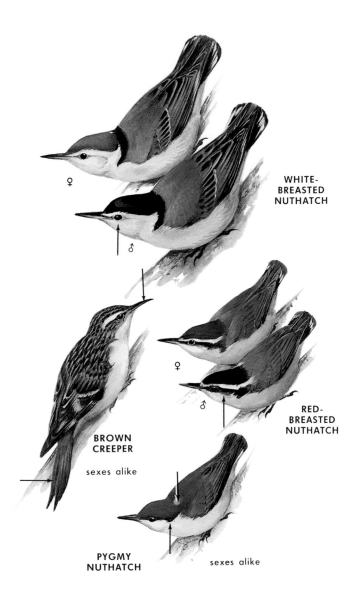

♀

WHITE-BREASTED NUTHATCH

♂

♀

♂

BROWN CREEPER

sexes alike

RED-BREASTED NUTHATCH

PYGMY NUTHATCH

sexes alike

■ **WRENS. Family Troglodytidae.** Small, energetic brown birds; stumpy, with slim, slightly curved bills; tails often cocked. **Food:** Insects, spiders. **Range:** N., Cen., and S. America; one (Winter Wren) in Eurasia. **No. of species:** World 67; West 9.

HOUSE WREN *Troglodytes aedon* M293
4½–5" (11–13 cm). A small, energetic gray-brown wren with a light eye-ring and no strong eyebrow stripe. A rustier form in the mountains of se. Arizona, the "Brown-throated Wren," was formerly rated a distinct species; it has a buff eyebrow.
Voice: A stuttering, gurgling song, rising in a musical burst, then falling at the end.
Range: S. Canada to Tierra del Fuego. **West:** Map 293. **Habitat:** Open woods, thickets, towns, gardens; often nests in bird boxes.

WINTER WREN *Troglodytes troglodytes* M294
4" (10 cm). A very small, round, dark wren, known from House Wren by its *much stubbier tail,* stronger eyebrow, and *dark, heavily barred belly.* Often bobs head. Mouse-like; stays near ground.
Voice: Song, rapid succession of high tinkling warbles, trills. Note, a hard, two-syllabled *kip-kip* (suggests Song Sparrow's *chip*).
Range: Northern parts of N. Hemisphere. **West:** Map 294. **Habitat:** Woodland underbrush; conifer forests (summer).

BEWICK'S WREN *Thryomanes bewickii* M292
5¼" (13 cm). Note the longish tail with *white corners* and the bold *white eyebrow stripe.* Western races are mouse-brown, less rusty.
Voice: Song suggests Song Sparrow's, but thinner, starting on two or three high notes, dropping lower, ending on a thin trill.
Range: S. Canada to Mexico. **West:** Map 292. **Habitat:** Thickets, underbrush, gardens. Often nests in bird boxes.

CAROLINA WREN *Thryothorus ludovicianus*
5¾" (14 cm). A large wren, near the size of a sparrow. *Warm rusty brown* above, buff below; conspicuous *white eyebrow stripe.*
Voice: A two- or three-syllabled chant. Variable; *tea-kettle, tea-kettle, tea kettle,* or *chirpity, chirpity, chirpity, chirp.*
Range: Resident, e. U.S., e. Mexico. **West:** Barely crosses our boundary in n. and w. Texas. Accidental, Wyoming, Colorado, New Mexico. **Habitat:** Tangles, undergrowth, suburbs, gardens, towns.

MARSH WREN *Cistothorus palustris* M295
(Long-billed Marsh Wren) 5" (13 cm). The *white stripes on the back* and the white eyebrow stripe identify this marsh dweller.
Voice: Song, reedy, gurgling, often ending in a guttural rattle: *cut-cut-turrrrrrrrr-ur;* sometimes at night. Note, a low *tsuck.*
Range: s. Canada to nw. Mexico. Winters to cen. Mexico. **West:** Map 295. **Habitat:** Marshes (cattail, bullrush, or brackish).

SEDGE WREN *Cistothorus platensis*
(Short-billed Marsh Wren) 4½" (11 cm). Stubbier than a Marsh Wren; buffier, with *buffy* undertail coverts, *streaked* crown.
Voice: Song, a dry staccato chattering: *chap chap chap chap chap chap chap chapper-rrrrr.* Note, a single or double *chap.*
Range: S. Canada locally to Tierra del Fuego. **West:** Breeds in e.-cen. Alberta, s. Saskatchewan. Rare migrant on Great Plains; accidental, California. **Habitat:** Grassy marshes, sedgy meadows.

HOUSE WREN

WINTER WREN

BEWICK'S WREN

CAROLINA WREN

MARSH WREN

SEDGE WREN

ROCK WREN
(p. 266)

265

CANYON WREN *Catherpes mexicanus*   **M291**

5¾" (14 cm). Note the white bib. Rusty, with a *dark rufous-brown belly* contrasting with a *white breast and throat.*
Voice: A gushing cadence of clear, curved notes tripping down the scale; sometimes picking up at the end: *te-you, te-you te-you tew tew tew tew* or *tee tee tee tee tew tew tew tew.* Note a shrill *beet.*
Range: Resident, sw. British Columbia to s. Mexico. Map 291. **Habitat:** Cliffs, canyons, rockslides; stone buildings.

ROCK WREN *Salpinctes obsoletus*   **M290**

5½–6½" (14–16 cm). A gray wren of the rocks; has a *finely streaked breast,* light belly, rusty rump, *buffy tail corners.*
Voice: Song, a harsh chant. A loud, dry trill; also *ti-keer.*
Range: Sw. Canada, w. U.S. to Costa Rica. Map 290. **Habitat:** Rocky slopes, canyons.

CACTUS WREN *Campylorhynchus brunneicapillus*   **M289**

7–8¾" (18–22 cm). A very large wren of arid country. Distinguished from other U.S. wrens by its much larger size and heavy spotting, which in adults gathers into a cluster on the upper breast. White stripe over eye and white spots in outer tail.
Similar species: Sage Thrasher (p. 270) is grayer; no back stripes.
Voice: A monotonous *chuh-chuh-chuh-chuh,* etc., or *chug-chug-chug-chug-chug,* on one pitch, gaining rapidity; unbird-like.
Range: Sw. U.S. to cen. Mexico. Map 289. **Habitat:** Cactus, yucca, mesquite; arid brush, deserts.

WRENTIT *Chamaea fasciata* Family Muscicapidae   **M311**

6–6½" (15–16 cm). Far more often heard than seen. The long, rounded, slightly cocked tail and obscurely *streaked* breast help identify this small, drab bird, which can be seen as it slips through the brush. Eye *white.* Behavior wren-like. Southern birds are grayer, northern ones browner.
Similar species: Bushtit (p. 260) is smaller; usually travels in flocks.
Voice: Song (heard throughout year), staccato ringing notes on one pitch; starting deliberately, running into a trill. Also a slower, double-noted version. Note, a soft *prr.*
Range: Oregon to n. Baja California. Map 311. **Habitat:** Chaparral, brush, parks, garden shrubs.

■ **DIPPERS. Family Cinclidae.** Plump, stub-tailed; like very large wrens. Solitary. Dippers dive and swim under water, where they walk on the bottom. **Food:** Insects, aquatic invertebrates, small fish.
Range: Eurasia, w. N. America, Andes of S. America. **No. of species:** World 5; West 1.

AMERICAN DIPPER *Cinclus mexicanus*   **M296**

(Water Ouzel) 7–8½" (18–21 cm). A chunky, *slate-colored* bird of rushing mountain streams. Shaped like a wren (size of a large thrush); *tail stubby.* Legs pale, eyelids *white.* Note bobbing motions, slaty color, flashing eyelid. Dives, submerges.
Voice: Note, a sharp *zeet.* Song clear and ringing, mockingbird-like in form (much repetition of notes), but higher, more wren-like.
Range: Resident, Alaska, w. Canada to w. Panama. Map 296. **Habitat:** Fast-flowing streams in mountains. Lower levels in winter.

CANYON
WREN

ROCK WREN

juv.

CACTUS WREN

adult

WRENTIT

northern
form

s. Calif.
form

AMERICAN
DIPPER

adult

juvenile

■ KINGLETS, GNATCATCHERS. Family Muscicapidae. (in part).

Subfamily Sylviinae. Tiny active birds with small slender bills. Kinglets are chubby, with short tails, bright crowns. Gnatcatchers are slender, with long mobile tails. See *Birding*, Feb. 1987.

RUBY-CROWNED KINGLET *Regulus calendula* **M298**

4" (10 cm). A tiny, stub-tailed birdlet; olive-gray, with a strong *black wing bar* below the white ones. Male with a *scarlet crown patch* (usually concealed; erect when excited). Flicks wings. *Broken white eye-ring* gives a big-eyed look. Any kinglet without a crown patch and eyestripe is this species. See Hutton's Vireo, p. 284.
Voice: A husky *ji-dit*. Song, three or four high notes, several lower notes and a chant, *tee tee tee-tew tew tew—ti-didee, ti-didee, ti-didee*. Variable.
Range: Canada, Alaska, w. U.S. Winters to Guatemala. **West:** Map 298. **Habitat:** Conifers; in winter, other woodlands.

GOLDEN-CROWNED KINGLET *Regulus satrapa* **M297**

3½" (9 cm). Note the bright crown patch (*yellow* in female, *orange* in male) *bordered by black*, and the *whitish eyebrow stripe*. Kinglets are tiny, olive-gray birds, smaller than most warblers. An upward flick of the wings is characteristic.
Voice: A high, wiry *see-see-see*. Song, a series of high thin notes, ascending, then dropping into a little chatter.
Range: S. Alaska, Canada to Guatemala. **West:** Map 297. **Habitat:** Conifers; in winter, also other trees.

BLUE-GRAY GNATCATCHER *Polioptila caerulea* **M299**

4½" (11 cm). Suggests a miniature Mockingbird. A tiny, slim mite, smaller than a chickadee; blue-gray above, whitish below, with a narrow *white eye-ring*. The *long, black and white tail* is often cocked like a wren's tail and flipped about.
Voice: Note, a thin, peevish *zpee* or *chee*. Song, a thin, squeaky, wheezy series of notes, easily overlooked.
Range: S. Utah, s. Ontario to Guatemala. Winters to Honduras. **West:** Map 299. **Habitat:** Open woods, oaks, pines, thickets.

BLACK-CAPPED GNATCATCHER *Polioptila nigriceps*

4½" (11 cm). *Male:* In breeding plumage puts on a *solid black cap*, lacking in winter and in females. Note the *largely white undertail* (largely black in Black-tailed Gnatcatcher).
Range: W. Mexico. Has bred in s. Arizona.

BLACK-TAILED GNATCATCHER *Polioptila melanura* **M300**

4½" (11 cm). Similar to Blue-gray Gnatcatcher, but breeding male has a black cap and much less white on the tail (outer web only). Winter male (without cap) and female are duller than Blue-gray Gnatcatcher. From below, the tail is largely *black*.
Voice: Note, a thin harsh *chee*, repeated two or three times (Blue-gray Gnatcatcher usually gives a single note); or *pee-ee-ee*.
Range: Resident, sw. U.S., n. Mexico. Map 300. **Habitat:** Desert brush, ravines, dry washes; mesquite, sage.

CALIFORNIA GNATCATCHER *Polioptila californica* **M300**

("Plumbeous Gnatcatcher") Formerly regarded as a race of Black-tailed Gnatcatcher, but dull gray below, less white on the underside of the tail. Resident, se. California and Baja California.

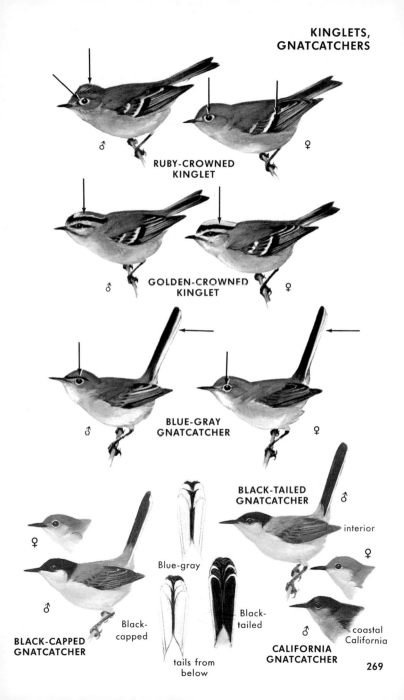

KINGLETS, GNATCATCHERS

RUBY-CROWNED KINGLET

♂   ♀

GOLDEN-CROWNED KINGLET

♂   ♀

BLUE-GRAY GNATCATCHER

♂   ♀

BLACK-TAILED GNATCATCHER   ♂

♀

interior

♀

Blue-gray

Black-capped

BLACK-CAPPED GNATCATCHER

Black-tailed

tails from below

♂

coastal California

CALIFORNIA GNATCATCHER

269

■ MOCKINGBIRDS AND THRASHERS. Family Mimidae.

Often called "mimic thrushes." Excellent songsters; some mimic other birds. Strong-legged; usually longer-tailed than true thrushes, bill usually more decurved. **Food:** Insects, fruits. **Range:** New World; Canada to Argentina. **No. of species:** World 35; West 9.

BROWN THRASHER *Toxostoma rufum*   M315

11½" (29 cm). Slimmer than a Robin; *bright rufous* above, *heavily striped* below. Note also the wing bars, the rather curved bill, the long tail, and the yellow eyes. The various brown thrushes (p. 276) have shorter tails, lack wing bars, are spotted (not striped), and have brown (not yellow) eyes.
Voice: Song, a succession of deliberate notes and phrases resembling the Catbird's song, but more musical and each phrase usually *in pairs*. Note, a harsh *chack!*
Range: S. Canada to Gulf states; east of Rockies. **West:** Map 315.
Habitat: Thickets, brush, shrubbery, thorn scrub.

GRAY CATBIRD *Dumetella carolinensis*   M312

9" (23 cm). Slate-gray; slim. Note the *black cap. Chestnut undertail coverts* (may not be noticeable). Flips tail jauntily.
Voice: *Catlike mewing;* distinctive. Also a grating *tcheck-tcheck.* Song, disjointed notes and phrases; not repetitious.
Range: S. Canada, e. and cen. U.S. Winters to Panama, W. Indies.
West: Map 312. **Habitat:** Undergrowth, brush, thorn scrub, suburban gardens.

NORTHERN MOCKINGBIRD *Mimus polyglottos*   M313

9–11" (23–28 cm). Gray; slimmer, longer-tailed than a Robin. Note the *large white patches* on the wings and tail, conspicuous in flight.
Similar species: Shrikes (pp. 280, 281) have black facial masks.
Voice: Song, a varied, prolonged succession of notes and phrases, each repeated a half-dozen times or more before changing. Often heard at night. Many Mockingbirds are excellent mimics of other species. Note, a loud *tchack;* also *chair.*
Range: S. Canada to s. Mexico, W. Indies, Hawaii (introduced). **West:** Map 313. **Habitat:** Towns, farms, roadsides, thickets.

SAGE THRASHER *Oreoscoptes montanus*   M314

8–9" (20–23 cm). A bit smaller than a Robin; similar in shape and some actions. Gray-backed, with a heavily streaked breast, white spots at tip of tail. The eyes are pale yellow. Small size, shorter tail, shorter bill, and striped breast distinguish it from other typically western thrashers.
Similar species: (1) See Cactus Wren (pp. 266, 267). (2) Young Mockingbirds, which are spotted below, have large white patches in the wings and tail. (3) See also Bendire's Thrasher (pp. 272, 273).
Voice: Song, clear, ecstatic warbled phrases, sometimes repeated in thrasher fashion; more often continuous, suggestive of a Black-headed Grosbeak. Note, a blackbird-like *chuck.*
Range: Sw. Canada, w. U.S. Map 314. **Habitat:** Sagebrush, brushy slopes, mesas; in winter, also deserts.

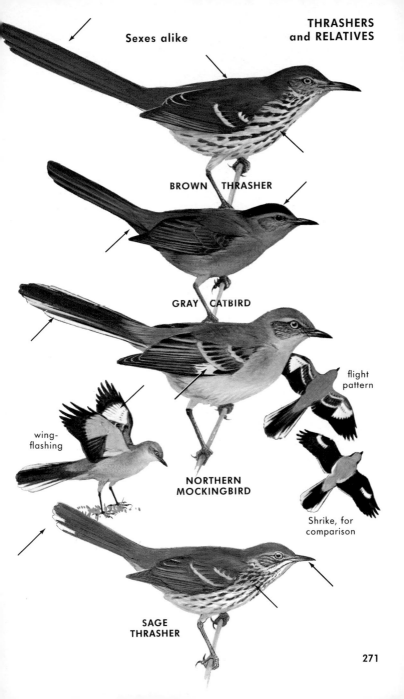

THRASHERS
and RELATIVES

Sexes alike

BROWN THRASHER

GRAY CATBIRD

NORTHERN
MOCKINGBIRD

flight
pattern

wing-
flashing

Shrike, for
comparison

SAGE
THRASHER

271

CALIFORNIA THRASHER *Toxostoma redivivum* **M317**

11–13″ (28–33 cm). A large, dull gray-brown thrasher, with a *pale cinnamon belly and undertail coverts;* tail long; bill *sickle-shaped.* The eyes are dark brown. It is the only thrasher of this type in California west of the desert divides (except very locally, where LeConte's and Crissal thrashers overlap).

Voice: Note, a dry *chak,* also a sharp *g-leek.* Song, a long, sustained series of notes and phrases, some musical, some harsh. Phrases may be *repeated* once or twice, but not several times as in Mockingbird; song more leisurely than Mocker's.

Range: California, n. Baja California. Map 317. **Habitat:** Chaparral, foothills, valley thickets, parks, gardens.

CRISSAL THRASHER *Toxostoma crissale* **M318**

10½–12½″ (27–31 cm). A rather dark thrasher of the desert, with a *deeply curved bill.* Note the dark *chestnut undertail coverts* (or crissum), darker than in other thrashers. No breast spots. The eyes are dull yellowish.

Voice: Song sweeter and less spasmodic than in other thrashers. Note, *pichoory* or *chideary,* repeated two or three times.

Range: Sw. U.S. to cen. Mexico. Map 318. **Habitat:** Dense brush along desert streams, mesquite thickets.

LeCONTE'S THRASHER *Toxostoma lecontei* **M319**

10–11″ (25–28 cm). A *very pale* thrasher of the desert, with a *darker tail.* The eyes are dark.

Similar species: (1) Crissal and California thrashers are much darker overall. (2) The other thrashers have spotted breasts.

Voice: Song (Jan.–Mar.) similar to songs of most other thrashers. Note, *ti-rup,* rising on second syllable.

Range: Sw. U.S., nw. Mexico. Map 319. **Habitat:** Desert flats with sparse bushes, *Atriplex.*

CURVE-BILLED THRASHER *Toxostoma curvirostre* **M317**

9½–11½″ (24–29 cm). This, the commonest desert thrasher, can be told from the others that have *well-curved* bills by the *mottled breast,* which is indistinct in the westernmost form, *palmeri.* Some individuals have narrow white wing bars. Eyes pale orange. Juvenile has yellow eyes, straighter bill.

Voice: Note, a sharp, liquid *whit-wheet!* (like a whistle to attract attention). Song, a musical series of notes and phrases, almost grosbeak-like in quality but faster. Not much repetition.

Range: Resident, sw. U.S. to s. Mexico. Map 317. **Habitat:** Deserts, arid brush.

BENDIRE'S THRASHER *Toxostoma bendirei* **M316**

9–11″ (23–28 cm). Of the various drab desert thrashers, this one may be known by its *shorter, more robin-like bill* (lower mandible quite straight). Breast lightly spotted. Eyes usually *yellow.*

Similar species: Curve-billed Thrasher usually has a longer, more curved bill; more blurry spotting; more orange eyes. *Caution:* Young Curve-bill may have a bill as short as Bendire's, and yellow eyes. **Voice:** Song, a *continuous,* clear, double-noted warble, not broken into phrases. Note, a soft *tirup.*

Range: Sw. U.S. to Sinaloa, Mexico. Map 316. **Habitat:** Desert, farmland; cholla, thorny bushes.

THRASHERS
Sexes alike

CALIFORNIA
THRASHER

CRISSAL
THRASHER

LeCONTE'S
THRASHER

curvirostre
se. Ariz. to Texas

CURVE-BILLED
THRASHER

palmeri, the more
widespread form

BENDIRE'S
THRASHER

■ **THRUSHES. Family Muscicapidae** (in part).* Subfamily Turdinae. Large-eyed, slender-billed, usually strong-legged songbirds. Most species that bear the name "thrush" are brown-backed, with *spotted* breasts. Robins and bluebirds, etc., suggest their relationship through their speckle-breasted young. Thrushes are often fine singers. **Food:** Insects, worms, snails, berries, fruits. **Range:** Nearly worldwide. **No. of species:** World 316; West 14 (+6 casual or accidental).

*__Note:__ Until recently the thrushes and their allies (robins, bluebirds, solitaires, etc.) were put in a family of their own, the *Turdidae,* but are now lumped with such unlikely and diverse associates as the kinglets, gnatcatchers, Old World warblers, Old World flycatchers, and the wrentit, under the catch-all family *Muscicapidae.*

AMERICAN ROBIN *Turdus migratorius*   M309
9–11″ (23–28 cm). A very familiar bird, often seen walking with an erect stance on lawns. Recognized by its dark gray back and brick-red breast. Dark stripes on a white throat. The head and tail of the male are blackish; those of the female grayer. The young bird has a speckled breast, but the rusty wash identifies it.
Voice: Song, a clear caroling; short phrases, rising and falling, often prolonged. Notes, *tyeep* and *tut-tut-tut.*
Range: Alaska, Canada to s. Mexico. **West:** Map 309. **Habitat:** Cities, towns, farmland, lawns, shade trees, forests; in winter, berry-bearing trees.

VARIED THRUSH *Ixoreus naevius*   M310
9–10″ (23–25 cm). Similar to the American Robin, but with an *orangish eyestripe, orange wing bars,* and a wide *black band* (male) or *gray band* (female) across the rusty breast. *Young:* Breastband imperfect or speckled; rusty wing bars and eyestripe distinguish it from a young Robin.
Voice: A long, eerie, quavering, whistled note, followed, after a pause, by one on a lower or higher pitch. A liquid *chup.*
Range: Alaska, w. Canada, nw. U.S. Map 310. **Habitat:** Thick, wet forest, conifers; in winter, woods, ravines, thickets.

RUFOUS-BACKED ROBIN *Turdus rufopalliatus*
9″ (23 cm). This rare Mexican visitor is like a pale American Robin (extensive cinnamon underparts; grayish head, wings, and tail), but with a *rufous back* and *no white* around the eye. A timid skulker.
Range: Western and S. Mexico. **West:** A rare but regular fall–winter visitor to s. Arizona. Accidental, Texas, California.

TOWNSEND'S SOLITAIRE *Myadestes townsendi*   M304
8″ (20 cm). A slim gray bird with a *white eye-ring, white sides on the tail,* and *buffy wing patches.* The pattern in the wing and tail give it a not-too-remote resemblance to a Mockingbird, but note the eye-ring, darker breast, and especially the buff wing patches.
Range: Alaska, nw. Canada, w. U.S., n. Mexico. Map 304. **Habitat:** Conifer forests in mountains, rocky cliffs, thickets; in winter, chaparral, pinyon-juniper, open woods, wooded streams.

ROBINS, THRUSHES

♀

juvenile

♂

AMERICAN
ROBIN

♂

♀

juvenile

VARIED
THRUSH

TOWNSEND'S
SOLITAIRE

sexes
similar

juvenile

sexes
similar

RUFOUS-
BACKED
ROBIN

VEERY *Catharus fuscescens* **M305**

6½–7½" (16–19 cm). Note the *uniform brown* cast above and the grayish tones on the flanks. No strong eye-ring (may have a dull whitish ring). Of all our brown thrushes, the least spotted; the spots may be indistinct in eastern birds, which are more tawny above than birds of the western mountains, which are darker brown.

Voice: Song, liquid, breezy, ethereal; wheeling downward: *vee-ur, vee-ur, veer, veer.* Note, a low *phew* or *view.*

Range: S. Canada, n. and cen. U.S. Winters from Colombia to Brazil. **West:** Map 305. **Habitat:** Damp deciduous woods.

SWAINSON'S THRUSH *Catharus ustulatus* **M307**

7" (18 cm). This spotted thrush is marked by its conspicuous *buffy eye-ring,* buff on cheeks and upper breast. Gray-cheeked Thrush has a less conspicuous eye-ring.

Voice: Song, breezy, flutelike phrases, each phrase sliding *upward.* Note, *whit,* or *foot.* Migrants at night (in sky), a short *heep,* or *quee-ah.*

Range: Alaska, Canada, w. and ne. U.S. Winters Mexico to Peru. **West:** Map 307. **Habitat:** Spruce forests; in migration, other woods.

GRAY-CHEEKED THRUSH *Catharus minimus* **M306**

7–8" (18–20 cm). A dull gray-brown thrush, distinguished from Swainson's by its *grayish* cheeks and less conspicuous eye-ring.

Voice: Song, thin and nasal; suggests Veery's, but often rising abruptly at close (Veery's goes down): *whee-wheeoo-titi-whee.* Note, *vee-a* or *quee-a,* higher and more nasal than Swainson's note.

Range: Ne. Siberia, Alaska, Canada, ne. U.S. Winters from W. Indies and Costa Rica to Brazil. **West:** Map 306. **Habitat:** Boreal forests, tundra scrub; in migration, other woodlands.

HERMIT THRUSH *Catharus guttatus* **M308**

7" (18 cm). A spot-breasted brown thrush with a *rufous* tail. When perched, it has a habit of cocking its tail and dropping it slowly.

Similar species: Fox Sparrow (some races have a rusty tail) is heavily streaked rather than spotted; note the conical bill.

Voice: Note, a low *chuck;* also a scolding *tuk-tuk-tuk* and a harsh *pay.* Song, clear, ethereal, flutelike; three or four phrases at *different pitches,* each with a *long introductory note.*

Range: Alaska, Canada, w. and ne. U.S. Winters U.S. to El Salvador. **West:** Map 308. **Habitat:** Conifer or mixed woods, forest floor; in winter, woods, thickets, parks.

WOOD THRUSH *Hylocichla mustelina*

8" (20 cm). *Rusty-headed.* Smaller than a Robin; plumper than the other brown thrushes, distinguished by the deepening rufous about the head, the *striped cheeks,* and the rounder, more numerous breast spots.

Range: Breeds se. Canada, e. and cen. U.S.; a very rare or casual stray in most western states west to Idaho, Oregon, and California.

Sexes similar

VEERY

russet-backed form

olive-backed form

SWAINSON'S THRUSH

GRAY-CHEEKED THRUSH

tail-lifting

WOOD THRUSH

HERMIT THRUSH

auduboni (western mts.)

guttatus (Pacific Coast)

277

WESTERN BLUEBIRD *Sialia mexicana* **M302**

6½–7" (16–18 cm). A bit larger than a sparrow; appears round-shouldered when perched. Head, wings, and tail *blue;* breast and back *rusty red.* (In some birds the back is partially or wholly blue.) *Throat blue.* Females are paler, duller, with rusty breast, *grayish* throat and belly. Young birds are speckle-breasted, grayish, devoid of red, but with some telltale blue in wings and tail.

Similar species: (1) Lazuli Bunting has white *wing bars.* (2) Male Mountain Bluebird has a *blue* breast (see also female).

Voice: A short *pew* or *mew.* Also a hard, chattering note.

Range: Breeds from s. British Columbia, western U.S. to mountains of cen. Mexico. Map 302. **Habitat:** Scattered trees, open conifer forests, farms; in winter, semi-open terrain, brush, deserts.

EASTERN BLUEBIRD *Sialia sialis* **M301**

7" (18 cm). Similar to Western Bluebird but *throat rusty,* not blue. Belly and undertail *whiter,* not as gray. Western Bluebird has a blue throat and usually some rust color on the back. Female duller than male; has a rusty throat and breast, *white* belly. *Juvenile:* Speckle-breasted; similar to juvenile Western Bluebird.

Voice: Note, a musical *chur-wi.* Song, 3 or 4 gurgling notes.

Range: East of Rockies; s. Canada to Gulf states; also se. Arizona to Nicaragua. **West:** Map 301. **Habitat:** Open country with scattered trees; farms, roadsides.

MOUNTAIN BLUEBIRD *Sialia currucoides* **M303**

7" (18 cm). *Male:* Turquoise blue, paler below; belly whitish. No rusty. *Female:* Dull brownish, with a touch of blue on rump, tail, and wings. Has a straighter posture than female Western Bluebird and lacks rusty wash on gray-brown breast.

Voice: A low *chur* or *phew.* Song, a short, subdued warble.

Range: Alaska, w. Canada to sw. U.S. **West:** Map 303. **Habitat:** Open country with some trees; in winter, also treeless terrain.

BLUETHROAT *Luscinia svecica*

5½" (14 cm). A small, sprightly bird; when flirted, the tail shows a *chestnut base.* Male in summer: *Blue throat patch,* with a *reddish spot* and a reddish band separating the blue from the white. Female has a white throat with a dark necklace.

Voice: A sharp *tac* and a soft *wheet.* Song, repetitious notes, musical and varied; often a cricketlike note.

Range: Eurasia, Alaska; winters to India, n. Africa. **West:** Breeds in n. and w. Alaska from Brooks Range to Seward Peninsula. **Habitat:** Dwarf willow, thick brush.

NORTHERN WHEATEAR *Oenanthe oenanthe*

6" (15 cm). A small, dapper bird of arctic barrens, flitting from rock to rock, fanning its tail and bobbing. Note the *white rump and sides of the tail.* The black on the tail forms a *broad inverted T.* Breeding male has a blue-gray back, black wings, and a black ear patch. Female and autumn male are buffier, with a brown back.

Voice: Note, a hard *chak-chak* or *chack-weet, weet-chack.*

Range: Eurasia, Alaska, Canada, Greenland. Migrates to Africa, India. **West:** Breeds from n. Alaska, n. Yukon to coastal Alaska, sw. Yukon. Accidental, British Columbia, Oregon, n. California.

BLUEBIRDS, and other small thrushes

juvenile

WESTERN BLUEBIRD

♂ ♀

EASTERN BLUEBIRD

♂ ♀

MOUNTAIN BLUEBIRD

♂ ♀

breeding ♂

BLUETHROAT

See also
Siberian
Ruby-throat,
Alaska strays,
pp. 354, 355.

breeding ♂   winter

NORTHERN WHEATEAR

279

■ **SHRIKES. Family Laniidae.** Songbirds with hook-tipped bills, hawk-like behavior. Shrikes perch watchfully on treetops, wires; often impale prey on thorns, barbed wire. **Food:** Insects, lizards, mice, small birds. **Range:** Widespread in Old World; 2 in N. America. **No. of species:** World 74; West 2 (+1 accidental).

NORTHERN SHRIKE *Lanius excubitor*   **M325**
9–10″ (23–25 cm). Similar to the Loggerhead Shrike; note the *faintly barred* breast and the *pale base* of the lower mandible. Bill longer, more hooked. *Juvenile:* Brown, with *fine bars* on breast.
Similar species: Adult Loggerhead Shrike has a solid black bill; black mask meets over base of bill. Juvenile may have faint bars, but is grayer than the young Northern.
Voice: Song, a disjointed, thrasher-like succession of harsh notes and musical notes. Note, *shek-shek;* a grating *jaaeg.*
Range: N. America, Eurasia, n. Africa. **West:** Map 325. **Habitat:** Semi-open country with lookout posts; trees, scrub.

LOGGERHEAD SHRIKE *Lanius ludovicianus*   **M326**
9″ (23 cm). Big-headed, slim-tailed; gray, black, and white, with a *black mask.* Sits quietly on wires or bush tops; taking off, flies low with flickering flight showing white patches, then swoops upward to its perch. Suggests a Mockingbird (p. 271).
Voice: Song, harsh, deliberate notes and phrases, repeated 3–20 times, suggesting Mockingbird's song; *queedle, queedle,* over and over, or *tsurp-see, tsurp-see.* Note, *shack shack.*
Range: S. Canada to s. Mexico. **West:** Map 326. **Habitat:** Semi-open country with lookout posts; wires, trees, scrub.

■ **STARLINGS. Family Sturnidae.** A varied family; some blackbird-like. Usually short-tailed, sharp-billed. Gregarious. **Food:** Insects, seeds, berries. **Range:** Widespread in Old World. **No. of species:** World 109; West 2 (introduced).

EUROPEAN STARLING *Sturnus vulgaris*   **M327**
7½–8½″ (19–21 cm). A gregarious, garrulous, short-tailed "blackbird"; shape of a meadowlark. In flight, looks triangular; flies swiftly and directly. In spring iridescent; bill *yellow.* In winter, *heavily speckled;* bill dark, changing to yellow in spring. Young Starling is dusky, a bit like female Cowbird, but tail shorter, bill longer.
Voice: A harsh *tseeeer;* a whistled *whooee.* Also clear whistles, clicks, chuckles; sometimes mimics other birds.
Range: Eurasia, n. Africa. Introduced N. America and elsewhere. **West:** Map 327. **Habitat:** Cities, parks, farms, open groves, fields.

CRESTED MYNA *Acridotheres cristatellus*
10½″ (26 cm). A large, chunky, short-tailed bird; black, with large *white wing patches;* bill *yellow;* legs yellow. The forehead is adorned with a short *bushy crest.*
Voice: Starling-like; repeated phrases. An accomplished mimic.
Range: Se. Asia. Introduced in Philippines and British Columbia. **West:** Resident in and near Vancouver, British Columbia; local, s. Vancouver I. Casual, w. Washington, nw. Oregon.

SHRIKES

immature

adult

NORTHERN SHRIKE

adult

See Mockingbird for comparison.

immature

LOGGERHEAD SHRIKE

STARLINGS

winter adult

juvenile

EUROPEAN STARLING

breeding

CRESTED MYNA

adult

281

■ **WAXWINGS. Family Bombycillidae.** The sleekest birds; a pointed crest may be raised or lowered. Waxy red tips on secondaries in most individuals. Gregarious. **Food:** Berries, insects. **Range:** N. Hemisphere. **No. of species:** World 3; West 2.

CEDAR WAXWING *Bombycilla cedrorum*   **M323**
7" (18 cm). Note the *yellow band* at the tip of the tail. A sleek, crested, brown bird, larger than a House Sparrow. Adults usually have *waxy red tips* on the secondaries. Differs from Bohemian Waxwing in having yellow on the belly, *white* (not rusty) undertail coverts. Juvenile is grayer, softly streaked below. Waxwings are gregarious; they fly and feed in compact flocks. Although they are berry-eaters, they often indulge in fly-catching.
Voice: A high, thin lisp or *zeee*; sometimes slightly trilled.
Range: Se. Alaska, Canada, to s.-cen. U.S. Winters s. Canada to Panama. **West:** Map 323. **Habitat:** Open woodlands, fruiting trees, orchards; in winter, widespread, including towns; nomadic.

BOHEMIAN WAXWING *Bombycilla garrulus*   **M322**
8" (20 cm). Similar to the Cedar Waxwing (yellow tip on tail), but larger and grayer, with no yellow on belly; wings with strong white or *white and yellow* markings. Note the *deep rusty* undertail coverts (these are white in Cedar Waxwing). Often travels in large nomadic flocks.
Voice: *Zreee*, rougher than thin note of Cedar Waxwing.
Range: N. Eurasia, nw. N. America. Winters to s. Eurasia, ne. and sw. U.S. **West:** Map 322. **Habitat:** In summer, boreal forests, muskeg; in winter, widespread in search of berries, especially in towns where plantings and fruiting trees attract them.

■ **SILKY-FLYCATCHERS. Family Ptilogonatidae.** Slim, crested, waxwing-like birds. **Range:** Sw. U.S. to Panama. **Food:** Berries, mistletoe; insects. **No. of species:** World 4; West 1 (+1 accidental).

PHAINOPEPLA *Phainopepla nitens*   **M324**
7–7¾" (18–19 cm). *Male:* A slim, *glossy black* bird with a *slender crest. White wing patches* are conspicuous in flight. *Female: Dark gray* with a slender crest; wing patches light gray, not conspicuous. Eats berries but also catches flies.
Similar species: (1) Cedar Waxwing is much browner than female Phainopepla, has a yellow tailband. (2) Mockingbird (white wing patches) is gray with much white in the tail.
Voice: Note, a soft low *wurp*. Song, a weak, casual warble, wheezy and disconnected.
Range: Sw. U.S. to s. Mexico. Map 324. **Habitat:** Desert scrub, mesquite, oak foothills, mistletoe, pepper trees.

WAXWINGS, PHAINOPEPLA

juvenile

♀

♂

CEDAR WAXWING

BOHEMIAN WAXWING

♀

♂

♀

♂

PHAINOPEPLA

283

■ **VIREOS. Family Vireonidae.** Small, olive- or gray-backed birds, much like wood warblers, usually less active. Bills with a more curved ridge and slight hook. May be divided into those with wing bars (and "spectacles") and those without (these have eyestripes). **Food:** Mostly insects. **Range:** Canada to Argentina. **No. of species:** World 43; West 9 (+ 1 accidental).

SOLITARY VIREO *Vireo solitarius* **M330**
5–6" (13–15 cm). *White "spectacles," gray head*, olive or gray back, *snow-white* throat. Two wing bars. See variation opposite.
Voice: Song, sweet whistled phrases; short deliberate pauses.
Range: Canada to El Salvador. Winters s. U.S. to Nicaragua, Cuba.
West: Map 330. **Habitat:** Mixed conifer-deciduous woods.

BLACK-CAPPED VIREO *Vireo atricapillus*
4½" (11 cm). A small, sprightly vireo; top and sides of head *glossy black* in male, slate gray in female. Two wing bars. White "spectacles" formed by eye-ring and loral patch; *eyes red.*
Voice: Song, hurried, harsh; phrases remarkable for restless, almost angry quality. Alarm note, a harsh *chit-ah.*
Range: Breeds sw. Kansas, cen. Oklahoma, w. and cen. Texas (through Edwards Plateau and Big Bend) to Coahuila, Mexico. Winters in w. Mexico. **Habitat:** Oak scrub, brushy hills, rocky canyons.

YELLOW-THROATED VIREO *Vireo flavifrons*
5" (13 cm). Note the *bright yellow* throat, *yellow* "spectacles," and white wing bars. See Pine Warbler (white tail spots, streaks).
Voice: Song, similar to Red-eyed Vireo's, but has a burry quality.
Range: Breeds e. U.S., se. Canada. **West:** Rare migrant east of Rockies; casual west to Utah, Nevada, California.

BELL'S VIREO *Vireo bellii* **M328**
4½–5" (11–13 cm). Small, grayish; nondescript. One or two light wing bars, pale yellowish-washed sides. Distinguished from Warbling Vireo by the wing bar(s) and whitish eye-ring. Flicks tail.
Voice: Sings as if through clenched teeth; husky phrases at short intervals: *cheedle cheedle chee! cheedle cheedle chew!*
Range: Cen. and sw. U.S., n. Mexico. Winters Mexico to Nicaragua.
West: Map 328. **Habitat:** Willows, streamsides.

HUTTON'S VIREO *Vireo huttoni* **M331**
4¼–4¾" (11–12 cm). Note the *incomplete eye-ring*, broken by a dark spot *above* the eye. A small, olive-brown vireo with two broad white wing bars, a *partial* eye-ring, and a large light loral spot. Suggests a Ruby-crowned Kinglet, but Hutton's Vireo is slightly larger, has a heavier bill, and lacks the dark wing bar. Does not twitch its wings like a kinglet.
Voice: A double-noted *zu-weep* (rising inflection), sometimes oft-repeated; vireo quality. A hoarse, deliberate *day dee dee.*
Range: Sw. British Columbia to Guatemala. Map 331. **Habitat:** Woods and adjacent brush; prefers oaks.

WHITE-EYED VIREO *Vireo griseus* (not shown)
Eastern. Barely reaches 100th meridian in Texas. Casual or accidental in Southwest (Colorado, Utah, New Mexico, Arizona, California). See *A Field Guide to the Birds* (Eastern).

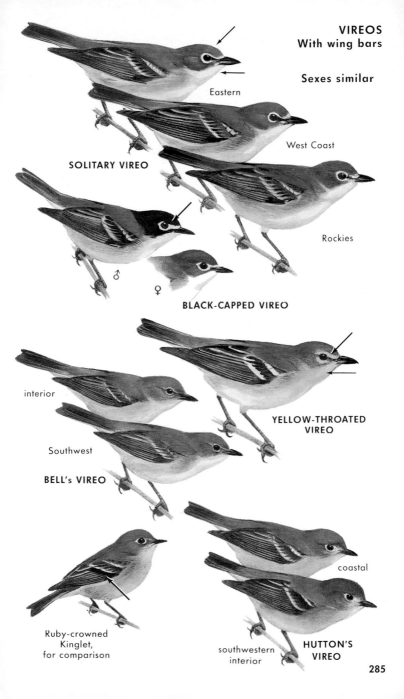

VIREOS
With wing bars

Sexes similar

Eastern

West Coast

SOLITARY VIREO

Rockies

♂

♀

BLACK-CAPPED VIREO

interior

YELLOW-THROATED VIREO

Southwest

BELL's VIREO

Ruby-crowned Kinglet, for comparison

coastal

southwestern interior

HUTTON'S VIREO

RED-EYED VIREO *Vireo olivaceus* M334

6″ (15 cm). Note the *gray cap* contrasting with the olive back, and the strong, *black-bordered white eyebrow stripe.* The red iris may not be obvious at a distance. The iris is brown in immature birds in fall.

Voice: Song, abrupt phrases, repeated as often as 40 times per minute; monotonous. Note, a nasal, whining *chway.*

Range: Canada to Gulf states. Winters in Amazon basin. **West:** Map 334. **Habitat:** Woodlands, shade trees, groves.

YELLOW-GREEN VIREO *Vireo flavoviridis*

6″ (15 cm). Very similar to Red-eyed Vireo (both in behavior and voice), but *strong yellow tones* on underparts; back greener; head stripes less distinct. Some authors lump the two species.

Range: Rio Grande delta, n. Mexico, to Panama. Winters in S. America. **West:** Casual fall visitor to southern and coastal California; recorded in summer in s. Arizona.

PHILADELPHIA VIREO *Vireo philadelphicus* M333

4¾″ (12 cm). This warbler-like vireo combines unbarred wings and strongly *yellow-tinged* underparts, especially on the breast.

Similar species: (1) Warbling Vireo usually lacks yellow (but may have a tinge on the sides). Note the *dark loral spot* (between eye and bill) in the Philadelphia. (2) Fall Tennessee Warbler (p. 300) has clear white (not yellow) undertail coverts.

Voice: Song similar to Red-eyed Vireo's; higher, slower.

Range: S. Canada, ne. edge of U.S. Winters in Cen. America. **West:** Map 333. **Habitat:** Second-growth woodlands, poplars, willows, alders.

WARBLING VIREO *Vireo gilvus* M332

5″ (13 cm). In this very plain vireo, note the whitish breast and the lack of black borders on the eyebrow stripe.

Similar species: (1) Philadelphia Vireo is yellowish below, has dark lores. (2) Red-eyed Vireo has black borders on the eyebrow stripe.

Voice: Song distinctive; a languid warble, unlike broken phrases of other vireos; suggests Purple Finch's song, but less spirited, with burry undertone. Note, a wheezy querulous *twee.*

Range: Canada to s. U.S., cen. Mexico. Winters Mexico to Nicaragua. **West:** Map 332. **Habitat:** Deciduous and mixed woods, aspen groves, poplars, shade trees.

GRAY VIREO *Vireo vicinior* M329

5–5¾″ (13–14 cm). This plain, gray-backed vireo of arid mountains has a *narrow white eye-ring* but differs from other vireos with eye-rings by having *no wing bars* or only one faint bar. Though drab, it has character, flopping its tail like a gnatcatcher.

Similar species: Bell's Vireo (p. 285) usually has two wing bars (sometimes only one). Habitat different (low stream edges).

Voice: Song similar to Solitary Vireo's, but more rapid, "patchy."

Range: Sw. U.S. to cen. Mexico. Map 329. **Habitat:** Brushy mountain slopes, mesas, open chaparral, scrub oak, junipers.

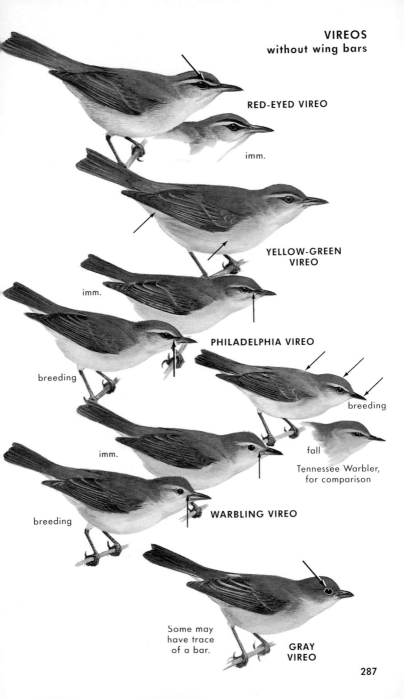

VIREOS
without wing bars

RED-EYED VIREO

imm.

YELLOW-GREEN
VIREO

imm.

PHILADELPHIA VIREO

breeding

breeding

fall

Tennessee Warbler,
for comparison

imm.

WARBLING VIREO

breeding

Some may
have trace
of a bar.

GRAY
VIREO

287

■ **WOOD WARBLERS. Family Emberizidae.** Subfamily Parulinae. Active, brightly colored birdlets, usually smaller than sparrows, with thin, needle-pointed bills. The majority have some yellow. Identification in autumn is often difficult. Until recently our wood warblers enjoyed full family status of their own, as *Parulidae.* Now they are lumped with tanagers, sparrows, blackbirds, and a number of others in the catch-all family *Emberizidae.* **Food:** Mainly insects. **Range:** Alaska and Canada to n. Argentina. **No. of species:** World 114; West 53 (including several that are purely casual or accidental, categories that are hard to define because recent intensive field work has shown they may be rare but regular as vagrants at certain coastal points and desert oases).

MAGNOLIA WARBLER *Dendroica magnolia*   **M342**
4¾" (12 cm). The "Black-and-yellow" Warbler. Upperparts blackish, with large white patches on wings and tail; underparts yellow, with heavy black stripes. Note the black tail crossed midway by a *broad white band* (from beneath, the tail is white with a broad black tip). Immature has weak breast stripes, but the tail pattern is distinctive.
Voice: Song suggests Yellow Warbler's but is shorter; *weeta weeta weetsee* (last note rising), or *weeta weeta wit-chew.*
Range: Canada, ne. U.S. Winters Mexico, W. Indies to Panama.
West: Map 342. **Habitat:** Low conifers, except in migration.

YELLOW-RUMPED WARBLER *Dendroica coronata*   **M344**
(Including "Audubon" and "Myrtle" Warblers.) 5–6" (13–15 cm). Note the bright *yellow rump* and the note (a loud *check* or *tchip*). *Male in spring:* Blue-gray above; heavy black breast patch (like an inverted U); throat, crown, side patches yellow. "Audubon" form (Western U.S., sw. Canada) differs from "Myrtle" form (Alaska, Canada, e. U.S.) in having a *yellow throat,* large white wing patches. *Female in spring:* Brown, not gray; pattern similar except for wing patch (has two white bars). *Winter adults and young:* Brownish above; whitish below, streaked; throat yellowish (sometimes dim) in western "Audubon" form, rump yellow.
Voice: Song, junco-like but two-parted, rising or dropping in pitch, *seet-seet-seet-seet-seet, trrrrrrrr.* Note, a loud *check.*
Range: Breeds Alaska, Canada, ne. and w. U.S. to Guatemala; winters to Panama. **West:** Map 344. **Habitat:** Conifer forests. In winter, varied; open woods, brush, thickets, gardens, even beaches.

CANADA WARBLER *Wilsonia canadensis*   **M361**
5–5¾" (13–14 cm). The "necklaced" warbler. *Male:* Solid gray above; bright yellow below, with *necklace of short black stripes. Female and immature:* Similar; necklace fainter or lacking. All have yellow "spectacles." No white in wings or tail.
Voice: Song, a staccato burst, irregularly arranged. *Chip, chupety swee-ditchety* (Gunn). Note, *tchip.*
Range: Canada, e. U.S. Winters Oaxaca, Mexico, to e. Peru. **West:** Map 361. **Habitat:** Forest undergrowth, shady thickets.

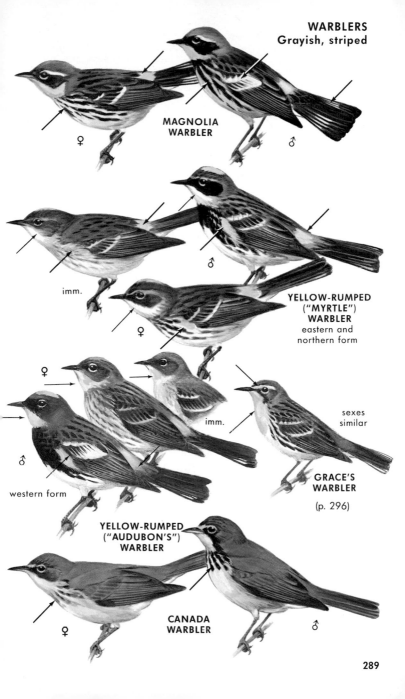

WARBLERS
Grayish, striped

MAGNOLIA WARBLER

♀

♂

YELLOW-RUMPED ("MYRTLE") WARBLER
eastern and northern form

imm.

♂

♀

♀

imm.

♂

western form

YELLOW-RUMPED ("AUDUBON'S") WARBLER

GRACE'S WARBLER

sexes similar

(p. 296)

CANADA WARBLER

♀

♂

TOWNSEND'S WARBLER *Dendroica townsendi* M346

4½–5″ (11–13 cm). *Male:* Easily distinguished by the *black and yellow pattern of the head*, with a *blackish cheek patch; underparts yellow*, with striped sides. *Female:* Throat largely yellow, not black; may be known by the *well-defined dark cheek patch, bordered by yellow* as in the male.

Similar species: Hermit Warbler lacks black cheek and crown.

Voice: Song, similar to Black-throated Gray's: *dzeer dzeer dzeer tseetsee* or *weazy, weazy, seesee.* "The first 3 or 4 notes similar in pitch, with a wheezy, buzzy quality, followed by 2 or more high-pitched sibilant notes" (H. H. Axtell).

Range: Breeds nw. N. America. Winters south to Nicaragua. Map 346. **Habitat:** Tall conifers, cool fir forests; in winter, also oaks, madroñas, laurels.

HERMIT WARBLER *Dendroica occidentalis* M347

4¾″ (12 cm). Note the bright *yellow face* set off by the *black throat and nape* and dark gray back. In the female the black of the throat is much reduced or wanting, but the yellow face, gray back, and whitish underparts identify it.

Similar species: (1) Male Townsend's Warbler has black cheek patches. Female has olive back, *yellow* breast. (2) In Canada (east of Rockies) see Black-throated Green Warbler.

Voice: Song, three high lisping notes followed by two abrupt lower ones: *sweety, sweety, sweety, chup'chup'* or *seedle, seedle, seedle, chup' chup'.* Abrupt end notes distinctive.

Range: Pacific states. Winters Mexico to California. Map 347. **Habitat:** Conifer forests; in migration, conifers and deciduous woods.

BLACK-THROATED GREEN WARBLER *Dendroica virens* M347

4½–5″ (11–13 cm). *Male:* The bright *yellow face* is framed by the black throat and olive-green crown. *Female:* Recognized by the yellow face; much less black on the throat.

Similar species: Hermit Warbler (Pacific states) has yellow on crown, lacks eye stripe. Back gray; no black on sides.

Voice: A lisping, dreamy *zoo zee zoo zoo zee* or *zee zee zee zee zoo zee;* the *zee* notes on same pitch, the *zoo* notes lower.

Range: Canada, ne. U.S. and south in mountains to Georgia. Winters s. Texas to Venezuela. **West:** Map 347. **Habitat:** Mainly conifers.

GOLDEN-CHEEKED WARBLER *Dendroica chrysoparia*

4½–5″ (11–13 cm). Breeds in the "cedar" hills of the Edwards Plateau, Texas; the warbler with yellow cheeks and a black throat usually found there. *Male:* Similar to Black-throated Green Warbler, but with a *black back* and blacker line through the eye. *Female:* Back olive-green; similar to a female Black-throated Green, but belly *snowy white* (lacking tinge of yellow).

Voice: Song, a hurried *tweeah, tweeah, tweesy* (H. P. Attwater) or *bzzzz, laysee, daysee* (E. Kincaid).

Range: Breeds only in Texas; mainly on Edwards Plateau; west to San Angelo, Rocksprings. Winters s. Mexico to Nicaragua. **Habitat:** Junipers, oaks; also streamside trees. *Endangered.*

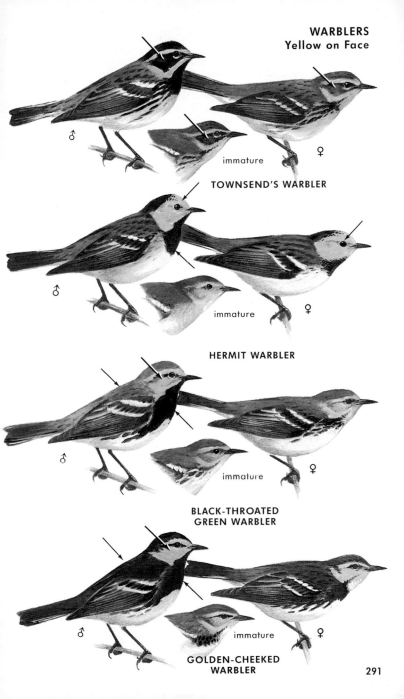

♂

immature

♀

TOWNSEND'S WARBLER

♂

immature

♀

HERMIT WARBLER

♂

immature

♀

**BLACK-THROATED
GREEN WARBLER**

♂

immature

♀

**GOLDEN-CHEEKED
WARBLER**

BLACK-AND-WHITE WARBLER *Mniotilta varia* **M352**
4½–5½" (11–14 cm). Creeps along trunks and branches. *Striped lengthwise* with *black and white;* has a *striped crown and white stripes on its back.* Female lacks the black throat and cheek.
Voice: Song, a thin *weesee weesee weesee weesee weesee weesee;* suggests one of Redstart's songs, but higher-pitched, longer.
Range: Canada to Gulf states. Winters s. U.S. to n. S. America.
West: Map 352. **Habitat:** Woods; trunks, limbs of trees.

BLACKPOLL WARBLER *Dendroica striata* **M351**
5" (13 cm). *Male, spring:* A striped gray warbler with a *black cap, white cheeks. Female, spring:* Less heavily streaked, lacking the black cap; greenish gray above, whitish below, streaked. *Autumn:* Olive above, greenish yellow below, faintly streaked; two wing bars; white undertail coverts; usually *pale yellowish* legs. Fall Bay-breasted Warbler (p. 295) has dark legs.
Voice: Song, a thin, deliberate, mechanical *zi-zi-zi zi-zi-zi-zi-zi-zi* on one pitch, becoming stronger, then diminishing.
Range: Alaska, Canada, ne. U.S. Winters in tropical S. America.
West: Map 351. **Habitat:** Conifers; broadleaf trees in migration.

BLACK-THROATED GRAY WARBLER *Dendroica nigrescens* **M345**
4½–5" (11–13 cm). *Male:* Gray, with a black throat, cheek, and crown patches separated by *white. Female: Slaty* crown and cheek; light throat. Suggests Black-and-white Warbler, but lacks the white stripes on the back and crown.
Voice: Song a buzzy chant, *zeedle zeedle zeedle zeet' che* (next to last or last note higher). Variable; "full of Z's."
Range: Western N. America. Map 345. Winters s. California to s. Mexico. **Habitat:** Dry oak slopes, pinyons, junipers, open mixed woods.

BLACK-THROATED BLUE WARBLER *Dendroica caerulescens*
5–5½" (13–14 cm). *Male:* Clean-cut; upperparts *deep blue;* throat and sides *black,* belly white; wing with white spot. *Female:* Brown-backed, with a light line over the eye and a small *white wing spot.* Immature and fall female may lack this white "pocket handkerchief," but note the *dark cheek.*
Voice: Song, a husky, lazy *zur, zur, zur, zreee,* or *beer, beer, beer, bree* (ending higher). May be shortened to two or three notes.
Range: Eastern N. America. Winters W. Indies. **West:** Casual migrant along w. edge of Plains from Alberta to Texas Panhandle; a few recorded west to Oregon, California, mainly in fall.

CERULEAN WARBLER *Dendroica cerulea*
4½" (11 cm). *Male: Blue* above, white below. Note the *narrow black ring* across the chest. *Female:* Blue-gray and olive-green above, whitish below; two white wing bars, whitish eyebrow.
Similar species: Female suggests (1) Tennessee Warbler (p. 301), which has no wing bars, or (2) a fall Blackpoll, but has a more conspicuous eyebrow; lacks stripes on the back.
Voice: Rapid buzzy notes on the same pitch, followed by a longer note on a higher pitch: *zray zray zray zreeeee.*
Range: Eastern U.S.; winters Colombia to Bolivia. **West:** Accidental stray west to Colorado, Nevada, Arizona, California.

WARBLERS
Black-striped, gray, or bluish

BLACK-AND-
WHITE WARBLER

♀

♂

BLACKPOLL
WARBLER

♂

summer

winter

♀

BLACK-THROATED
GRAY WARBLER
(accidental)

♂

♀

imm.

BLACK-THROATED
BLUE WARBLER

♂

♀

CERULEAN
WARBLER

♀

♂

293

CAPE MAY WARBLER *Dendroica tigrina*   **M343**
5″ (13 cm). *Male, breeding:* Note the *chestnut* cheeks. Yellow below, striped with black; rump yellow, crown black. *Female and autumn birds:* Lack chestnut cheeks; duller, breast often whitish, streaked. Note the dull *patch of yellow behind the ear.*
Voice: Song, a very high, thin *seet seet seet seet.* May be confused with song of Bay-breasted or Black-and-white Warbler.
Range: Canada, ne. edge of U.S. Winters in Caribbean area. **West:** Map 343. **Habitat:** Spruce forest; broadleaf trees in migration.

CHESTNUT-SIDED WARBLER *Dendroica pensylvanica*   **M341**
4½–5½″ (11–14 cm). *Adult, breeding:* Identified by combination of *yellow crown, chestnut sides. Autumn:* Lemon-greenish above, whitish below; narrow white eye-ring, *two pale yellow* wing bars. Adults retain some chestnut, immatures do not.
Voice: Song, similar to Yellow Warbler's: *see see see see Miss Beech'er* or *please please pleased to meet'cha;* penultimate note accented, last note dropping. Also a more rambling song.
Range: Mainly s. Canada, ne. U.S. Winters se. Mexico to n. S. America. **West:** Map 341. **Habitat:** Slashings, bushy pastures.

BAY-BREASTED WARBLER *Dendroica castanea*   **M350**
5–6″ (13–15 cm). *Male, spring:* Dark-looking, with a *chestnut throat, upper breast,* and sides. Note the *large spot of pale buff* on the neck. *Female, spring:* Paler, more washed out. *Autumn:* Olive-green above; two white wing bars; dull buff-white below. May have trace of bay on sides. *Buff* undertail coverts, *dark* legs. Fall Blackpoll (p. 293) usually has pale legs.
Voice: A high, sibilant *tees teesi teesi;* resembles song of Black-and-white Warbler; thinner, shorter, more on one pitch.
Range: Canada, ne. edge of U.S. Winters Panama to Venezuela. **West:** Map 350. **Habitat:** Woodlands, conifers in summer.

BLACKBURNIAN WARBLER *Dendroica fusca*
5″ (13 cm). The "Fire Throat." *Male, spring:* Black and white, with *flame orange* on head and throat. *Female and autumn birds:* Paler orange on throat. Note the yellow head stripes, pale back stripes.
Voice: Song, *zip zip zip titi tseeeeee,* ending on a very high, up-slurred note (inaudible to some ears). Also a two-parted *teetsa teetsa teetsa teetsa zizizizizi,* more like Nashville's.
Range: Canada, e. U.S. Winters Costa Rica to Bolivia. **West:** Breeds locally in cen. Saskatchewan, cen. Alberta. Rare migrant on Plains west to Rockies; each year a few strays reach California coast. **Habitat:** Woodlands; conifers in summer.

AMERICAN REDSTART *Setophaga ruticilla*   **M353**
5″ (13 cm). Butterfly-like; actively flitting, with drooping wings and spread tail. *Male:* Black; *bright orange patches* on wings and tail. *Female:* Olive-brown; *yellow flash-patches* on wings and tail. *Immature male:* Like female, but tinged with orange on the chest.
Voice: Songs (often alternated), *zee zee zee zee zwee* (last note higher), *tsee tsee tsee tsee tsee-o* (last syllable dropping), and *teetsa teetsa teetsa teetsa teet* (notes paired).
Range: Canada, e. U.S. Winters Mexico, W. Indies to nw. Brazil. **West:** Map 353. **Habitat:** Second-growth woods, river groves.

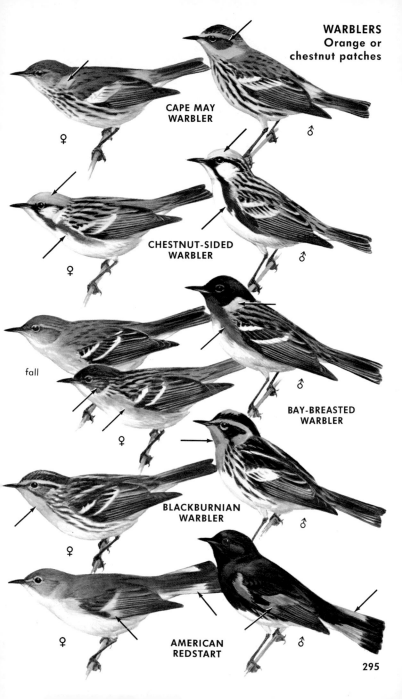

WARBLERS
Orange or
chestnut patches

CAPE MAY
WARBLER

♀

♂

CHESTNUT-SIDED
WARBLER

♀

♂

fall

♀

♂

BAY-BREASTED
WARBLER

BLACKBURNIAN
WARBLER

♀

♂

♀

AMERICAN
REDSTART

♂

PAINTED REDSTART *Myioborus picta* **M363**

5½″ (14 cm). Beautiful; postures with half-spread wings and tail, showing off *large white patches*. Black head and upperparts; *large bright red patch* on lower breast. Also called Painted Whitestart.

Voice: Song, a repetitious *weeta weeta weeta wee* or *weeta weeta chilp chilp chilp*. Note, an unwarbler-like *clee-ip*.

Range: Sw. U.S. to n. Nicaragua. Map 363. **Habitat:** Oak canyons, pine-oak forests in mountains.

RED-FACED WARBLER *Cardellina rubrifrons* **M362**

5–5½″ (13–14 cm). The only U.S. warbler with a *bright-red face*. It has a gray back, a black patch on the head, and a white nape.

Voice: A clear, sweet song, similar to that of Yellow Warbler.

Range: Sw. U.S. to Durango, Mexico. Map 362. Winters Mexico, Guatemala. **Habitat:** Open pine-oak forests in high mountains.

OLIVE WARBLER *Peucedramus taeniatus* **M365**

4½–5″ (11–13 cm). *Male:* Note the *orange-brown head and chest* and the *black ear patch. Female:* Duller crown, nape olive, breast yellowish. It has the dusky ear patch.

Voice: Song, a ringing *peter peter peter peter*. Variable.

Range: Sw. U.S. to Nicaragua. Map 365. **Habitat:** Pine and fir forests of high mountains.

COLIMA WARBLER *Vermivora crissalis*

5½″ (14 cm). Found in the high Chisos Mts. in Texas. Drab, with a *yellow rump* and undertail coverts. Larger than Virginia's Warbler; sides *brownish;* lacks yellow on the breast.

Voice: Song, "a simple trill, like that of Chipping Sparrow but more musical and ending in two lower notes" (J. Van Tyne).

Range: Breeds in w. Texas (Chisos Mts.), n.-cen. Mexico. Winters in Mexico to Colima, Guerrero. **Habitat:** Oak-pine canyons.

GRACE'S WARBLER *Dendroica graciae* **M348**

4½–5″ (11–13 cm). *Gray-backed, with a yellow throat,* two wing bars, *yellowish eyebrow stripe,* stripes on sides. Resembles Yellow-throated Warbler, which has a white patch behind the ear.

Voice: *Cheedle cheedle che che che che,* etc. (ends in a trill).

Range: Breeds from sw. U.S. to n. Nicaragua. Map 348. Winters south of U.S. **Habitat:** Pine-oak forests of mountains.

VIRGINIA'S WARBLER *Vermivora virginiae* **M338**

4–4½″ (10–11 cm). *Male:* A small *gray* warbler, with a *yellowish rump and undertail coverts,* narrow white eye-ring, rufous spot on the crown (usually concealed), and touch of yellow on the breast. Flicks tail. *Female* duller. Immature may lack the yellow.

Voice: Song, loose, colorless notes on nearly the same pitch; *chlip-chlip-chlip-chlip-chlip-wick-wick.*

Range: Sw. U.S. Map 338. Winters in s. Mexico. **Habitat:** Oak canyons, brushy slopes, pinyons.

LUCY'S WARBLER *Vermivora luciae* **M339**

4″ (10 cm). A small desert warbler; known by its *chestnut rump patch.* White eye-ring, small patch of chestnut on the crown.

Voice: A high *weeta weeta weeta che che che che,* on two pitches.

Range: Breeds sw. U.S., nw. Mexico. Map 339. **Habitat:** Mesquite along desert streams and washes; willows, cottonwoods.

Strictly western
specialties

WARBLERS

juvenile

adult

**PAINTED
REDSTART**

adult

**RED-FACED
WARBLER**

♂   **OLIVE WARBLER**   ♀

**COLIMA
WARBLER**

♂   **GRACE'S
WARBLER**

♂

Yellow-throated
Warbler, for
comparison

♂   **VIRGINIA'S
WARBLER**   ♀

♂   **LUCY'S WARBLER**   ♀

297

NASHVILLE WARBLER *Vermivora ruficapilla* **M337**

4¾" (12 cm). Note the *white eye-ring* in combination with the *yellow* throat. *Head gray*, contrasting with the olive-green back. No wing bars. The yellow undertail coverts are separated from the yellow of the belly by a white area. Males may show a dull chestnut crown patch (seldom visible).

Similar species: Male Connecticut Warbler also has a complete white eye-ring and lacks wing bars, but its throat is *grayish*.

Voice: Song, two-parted: *seebit, seebit, seebit, seebit, tititititi* (ends like Chipping Sparrow's song).

Range: S. Canada, w. and n. U.S. Winters to Honduras. **West:** Map 337. **Habitat:** Cool, open mixed woods with undergrowth; forest edges, bogs.

CONNECTICUT WARBLER *Oporornis agilis* **M356**

5¼–6" (13–15 cm). Similar to MacGillivray's and Mourning warblers (gray hood, yellow and olive body), but note the *complete white eye-ring*. Fall female and young are duller and lack the gray hood, but have a suggestion of one (a brownish stain across the upper breast). The eye-ring is always present. This species walks.

Similar species: (1) Breeding Mourning Warbler lacks eye-ring (in fall, often has a broken one). Breeding male has a black throat. The yellow undertail coverts reach the middle of the tail (nearly to the end in Connecticut). (2) Nashville Warbler also has an eye-ring, but the bird is much smaller. It has a *yellow throat* and is more active.

Voice: A repetitious *chip-chup-ee, chip-chup-ee, chip-chup-ee, chip,* or *sugar-tweet, sugar-tweet, sugar-tweet* (W. Gunn).

Range: Cen.-s. Canada, cen.-n. U.S. Winters n. S. America. **West:** Map 356. **Habitat:** Poplar bluffs, muskeg, mixed woods near water; in migration, undergrowth. Feeds mostly on the ground.

MOURNING WARBLER *Oporornis philadelphia* **M357**

5–5¾" (13–14 cm). Similar to MacGillivray's Warbler, but the male has *no* eye-ring. Female and immature may have a very light broken eye-ring and are therefore very difficult to separate from Mac-Gillivray's. See basic ranges on maps.

Voice: Song, *chirry, chirry, chorry, chorry* (*chorry* lower). Considerable variation.

Range: Canada, ne. U.S. Winters Nicaragua to nw. Amazonia. **West:** Map 357. **Habitat:** Clearings, thickets, slashings, undergrowth.

MacGILLIVRAY'S WARBLER *Oporornis tolmiei* **M358**

4¾–5½" (12–14 cm). *Male:* Olive above, yellow below, with a *slate-gray hood* (blackish on the throat) completely encircling the head and neck. *Partial white eye-ring is broken fore and aft. Female:* Similar, but the hood is much paler, washed out on the throat. Immature may have only a suggestion of the hood and is difficult to separate from immature Mourning Warbler, which breeds in Canada east of the Rockies.

Voice: Song, a rolling *chiddle-chiddle-chiddle, turtle-turtle,* last notes dropping; or *sweeter-sweeter-sweeter, sugar-sugar.*

Range: Breeds w. N. America. Map 358. Winters Sonora to w. Panama. **Habitat:** Low dense undergrowth; shady thickets.

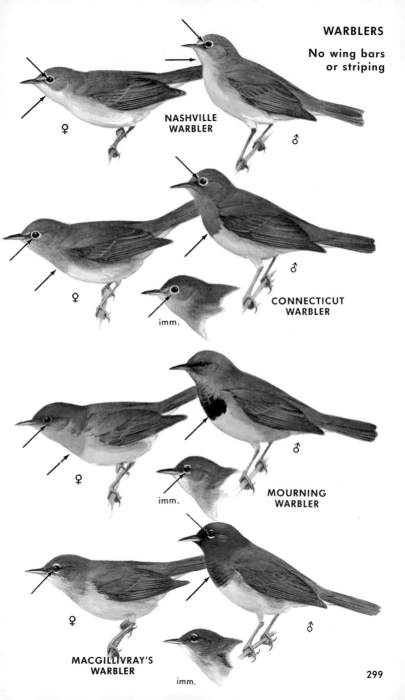

WARBLERS

No wing bars
or striping

♀   **NASHVILLE WARBLER**   ♂

♀   imm.   ♂   **CONNECTICUT WARBLER**

♀   imm.   ♂   **MOURNING WARBLER**

♀   **MACGILLIVRAY'S WARBLER**   imm.   ♂

YELLOW WARBLER *Dendroica petechia* **M340**

5" (13 cm). No other warbler is so extensively yellow. Even the *tail spots are yellow* (other warblers have white tail spots or none). Male has *rusty breast streaks* (in female, these are faint or lacking).
Voice: Song, a bright cheerful *tsee-tsee-tsee-tsee-titi-wee* or *weet weet weet weet tsee tsee*, given rapidly. Variable.
Range: Alaska, Canada to Peru. Winters Mexico to Peru. **West:** Map 340. **Habitat:** Bushes, swamp edges, streams, gardens.

PALM WARBLER *Dendroica palmarum* **M349**

4½–5½" (11–14 cm). Note the constant *bobbing* of the tail. Brown above; yellowish or whitish below, narrowly streaked; *yellow* undertail coverts, white spots in tail corners. In spring, has a *chestnut cap* (obscure in fall, winter). Sexes similar.
Voice: Song, weak, repetitious notes: *zhe-zhe-zhe-zhe-zhe-zhe.*
Range: Canada, ne. edge of U.S. Winters in s. U.S., Caribbean area.
West: Map 349. **Habitat:** Wooded borders of muskeg (summer). In migration, low trees, bushes, ground. A ground-loving warbler.

ORANGE-CROWNED WARBLER *Vermivora celata* **M336**

4½–5½" (11–14 cm). Dingy, without wing bars or other distinctive marks; olive-green above, greenish yellow below. Note the faint breast streaks and lack of wing bars. "Orange" of crown is seldom visible. In fall and winter many birds are quite gray.
Similar species: Autumn Tennessee Warbler has white undertail coverts.
Voice: Song, a colorless trill, becoming weaker toward the end. Often changes pitch, rising then dropping.
Range: Alaska, Canada, w. U.S. Winters to Guatemala. **West:** Map 336. **Habitat:** Brushy clearings, aspens, undergrowth.

TENNESSEE WARBLER *Vermivora peregrina* **M335**

4¾" (12 cm). Quite plain. *Male, spring:* Note the white eyebrow stripe and *gray head contrasting with its greenish back. Female, spring:* Similar; head less gray, underparts slightly yellowish. *Fall:* Greenish; note the *unstreaked* yellowish breast, strong yellowish eyebrow stripe, and trace of a wing bar. A vireo-like species.
Similar species: (1) Autumn Orange-crowned Warbler has yellow undertail coverts. (2) See also vireos without wing bars (pp. 286, 287).
Voice: Song, staccato, two- or three-parted: *ticka ticka ticka ticka, swit swit, chew-chew-chew-chew-chew* (Gunn). Suggests Nashville Warbler's song, but louder, more tirelessly repeated.
Range: Canada, ne. edge of U.S. Winters Mexico to Venezuela. **West:** Map 335. **Habitat:** Deciduous and mixed forests; in migration, groves, brush.

ARCTIC WARBLER *Phylloscopus borealis* Family Musicapidae

4¾" (12 cm). A small, plain, Old World warbler. Dull greenish brown above, whitish below; light stripe over eye, a trace of a narrow whitish wing bar; pale legs. Sexes similar. Keep in mind Orange-crowned and Tennessee warblers.
Voice: Song, a repeated *tchick* followed by a short trill.
Range: Near tree limit, n. Eurasia, Alaska. Winters tropical Asia.
West: Breeds in w. Alaska from w. Brooks Range, Colville R., south to Katmai, Mt. McKinley, Denali. **Habitat:** Willow scrub.

WARBLERS
Olive or yellowish

immature

♂

**YELLOW
WARBLER**

♀

breeding

**PALM
WARBLER**

winter

rthern

typical
sexes similar

**ORANGE-
CROWNED
WARBLER**

immature

breeding

♂

♀

fall

**TENNESSEE
WARBLER**

**ARCTIC
WARBLER**

(an Old World
Warbler)

COMMON YELLOWTHROAT *Geothlypis trichas* **M359**

4½–5½" (11–14 cm). Wren-like. *Male* with a *black (Lone Ranger) mask*, yellow throat. *Female* and *immature:* Olive-brown, with a rich yellow throat, buffy yellow breast; no black mask. Known from similar warblers by its whitish belly, tan sides, and habitat.

Voice: A bright rapid chant, *witchity-witchity-witchity-witch;* sometimes *witchy-witchy-witchy-witch.* Note, a husky *tchep.*

Range: Canada to s. Mexico. Winters s. U.S. to W. Indies, Panama. **West:** Map 359. **Habitat:** Swamps, marshes, wet thickets, edges.

YELLOW-BREASTED CHAT *Icteria virens* **M364**

7" (18 cm). Note the *white* "spectacles," bright *yellow* throat and breast. No wing bars. Size (very large for a warbler), bill, long tail, actions, and habitat suggest a mimic thrush.

Voice: Repeated whistles, alternating with harsh notes and soft *caw's.* Suggests a Mockingbird, but repertoire more limited; much longer pauses between phrases. Single notes: *whoit, kook,* etc.

Range: S. Canada to cen. Mexico. Winters s. U.S. to Panama. **West:** Map 364. **Habitat:** Brushy tangles, briars, stream thickets.

WILSON'S WARBLER *Wilsonia pusilla* **M360**

4¾" (12 cm). *Male:* Golden, with a *round black cap. Female* may show trace of a cap; immature does not. They are small, golden-looking birds with a yellow stripe above the beady eye.

Voice: Song, a thin, rapid little chatter, dropping in pitch at the end: *chi chi chi chi chi chet chet.*

Range: Alaska, Canada, w. and ne. U.S. Winters Mexico to Panama. **West:** Map 360. **Habitat:** Thickets along wooded streams, moist tangles, low shrubs, willows, alders.

HOODED WARBLER *Wilsonia citrina*

5½" (14 cm). The *black hood* or cowl of the *male* encircles the yellow face and forehead. *Female* and *young* lack the hood, although the yellow face may be sharply outlined in some females. Aside from *white tail spots,* they may lack other marks.

Range: E. and cen. U.S. Winters in Cen. America. **West:** Casual or accidental vagrant in most western states. **Habitat:** Forest undergrowth.

NORTHERN PARULA *Parula americana*

4½" (11 cm). Bluish, with a yellow throat and breast and two white wing bars. A suffused *greenish patch* on back. The male's best mark is a *dark breastband* (indistinct or lacking in the female).

Voice: Song, a buzzy trill or rattle that climbs the scale and trips over the top: *zeeeeeeeee-up.* Also *zh-zh-zh-zheeeeee.*

Range: Se. Canada, e. U.S. Winters Florida, Mexico to W. Indies, Nicaragua. **West:** Rare or casual vagrant west to Pacific states, but found annually in California (has bred there).

NORTHERN WATERTHRUSH Text on p. 304.

OVENBIRD *Seiurus aurocapillus* **M354**

6" (15 cm). When breeding, more often heard than seen. Usually seen walking on pale *pinkish* legs on the leafy floor of the woods. Suggests a small thrush, but striped rather than spotted beneath. *Orangish patch on the crown.* Song, an emphatic *teach'er,* *TEACH'ER,* **TEACH'ER,** etc., in crescendo. In some areas, monosyllabic, *TEACH, TEACH, TEACH,* etc. (continued on p. 304)

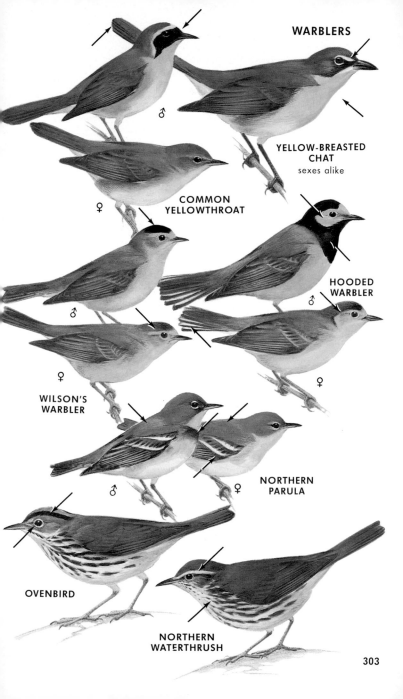

WARBLERS

YELLOW-BREASTED CHAT
sexes alike

♂

♀ **COMMON YELLOWTHROAT**

♂

HOODED WARBLER
♂

♀

♀ **WILSON'S WARBLER**

♂ ♀ **NORTHERN PARULA**

OVENBIRD

NORTHERN WATERTHRUSH

OVENBIRD (continued). **Range:** S. Canada, U.S. mainly east of Rockies. Winters se. U.S. to n. S. America. **West:** Map 354. **Habitat:** Near ground in leafy woods; in migration, thickets.

NORTHERN WATERTHRUSH *Seiurus noveboracensis*   **M355**
(Illustrated on p. 303.) 6″ (15 cm). Suggests a small thrush. *Walks* along the water's edge and *teeters* like a Spotted Sandpiper. Brown-backed, with *striped* underparts, strong eyebrow stripe.
Voice: Note, a sharp *chip.* Song, a vigorous, rapid *twit twit twit sweet sweet sweet chew chew chew* (*chew's* drop in pitch).
Range: Alaska, Canada, n. edge of U.S. Winters mainly in tropics. **West:** Map 355. **Habitat:** Swampy or wet woods, streamsides, lake shores; in migration, also thickets.

■ **MISCELLANEOUS STRAY WARBLERS FROM THE EAST.** For further details see the eastern *Field Guide to the Birds.*

PROTHONOTARY WARBLER *Protonotaria citrea*
5½″ (14 cm). A bird of wooded swamps. Head and breast deep yellow. Wings blue-gray, with no bars. Female duller. Casual stray, Colo., N.M., Ariz., Calif. Accidental, Ore., Wash.

PINE WARBLER *Dendroica pinus*
5–5½″ (13–14 cm). Yellow-breasted, with *white wing bars;* no other obvious field marks. Breast dimly streaked; back *unstreaked.* White spots in tail corners. Female duller; autumn birds often obscure (see eastern *Field Guide*). Casual west to Great Plains. Accidental, coast of Calif. Not always in pines.

BLUE-WINGED WARBLER *Vermivora pinus*
4½–5″ (11–13 cm). Face and underparts yellow; wings blue-gray, with *two white bars.* Note the narrow *black mark through the eye.* Accidental, Colo., Utah, N.M., Ariz., Calif.

WORM-EATING WARBLER *Helmitheros vermivorus*
5–5½″ (13–14 cm). A modest forager of leafy wooded slopes. Dull olive, with *black stripes* on a buffy head. Breast rich buff. Accidental, Wyo., Nev. Casual stray w. Texas, Colo., N.M., Ariz., Calif., Nev., Wyo., Sask.

PRAIRIE WARBLER *Dendroica discolor*
5″ (13 cm). *Bobs its tail* (like Palm Warbler). Yellow below; black stripes *confined to the sides. Two black face marks;* one through the eye, one below. Very rare but regular fall vagrant, Calif. Accidental, Ore., Mont., Colo., Ariz., N.M.

KENTUCKY WARBLER *Oporornis formosus*
5½″ (14 cm). Black *sideburns* below the eyes; *yellow "spectacles."* Casual stray through sw. border states to Calif. Accidental, Nev., Colo., Wyo., Mont., Sask., Alaska.

GOLDEN-WINGED WARBLER *Vermivora chrysoptera*
5–5½″ (13–14 cm). Note the combination of *yellow wing patch* and *black throat* (female, gray); also yellow forehead, black ear patch. Accidental, Idaho, Ore., Colo., N.M., Ariz., Calif.

YELLOW-THROATED WARBLER *Dendroica dominica*
5–5½″ (13–14 cm). Very similar to Grace's Warbler, but note the *white patch* behind the ear. Creeps about branches. Accidental west to Rocky Mt. states; very rare in Southwest to Calif.

WARBLERS
Mostly eastern strays

PROTHONOTARY
WARBLER

♂

♀

PINE
WARBLER

♂

immature

BLUE-WINGED
WARBLER

♂

WORM-EATING
WARBLER

PRAIRIE
WARBLER

♂

♀

KENTUCKY
WARBLER

♂

GOLDEN-WINGED
WARBLER

♂

♀

YELLOW-THROATED
WARBLER

♂

Grace's Warbler,
for comparison

♂

305

■ BLACKBIRDS, ORIOLES, etc. Family Emberizidae. Subfamily Icterinae.

A varied group of birds with conical, sharp-pointed bills and rather flat profiles. Collectively known as "icterids." Some are black and iridescent; others, such as orioles (p. 313), are highly colored. Sexes usually not alike. **Food:** Insects, small fruits, seeds, waste grain, small aquatic life. **Range:** New World; most in tropics. **No. of species:** World 94; West 16 (+2 casual or accidental).

BREWER'S BLACKBIRD *Euphagus cyanocephalus*   M421
9" (23 cm). A very common and familiar blackbird. *Male:* All black, with a whitish eye; in good light, *purplish* reflections may be seen on the head and greenish reflections on the body. *Female:* Brownish gray, with a *dark* eye.
Similar species: Breeding male Rusty Blackbird has dull *greenish* head reflections (hard to see); the bill is longer. Female Rusty has a *light* eye. Unlike the Rusty (both sexes), Brewer's does not acquire an extensive rusty look in fall and winter (but may have a trace).
Voice: Song, a harsh wheezy, creaking *ksh-eee*. Note, *chack*.
Range: Sw. Canada, w. and n.-cen. U.S. Winters to s. Mexico. **West:** Map 421. **Habitat:** Fields, prairies, farms, parks.

RUSTY BLACKBIRD *Euphagus carolinus*   M420
9" (23 cm). Rusty only in fall or winter; otherwise suggests Brewer's Blackbird. *Male, spring:* A Robin-sized blackbird with a pale yellow eye. Black head of breeding male may show faint *greenish* gloss (not purplish). *Female, spring:* Slate-colored, with a *light eye. Fall and winter adults:* Washed with rusty; males *barred* below.
Voice: Note, a loud *chack*. "Song," a split creak, like a rusty hinge: *kush-a-lee*, alternating with *ksh-lay*.
Range: Alaska, Canada, ne. edge of U.S. Winters mainly to se. U.S. **West:** Map 420. **Habitat:** River groves, wooded swamps; muskeg.

COMMON GRACKLE *Quiscalus quiscula*   M423
11–13½" (28–34 cm). *Male:* A large, *very iridescent*, yellow-eyed blackbird, larger than a Robin, with a long, wedge-shaped or *keel-shaped tail*. Flight more level than that of other blackbirds. Iridescent purple on head, deep bronze on back. Females are somewhat smaller and duller; juveniles are sooty, with dark eyes.
Voice: Note, *chuck* or *chack*. "Song," a split rasping note.
Range: Canada, U.S., mainly east of Rockies. **West:** Map 423. **Habitat:** Croplands, towns, groves, streamsides.

GREAT-TAILED GRACKLE *Quiscalus mexicanus*   M422
Male, 18" (45 cm); female, 14" (35 cm). Male, a very large, purple-glossed blackbird, much larger than the Common Grackle and with a longer, more ample tail. Female is much smaller than the male; brown, with a pale breast. Adults have yellow eyes.
Voice: A harsh *check check check*; also a high *kee-kee-kee-kee*. Shrill, discordant notes, whistles, and clucks. A rapid, upward-slurring *ma-ree*.
Range: Sw. U.S. to Peru. **West:** Map 422. **Habitat:** Groves, thickets, farms, towns, city parks.

ICTERIDS
(BLACKBIRDS, GRACKLES)

♀

♂ fall

♂ breeding

**BREWER'S
BLACKBIRD**

♀

♂ fall

♂ breeding

**RUSTY
BLACKBIRD**

♀

♂

**COMMON
GRACKLE**

♂

Cowbird, for
comparison

winter

breeding

Starling,
for
comparison

♀

**GREAT-TAILED
GRACKLE**

307

RED-WINGED BLACKBIRD *Agelaius phoeniceus* **M415**

7–9½″ (18–24 cm). *Male:* Black, with *bright red epaulets*, most conspicuous in spring display. Much of the time the scarlet is concealed and only the yellowish margin shows. *Immature male:* Sooty brown, mottled, but with red shoulders. *Female:* Brownish, with a sharply pointed bill, "blackbird" appearance, and *well-defined dark stripings* below; may have pinkish tinge around throat. Gregarious, traveling and roosting in flocks. One race, the "Bicolored Blackbird" of cen. California, has solid red epaulets *without* the yellow border.
Voice: Notes, a loud *check* and a high, slurred *tee-err.* Song, a liquid, gurgling *konk-la-ree* or *o-ka-lay.*
Range: Canada to W. Indies, Costa Rica. **West:** Map 415. **Habitat:** Breeds in marshes, brushy swamps, hayfields; forages also in cultivated land, along edges of water, etc.

TRICOLORED BLACKBIRD *Agelaius tricolor* **M416**

7½–9″ (19–23 cm). *Male:* Similar to the Red-winged Blackbird, but the red shoulder patch is darker, with a conspicuous *white margin.* *Female:* Much darker than most races of the Red-wing; bill thicker at the base, more sharply pointed. Highly gregarious. Nests in dense colonies often numbering many thousands, whereas the Red-wing is territorial.
Voice: More nasal than Red-wing's: *on-ke-kaangh.* A nasal *kemp.*
Range: Breeds from s. Oregon to nw. Baja California. Map 416. **Habitat:** Cattail or tule marshes; forages in fields, farms.

YELLOW-HEADED BLACKBIRD **M419**
Xanthocephalus xanthocephalus

8–11″ (20–28 cm). *Male:* A Robin-sized marsh blackbird, with an *orange-yellow head and breast;* in flight, shows a *white wing patch.* *Female:* Smaller and browner; most of the yellow is confined to the throat and chest; lower breast streaked with white. Gregarious.
Voice: Song, low, hoarse rasping notes produced with much effort; suggests rusty hinges. Note, a low *kruck* or *kack.*
Range: S. Canada, w. U.S., upper Mississippi Valley to nw. Mexico. Winters sw. U.S., Mexico. **West:** Map 419. **Habitat:** Fresh marshes. Forages in fields, open country.

BOBOLINK *Dolichonyx oryzivorus* **M414**

6–8″ (15–20 cm). *Male, spring:* Our only songbird that is *solid black below and largely white above,* suggesting a dress suit on backward. Has a buff-yellow nape. *Female and autumn male:* A bit larger than a House Sparrow; rich buff, with dark stripings on crown and back. Bill is more like a sparrow's than a blackbird's.
Similar species: (1) Male Lark Bunting has white confined to wings; (2) female Red-wing is heavily striped below and has a longer bill.
Voice: Song, in hovering flight and quivering descent, ecstatic and bubbling: starts with low, reedy notes and rollicks upward. Flight note, a clear *pink,* often heard overhead in migration.
Range: S. Canada, n. U.S. Winters in s. S. America. **West:** Map 414.
Habitat: Hayfields, meadows. In migration, marshes.

ICTERIDS
(BLACKBIRDS, etc.)

red epaulettes
hidden

♂

**RED-WINGED
BLACKBIRD**

♀

♂

imm. ♂
Red-winged

bicolored
form

♀

♂

**TRICOLORED
BLACKBIRD**

Tricolored

♂

♀

**YELLOW-HEADED
BLACKBIRD**

♀

♂

♀

BOBOLINK

♂ fall

EASTERN MEADOWLARK *Sturnella magna* M417

9″ (23 cm). Nearly identical with Western Meadowlark; darker brown above; yellow of throat does not invade the cheek. Easily recognized by song. Pale southwestern form has more white in the tail.

Voice: Song, unlike the flutelike gurgling of Western Meadowlark, is composed of two clear, slurred whistles, musical and pulled out, *tee-yah, tee-yair* (last note skewy and descending). Note, a rasping or buzzy *dzrrt;* also a guttural chatter.

Range: Se. Canada through e. and cen. U.S. to Brazil. **West:** Map 417. **Habitat:** Open fields and pastures, meadows, prairies.

WESTERN MEADOWLARK *Sturnella neglecta* M418

9″ (23 cm). In grassy country, a chunky brown bird flushes, showing a conspicuous patch of *white* on each side of its short wide tail. Several rapid wingbeats alternate with short glides. Should it perch on a post, the glass reveals a bright yellow breast crossed by a *black V.* Walking, the bird flicks its tail open and shut. Starling shape.

Voice: Song variable; 7–10 flutelike notes, gurgling and double-noted, unlike the clear whistles of Eastern Meadowlark. Note, *chupp,* lower than the rasping *dzrrt* of Eastern Meadowlark.

Range: Sw. Canada, through w. U.S. to highlands of cen. Mexico. **West:** Map 418. **Habitat:** Grasslands, cultivated fields and pastures, meadows, prairies.

BROWN-HEADED COWBIRD *Molothrus ater* M424

7″ (18 cm). A rather small blackbird with a short, sparrow-like bill. *Male:* Black, with a *brown head. Female:* Mouse-gray with a lighter throat; note the short *finch-like bill. Juvenile:* Paler than female—buffy gray, with soft breast streaks; often seen being fed by smaller birds whose nests have been parasitized. Young males in late summer molt may be bizarrely patterned with tan and black. When flocking or with other blackbirds, Cowbirds are smaller and feed on the ground with their tails lifted high.

Similar species: Gray female Cowbird can be told from (1) female Brewer's and (2) female Rusty Blackbird by its stubby bill and smaller size. (3) Young Starling has a longer bill and a shorter tail.

Voice: Flight call, *weee-titi* (high whistle, two lower notes). Song, a bubbly and creaky *glug-glug-gleeee.* Note, *chuck.*

Range: S. Canada to Mexico. **West:** Map 424. **Habitat:** Farms, fields, barnyards, roadsides, wood edges, river groves.

BRONZED COWBIRD *Molothrus aeneus*

6½–8¾″ (16–22 cm). *Male:* Larger than Brown-headed Cowbird; does *not* have a brown head. Bill longer. Red eye can be seen only at close range. In breeding season, a conspicuous *ruff* on the nape. *Female:* Smaller, with a smaller ruff; dull blackish, much like male, not gray like female of other Cowbird.

Voice: High-pitched mechanical creakings.

Range: Southwestern U.S. to w. Panama. Summers in extreme se. California, cen. and s. Arizona, sw. New Mexico, s. Texas (north to Eagle Pass). Winters in s. Arizona (rarely), s. Texas. **Habitat:** Croplands, brush, semi-open country, feedlots.

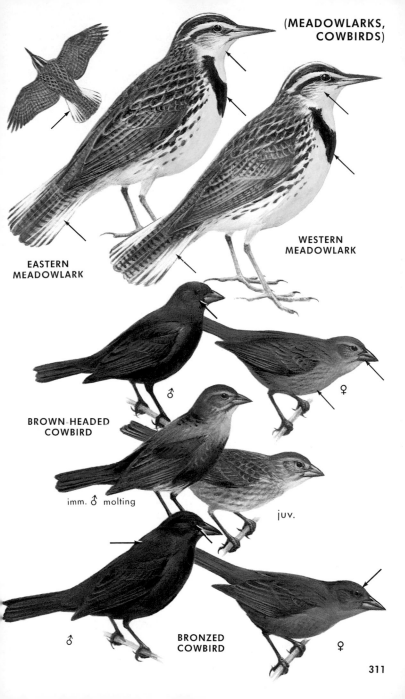

(MEADOWLARKS, COWBIRDS)

EASTERN MEADOWLARK

WESTERN MEADOWLARK

BROWN-HEADED COWBIRD

♂

♀

imm. ♂ molting

juv.

BRONZED COWBIRD

♂

♀

■ **ORIOLES.** Smaller, slimmer than a Robin; a brightly colored genus (*Icterus*) of subfamily Icterinae (blackbirds, etc.).

"BALTIMORE" ORIOLE or NORTHERN ORIOLE (in part)   M426
Icterus galbula galbula
7–8" (18–20 cm). *Male:* Flame-orange and black, with a solid black head. *Female and young:* Olive-brown above, burnt orange-yellow below; two white wing bars. Some females may have traces of black on the head, suggesting the hood of the male.
Note: This eastern form of the Northern Oriole was formerly regarded as a separate species; systematists may yet restore it.
Voice: S. Rich, piping whistles. Note, a low, whistled *hewli.*
Range: S. Canada, e. and cen. U.S. Winters se. U.S. to Venezuela.
West: Map 426. **Habitat:** Open woods, elms, shade trees.

"BULLOCK'S" ORIOLE or NORTHERN ORIOLE (in part)   M426
Icterus galbula bullockii
7–8½" (18–21 cm). The western form. *Male:* Differs from male "Baltimore" by *orange cheeks, large white wing patches,* tail pattern. *Female:* Differs from female "Baltimore" by grayer back, *whiter belly. Immature male:* Similar to female, but throat black.
Voice: Accented double notes and one or two piping notes.
Range: Breeds sw. Canada, w. U.S., n. Mexico. Winters s. U.S. to Guatemala. **West:** Map 426. Breeds east to Great Plains (S. Dakota, cen. Nebraska, w. Kansas, w. Oklahoma), where it may hybridize with "Baltimore" Oriole.

HOODED ORIOLE *Icterus cucullatus*   M425
7½" (19 cm). *Male:* Orange and black, with a black throat and an *orange crown.* In winter, back obscurely scaled. *Female:* Similar to female Bullock's Oriole, but entire underparts yellowish; bill longer, more curved. Back olive-gray; head and tail more yellowish.
Voice: Song, throaty notes and piping whistles: *chut chut chut whew whew;* opening notes throaty. Note, a sharp *eek* or *wheenk.*
Range: Breeds sw. U.S. to s. Mexico. Map 425. Winters in Mexico; rarely sw. U.S. **Habitat:** Open woods, shade trees, palms.

SCOTT'S ORIOLE *Icterus parisorum*   M427
7¾" (19 cm). *Male:* Solid black head and back and *lemon-yellow* pattern distinguish it. *Female:* More greenish yellow beneath than most other females (except Orchard Oriole). *Immature male:* Throat black; similar to other young male orioles, but more black on face.
Voice: Song, rich whistles; suggests Western Meadowlark.
Range: Sw. U.S., n. Mexico. Map 427. **Habitat:** Dry woods and scrub in desert mountains, yucca "forests," Joshua-trees, pinyons.

ORCHARD ORIOLE *Icterus spurius*   M416
6–7" (15–18 cm). *Male:* An all-dark oriole. Rump and underparts *deep chestnut. Female, young:* Olive-green above, yellowish below; two white wing bars. *Immature male:* Black bib down to chest.
Voice: A fast-moving outburst interspersed with piping whistles and guttural notes. Suggests Purple Finch's song.
Range: Se. Canada, e. and cen. U.S. to cen. Mexico. Winters from Sinaloa to Venezuela. **West:** Map 416. **Habitat:** Wood edges, orchards, shade trees.

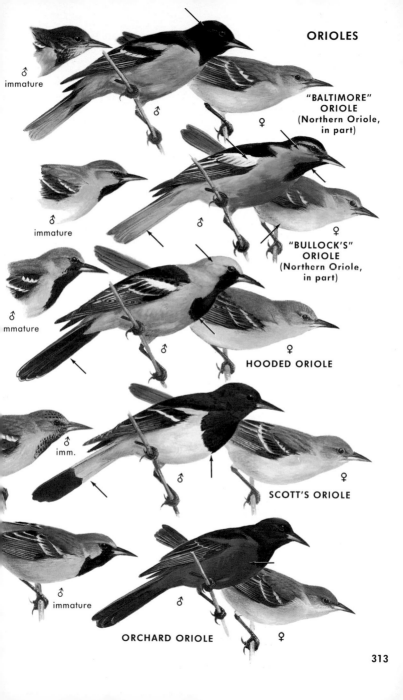

ORIOLES

♂
immature

"BALTIMORE" ORIOLE
(Northern Oriole, in part)

♂

♀

♂
immature

♂

♀

"BULLOCK'S" ORIOLE
(Northern Oriole, in part)

♂
immature

♂

♀

HOODED ORIOLE

♂
imm.

♂

♀

SCOTT'S ORIOLE

♂
immature

♂

♀

ORCHARD ORIOLE

■ **TANAGERS. Family Emberizidae** (in part). Subfamily Thraupinae. Male tanagers are brightly colored; females of our species are greenish above and yellow below, suggesting large, thick-billed vireos. Females may be confused with female orioles, but have darker cheeks and most species lack wing bars. The rather stout bills are *notched*. **Food:** Insects, fruits. **Range:** New World; most species in tropics. **No. of species:** World 215; West 4.

WESTERN TANAGER *Piranga ludoviciana*   M368
7″ (18 cm). The only U.S. tanager with strong *wing bars*. *Male:* Yellow, with a black back, wings, and tail, two wing bars, and a *red head*. The red disappears in autumn and winter. *Female:* Yellowish below; dull olive above, with white and yellow wing bars. Resembles female orioles (pp. 312, 313), but the tail and sides of the face are darker, and the bill is less sharply pointed.
Voice: Song, short phrases; similar to Robin's in form, but less sustained, hoarser. Note, a dry *pi-tic* or *pit-i-tic.*
Range: Western N. America; winters w. Mexico to Costa Rica. Map 368. **Habitat:** Open conifer or mixed forests; widespread in migration.

SUMMER TANAGER *Piranga rubra*   M367
7–7¾″ (18–19 cm). *Male: Rose-red all over*, with a *yellowish* bill; no crest. *Female:* Olive above, deep yellow below; yellowish bill. Young males acquiring adult plumage may be patched with red, yellow, and green.
Similar species: (1) Male Cardinal has a crest and a black face. (2) Hepatic Tanager is darker, with a blackish bill.
Voice: Note, a staccato *pi-tuk* or *pik-i-tuk-i-tuk.* Song, robin-like phrases, less nasal and resonant than Scarlet Tanager's.
Range: Cen. and s. U.S. to n. Mexico. Winters Mexico to Brazil. **West:** Map 367. **Habitat:** Woods, groves (especially oaks).

HEPATIC TANAGER *Piranga flava*   M366
7½″ (19 cm). *Male:* Darker than Summer Tanager; orange-red, with a *dark ear patch, blackish bill.* Male Summer Tanager is rosier, has a *pale yellow bill. Female:* Known from female Summer Tanager by its more orange-yellow throat, gray ear patch, *blackish bill.*
Voice: Song, very similar to Black-headed Grosbeak's (Summer Tanager sounds more like a Robin). Call note, a single *chuck.*
Range: Breeds sw. U.S. to Argentina. Winters mainly south of U.S. Map 366. **Habitat:** Open mountain forests, oaks, pines.

SCARLET TANAGER *Piranga olivacea*
7″ (18 cm). *Male: Flaming scarlet*, with *jet-black* wings and tail. *Female, immature*, and *winter male:* Dull greenish above, yellowish below; has dark *brownish or blackish wings*; normally no wing bars, but young birds may. Molting male patched with red.
Voice: Song, four or five short phrases, robin-like but hoarse (suggesting a Robin with a sore throat). Note, *chip-burr.*
Range: Se. Canada, e. U.S. Winters S. America. **West:** Breeds east of 100th meridian. In migration, a few wander onto Great Plains from Saskatchewan to Texas Panhandle. Rare or casual stray to sw. states, especially California. Accidental in Northwest to British Columbia, Alaska. **Habitat:** Forests and shade trees (especially oaks).

TANAGERS

breeding ♂

♂ winter

♀

WESTERN TANAGER

♂ all seasons

♀

♂ imm. changing to adult

SUMMER TANAGER

♀

♂ imm.

♂

HEPATIC TANAGER

♂

♀

changing

♂ winter

♂ breeding

♂ orange variant

SCARLET TANAGER

■ SPARROWS. Family Emberizidae (in part).

WHITE-THROATED SPARROW *Zonotrichia albicollis*   **M404**
6½–7″ (16–18 cm). A gray-breasted sparrow, similar to White-crown but browner, with a *well-defined white throat patch* and a *yellow spot* between the eye and bill. Bill *blackish*, not pink. Polymorphic; adults with *black and white head stripes* mate with birds having *brown and tan head stripes. Winter:* Duller; head stripes vary.
Voice: Song, several clear pensive whistles, easily imitated; one or two clear notes, followed by three quavering notes on a different pitch. Note, a slurred *tseet;* also a hard *chink.*
Range: Canada, ne. U.S. Winters to s. U.S., ne. Mexico (rarely).
West: Map 404. **Habitat:** Thickets, brush, undergrowth of conifer and mixed woodlands. Patronizes bird feeders.

WHITE-CROWNED SPARROW *Zonotrichia leucophrys*   **M406**
6½–7½″ (16–19 cm). *Adult:* Clear grayish breast and puffy crown *striped with black and white.* Bill *pink* or *yellowish. Immature:* Browner, with head stripes of dark red-brown and light buff; *bill pinkish.* In birds of high Sierra and Rockies, the white eyestripe extends *from the eye* instead of from the bill.
Voice: Song, one or more clear, plaintive whistles, followed by husky trilled whistles. Variable; many local dialects.
Range: Across Canada to Alaska; south through w. U.S. Winters w. and s. U.S., Mexico, Cuba. **West:** Map 406. **Habitat:** Brushland, forest edges, thickets, chaparral, gardens, parks; in winter also farms and desert washes. Patronizes feeders.

GOLDEN-CROWNED SPARROW *Zonotrichia atricapilla*   **M405**
6–7″ (15–18 cm). Similar to White-crowned Sparrow, but without white head stripes; instead a *dull yellow central crown stripe,* usually bordered broadly with black. Immature birds and some winter adults may look like large female House Sparrows, but are longer-tailed and darker, usually with a dull yellow suffusion on the fore-crown. Some lack the yellow and have little to distinguish them except the fine streaking on the crown.
Voice: Song, 3–5 high whistled notes of plaintive minor quality, coming down the scale, "oh-dear-me." Sometimes a faint trill.
Range: Nw. N. America, wintering through Pacific states. Map 405.
Habitat: Boreal scrub, spruce; in winter, similar to that of White-crown, but Golden-crown favors denser shrubs.

HARRIS'S SPARROW *Zonotrichia querula*   **M407**
7½″ (19 cm). Large; size of Fox Sparrow. In breeding plumage, has a *black crown, face, and bib encircling a pink bill.* In winter adults, the black crown is scaled with gray. First-winter young have *white on the throat,* less black on the crown, buffy brown on the rest of the head; blotched and streaked on the breast. In the second winter the chin is black.
Voice: Song has quavering quality of White-throat's: clear whistles on same pitch, or one or two at one pitch, the rest slightly lower; general effect *minor.* Alarm note, *wink.*
Range: N.-cen. Canada. Winters s.-cen. U.S. **West:** Map 407. **Habitat:** Stunted boreal forest; in winter, brush, open woods.

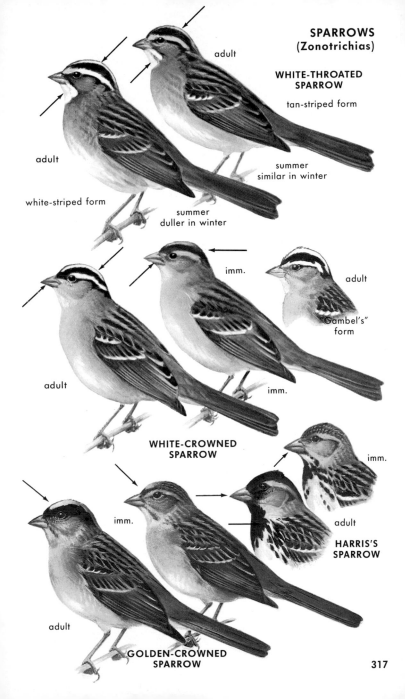

SPARROWS (Zonotrichias)

WHITE-THROATED SPARROW

tan-striped form

adult

summer
similar in winter

adult

white-striped form

summer
duller in winter

imm.

adult

"Gambel's" form

adult

imm.

WHITE-CROWNED SPARROW

imm.

imm.

adult

HARRIS'S SPARROW

adult

GOLDEN-CROWNED SPARROW

LARK SPARROW *Chondestes grammacus* **M391**
5½–6½" (14–16 cm). Note the *black tail with much white in the corners;* also the single dark *central breast spot* and *quail-like head pattern,* with the chestnut ear patch and striped crown. Young birds are duller; finely streaked on the sides of the breast.
Voice: A broken song; clear notes and trills with pauses between; characterized by buzzing and churring passages.
Range: S. Canada south (west of Appalachians) to n. Mexico. Winters s. U.S. to El Salvador. **West:** Map 391. **Habitat:** Open country with bushes, trees; pastures, farms, roadsides.

SAGE SPARROW *Amphispiza belli* **M393**
5–6" (13–15 cm). A gray sparrow of arid brush. Note the combination of a *single breast spot* and *heavy dark "whiskers" on each side of the throat.* Dark cheek, white eye-ring, touch of whitish over the eye. "Bell's" Sparrow, a race resident west of the Sierra in California, was until recently regarded as a distinct species. It is much darker, with heavier black whiskers.
Voice: Song, four to seven notes, *tsit-tsoo-tseee-tsay* (third note highest). Or, *tsit, tsit, tsi you, tee a-tee.*
Range: Western U.S. to n. Mexico. Map 393. **Habitat:** Dry brushy foothills; chaparral, sage; in winter, also deserts.

FIVE-STRIPED SPARROW *Amphispiza quinquestriata*
6" (15 cm). A rare Mexican sparrow. *Dusky,* with *five white stripes* on the head (white throat, eyebrows, and jaw lines) and a single black spot on the dark gray breast.
Range: Very local in se. Arizona; found in dense shrubs on dry canyon slopes, rocky arid hillsides.

BLACK-THROATED SPARROW *Amphispiza bilineata* **M392**
4¾–5¼" (12–13 cm). Note the face pattern. A pretty, gray desert sparrow, with *white face stripes* and a *jet-black throat and chest.* Young birds lack the black throat, but have a similar cheek pattern; the breast is finely streaked.
Similar species: (1) Young birds somewhat resemble Sage Sparrow. (2) Black-throated Gray Warbler (similar face pattern) has wing bars and a thin, warbler-like bill (see p. 293).
Voice: Song, a sweet *cheet cheet cheeeeeeee* (two short, clear opening notes and a fine trill on a lower or higher pitch).
Range: Western U.S., n. Mexico. Map 392. **Habitat:** Arid brush, creosote-bush deserts, "cholla gardens."

BLACK-CHINNED SPARROW *Spizella atrogularis* **M389**
5–5½" (13–14 cm). A somewhat junco-like sparrow (with no white in the tail); it has a streaked brown back, but *head and underparts are gray.* In the male the *pinkish bill* is encircled by a *black chin* and facial patch. Females lack the black and can be told by the *unmarked gray head and breast,* striped brown back.
Voice: Song, a series of notes on about the same pitch, or descending slightly; starts with several high, thin, clear notes and ends in a rough trill, *sweet, sweet, sweet, weet-trrrrrrr.*
Range: Sw. U.S. to s. Mexico. **West:** Map 389. **Habitat:** Brushy mountain slopes, open chaparral, sagebrush.

SPARROWS

LARK SPARROW

adult

juvenile

SAGE SPARROW

"Bell's" form (coastal)

adult

juvenile

adult

adult

FIVE-STRIPED SPARROW

LACK-THROATED SPARROW

adult

juv.

BLACK-CHINNED SPARROW

♂

♀

CHIPPING SPARROW *Spizella passerina* **M385**

5¼" (13 cm). *Breeding:* A small, gray-breasted sparrow with a bright *rufous cap*, a *black line* through the eye, and a *white line* over it. *Winter:* Browner, not so gray-breasted; cap and eyebrow line duller. *Immature:* Browner; light crown stripe, *gray* rump.
Similar species: See Clay-colored Sparrow.
Voice: Song, a chipping rattle on one pitch. Note, a dry *chip.*
Range: Canada to Nicaragua. Winters s. U.S. to Nicaragua. **West:** Map 385. **Habitat:** Open woods, conifers, especially yellow pine, Douglas fir; orchards, farms, towns.

FIELD SPARROW *Spizella pusilla* **M388**

5" (13 cm). Note the *pink bill* of this rusty-capped sparrow. A narrow light *eye-ring* gives it a big-eyed expression. It has rather rusty upperparts and a clear breast; facial striping less noticeable than on the other rusty-capped sparrows. The juvenile has a finely streaked breast; note the eye-ring.
Voice: Song, opening on deliberate, sweet, slurring notes, speeding into a trill (which ascends, descends, or stays on the same pitch). Note, *tsee;* has a querulous quality.
Range: Se. Canada, U.S. (east of Rockies). Winters to ne. Mexico. **West:** Map 388. **Habitat:** Bushy pastures, brush, scrub, feeders.

SWAMP SPARROW *Melospiza georgiana* **M403**

5–5¾" (13–14 cm). A rather stout, dark, rusty-winged sparrow with a dull gray breast, outlined *white throat, rusty cap. No prominent wing bars.* Winter birds and immatures are dimly streaked and have little rusty on the striped crown. They are sometimes misidentified as Lincoln's Sparrow (p. 324).
Voice: Song, a loose trill, similar to Chipping Sparrow's, but slower, sweeter, and stronger (sometimes on two pitches simultaneously). Note, a hard *chink* similar to White-throat's.
Range: Canada (east of Rockies), ne. U.S. Winters s. U.S., n. Mexico. **West:** Map 403. **Habitat:** Fresh marshes with tussocks, bushes, or cattails; sedgy swamps.

AMERICAN TREE SPARROW *Spizella arborea* **M384**

6–6½" (15–16 cm). To identify this bird of the North, note the single *dark spot or "stickpin"* on the breast, and the *red-brown cap.* Bill dark above, yellow below; two white wing bars.
Voice: Song, sweet, variable, opening on one or two high clear notes. Note, *tseet;* feeding note, a musical *teelwit.*
Range: Alaska, n. Canada. Winters s. Canada to cen. U.S. **West:** Map 384. **Habitat:** Arctic scrub, willow thickets; in winter, brushy roadsides, weedy edges, marshes; may patronize feeders.

RUFOUS-CROWNED SPARROW *Aimophila ruficeps* **M383**

5–6" (13–15 cm). A dark sparrow of the arid Southwest, with a plain dusky breast, rufous cap, and rounded tail. Note the *black whisker* bordering the throat.
Voice: Song, stuttering, gurgling. Note, a nasal *dear, dear, dear.*
Range: Sw. U.S. Map 383. **Habitat:** Grassy or rocky slopes with sparse low bushes; open pine-oak woods.

RUSTY-CAPPED SPARROWS

sexes similar

winter

summer

CHIPPING SPARROW

juv.

for comparison with winter Chipping Sparrow, above

FIELD SPARROW

juv.

CLAY-COLORED SPARROW
(see next page)

SWAMP SPARROW

imm.

AMERICAN TREE SPARROW

RUFOUS-CROWNED SPARROW

CLAY-COLORED SPARROW *Spizella pallida* **M386**
5¼" (13 cm). Like a pale Chipping Sparrow, but buffier, with a *sharply outlined ear patch.* Chipping and Clay-colored sparrows are more obscure in fall and winter, with similar head markings, but the rump is *brown* in Clay-color, *gray* in Chipping.
Voice: Unbirdlike; 3–4 low, flat buzzes: *bzzz, bzzz, bzzz.*
Range: W. and cen. Canada, n.-cen. U.S. In winter, s. U.S. to Mexico. **West:** Map 386. **Habitat:** Scrub, brushy prairies, jack pines.

RUFOUS-WINGED SPARROW *Aimophila carpalis*
5–5½" (13–14 cm). An Arizona specialty. Suggests a Chipping Sparrow, but tail not notched. *Double black "whiskers;"* gray stripe through rufous crown. *Rufous shoulder* not easily seen.
Voice: Song, one or two sweet introductory notes and a rapid series of musical chips on one pitch.
Range: Resident from cen. to s. Arizona (local) and Sonora to Sinaloa. **Habitat:** Tall desert grass, thorn brush, desert hackberry.

BREWER'S SPARROW *Spizella breweri* **M387**
5¼" (13 cm). A small pale sparrow of the sagebrush. Clear-breasted; resembles a Chipping Sparrow but sandier; *crown finely streaked,* with no hint of a median line (as in Chipping and Clay-colored sparrows in fall and winter).
Voice: Song, long, musical buzzy trills on different pitches; sounds like a Chipping Sparrow trying to sing like a Canary.
Range: Breeds w. Canada, w. U.S. Winters s. U.S. to n. Mexico. Map 387. **Habitat:** Sagebrush, brushy plains; also near tree line in n. Rockies; in winter, also weedy fields.

GRASSHOPPER SPARROW *Ammodramus savannarum* **M397**
4½–5¼" (11–13 cm). A little sparrow of open fields, with a short sharp tail, flat head, and yellow shoulder (hard to see). Crown with a pale median stripe; note the relatively unstriped buffy breast. However, the juvenile (p. 327) has a streaked breast.
Voice: A thin dry buzz, *pi-tup zeeeeeeeeeee.*
Range: S. Canada to s. U.S., W. Indies; also Mexico to Ecuador. **West:** Map 397. **Habitat:** Grassland, hayfields, prairies.

BOTTERI'S SPARROW *Aimophila botterii*
5¼–6¼" (13–16 cm). Very local; nondescript. Cassin's Sparrow, breeding in the same habitat, is almost identical, but grayer. Botteri's has a buffy breast, plain brown tail. Best told by voice.
Voice: Song, a constant tinkling and "pitting," sometimes running into a dry trill on same pitch. Very unlike song of Cassin's.
Range: Se. Arizona (local), s. tip of Texas to Costa Rica. Winters south of U.S. **Habitat:** In Arizona, desert grass.

CASSIN'S SPARROW *Aimophila cassinii* **M382**
5½" (14 cm). A drab sparrow of open arid country; underparts dingy without markings, or with faint streaking on flanks. *Pale or whitish tips* on gray-brown outer tail feathers. Best clue is the "skylarking" song. Botteri's Sparrow (very local) does not skylark.
Voice: Song, one or two short notes, a high sweet trill, and two lower notes: *ti ti tseeeeeee tay tay;* vaguely suggests Savannah Sparrow. Often "skylarks" in the air, giving trill at climax.
Range: Sw. U.S., ne. Mexico. Map 382. **Habitat:** Grassland, bushes.

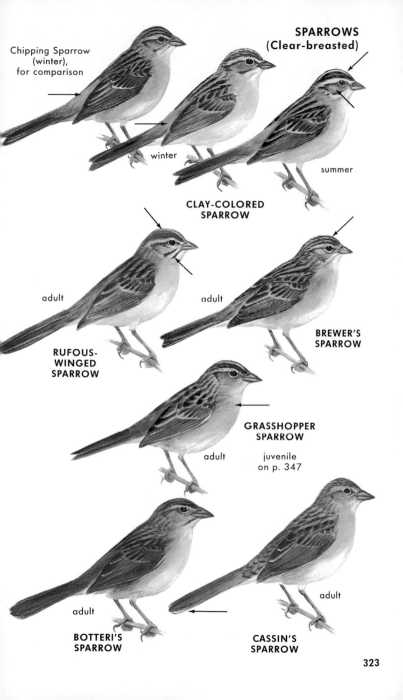

SPARROWS
(Clear-breasted)

Chipping Sparrow
(winter),
for comparison

winter

summer

CLAY-COLORED
SPARROW

adult

adult

RUFOUS-
WINGED
SPARROW

BREWER'S
SPARROW

GRASSHOPPER
SPARROW

adult

juvenile
on p. 347

adult

adult

BOTTERI'S
SPARROW

CASSIN'S
SPARROW

FOX SPARROW *Passerella iliaca* **M400**

6¾–7½" (17–19 cm). Larger than a House Sparrow; most forms have a *rusty rump and tail*. Action towhee-like, kicking among dead leaves. Breast heavily streaked with triangular spots, shaped like inverted V's; these often cluster in a large blotch on the upper breast. Fox Sparrows vary widely. Many races; can be roughly divided into three basic types: (1) bright rusty (northern and eastern); (2) dusky head, back, and upper breast (humid Northwest); (3) gray-headed, large yellowish bills (Rockies, Great Basin, Sierra). It is frustrating to try to separate them further; in winter they intermingle.
Voice: Song, brilliant and musical; a varied arrangement of short clear notes and sliding whistles.
Range: Alaska, Canada; western mountains to cen.-w. U.S. Winters to s. U.S. **West:** Map 400. **Habitat:** Wooded undergrowth, brush.

SONG SPARROW *Melospiza melodia* **M401**

5–6½" (13–16 cm). The heavy breast streaks merge into a *large central spot*. The bird pumps its rounded tail as it flies. Young birds, more finely streaked, often lack the central spot. Song Sparrows vary widely in color and size, as shown opposite, from typical birds, to small pale forms in the sw. deserts, and very large dark forms in Alaska and Aleutians. Many races are recognized by taxonomists.
Voice: Song, a variable series of notes, some musical, some buzzy; usually starts with three or four bright repetitious notes, *sweet sweet sweet*, etc. Call note, a low, nasal *tchep*.
Range: Alaska, Canada to cen. Mexico. **West:** Map 401. **Habitat:** Thickets, brush, marshes, roadsides, gardens.

LINCOLN'S SPARROW *Melospiza lincolnii* **M402**

5½" (14 cm). A skulker, "afraid of its shadow." Similar to a Song Sparrow, but trimmer, side of face grayer, breast streaks *much finer* and often not aggregated into a central spot. Note the band of *creamy buff* across the breast and the narrow eye-ring.
Similar species: Immature or winter Swamp Sparrow, sometimes mistaken for Lincoln's Sparrow, has a duller breast, with blurry streaks. Lincoln's is grayer, with a more striped crown.
Voice: Song, sweet and gurgling; suggests both House Wren's and Purple Finch's; starts with low passages, rises abruptly, drops.
Range: Alaska, Canada, w. and ne. U.S. Winters s. U.S. to Panama. **West:** Map 402. **Habitat:** Willow and alder thickets, muskeg, brushy bogs. In winter, thickets, weeds, bushes.

VESPER SPARROW *Pooecetes gramineus* **M390**

6" (15 cm). The *white outer tail feathers* are conspicuous when the bird flies. Otherwise it suggests a grayish Song Sparrow, but has a *whitish eye-ring*. Bend of wing *chestnut*.
Similar species: Other sparrow-like field birds with white tail sides are pipits, longspurs, and Lark Sparrow.
Voice: Song, throatier than a Song Sparrow's; usually begins with two clear minor notes, followed by two higher ones.
Range: Canada to cen. U.S. Winters to s. Mexico. **West:** Map 390.
Habitat: Meadows, fields, prairies, roadsides.

STREAKED SPARROWS

Rockies

large-billed s. Calif. form

head of eastern form

FOX SPARROW

Pacific Northwest

There are many races; 4 are shown here.

large, dark Alaskan form

small, pale desert form

SONG SPARROW

There are nearly 30 western races; only 3 are shown here.

LINCOLN'S SPARROW

VESPER SPARROW

SAVANNAH SPARROW *Passerculus sandwichensis*   **M395**
4½–5¾" (11–14 cm). This streaked open-country sparrow suggests a Song Sparrow, but usually has a *yellowish eyebrow stripe*, whitish stripe through the crown, a short notched tail, pinker legs. Some birds may lack the yellowish on the eyebrow. The tail notch is an aid to recognition when flushing sparrows (Song Sparrow's tail is longer, *rounded*). A small dark race, "Belding's Sparrow" (*beldingi*), resident in salt marshes of s. California was formerly regarded as a species. Its breast streaks are heavier, the median line on the crown is indistinct, the legs browner. A larger Mexican race, "Large-billed Sparrow" (*rostratus*), which winters north to cen. California, is pale without well-defined markings on the back and crown; the breast streaks are more diffuse. It too was regarded as a species.
Voice: Song, a dreamy, lisping *tsit-tsit-tsit, tseeee-tsaaay* (last note lower). Note, a light *tsip*.
Range: Alaska, Canada to Guatemala. Winters to Honduras, W. Indies. **West:** Map 395. **Habitat:** Open fields, meadows, salt marshes, prairies, dunes, shores.

LeCONTE'S SPARROW *Ammodramus leconteii*   **M398**
4½–5½" (11–14 cm). A sharp-tailed sparrow of weedy prairie marshes. Note the *bright buff-ochre* eyebrow stripe and breast (with streaks *confined to the sides*). Other points are the *pinkish brown nape*, white stripe through the crown, strong stripes on the back.
Voice: Song, two extremely thin, grasshopper-like hisses.
Range: S.-cen. Canada to n. prairie states. Winters se. U.S. **West:** Map 398. **Habitat:** Tall grass, weedy hayfields, marshes.

BAIRD'S SPARROW *Ammodramus bairdii*   **M396**
5¼" (13 cm). An elusive prairie sparrow. Light breast crossed by a *narrow band* of fine black streaks. Head yellow-brown, streaked. The key mark is a broad *ochre* median crown stripe.
Similar species: Savannah Sparrow has more extensive streaking; stripe on midcrown is narrower (whitish, not ochre).
Voice: Song begins with 2–3 high musical *zip's*, and ends with a trill on a lower pitch; more musical than Savannah's.
Range: N. Great Plains. Winters sw. U.S., n. Mexico. **West:** Map 396. **Habitat:** Native longgrass prairies; local.

SHARP-TAILED SPARROW *Ammodramus caudacutus*
5–6" (13–15 cm). A marsh sparrow. Note the bright *ochre-orange on the face*, completely surrounding the gray ear patch. Breast very warm ochre, with faint blurry streaks, mostly on the sides. Back sharply striped with white.
Similar species: LeConte's Sparrow of the prairies has sharp stripes on the sides, a white median stripe through the crown.
Voice: Song, a gasping buzz, *tuptup-sheeeeeeeee*.
Range: Canadian prairies; Atlantic Coast. Winters mainly on Atlantic and Gulf coasts. **West:** Breeds ne. British Columbia, Great Slave Lake to cen. Alberta; e. Montana, North Dakota. Very rare winter visitor to California coast. **Habitat:** Prairie marshes, muskeg; in winter, coastal marshes.

Birds of
open country

STREAKED
SPARROWS

dark "Belding's"
form (coastal
California)

SAVANNAH
SPARROW

large, pale
"large-billed"
form (coastal
California)

LeCONTE'S
SPARROW

BAIRD'S
SPARROW

GRASSHOPPER
SPARROW

juvenile;
see adult
on p. 323

SHARP-TAILED
SPARROW

327

LAPLAND LONGSPUR *Calcarius lapponicus* **M410**
6½" (16 cm). Lapland Longspurs, like Horned Larks, the pipits, and the other longspurs, are birds of open country; in flight, they appear to have shorter tails. *Male, breeding: The black face outlined with white* is distinctive. Rusty collar. *Male, winter:* Sparse black streaks on the sides, a rusty nape, and a smudge across the breast help identify it. *Female, breeding:* Resembles a winter male. *Female, winter:* More nondescript; note the tail pattern (opposite).
Similar species: (1) Other longspurs have more white in the tail (see opposite). (2) Pipits and Horned Lark have thin bills.
Voice: A musical *teew;* also a rattle and a whistle, *ticky-tick-tew.* Song in display flight, vigorous, musical.
Range: Arctic, circumpolar. Winters from s. Canada to s. U.S. **West:** Map 410. **Habitat:** In summer, tundra; in winter, fields, prairies.

CHESTNUT-COLLARED LONGSPUR *Calcarius ornatus* **M412**
5½–6½" (14–16 cm). *Male, breeding:* Solid *black* below, except on the throat and lower belly; nape *chestnut. Female and winter:* Sparrow-like; the best field mark is the tail pattern (a dark triangle on a white tail).
Voice: Song, short, feeble, but musical; suggestive of Western Meadowlark's. Note, a finch-like *ji-jiv* or *kittle.*
Range: S. Canadian prairies; n. prairie states. Winters sw. U.S., n. Mexico. **West:** Map 412. **Habitat:** Plains, prairies.

McCOWN'S LONGSPUR *Calcarius mccownii* **M409**
6" (15 cm). *Male, breeding:* Crown and patch on breast black, tail largely white. Hind-neck *gray* (brown or chestnut in other longspurs). *Female and winter male:* Sparrow-like; note the tail pattern (an inverted T of black on white).
Similar species: (1) Male Chestnut-collared Longspur in summer has a chestnut collar, black belly. (2) Horned Lark (similar breast splotch) has a thin bill, yellow throat.
Voice: Song in display flight, clear sweet warbles, suggestive of Lark Bunting. Note, a dry rattle, softer than Lapland's. Also a soft *pink.*
Range: Prairies of s.-cen. Canada, n.-cen. U.S. Winters sw. U.S. to n. Mexico. **West:** Map 409. **Habitat:** Plains, prairies.

SMITH'S LONGSPUR *Calcarius pictus* **M411**
6" (15 cm). A *buffy* longspur; warm buff on entire underparts. Tail edged with white, as in Vesper Sparrow (no dark band at tip). *Male, breeding: Deep buff;* ear patch with a *white spot,* strikingly outlined by a *black triangle. Female and winter:* Less distinctive; buffish breast lightly streaked; some males may show a white shoulder.
Similar species: See (1) Vesper Sparrow (p. 324), (2) Sprague's Pipit (p. 244), and (3) other longspurs (study the tail diagrams opposite).
Voice: Rattling or clicking notes in flight (has been likened to the winding of a cheap watch). Song, sweet, warbler-like, terminating in *we'chew.* Does not sing in flight.
Range: N. Alaska to Hudson Bay. Winters s.-cen. U.S. **West:** Map 411. **Habitat:** Prairies, fields, airports; in summer, tundra.

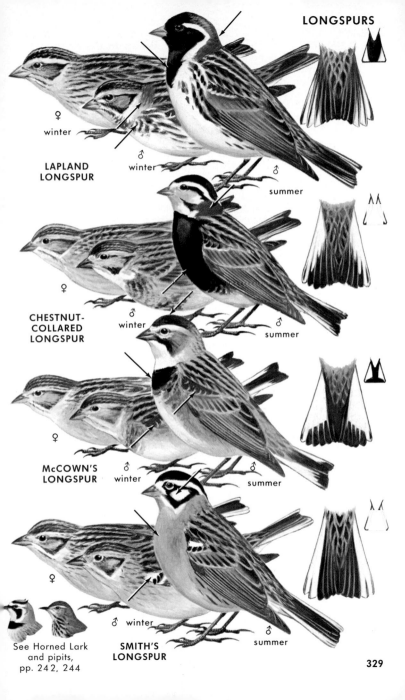

LONGSPURS

♀
winter

LAPLAND LONGSPUR

♂
winter

♂
summer

♀

CHESTNUT-COLLARED LONGSPUR

♂
winter

♂
summer

♀

McCOWN'S LONGSPUR

♂
winter

♂
summer

♀

SMITH'S LONGSPUR

♂
winter

♂
summer

See Horned Lark
and pipits,
pp. 242, 244

329

RUFOUS-SIDED TOWHEE *Pipilo erythrophthalmus* **M379**
7–8½″ (18–21 cm). Smaller and more slender than a Robin, this towhee rummages noisily among the dead leaves. It is readily recognized by its *rufous sides*. *Male:* Head and chest black; sides robin-red, belly white, *back heavily spotted with white*. It flashes *large white patches* in the tail corners. Eye fiery red. *Female:* Similar, but dusky brown where the male is black. *Juvenile, summer:* Streaked below, like a large sparrow, but with the flash pattern in the tail.
Voice: Song, a drawn-out, buzzy *chweeeeee*. Sometimes *chup chup chup zeeeeeeee*; variable. Note, a cat-like *guee* or *cheeee*.
Range: S. Canada to Guatemala, Florida. Migrant in North. **West:** Map 379. **Habitat:** Open woods, undergrowth, brushy edges.

CALIFORNIA TOWHEE *Pipilo crissalis* **M380**
(Brown Towhee) 8½–10″ (21–25 cm). A common, dull brown, ground-loving bird, with a moderately long dark tail; suggests a very plain, slim, overgrown sparrow. Note the pale *rusty undertail coverts* and the streaked buffy or rusty throat.
Similar species: See (1) Canyon Towhee and (2) Abert's Towhee. Most thrashers (pp. 272–273) are larger, with slim curved bills.
Voice: Note, a metallic *chink*. Song, a rapid *chink-chink-ink-ink-ink-ink-ink-ink* on one pitch. Often ends in a trill.
Range: Resident from sw. Oregon to Baja California. Map 380.
Habitat: Brushy, stony areas, open chaparral, open woods, canyons, pinyon, junipers, gardens.

CANYON TOWHEE *Pipilo fuscus* **M380**
Formerly regarded as conspecific with the preceding species under the name of "Brown Towhee"; it has now been split. Paler and grayer than California Towhee, with a rufous crown and black spot on the breast. Vocalizations differ.
Range: Resident from Arizona, n. New Mexico, Colorado, w. Texas to s. Mexico. Map 380. **Habitat:** Similar to California Towhee's, but drier.

ABERT'S TOWHEE *Pipilo aberti* **M381**
8–9″ (20–23 cm). A shy, skulking desert species, similar to the California Towhee, but paler and browner, the entire underparts buffy brown. Note the *black patch* embracing the base of the bill.
Voice: Note, a sharp *peek*. Song similar to Canyon Towhee's.
Range: Resident sw. U.S., nw. Mexico. Map 381. **Habitat:** Desert streams, brush, mesquite.

GREEN-TAILED TOWHEE *Pipilo chlorurus* **M378**
6½″ (16 cm). This slender finch-like bird of the mountains may be known by its *rufous cap*, conspicuous *white throat*, black mustache, gray chest, and plain *olive-green upperparts*.
Voice: A cat-like mewing note, and a *chink* like that of California Towhee. Song variable; opening with sweet notes, followed by burry notes; *weet-churr-cheeeeee-churr*.
Range: Breeds w. U.S. Map 378. Winters sw. U.S. to s. Mexico. **Habitat:** Dry brushy mountain slopes, low chaparral, open pines, sage, manzanita, riverine woods.

TOWHEES

♂

RUFOUS-SIDED
TOWHEE

juvenile

RUFOUS-SIDED
TOWHEE

♀

CANYON
TOWHEE

CALIFORNIA
TOWHEE

(formerly
Brown
Towhee)

ABERT'S TOWHEE

GREEN-TAILED
TOWHEE

DARK-EYED JUNCO *Junco hyemalis*

5½–6¾" (14–17 cm). This hooded, sparrow-shaped bird is characterized by *white outer tail* feathers that flash conspicuously as it flies away. The bill and belly are usually whitish. Males may have dark hoods; females and immatures are duller. The juvenile bird in summer is finely streaked on the breast, hence its white outer tail feathers might even suggest a Vesper Sparrow.

Note: Until recently this species was divided into four full species (plus several subspecies) in N. America. Some have gray sides, others rusty or "pinkish." They tend to hybridize or intergrade and are now lumped as one highly complex species. Treated separately, the main forms were known as follows:

(1) **"OREGON JUNCO"** (*J. h. oreganus*) of se. coastal Alaska, sw. Canada southward in Pacific states to Baja California and in Rockies to s. Idaho, n. Wyoming. Male *rusty-backed*, with a *black head* and *buffy or rusty sides*.

(2) **"GRAY-HEADED JUNCO"** (*J. h. caniceps*) of the Great Basin and s. Rockies. Rufous back like that of "Oregon Junco," but differs in having *gray sides* and a *gray head*.

(3) **"SLATE-COLORED JUNCO"** (*J. h. hyemalis*), the northern and eastern form, wintering mainly east of the Rockies, sparingly westward. A gray junco with a *gray back* and white belly. The uniform coloration, lacking rusty or brown areas, is distinctive.

(4) **"WHITE-WINGED JUNCO"** (*J. h. aikeni*), of the Black Hills area. A large pale form with a gray back; it usually has *two whitish wing bars* and exhibits considerably more white in the tail (four outer feathers on each side).

Voice: Song, a loose trill, suggestive of Chipping Sparrow's song, but more musical. Note, a light *smack*; also clicking or tickering notes.

Range: Breeds Alaska, Canada; south in mountains to n. Georgia, sw. U.S. Winters to Gulf states, n. Mexico. **West:** Map 408. **Habitat:** Conifer and mixed woods. In winter, open woods, undergrowth, roadsides, brush; also patronizes feeders.

YELLOW-EYED JUNCO *Junco phaeonotus*

(Mexican Junco) 5½–6½" (14–16 cm). Our only junco with *yellow eyes*. It also lacks the hooded effect and is whitish-throated. Walks rather than hops. The combination of grayish sides and *bright rufous* back distinguishes this pale-breasted species from all other juncos except the "Gray-headed" form of the Dark-eyed Junco.

Voice: Song, musical, unjunco-like; more complicated, three-parted: *chip chip chip, wheedle wheedle, che che che che che.*

Range: Resident in high mountains of se. Arizona, extreme sw. New Mexico; south to Guatemala. **Habitat:** Conifer forests, pine-oak woods.

JUNCOS

♀

♂

DARK-EYED JUNCO ("Oregon")

juvenile

DARK-EYED JUNCO ("Pink-sided" form)

♂

southern Rockies

♂

DARK-EYED JUNCO ("Gray-headed" form)

♀

DARK-EYED JUNCO ("Slate-colored" form)

♂

DARK-EYED JUNCO ("White-winged" form)

♂

♂

YELLOW-EYED JUNCO

333

■ BUNTINGS. Family Emberizidae (in part).

SNOW BUNTING *Plectrophenax nivalis*   M413
6–7½″ (15–19 cm). Snow Buntings often swirl over snowy fields in large flocks. No other songbird (except McKay's Bunting) shows so much white. In winter some individuals, especially females, may look quite brown, but when they fly their flashing *white wing patches* identify them. Overhead, Snow Buntings look almost entirely white, whereas American Pipits and Horned Larks are black-tailed. In summer in the Arctic the male has a black back, contrasting with its white head and underparts.
Voice: Note, a sharp, whistled *teer* or *tew;* also a rough, purring *brrt.* Song, a musical *ti-ti-chu-ree,* repeated.
Range: Arctic, circumpolar; in winter to cen. Eurasia, cen. U.S.
West: Map 413. **Habitat:** Prairies, fields, dunes, shores. In summer, tundra.

McKAY'S BUNTING *Plectrophenax hyperboreus*
7″ (18 cm). An Alaskan specialty. The male in breeding plumage is almost pure white, except for the ends of the primaries and scapulars and the tips of the central tail feathers. Females show some dark on the back. In winter, there are light touches of brown, but less than in the Snow Bunting.
Similar species: Breeding male Snow Bunting has a *black* back. Females and winter birds are much browner.
Voice: Song of male is said to suggest an American Goldfinch.
Range: Breeds mainly on Hall I. and St. Matthew I. in Bering Sea; rarely on Pribilofs and St. Lawrence I. Winters to coast of w. Alaska, Nunivak; casual, Aleutians, coastal s. Alaska; accidental, Vancouver I., Washington, Oregon. **Habitat:** Tundra, barrens, shores.

■ FINCHES. Family Fringillidae (in part).

ROSY FINCH *Leucosticte arctoa*   M428
(Including "Gray-crowned," "Brown-capped," and "Black" Rosy finches.) 5¾–6¾″ (14–17 cm). Rosy Finches are sparrow-sized birds of the high snowfields; they walk, not hop, and are *dark brown* or *blackish,* with a *pinkish wash* on the belly, wings, and rump; some have a *light gray patch* on the back of the head. Females are duller; the gray patch reduced or almost wanting. Formerly the various races of the Rosy Finch were regarded as three distinct species:
(1) **"GRAY-CROWNED" ROSY FINCH:** Widespread in Alaska, Canada, nw. U.S. (Aleutian birds are largest);
(2) **"BROWN-CAPPED" ROSY FINCH** (male lacks pale gray on head): High mountains of s. Wyoming, Colorado, n. New Mexico;
(3) **"BLACK" ROSY FINCH** (blackish rather than brown): Sw. Montana, cen. Idaho, w. Wyoming, ne. Nevada, n. Utah.
Voice: High chirping notes, suggestive of House Sparrow.
Range: Breeds from islands in Bering Sea, Aleutians, n.-cen. Alaska, nw. Canada south through the high mountains of w. U.S. Map 428.
Habitat: Rocky summits, alpine cirques and snowfields; rocky islands (off Alaska); winters in open country at lower levels, spreading onto plains.

"SNOWBIRDS"

winter ♂

winter ♀

SNOW
BUNTING

♂ summer

Snow
Bunting

♀

♂

summer ♀

♂ summer

McKay's
Bunting

♂

McKAY'S BUNTING

♂ winter

♀

juvenile

"Black"

♂

"Brown-capped"

♂

"Hepburn's"

Pribilofs

♂

"Gray-crowned"

ROSY
FINCH

■ **GROSBEAKS. Family Emberizidae** (in part). Finch-like birds, larger than sparrows, with thick, strong triangular bills adapted for seed-cracking. See also pp. 338, 340.

ROSE-BREASTED GROSBEAK *Pheucticus ludovicianus*   **M371**
7–8½" (18–21 cm). Size and shape of Black-headed Grosbeak. *Male:* Black and white, with a *large triangle of rose-red* on the breast and a *thick pale bill.* In flight, a pattern of white flashes across the black upper plumage; from below, rose-red wing linings. *Female:* Streaked, like a large sparrow or female Purple Finch; recognized by the large "grosbeak" bill, white wing bars, striped crown, broad white eyebrow stripe, and dark cheek. Wing linings yellow. Differs from the female Black-headed Grosbeak in being *heavily striped* on the underparts.
Voice: Song very similar to Black-headed Grosbeak's; resembles Robin's song, but mellower (suggesting a Robin that has taken voice lessons). Note, a metallic *kik* or *kek.*
Range: S. Canada, e. and cen. U.S. Winters W. Indies, Mexico to e. Peru. **West:** Map 371. **Habitat:** Deciduous woods, orchards, groves.

BLACK-HEADED GROSBEAK *Pheucticus melanocephalus*   **M372**
6½–7¾" (16–19 cm). A stocky bird, larger than a sparrow, with an outsized bill. *Male:* Breast, collar, and rump *dull orange-brown.* Otherwise, the black head; bold, black and white wing and tail pattern; and pale bill are similar to those of its eastern counterpart, the Rose-breasted Grosbeak. *Female:* Largely brown, with sparrowlike streaks above; head strongly patterned with light stripes and dark ear patch. Breast strongly *washed with ochre-brown;* streaks on sides fine, nearly absent across the chest. Female Rose-breast is more heavily striped below, lacks the strong ochre.
Voice: Song, rising and falling passages; resembles a Robin's song but more fluent and mellow. Note, a flat *ik* or *eek.*
Range: Sw. Canada, w. U.S. to s. Mexico. Winters in Mexico. Map 372. Sometimes hybridizes with Rose-breasted Grosbeak where ranges overlap.

PYRRHULOXIA *Cardinalis sinuatus*   **M370**
7½–8½" (19–21 cm). *Male:* A slender, *gray and red bird, with a crest* and a *red, stubby, almost parrot-like bill.* The rose-colored breast and crest suggest a Cardinal, but the gray back and *yellow bill* set it apart. *Female:* Note the *yellow bill.* The gray back, buff breast, and touch of red in the wings and crest separate it from the female Cardinal, which is browner with a reddish bill.
Voice: Song, a clear *quink quink quink quink quink,* on one pitch; also a slurred, whistled *what-cheer, what-cheer,* etc., thinner and shorter than Cardinal's song.
Range: Sw. U.S. to cen. Mexico. Map 370. **Habitat:** Mesquite, thorn scrub, deserts.

GROSBEAKS

ROSE-
BREASTED
GROSBEAK

♀

♂

juvenile

♀

♂

BLACK-
HEADED
GROSBEAK

♂

♀

head of
♀ Cardinal

♂

juv.

PYRRHULOXIA

BLUE GROSBEAK *Guiraca caerulea*   **M373**

6–7½" (15–19 cm). *Male:* Deep *dull blue*, with a thick bill, *two broad tan wing bars*. Often flips tail. Immature male, a mixture of brown and blue. *Female:* About size of Cowbird; warm brown, lighter below, with two *tan wing bars*; rump tinged with blue.

Similar species: Indigo Bunting is smaller, lacks the wing bars.

Voice: A warbling song, phrases rising and falling; suggests Purple or House Finch; slower, more guttural. A sharp *chink*.

Range: Cen. U.S. to Costa Rica. Winters Mexico to Panama. **West:** Map 373. **Habitat:** Brush, roadsides, streamside thickets.

INDIGO BUNTING *Passerina cyanea*

5½" (14 cm). *Male:* A small finch; *rich deep blue all over*. In autumn more like the brown female, but usually with some blue in the wings and tail. *Female:* A small, plain brown finch; breast paler, with faint streaks; no strong wing bars or other obvious marks. May hybridize with Lazuli Bunting where their ranges overlap.

Voice: Song, lively, high, and strident; measured phrases, usually paired: *sweet-sweet*, *chew-chew*, etc. Note, a sharp, thin *spit*.

Range: Breeds se. Canada, U.S. west to Great Plains and recently through New Mexico and Arizona locally to se. California (Colorado R.). Rare or casual elsewhere in West. Winters from se. U.S., Mexico to nw. Colombia. **Habitat:** Brushy pastures, bushy wood edges.

LAZULI BUNTING *Passerina amoena*   **M374**

5–5½" (13–14 cm). *Male:* A small, turquoise-blue finch, suggesting a Bluebird, but with *two white wing bars*. *Female:* A small finch with an unstreaked brown back, a trace of blue in wings and tail, and two pale wing bars (stronger than in female Indigo Bunting). Hybrids are frequent where range overlaps that of Indigo.

Voice: Song, similar to Indigo Bunting's, but faster.

Range: Sw. Canada, w. U.S. Winters in Mexico. Map 374. **Habitat:** Open brush, streamside shrubs.

PAINTED BUNTING *Passerina ciris*   **M376**

5½" (14 cm). The most gaudily colored North American songbird. *Male:* A patchwork of *blue-violet* on head, *green* on back, red on rump and underparts. *Female:* Very plain; greenish above, paling to lemon-green below; *no other small finch is so uniformly green*.

Voice: Song, a wiry warble; suggests song of Warbling Vireo.

Range: S. U.S., ne. Mexico. Winters to Panama. **West:** Map 376. **Habitat:** Woodland edges, roadsides, brush, towns, gardens.

VARIED BUNTING *Passerina versicolor*   **M375**

4½–5½" (11–14 cm). *Male:* A small dark finch with a plum-purple body (looks black at a distance). Crown, face, and rump blue, with *a bright red patch on the nape*; "colored like an Easter egg." *Female:* A small, plain *gray-brown* finch with lighter underparts. *No strong wing bars, stripes, or distinctive marks of any kind*.

Similar species: Male Painted Bunting has a bright red breast. Female Indigo is browner, with a hint of breast streaks.

Voice: Song thin, bright, more distinctly phrased, less warbled than Painted Bunting's; notes not as paired as in Lazuli's.

Range: Breeds sw. U.S. to Guatemala. Map 375. Winters from n. Mexico south. **Habitat:** Streamside thickets, brush.

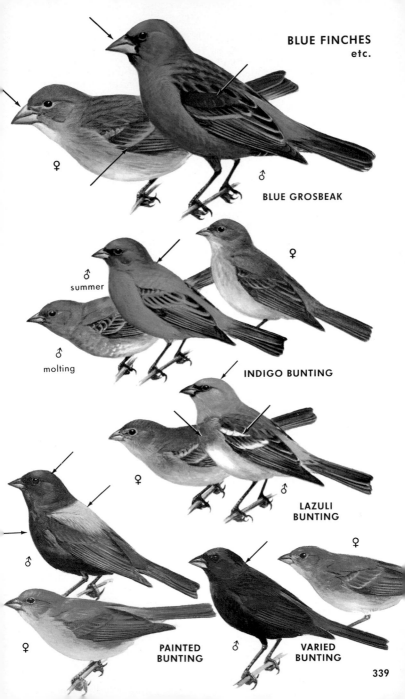

BLUE FINCHES
etc.

♀

♂

BLUE GROSBEAK

♂
summer

♀

♂
molting

INDIGO BUNTING

♀

♂

LAZULI BUNTING

♂

♀

♀

♂

PAINTED BUNTING

VARIED BUNTING

339

NORTHERN CARDINAL *Cardinalis cardinalis* **M369**
7½–9" (19–23 cm). *Male:* An all-red bird with a pointed crest and
a black patch at the base of its heavy, triangular red bill. *Female:*
Buff-brown, with some red on the wings and tail. The crest, dark
face, and heavy red bill are distinctive. *Immature:* Similar to the
female, but with a blackish bill (see Pyrrhuloxia, p. 337, and Hepatic
Tanager, p. 315).
Similar species: Male Summer and Hepatic tanagers, the other all-
red birds of the Southwest, have no crests.
Voice: Song, clear, slurred whistles; repeated. Several variations:
what-cheer cheer cheer, etc.; *whoit whoit whoit* or *birdy birdy
birdy,* etc. Note, a short, light *tik.*
Range: S. Quebec to Gulf states; sw. U.S., Mexico to Belize. **West:**
Map 369. **Habitat:** Woodland edges, thickets, suburban gardens,
towns, bird feeders.

■ **FINCHES. Family Fringillidae.** These birds have seed-cracking
bills of three main types: (1) very large and grosbeak-like, as in the
Evening Grosbeak; (2) rather canary-like, as in most of the lesser
finches such as the Goldfinch; and (3) cross-tipped, as in the two
crossbills. Until recently, all the other grosbeaks as well as the sparrows and buntings were also put into this family, but now they are
lumped with such unlikely associates as the tanagers, warblers,
blackbirds, and orioles in the catch-all family *Emberizidae.* See the
Systematic Checklist, pp. 409–416.

RED CROSSBILL *Loxia curvirostra* **M433**
5½–6½" (14–16 cm). Near the size of a House Sparrow, with a heavy
head and short tail. Note the *crossed mandibles.* The sound when
it cracks the cones of evergreens often betrays its presence. It acts
like a small parrot as it dangles while feeding. *Male:* Dull red,
brighter on the rump; wings and tail blackish. Young males are
more orange. *Female:* Dull olive-gray; yellowish on the rump and
underparts. *Juvenile:* Striped above and below, suggesting a large
Pine Siskin; note the bill.
Voice: Note, a hard *jip-jip* or *jip-jip-jip.* Song, finch-like warbled
passages, *jip-jip-jip-jeeaa-jeeaa;* trills, chips.
Range: Conifer forests of N. Hemisphere. In N. America, south in
mountains to Nicaragua; in East, locally to s. Appalachians. Erratic
wanderings in winter. **West:** Map 433. **Habitat:** Conifers.

WHITE-WINGED CROSSBILL *Loxia leucoptera* **M434**
6–6¾" (15–17 cm). Note the wing bars and crossed mandibles.
Male: Dull *rose-pink,* with black wings crossed by *two broad white
wing bars;* tail black. *Female:* Olive-gray, with a yellowish rump
similar to female Red Crossbill's, but with *two broad white wing
bars.* The wing bars are often quite evident in flight and help pick
out this species in mixed flocks of crossbills.
Voice: Notes, a liquid *peet* and a dry *chif-chif.* Song, a succession
of loud trills on different pitches.
Range: Boreal forests of N. Hemisphere. Also Hispaniola. **West:** Map
434. **Habitat:** Spruce and fir forests, hemlocks.

RED FINCHES
etc.

NORTHERN
CARDINAL

♂

♀

juv.

RED
CROSSBILL

♂

♀

imm.

WHITE-WINGED
CROSSBILL

♂

♀

341

REDPOLL *Carduelis flammea*   **M435**

5–5½" (13–14 cm). Note the *bright red cap* on the forehead of this
little winter finch. Gray-brown, streaked; note the *black chin* and
dark flank streaks. Male has a *pink breast.* Among the more typical
Redpolls, look for "frostier" birds. If the rump is *without streaks*
and the bill is *smaller,* the bird is a "Hoary" Redpoll—until recently
designated a species *(Carduelis hornemanni),* but now regarded as
a northern population of the "Common" Redpoll.
Voice: In flight, a rattling *chet-chet-chet-chet.* Song, a trill, followed
by the rattling *chet-chet-chet-chet.*
Range: Circumboreal. **West:** Map 435. **Habitat:** Birches, tundra
scrub. In winter, weeds, brush.

HOUSE FINCH *Carpodacus mexicanus*   **M432**

5–5¾" (13–14 cm). *Male: Bright red* breast, forehead, stripe over the
eye and rump. Resembles male Purple and Cassin's finches but
slighter; male brighter red. Note the *dark stripes* on the sides and
belly. The striped brown female is separated from female Purple and
Cassin's finches by its smaller head, bill, and *bland face* (no heavy
mustache or dark cheek patch). Some males may be orange.
Voice: Song, bright, loose and disjointed; often ends in a nasal
wheer. Notes suggest a House Sparrow's, but more musical.
Range: British Columbia to s. Mexico. Introduced in e. U.S.; spreading. **West:** Map 432. **Habitat:** Cities, suburbs, farms, canyons; feeders.

PURPLE FINCH *Carpodacus purpureus*   **M430**

5½–6" (14–15 cm). Like a sparrow dipped in raspberry juice. *Male:*
Dull rose-red, brightest on the head, chest, and rump. *Female and
immature:* Heavily striped, brown; similar to a female House Finch,
but note the *broad dark jaw stripe,* dark *ear patch,* and broad light
stripe behind the eye.
Voice: Song, a fast lively warble; note, a dull metallic *tick.*
Range: Canada, Pacific states, n. Baja California, ne. U.S. Winters
to s. U.S. **West:** Map 430. **Habitat:** Woods, groves, suburbs, feeders.

CASSIN'S FINCH *Carpodacus cassinii*   **M431**

6–6½" (15–16 cm). *Male:* Very similar to Purple Finch, but red of
breast paler; *squarish red crown patch contrasts abruptly* with the
brown of the nape; bill has a straighter ridge. Note, a musical *chi-
diup. Female:* Whiter underparts, sharper stripings, streaked undertail coverts, and bill shape distinguish it from female Purple Finch.
Range: Sw. Canada, w. U.S. Winters to mountains of Mexico. Map
431. **Habitat:** Conifers in high mountains; lower levels in winter.

PINE GROSBEAK *Pinicola enucleator*   **M429**

8–10" (20–25 cm). Near size of Robin; a large, tame "winter" finch
with a stubby bill, longish tail. Not a true Grosbeak. Flight undu-
lates deeply. *Male, adult:* Dull *rose-red,* dark wings with *two white
bars. Male, immature:* Similar to the gray female, but with a touch
of russet on the head and rump. *Female:* Gray, with two white wing
bars; head and rump tinged with dull yellow.
Voice: Call, a whistled *tee-tew-tew,* suggesting that of Greater Yellowlegs, but finch-like; also a musical *chee-vli.*
Range: Boreal forests of N. Hemisphere; winters irruptively southward. **West:** Map 429. **Habitat:** Conifers; in winter, other trees.

RED FINCHES
etc.

orange
variant

♀

♂

HOUSE
FINCH

♂ ♀

REDPOLL

"HOARY"
REDPOLL

♀

♂

PURPLE
FINCH

CASSIN'S
FINCH

♂ ♀

PINE GROSBEAK

343

EVENING GROSBEAK *Coccothraustes vespertina* **M440**

8″ (20 cm). Size of a Starling. A *chunky, short-tailed* finch with a *very large, pale, conical bill. Male:* Dull yellow, with a dark head, yellow eyebrow, and black and white wings; suggests an overgrown Goldfinch. *Female:* Silver-gray, with enough yellow, black, and white to be recognized. Gregarious. Undulating flight, shape, and *large white wing patches* identify them.

Voice: A ringing, finch-like *clee-ip*; a high, clear *thew.*
Range: Spruce belt of Canada, ne. and w. U.S. to Oaxaca. Winters to se. U.S., Mexico. **West:** Map 440. **Habitat:** Conifer forests; in winter, box-elders and other maples; also fruiting shrubs; often swarm at feeding trays.

AMERICAN GOLDFINCH *Carduelis tristis* **M439**

5″ (13 cm). *Male, summer: A small yellow bird with black wings;* tail and forehead also black. *Female, summer:* Dull yellow-olive; darker above, with blackish wings and conspicuous wing bars. Goldfinches are distinguished from other small, olive-yellow birds (warblers, etc.) by their short, conical bills. *Winter, both sexes:* Much like summer female, but gray-brown; yellow on throat.

Voice: Song, clear, light, canary-like. In undulating flight, each dip is punctuated by *ti-dee'-di-di* or *per-chik-o-ree,* or *"po-ta-to-chip."*
Range: S. Canada to s. U.S., n. Baja California. **West:** Map 439. **Habitat:** Patches of thistles and weeds, dandelions on lawns, roadsides, open woods, edges; in winter, also feeders.

LESSER GOLDFINCH *Carduelis psaltria* **M437**

3¾–4¼″ (9–11 cm). *Male:* A very small finch with a *black cap,* black or greenish back, and bright yellow underparts; white on the wings. Black cap retained in winter. Males of race *psaltria* (s. Rockies) have *black* backs; males of western race *hesperophilus* have *greenish* backs. *Female:* Similar to American Goldfinch, but smaller, more greenish; *rump dark* (not pale).

Voice: Sweet, plaintive notes *tee-yee* (rising) and *tee-yer* (dropping). Song, more phrased than American Goldfinch's.
Range: Breeds from w. U.S. to Peru. Map 437. **Habitat:** Open brushy country, open woods, wooded streams, gardens.

LAWRENCE'S GOLDFINCH *Carduelis lawrencei* **M438**

4½″ (11 cm). In all plumages known by the *large amount of yellow in the wings.* Male has a *black face* (including chin).

Voice: Song similar to that of American Goldfinch. Call note, distinctive: *tink-oo,* syllables emphasized equally.
Range: Breeds n. California to n. Baja California. Winters sw. U.S., nw. Mexico. Map 438. **Habitat:** Oak-pine woods, chaparral.

PINE SISKIN *Carduelis pinus* **M436**

4½–5″ (11–13 cm). Size of a Goldfinch. A small, dark, *heavily streaked* finch with a deeply notched tail, sharply pointed bill. *A touch of yellow in the wings* and at the *base of the tail* (not always evident). Most Siskins are detected by voice, flying over.

Voice: Call, a loud *chlee-ip*; also a light *tit-i-tit*; a buzzy *shreeeee.* Song suggests Goldfinch's, but coarser, wheezy.
Range: S. Canada to s. U.S. Winters to cen. Mexico. **West:** Map 436. **Habitat:** Conifers, mixed woods, alders, weedy areas, feeders.

YELLOW
FINCHES
etc.

♂

♀

**EVENING
GROSBEAK**

♂ winter

♂ summer

♀

**AMERICAN
GOLDFINCH**

♂

♀

black-backed
("Arkansas")

♂

♀

**LESSER
GOLDFINCH**

green-backed

♀

**LAWRENCE'S
GOLDFINCH**

♂

♂

**PINE
SISKIN**

- **WEAVER FINCHES. Family Passeridae.** Old World sparrows, unrelated to our native sparrows, which are lumped with the *Emberizidae*. **Food:** Insects, seeds. **Range:** Widespread in Old World; 301 species (sparrow-weavers, 35); West 2 (introduced).

HOUSE SPARROW *Passer domesticus*   M441
6″ (15 cm). Familiar to everyone. Sooty city birds often bear little resemblance to clean country males with the *black throat, white cheeks, chestnut nape.* Females and young lack the black throat, have a dingy breast, rusty wings, and dull eyestripe.
Range: Eurasia, n. Africa. Introduced N. and S. America, S. Africa, Australia. **West:** Map 441. **Habitat:** Cities, farms.

EURASIAN TREE SPARROW *Passer montanus* (not shown)
5½″ (14 cm). Both sexes resemble male House Sparrow, but black throat patch smaller. Key mark is a *black ear spot.* Crown brown. Illustrated in the eastern *Field Guide.*
Range: Eurasia. Introduced; local resident in vicinity of St. Louis, Missouri **West:** Reported recently from s. Vancouver I.

- **MISCELLANEOUS SPARROW-LIKE EMBERIZIDS.**

BROWN-HEADED COWBIRD *Molothrus aeneus*
7″ (18 cm). The gray-brown female and the juvenile with its soft streakings may be taken for sparrows of some sort because of their short, finch-like bills. See fuller coverage on p. 310.

DICKCISSEL *Spiza americana*   M377
6–7″ (15–18 cm). A grassland bird; often travels in large flocks. Sits on fenceposts. *Male:* Suggests a miniature Meadowlark (black bib, yellow chest). In fall the bib is obscure or lacking. *Female:* Very much like a female House Sparrow, but paler, with a lighter stripe over the eye, touch of yellow on the breast, and a bluish bill. The chestnut shoulder is also an aid.
Voice: Song, a staccato *dick-ciss-ciss-ciss* or *chup-chup-klip-klip-klip.* A short buzzing call is often heard at night in migration.
Range: S. Canada and interior of U.S. Winters mainly from Mexico to n. S. America. Very rare migrant and winter visitor to California. **West:** Map 377. **Habitat:** Alfalfa and other fields, meadows, prairies.

BOBOLINK *Dolichonyx oryzivorus*
Because of the short bill, female Bobolinks and autumn males may suggest sparrows or finches. They are a bit larger than House Sparrows; rich buff, with dark stripings on the crown and back. For a fuller discussion, see p. 308.

LARK BUNTING *Calamospiza melanocorys*   M394
7″ (18 cm). A prairie bird. Gregarious. *Male in spring: Black,* with *large white wing patches* (male Bobolink has white patches on the body, not on the wings). *Female, young, and winter male:* Brown, streaked; pattern suggests female Purple Finch. Usually some birds in the flock show *whitish wing patches.*
Voice: Song, cardinal-like slurs, unmusical chat-like *chug's;* piping whistles and trills; each note repeated 3–11 times.
Range: Prairies of s. Canada to n. Texas. Winters sw. U.S. to cen. Mexico. **West:** Map 394. **Habitat:** Plains, prairies.

FINCHLIKE BIRDS

♂

♀

juvenile

HOUSE
SPARROW

♀

BROWN-
HEADED
COWBIRD

♂

♀

DICKCISSEL

fall

BOBOLINK

♂ summer

♀

LARK
BUNTING

347

■ **MISCELLANEOUS STRAYS FROM MEXICO.** The birds shown opposite and on the next plate may be found by the birder who travels to Mexico to sample its rich avifauna. On very rare occasion, one of these strays from the neotropics slips across the border to our side. Arizona has been especially favored. A few other Mexican rarities or accidentals have been treated earlier in this book—the Eared Trogon (p. 206), a few hummingbirds (pp. 220–221), and the Rufous-backed Robin (pp. 274–275). Still others may eventually be added to our U.S. list by perceptive birders. To prepare for the unexpected, study *A Field Guide to Mexican Birds.*

STREAK-BACKED ORIOLE *Icterus pustulatus* (Scarlet-headed Oriole)
8″ (20 cm). The breeding adult has a *striped back.* Much white in the wing. Otherwise resembles Hooded Oriole. *Male* is basically yellow-orange, head becoming almost red. *Female* is duller, back more olivaceous, but the streaking is still obvious. **West:** Sparse wanderer in fall and winter to s. Arizona (where it has visited hummingbird feeders around Tucson). Casual stray, s. California.

BLACK-VENTED ORIOLE *Icterus wagleri*
7½–9″ (19–23 cm). This black-hooded oriole differs from the yellow and black Scott's Oriole in being more orangish, with *no white in the wing.* Note the *black vent (undertail coverts),* all-black tail. Sexes alike. **West:** Accidental, w. Texas (Big Bend, San Ygnacio).

RUFOUS-BACKED ROBIN *Turdus rufopalliatus*
9″ (23 cm). Like a pale American Robin, but with a *rufous back* and no white around the eye. **West:** Rare fall and winter visitor s. Arizona. Accidental, Texas, New Mexico, California. See also p. 275.

AZTEC THRUSH *Ridgwayia pinicola*
8½″ (21 cm). A robin-like thrush with a *dark hood,* white belly, white rump. Wings strikingly *patched with white. Male,* blackish on head, breast, and back; *female* brownish. **West:** Casual stray near Mexican border of w. Texas (Big Bend) and mountains of se. Arizona.

FLAME-COLORED TANAGER *Piranga bidentata*
(Stripe-backed Tanager) 6–7½″ (15–19 cm). The male is *fire-red* with a *striped back,* dusky ear patch and two whitish wing bars. Dark tail tipped in corners with white. The female looks somewhat like a female Western Tanager (two white wing bars), but the *striped back* is a giveaway. **West:** Accidental, se. Arizona (Chiricahua Mts., where a male apparently nested with a female Western Tanager).

YELLOW GROSBEAK *Pheucticus chrysopeplus*
8½″ (21 cm). Size and shape of Black-headed Grosbeak; male *golden yellow and black,* suggesting an overblown Goldfinch except for the large, black grosbeak bill. *Female* duller, with a streaked back and crown. **West:** Casual vagrant in summer, s. Arizona.

RUDDY GROUND-DOVE *Columbina talpacoti*
6–7″ (15–18 cm). Male, a small, *reddish-looking* dove with a light *blue-gray* crown and black underwing coverts. The dull gray-brown female resembles the Common Ground-Dove somewhat, but lacks the scaly appearance on the sides of the breast. **West:** Accidental, California, Arizona, New Mexico, Texas.

To be looked for in southwestern border states

ACCIDENTAL STRAYS FROM MEXICO

BLACK-VENTED ORIOLE   adult

STREAK-BACKED ORIOLE ♂

♂   ♀

AZTEC THRUSH

RUFOUS-BACKED ROBIN

♂

See Rufous-backed Robin on p. 277.

FLAME-COLORED TANAGER

♀   ♂

♂

♀

RUDDY GROUND-DOVE

YELLOW GROSBEAK

349

CRESCENT-CHESTED WARBLER *Parula superciliosa*
4–4¾" (10–12 cm). Note the *chestnut crescent* on a yellow breast, and the strong *white eyebrow stripe* on a gray head. Back olive-green. **West:** Accidental, Texas, s. Arizona.

RUFOUS-CAPPED WARBLER *Basileuterus rufifrons*
4½–5" (11–13 cm). *Rufous cap and cheek* separated by a white eyebrow stripe. Breast yellow, upperparts olive. **West:** Casual, w. Texas, s. Arizona (has bred).

FAN-TAILED WARBLER *Euthlypis lachrymosa*
5½–6" (14–15 cm). A large warbler, blackish above, yellow below. Note the *yellow crown spot* and *tawny orange* wash on the breast. Flicks its long, fan-shaped, white-tipped tail a great deal. **West:** Accidental, se. Arizona.

SLATE-THROATED REDSTART *Myioborus miniatus*
5" (13 cm). Very much like Painted Redstart, but *lacks the white wing patch.* Breast *orange-red* rather than rose-red. Female has a salmon-pink breast. **West:** Accidental, New Mexico, s. Arizona.

XANTUS' (BLACK-FRONTED) HUMMINGBIRD *Hylocharis xantusii*
3½" (9 cm). A female of this Baja California species has occurred once in s. California, where it actually nested and laid eggs that did not hatch. Female resembles White-eared Hummingbird, but has buff underparts, rusty sides of tail. The male has a green throat, cinnamon belly, chestnut tail, and white stripe behind the eye.
Note: On p. 221, see other rare or vagrant hummingbirds from Mexico (Berylline, Bumblebee, and Plain-capped Starthroat).

NUTTING'S FLYCATCHER *Myiarchus nuttingi*
7" (18 cm). Similar to Ash-throated Flycatcher (p. 234), but a shade smaller, and a bit browner above. Interior of mouth *orange.* Probably not safely separable in the field except by voice—a clear, whistled *peer;* suggests voice of Dusky-capped Flycatcher, but higher, less plaintive. **West:** Accidental, s. Arizona, w. Texas (Big Bend).

GRAY SILKY-FLYCATCHER *Ptilogonys cinereus*
7½–8½" (19–21 cm). Related to the Phainopepla. A slim, crested, waxwing-like bird with a long, strikingly patterned black and white tail and yellow undertail coverts. *Male:* gray; *female:* brown. **West:** Accidental, s. Texas (confirmed by photograph), se. Ariz., s. Calif.(?).

CRIMSON-COLLARED GROSBEAK *Rhodothraupis celaeno*
7–8" (18–20 cm). *Male:* A blackish grosbeak with a *dark red collar* encircling the black head and chest. The red underparts are often spotted or blotched with black. *Female and immature:* Patterned like the male, but *dull green* replaces the red. **West:** Casual stray, s. Texas just south of our area.

MOTTLED OWL *Ciccaba virgata* (not shown)
12–15" (30–38 cm). This dark Mexican owl, unlike the somewhat larger Barred Owl, is uniformly dark above (with fine mottlings). Streaked lengthwise below. No ear tufts. Eyes *brown.* **West:** A road-killed specimen has been recorded from s. Texas near the Rio Grande, but south of our area.

IMPERIAL WOODPECKER *Campephilus imperiatis* (not shown)
21" (53 cm). This very large (near extinct) woodpecker was possibly seen but not confirmed in Big Bend National Park in 1958. See illustration in *A Field Guide to Mexican Birds.*

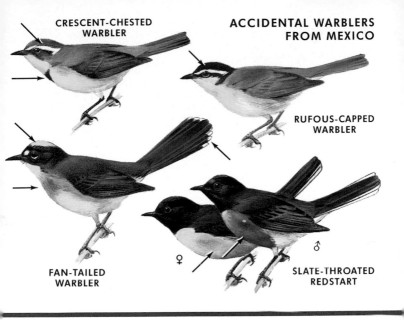

ACCIDENTAL WARBLERS FROM MEXICO

CRESCENT-CHESTED WARBLER

RUFOUS-CAPPED WARBLER

FAN-TAILED WARBLER

♀   ♂

SLATE-THROATED REDSTART

OTHER ACCIDENTALS FROM MEXICO

XANTUS' HUMMINGBIRD

♀

♂

NUTTING'S FLYCATCHER

GRAY SILKY-FLYCATCHER

♂

♀

GRAY SILKY-FLYCATCHER

♀

♂

CRIMSON-COLLARED GROSBEAK

■ ALASKAN STRAYS FROM ASIA. On the next three plates a number of rarities from Asia are shown. Whereas the shores and islands of the Bering Sea have produced most records, a very few have occurred south along the Pacific Coast. A few other Alaskan strays have been shown on previous plates: waterfowl (pp. 49, 63); sandpipers (pp. 151, 153, 155, 157); wagtails (p. 243); pipits (p. 245); swifts (p. 247). For further information, consult *A Field Guide to the Birds of Britain and Europe*. For other possibilities, see *A Field Guide to the Birds of Japan* (Wild Bird Society of Japan).

COMMON HOUSE MARTIN *Delichon urbica* 8″ (20 cm). Like a Tree Swallow with a *white patch completely across the rump*. **West:** Accidental, Bering Sea area (Nome, St. Paul I., St. Matthew I.).

EYEBROWED THRUSH *Turdus obscurus*
7½″ (19 cm). Robin-like; smaller, with *reddish confined to the sides*. Gray back and breast; *white eyebrow*, chin and belly. **West:** Rare in spring, w. Aleutians; casual, Pribilofs, w. and n. Alaska.

FIELDFARE *Turdus pilaris*
10″ (25 cm). Robin-like, with a heavily striped tawny breast. *Back rusty*; head, rump gray. **West:** Accidental, n. Alaska, St. Lawrence I.

DUSKY THRUSH *Turdus naumanni*
9″ (23 cm). Robin-like. Head and underparts dusky; *heavily scaled*. Rufous wings. **West:** Casual, w. Aleutians and St. Lawrence I.; accidental, n. Alaska (Pt. Barrow).

BROWN SHRIKE *Lanius cristatus*
8″ (20 cm). A small shrike, *brown* above, white below, with a *dark mask*. **West:** Accidental, w. Aleutians, St. Lawrence I., Anchorage, Alaska; also California (Farallons).

STONECHAT *Saxicola torquata*
5″ (13 cm). Small, plump, upright. Male has a black head and throat, *white half-collar*, rusty breast. **West:** Accidental, St. Lawrence I.

EURASIAN WRYNECK *Jynx torquilla*
6½″ (16 cm). Woodpecker-like; mottled gray-brown, underparts finely barred. **West:** Accidental, nw. Alaska (Seward Peninsula).

HOOPOE *Upupa epops*
11″ (28 cm). Pinkish brown with *boldly barred, black and white wings and tail* and a long *erectile crest* (usually depressed). **West:** Accidental, w. Alaska (Old Chevak).

RUFOUS TURTLE-DOVE *Streptopelia orientalis*
13″ (33 cm). Striped patch on neck; rufous in wings. **West:** Accidental, Attu, Pribilofs.

COMMON CUCKOO *Cuculus canorus*
13″ (33 cm). Slender; looks falconlike. Gray, with *barred underparts*. Rufous morph of female (rare) is barred except on rump. **West:** Rare overshoot in outer Aleutians, Pribilofs. Accidental, mainland of w. Alaska.

ORIENTAL CUCKOO *Cuculus saturatus*
13″ (33 cm). Darker than the Common Cuckoo, with a shorter bill and *wider bars* on the belly. Rufous morph of the female has heavier barring; has strong barring on the rump. **West:** Very rare vagrant (June–July) in outer Aleutians.

VAGRANTS or STRAYS FROM ASIA

HOUSE MARTIN

FIELDFARE

DUSKY THRUSH

EYEBROWED THRUSH

♂

BROWN SHRIKE

EURASIAN WRYNECK

♀ ♂

STONECHAT

HOOPOE

COMMON CUCKOO rufous morph ♀

RUFOUS TURTLE-DOVE

COMMON CUCKOO

ORIENTAL CUCKOO rufous morph ♀

ORIENTAL CUCKOO

353

LANCEOLATED WARBLER *Locustella lanceolata*
4½″ (11 cm). Small, skulking. Streaked brown upperparts, band of *fine streaks* on whitish breast. Light eyebrow stripe, white throat. **West:** Casual or accidental, outer Aleutians (Attu).

MIDDENDORFF'S GRASSHOPPER-WARBLER *Locustella ochotensis*
6½″ (16 cm). A rather large Old World warbler; brown above, white below, with *tan sides* and a *tapered white-tipped tail.* Light eyebrow. **West:** Summer and fall vagrant to Bering Sea islands (Attu, Nunivak, Pribilofs, St. Lawrence I.).

DUSKY WARBLER *Phylloscopus fuscatus*
4½″ (11 cm). A small, very plain Old World warbler; dusky-brown above, no wing bars. Whitish below, with buffy eyebrows, sides, and undertail coverts. **West:** Casual or accidental in fall, Gambell, outer Aleutians; accidental, California.

SIBERIAN BLUE ROBIN *Luscinia cyane*
5½″ (14 cm). Dull blue above, pure white below, separated by black on the sides of the face and neck. *Female:* Brown above, mottled buff below, tail bluish. **West:** Accidental, outer Aleutians (Attu).

SIBERIAN RUBYTHROAT *Luscinia calliope*
6″ (15 cm). Small and dark; note the *ruby-red throat,* gray breast. *White eyebrows and whiskers.* Female has a *white throat.* **West:** Rare but regular migrant, w. Aleutians; casual, Pribilofs, St. Lawrence I.

RED-FLANKED BLUETAIL *Tarsiger cyanurus*
5½″ (14 cm). *Male:* Deep blue above with *bright orange-red flanks,* white throat. *Female:* Dusky brown, with a dark chest, white throat, *orange flanks.* **West:** Accidental, outer Aleutians (Attu).

RED-BREASTED FLYCATCHER *Ficedula parva*
4½″ (11 cm). A tiny flycatcher. *Male:* Orange throat, gray cheeks, narrow eye-ring, *white tail patches. Female:* Browner, without the orange throat. **West:** Casual, w. Aleutians; accidental, St. Lawrence I.

GRAY-SPOTTED FLYCATCHER *Muscicapa griseisticta*
5½″ (14 cm). *Empidonax*-like. *Strongly streaked* breast and flanks. **West:** Rare, irregular, perhaps regular (May–June), w. Aleutians.

SIBERIAN FLYCATCHER *Muscicapa sibirica* (Sooty Flycatcher) 5″ (13 cm). Suggests a sooty *Empidonax* flycatcher (eye-ring, wing bar, etc.). Note the *broad dark band across the breast.* **West:** Accidental, w. Aleutians.

ASIAN BROWN FLYCATCHER *Muscicapa latirostris*
5″ (13 cm). Similar to Siberian Flycatcher, but smaller, and much paler on the breast. **West:** Accidental, w. Aleutians (Attu).

NARCISSUS FLYCATCHER *Ficedula narcissina*
5″ (13 cm). Black back, *orange throat* (male), *yellow rump and eyebrow,* white wing patch. **West:** Accidental, w. Aleutians (Attu).

GREAT TIT *Parus major* 5½″ (14 cm). A large "chickadee" with a *black stripe* extending from its black throat through its *whitish underparts.* **West:** Accidental, Little Diomede I. (at a feeder).

SIBERIAN ACCENTOR *Prunella montanella* (Family Prunellidae)
5½″ (14 cm). *Dark cheeks* separate *ochre eyebrows* from the *bright ochre-buff throat and underparts.* Sides striped; bill *warbler-like.* **West:** Casual fall visitor, Nunivak I., St. Lawrence I. and mainland Alaska. Accidental, Washington.

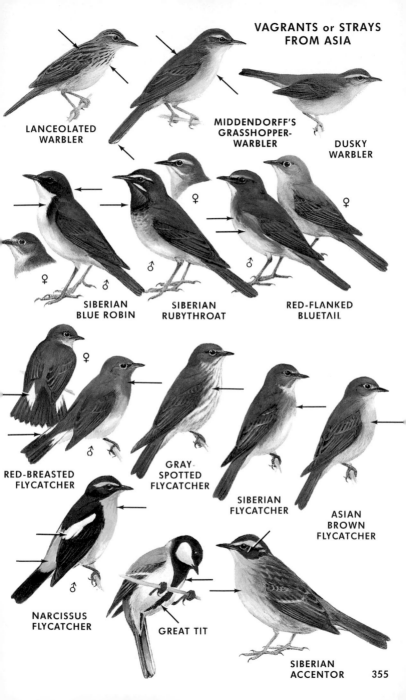

VAGRANTS or STRAYS FROM ASIA

LANCEOLATED
WARBLER

MIDDENDORFF'S
GRASSHOPPER-
WARBLER

DUSKY
WARBLER

SIBERIAN
BLUE ROBIN

♀

♂

SIBERIAN
RUBYTHROAT

♀

♂

♀

RED-FLANKED
BLUETAIL

♂

♀

♂

RED-BREASTED
FLYCATCHER

GRAY-
SPOTTED
FLYCATCHER

SIBERIAN
FLYCATCHER

ASIAN
BROWN
FLYCATCHER

NARCISSUS
FLYCATCHER

♂

GREAT TIT

SIBERIAN
ACCENTOR

355

YELLOW-BREASTED BUNTING *Emberiza aureola*
5½" (14 cm). Male has a black head, *chestnut band across its yellow breast*. **West:** Accidental, Attu, Buldir, St. Lawrence I.

RUSTIC BUNTING *Emberiza rustica*
5¾" (15 cm). A *rusty*, sparrow-like bird with a *rusty* breast band, black crown, and *black cheek outlined in white*. Female has a light spot on its brown cheek patch. Regular but scarce; mainly in spring, outer Aleutians. **West:** Casual, St. Lawrence I. Accidental, British Columbia, Oregon, California

LITTLE BUNTING *Emberiza pusilla* 5" (13 cm). Suggests a Savannah Sparrow, but the *rufous crown* and *rufous cheek patches* are outlined with black. **West:** Accidental, outer Aleutians, Chukchi Sea.

COMMON REED-BUNTING *Emberiza schoeniclus* 6" (15 cm). Male has a *black head and bib, white collar and malar stripe* in summer. Rusty wings. **West:** Casual or accidental in spring in outer Aleutians.

PALLAS'S REED-BUNTING *Emberiza pallasi*
5½" (14 cm). Similar to Common Reed-Bunting, but smaller. Shoulders blue-gray, lacking the bright rusty tone. Upper ridge of bill straight. Rump paler. **West:** Accidental, n. Alaska (St. Lawrence I., Barrow).

GRAY BUNTING *Emberiza variabilis* 6" (15 cm). *Male: Dark slate gray* above and below. *Female:* Dark brown, paler below; *chestnut rump*, no white in tail. **West:** Accidental, outer Aleutians.

HAWFINCH *Coccothraustes coccothraustes*
7" (18 cm). A chunky finch with a *massive bill* and a short tail. Bold *white patches* high on black wings. Female paler; less rufous on crown. **West:** A rare stray, mainly in spring, Bering Sea area (Aleutians, Pribilofs, St. Lawrence I.).

EURASIAN BULLFINCH *Pyrrhula pyrrhula*
5¾" (15 cm). A stubby-billed finch with a black cap and a *white rump. Male:* Rose-red breast and cheeks. *Female:* Similar pattern, but breast is warm pinkish brown. **West:** Casual stray in Bering Sea islands (outer Aleutians, Nunivak I., St. Lawrence I.). Accidental in winter on mainland Alaska.

ORIENTAL GREENFINCH *Carduelis sinica*
6" (15 cm). An olive and brown, siskin-like bird without striping. *Large yellow patches* on wings and tail. Female browner than male. **West:** Rare vagrant, outer Aleutians. Accidental, California.

BRAMBLING *Fringilla montifringilla*
5¾" (15 cm). *Tawny* breast and shoulders, white rump. *Male* in summer has black head and back. **West:** Rare stray, Bering Sea area (Aleutians, Pribilofs, St. Lawrence I.), and various points in Alaska. Accidental, British Columbia, Manitoba, Washington, Oregon, California, Nevada, Montana, Wyoming, Utah, Colorado.

COMMON ROSEFINCH *Carpodacus erythrinus*
5¾" (15 cm). Resembles Purple Finch, but without the facial striping. Upper ridge of bill more curved. **West:** Rare in spring in outer Aleutians (Purple Finch does not occur within 2,000 miles). Casual, St. Paul, Gambell. Accidental on mainland Alaska.

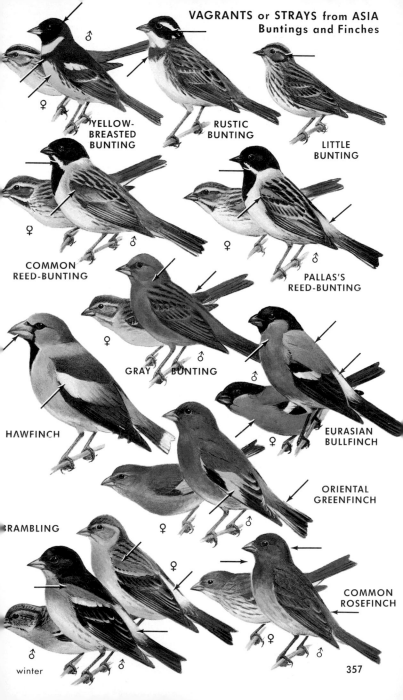

VAGRANTS or STRAYS from ASIA
Buntings and Finches

YELLOW-
BREASTED
BUNTING

♂
♀

RUSTIC
BUNTING

LITTLE
BUNTING

COMMON
REED-BUNTING

♀
♂

PALLAS'S
REED-BUNTING

♀
♂

GRAY BUNTING

♀
♂

HAWFINCH

EURASIAN
BULLFINCH

♂
♀

ORIENTAL
GREENFINCH

BRAMBLING

♀
♂

♀
♂

COMMON
ROSEFINCH

♀
♂

winter

357

■ **OTHER ASIAN STRAYS** (not shown). The following species have been recorded only once or twice in Alaska and (with two exceptions) are not illustrated in this book. They could occur again, as could others. For further possibilities, see *A Field Guide to the Birds of Japan* (Wild Bird Society of Japan).

CHINESE EGRET *Egretta eulophotes*
See illus., p. 113. When breeding, resembles Snowy Egret (black legs, yellow feet), but bill *yellow*, lores *dark*. This endangered Asiatic has occurred once in the w. Aleutians (Aggatu I.).

CHINESE LITTLE BITTERN *Ixobrychus sinensis*
14" (36 cm). Rather like our Least Bittern. Has occurred as an accidental at Attu in the Aleutians, where Least Bittern would not occur.

GREYLAG GOOSE *Anser anser*
An unconfirmed sighting of this large, pale gray Eurasian goose was reported at Attu.

EURASIAN KESTREL *Falco tinnunculus*
Larger than the American Kestrel, with a longer tail, which in males is *gray*. Wings largely rufous (blue-gray in American). Female Eurasian Kestrel has only one black facial bar. **West:** Accidental, w. Aleutians (where American Kestrel would not occur).

NORTHERN HOBBY *Falco subbuteo*
Near size of a Merlin; suggests a small Peregrine. Slaty-backed, heavily striped below, with *rufous "trousers"*; narrow mustache. **West:** Accidental at sea near Aleutians, Pribilofs.

EURASIAN COOT *Fulica atra*
See illus. of head, p. 63. Similar to the American Coot, but with an *entirely white frontal shield* above the bill. *No white* on the undertail coverts. **West:** Accidental, Pribilofs.

BLACK-WINGED STILT *Himantopus himantopus*
Like the Black-necked Stilt, but head and neck largely white, without black pattern. **West:** Accidental, Nizki I., Alaska.

BLACK-TAILED GULL *Larus crassirostris*
A medium-sized gull with a dark mantle and a *broad black band* across the white tail. Yellow legs; yellow bill with a *black ring and red tip*. **West:** Accidental, w. Aleutians; also San Diego, California (perhaps an escape?).

ORIENTAL SCOPS-OWL *Otus sunia*
Resembles a small Screech-Owl. **West:** Accidental, w. Aleutians (nearly 2,000 miles west of Screech-Owl's normal range).

JUNGLE NIGHTJAR *Caprimulgus indicus*
Similar to a Nighthawk (white bar near wing tip, but grayer, tail rounded, breast not barred. **West:** Accidental, w. Aleutians.

GREAT SPOTTED WOODPECKER *Dendrocopos major*
Size of a Hairy Woodpecker, with a black back separating the *large white scapular patches*. *Undertail coverts crimson*. **West:** Accidental outer Aleutians (Attu).

Range Maps

BY VIRGINIA MARIE PETERSON

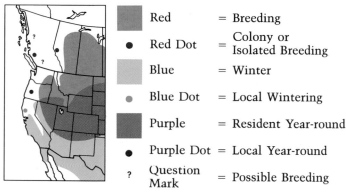

	Red	= Breeding
	Red Dot	= Colony or Isolated Breeding
	Blue	= Winter
	Blue Dot	= Local Wintering
	Purple	= Resident Year-round
	Purple Dot	= Local Year-round
?	Question Mark	= Possible Breeding

The maps on the following pages are approximate, giving the general outline of the range of each species. Within these broad outlines may be many gaps—areas that are ecologically unsuitable for the species. A Marsh Wren must have a marsh, a Meadowlark a meadow, a Ruffed Grouse a woodland or a forest. Certain species may be extremely local or sporadic for reasons that are not clear. Some birds are extending their ranges, a few explosively. Others are declining or even disappearing from large areas where they were formerly found. Some of these increases and declines, as well as extralimital occurrences, are noted on the maps. The maps are based on data from many state and regional publications and modified by the observations of a myriad of birders as reported in *American Birds, Birding, NARBA, Western Birds,* and various other journals and checklists.

Winter ranges are not as definite as breeding ranges. A species may exist at a very low density near the northern limits of its winter range, surviving in mild seasons through December but often succumbing to the bitter conditions of January and February.

The maps are specific only for the area covered by this *Field Guide.* The Mallard, for example, is found over a large part of the globe. Its world range is briefly stated in the main text. The map shows only its range in western North America. The maps are in phylogenetic sequence (see the Systematic Checklist on p. 409) and are not arranged in the arbitrary visual order in which the species appear in this book. The small page number under the map number refers back to the main text.

Note: The Aleutian Chain, extending for another 1,000 miles to the west, is not shown, but pertinent information applying to these islands is included on the maps.

1 (p. 24)

Resident in
Aleutians

?

Rare in
migration
or in winter
in interior

RED-
THROATED
LOON

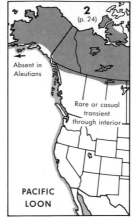

2 (p. 24)

Absent in
Aleutians

Rare or casual
transient
through interior

PACIFIC
LOON

3 (p. 24)

Throughout
Aleutians

?

Transient
through
interior;
wintering
locally

COMMON
LOON

4 (p. 24)

Winters in
Aleutians

Winters
rarely
south to
coastal
Calif.

Very rare
vagrant
inland

YELLOW-
BILLED
LOON

5 (p. 26)

Very rare
in Alaska;
has bred

Winters
locally
on open
water
south of
dash line

Breeds
locally
on fresh
water

PIED-BILLED
GREBE

6 (p. 26)

Winters in
Aleutians

Transient
through
interior;
winters
locally
on open
water

HORNED
GREBE

7 (p. 26)

Winters in
Aleutians

Migrates
mainly
east of
Rockies
and along
coast

RED-NECKED
GREBE

8 (p. 26)

May
winter
locally
elsewhere
on open
water
inland

Breeds
west of
Sierra
only when
conditions
favorable

Great
staging
areas at
Mono Lake,
Salton Sea

EARED
GREBE

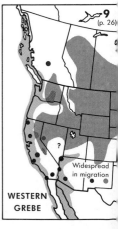

9 (p. 26)

?

Widespread
in migration

WESTERN
GREBE

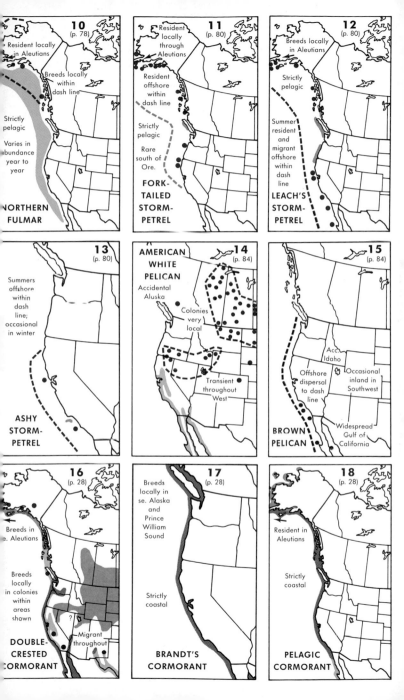

10 (p. 78)

Resident locally in Aleutians

Breeds locally within dash line

Strictly pelagic

Varies in abundance year to year

NORTHERN FULMAR

11 (p. 80)

Resident locally through Aleutians

Resident offshore within dash line

Strictly pelagic

Rare south of Ore.

FORK-TAILED STORM-PETREL

12 (p. 80)

Breeds locally in Aleutians

Strictly pelagic

Summer resident and migrant offshore within dash line

LEACH'S STORM-PETREL

13 (p. 80)

Summers offshore within dash line; occasional in winter

ASHY STORM-PETREL

14 (p. 84)

AMERICAN WHITE PELICAN

Accidental Aluska

Colonies very local

Transient throughout West

15 (p. 84)

Acc. Idaho

Offshore dispersal to dash line

Occasional inland in Southwest

Widespread Gulf of California

BROWN PELICAN

16 (p. 28)

Breeds in e. Aleutians

Breeds locally in colonies within areas shown

?

Migrant throughout

DOUBLE-CRESTED CORMORANT

17 (p. 28)

Breeds locally in se. Alaska and Prince William Sound

Strictly coastal

BRANDT'S CORMORANT

18 (p. 28)

Resident in Aleutians

Strictly coastal

PELAGIC CORMORANT

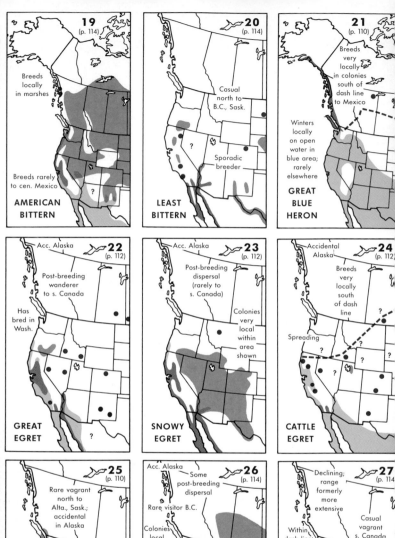

19 (p. 114)
Breeds locally in marshes
Breeds rarely to cen. Mexico
?
AMERICAN BITTERN

20 (p. 114)
Casual north to B.C., Sask.
?
Sporadic breeder
LEAST BITTERN

21 (p. 110)
Breeds very locally in colonies south of dash line to Mexico
Winters locally on open water in blue area; rarely elsewhere
GREAT BLUE HERON

22 (p. 112)
Acc. Alaska
Post-breeding wanderer to s. Canada
Has bred in Wash.
?
GREAT EGRET

23 (p. 112)
Acc. Alaska
Post-breeding dispersal (rarely to s. Canada)
Colonies very local within area shown
SNOWY EGRET

24 (p. 112)
Accidental Alaska
Breeds very locally south of dash line
Spreading
?
?
?
?
?
CATTLE EGRET

25 (p. 110)
Rare vagrant north to Alta., Sask.; accidental in Alaska
GREEN-BACKED HERON

26 (p. 114)
Acc. Alaska
Some post-breeding dispersal
Rare visitor B.C.
Colonies local within range shown
?
BLACK-CROWNED NIGHT-HERON

27 (p. 114)
Declining; range formerly more extensive
Casual vagrant s. Canada
Within dash line colonies local and intermittent
?
?
WHITE-FACED IBIS

28 (p. 38)

Breeds west to Cold Bay

Hundreds winter at end of Alaska Peninsula

Migrant throughout

TUNDRA SWAN

29 (p. 38)

Breeding range now expanding due to restoration program

Winters very rarely south to n. Calif., N.M.

Accidental s. Calif.

TRUMPETER SWAN

30 (p. 40)

A few in winter north to Wash.

Widespread migrant through interior

GREATER WHITE-FRONTED GOOSE

31 (p. 38)

Migrant through interior

SNOW GOOSE

32 (p. 38)

Acc. Alaska, B.C.

Migrant through Plains and west to Pacific states

Increasing as strays eastward

ROSS'S GOOSE

33 (p. 40)

Winters throughout Aleutians

Rare vagrant south to s. Calif.

Casual to inland valleys of Pacific states with other geese

EMPEROR GOOSE

34 (p. 40)

Casual or acc. in most inland states and provinces

Local concentrations on coast in winter within dash line

BRANT

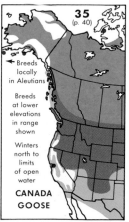

35 (p. 40)

Breeds locally in Aleutians

Breeds at lower elevations in range shown

Winters north to limits of open water

CANADA GOOSE

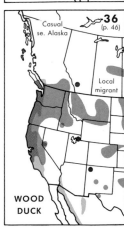

36 (p. 46)

Casual se. Alaska

Local migrant

WOOD DUCK

37 (p. 48)

Resident in Aleutians (Eurasian form resident east to Akutan)

GREEN-WINGED TEAL

38 (p. 44)

Resident throughout Aleutians

Winters north locally as ice-free waters permit

MALLARD

39 (p. 46)

Breeds in Aleutians

NORTHERN PINTAIL

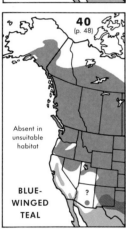

40 (p. 48)

Absent in unsuitable habitat

BLUE-WINGED TEAL

41 (p. 48)

Rare vagrant Alaska

Absent from higher mts. in area shown

?

?

?

?

CINNAMON TEAL

42 (p. 48)

Not in Aleutians

NORTHERN SHOVELER

43 (p. 44)

Sporadic in n. part of winter range

GADWALL

44 (p. 46)

Not in Aleutians

AMERICAN WIGEON

45 (p. 56)

A few winter north to Idaho, Mont.

CANVASBACK

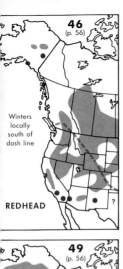

46
(p. 56)

Winters locally south of dash line

REDHEAD

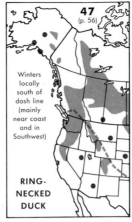

47
(p. 56)

Winters locally south of dash line (mainly near coast and in Southwest)

RING-NECKED DUCK

48
(p. 56)

Breeds sparingly in Aleutians, Bering Sea islands

?

Rare transient, in interior; winters locally south of dash line

GREATER SCAUP

49
(p. 56)

May winter rarely elsewhere below dash line

LESSER SCAUP

50
(p. 52)

Resident in Aleutians

Accidental B.C., Sask.

COMMON EIDER

51
(p. 52)

Winters in Aleutians

Acc. Alberta, Sask.

Casual stray south to Calif.

KING EIDER

52
(p. 52)

Assumed to winter well out in Bering Sea at edge of ice pack

Acc. B.C.

SPECTACLED EIDER

53
(p. 54)

Winters throughout Aleutians

Acc. s. B.C., Wash., Calif.

STELLER'S EIDER

54
(p. 54)

Year round Aleutians; not breeding

Mainly coastal in winter

?

Accidental south to Nev., Utah, N.M.

HARLEQUIN DUCK

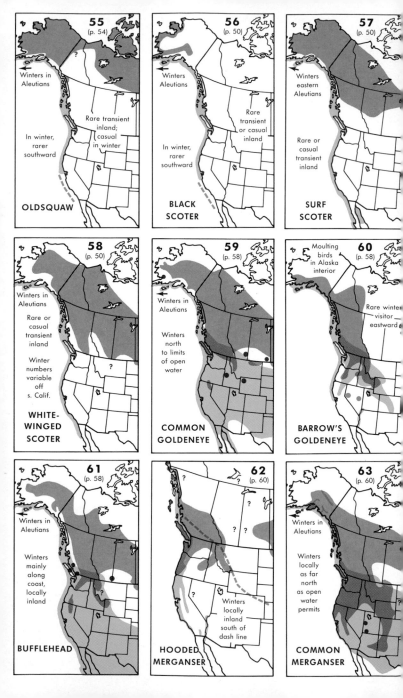

55 (p. 54)

Winters in Aleutians

In winter, rarer southward

?

Rare transient inland; casual in winter

OLDSQUAW

56 (p. 50)

Winters Aleutians

In winter, rarer southward

Rare transient or casual inland

BLACK SCOTER

57 (p. 50)

Winters eastern Aleutians

Rare or casual transient inland

SURF SCOTER

58 (p. 50)

Winters in Aleutians

Rare or casual transient inland

Winter numbers variable off s. Calif.

?

WHITE-WINGED SCOTER

59 (p. 58)

Winters in Aleutians

Winters north to limits of open water

COMMON GOLDENEYE

60 (p. 58)

Moulting birds in Alaska interior

Rare winter visitor eastward

BARROW'S GOLDENEYE

61 (p. 58)

Winters in Aleutians

Winters mainly along coast, locally inland

BUFFLEHEAD

62 (p. 60)

?
?
?
?
?
?

Winters locally inland south of dash line

HOODED MERGANSER

63 (p. 60)

Winters in Aleutians

Winters locally as far north as open water permits

COMMON MERGANSER

64 (p. 60)

esident in Aleutians

Mainly coastal in winter; very few winter locally in interior

RED-BREASTED MERGANSER

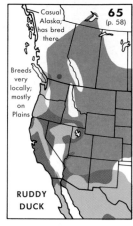

65 (p. 58)

Casual Alaska; has bred there

Breeds very locally; mostly on Plains

RUDDY DUCK

66 (p. 182)

Accidental Alaska

Occasional in winter to s. B.C.

Breeds very locally; ranges widely

TURKEY VULTURE

67 (p. 184)

Breeds very locally in area shown

May breed elsewhere in Southwest

Winters rarely on inland lakes of Calif.

OSPREY

68 (p. 170)

Expanding range in Pacific states

Casual or acc. east to Utah, Idaho, Wyo., S.D., N.M., w. Texas

Wanders in winter

BLACK-SHOULDERED KITE

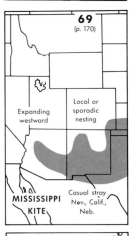

69 (p. 170)

Expanding westward

Local or sporadic nesting

Casual stray Nev., Calif., Neb.

MISSISSIPPI KITE

70 (p. 180)

Resident to w. Aleutians (Buldir I.)

Breeds locally near water in range shown

BALD EAGLE

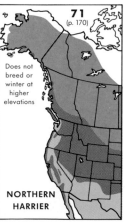

71 (p. 170)

Does not breed or winter at higher elevations

NORTHERN HARRIER

72 (p. 172)

Breeds very locally within area shown

SHARP-SHINNED HAWK

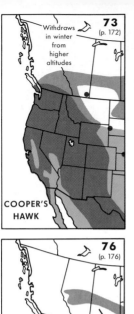

Withdraws in winter from higher altitudes

73 (p. 172)

COOPER'S HAWK

74 (p. 172)

Widespread wandering in winter

NORTHERN GOSHAWK

RED-SHOULDERED HAWK

75 (p. 17...)

Accidental north to Wash., B.C., Mont., Dakotas

Spreading; partially migratory

Widespread in e. U.S.

76 (p. 176)

Winters rarely s. Calif.

Migrates mainly east of Rockies to tropics; a very few west to coast

BROAD-WINGED HAWK

77 (p. 174)

Numbers reduced in recent years

A few reach coast in migration

SWAINSON'S HAWK

78 (p. 174)

Withdraws in winter from higher elevations

RED-TAILED HAWK

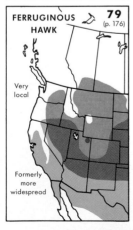

FERRUGINOUS HAWK

79 (p. 176)

Very local

Formerly more widespread

80 (p. 176)

Breeds in e. Aleutians

Winters rarely to Mexican border

ROUGH-LEGGED HAWK

81 (p. 180)

Breeds to Unimak I.

Breeds locally in area indicated

GOLDEN EAGLE

82 (p. 186)

Widespread breeder except in higher mts. and some deserts

Withdraws from higher elevations in winter

AMERICAN KESTREL

83 (p. 186)

Winters below dash line; most frequent southward and along coast

MERLIN

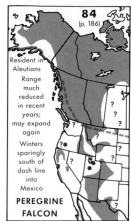

84 (p. 186)

Resident in Aleutians

Range much reduced in recent years; may expand again

Winters sparingly south of dash line into Mexico

PEREGRINE FALCON

85 (p. 184)

Breeds in e. Aleutians

Irregular winter visitor south to dash line; accidental further (n. Calif., Utah, Colo.)

GYRFALCON

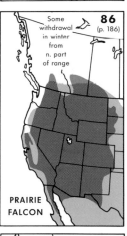

86 (p. 186)

Some withdrawal in winter from n. part of range

PRAIRIE FALCON

87 (p. 164)

European import; introduced widely and successfully

GRAY PARTRIDGE

88 (p. 164)

An Asian import; introduced widely and successfully

CHUKAR

89 (p. 158)

Introduced. Stocked in many localities; does not always persist

RING-NECKED PHEASANT

90 (p. 164)

SPRUCE GROUSE

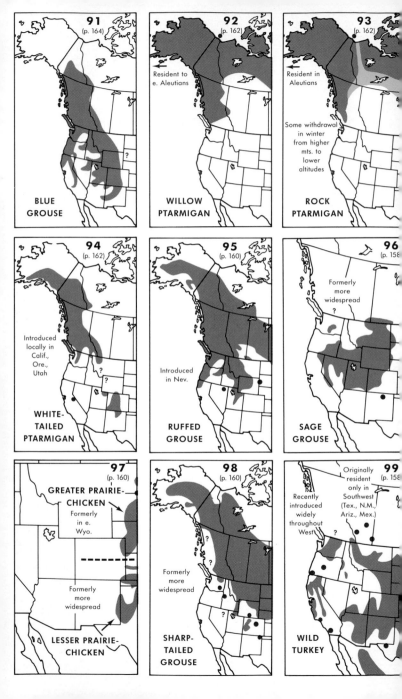

91 (p. 164)

BLUE GROUSE

92 (p. 162)

← Resident to e. Aleutians

WILLOW PTARMIGAN

93 (p. 162)

← Resident in Aleutians

Some withdrawal in winter from higher mts. to lower altitudes

ROCK PTARMIGAN

94 (p. 162)

Introduced locally in Calif., Ore., Utah

WHITE-TAILED PTARMIGAN

95 (p. 160)

Introduced in Nev.

RUFFED GROUSE

96 (p. 158)

Formerly more widespread ?

SAGE GROUSE

97 (p. 160)

GREATER PRAIRIE-CHICKEN →

Formerly in e. Wyo.

Formerly more widespread

LESSER PRAIRIE-CHICKEN

98 (p. 160)

Formerly more widespread

SHARP-TAILED GROUSE

99 (p. 158)

Originally resident only in Southwest (Tex., N.M., Ariz., Mex.)

Recently introduced widely throughout West

WILD TURKEY

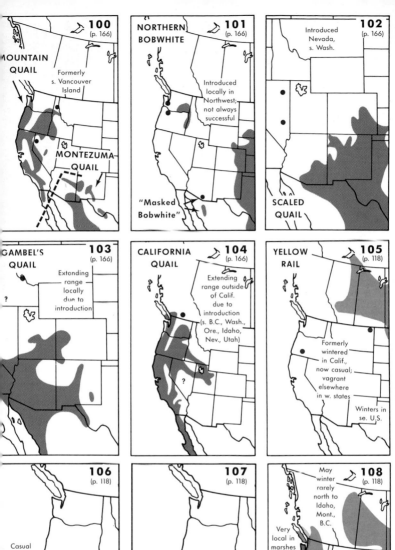

100 (p. 166)

MOUNTAIN QUAIL

Formerly s. Vancouver Island

MONTEZUMA QUAIL

NORTHERN BOBWHITE **101** (p. 166)

Introduced locally in Northwest; not always successful

"Masked Bobwhite"

102 (p. 166)

Introduced Nevada, s. Wash.

SCALED QUAIL

GAMBEL'S QUAIL **103** (p. 166)

Extending range locally due to introduction

?

CALIFORNIA QUAIL **104** (p. 166)

Extending range outside of Calif. due to introduction (s. B.C., Wash., Ore., Idaho, Nev., Utah)

?

YELLOW RAIL **105** (p. 118)

Formerly wintered in Calif., now casual; vagrant elsewhere in w. states

Winters in se. U.S.

106 (p. 118)

Casual elsewhere in Ariz., casual also in Colo., N.D., N. Mex.

?

BLACK RAIL

107 (p. 118)

Very local in coastal marshes

Also recorded locally near Phoenix, Ariz.

CLAPPER RAIL

108 (p. 118)

May winter rarely north to Idaho, Mont., B.C.

Very local in marshes in area shown

? ? ?

?

VIRGINIA RAIL

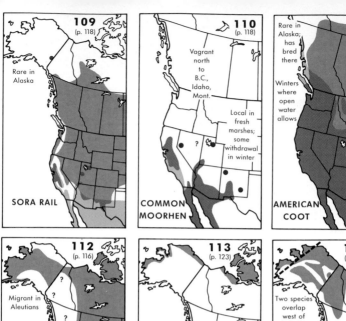

109 (p. 118)

Rare in Alaska

SORA RAIL

110 (p. 118)

Vagrant north to B.C., Idaho, Mont.

Local in fresh marshes; some withdrawal in winter

COMMON MOORHEN

11 (p. 11)

Rare in Alaska; has bred there

Winters where open water allows

AMERICAN COOT

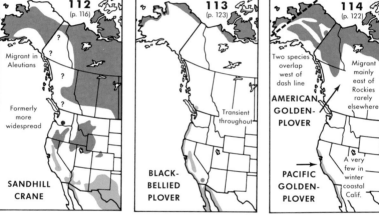

112 (p. 116)

Migrant in Aleutians

Formerly more widespread

SANDHILL CRANE

113 (p. 123)

Transient throughout

BLACK-BELLIED PLOVER

114 (p. 122)

Two species overlap west of dash line

AMERICAN GOLDEN-PLOVER

Migrant mainly east of Rockies rarely elsewhere

PACIFIC GOLDEN-PLOVER

A very few in winter coastal Calif.

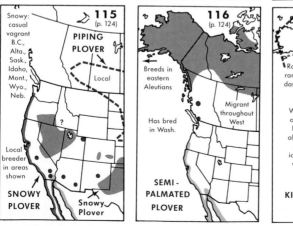

115 (p. 124)

Snowy: casual vagrant B.C., Alta., Sask., Idaho, Mont., Wyo., Neb.

PIPING PLOVER

Local

Local breeder in areas shown

SNOWY PLOVER

Snowy Plover

116 (p. 124)

Breeds in eastern Aleutians

Has bred in Wash.

Migrant throughout West

SEMI-PALMATED PLOVER

117 (p. 126)

Ranges rarely to dash line

Winters only at lower altitudes near ice-free water

KILLDEER

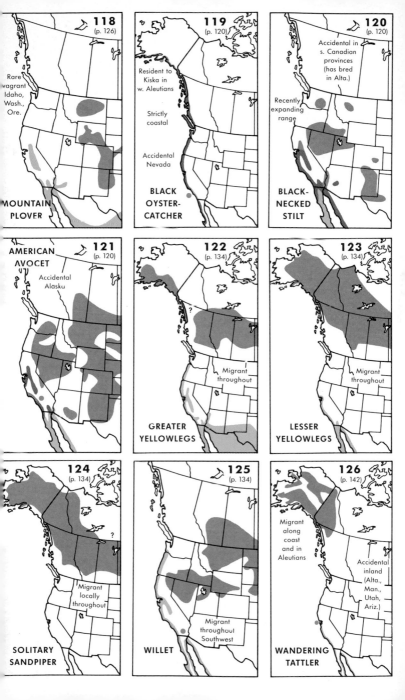

118 (p. 126)

Rare vagrant Idaho, Wash., Ore.

MOUNTAIN PLOVER

119 (p. 120)

Resident to Kiska in w. Aleutians

Strictly coastal

Accidental Nevada

BLACK OYSTER-CATCHER

120 (p. 120)

Accidental in s. Canadian provinces (has bred in Alta.)

Recently expanding range

BLACK-NECKED STILT

121 (p. 120)

AMERICAN AVOCET

Accidental Alaska

122 (p. 134)

?

Migrant throughout

GREATER YELLOWLEGS

123 (p. 134)

Migrant throughout

LESSER YELLOWLEGS

124 (p. 134)

?

Migrant locally throughout

SOLITARY SANDPIPER

125 (p. 134)

Migrant throughout Southwest

WILLET

126 (p. 142)

Migrant along coast and in Aleutians

Accidental inland (Alta., Man., Utah, Ariz.)

WANDERING TATTLER

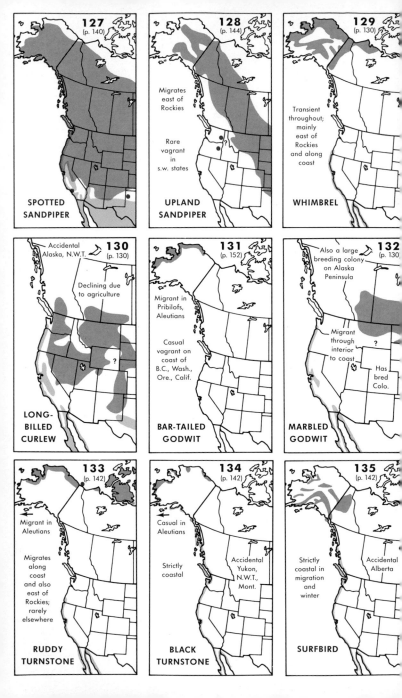

127 (p. 140)

SPOTTED SANDPIPER

128 (p. 144)

Migrates east of Rockies

Rare vagrant in s.w. states

UPLAND SANDPIPER

129 (p. 130)

Transient throughout; mainly east of Rockies and along coast

WHIMBREL

130 (p. 130)

Accidental Alaska, N.W.T.

Declining due to agriculture

?

LONG-BILLED CURLEW

131 (p. 152)

Migrant in Pribilofs, Aleutians

Casual vagrant on coast of B.C., Wash., Ore., Calif.

BAR-TAILED GODWIT

132 (p. 130)

Also a large breeding colony on Alaska Peninsula

Migrant through interior to coast

?

Has bred Colo.

MARBLED GODWIT

133 (p. 142)

Migrant in Aleutians

Migrates along coast and also east of Rockies; rarely elsewhere

RUDDY TURNSTONE

134 (p. 142)

Casual in Aleutians

Strictly coastal

Accidental Yukon, N.W.T., Mont.

BLACK TURNSTONE

135 (p. 142)

Strictly coastal in migration and winter

Accidental Alberta

SURFBIRD

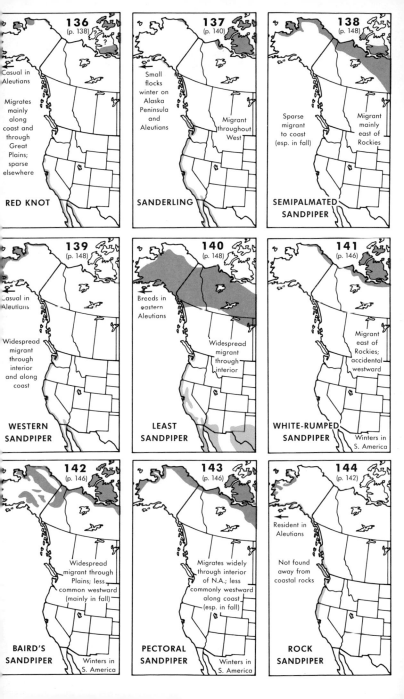

136 (p. 138)

Casual in Aleutians

Migrates mainly along coast and through Great Plains; sparse elsewhere

RED KNOT

137 (p. 140)

Small flocks winter on Alaska Peninsula and Aleutians

Migrant throughout West

SANDERLING

138 (p. 148)

Sparse migrant to coast (esp. in fall)

Migrant mainly east of Rockies

SEMIPALMATED SANDPIPER

139 (p. 148)

Casual in Aleutians

Widespread migrant through interior and along coast

WESTERN SANDPIPER

140 (p. 148)

Breeds in eastern Aleutians

Widespread migrant through interior

LEAST SANDPIPER

141 (p. 146)

Migrant east of Rockies; accidental westward

Winters in S. America

WHITE-RUMPED SANDPIPER

142 (p. 146)

Widespread migrant through Plains; less common westward (mainly in fall)

BAIRD'S SANDPIPER

Winters in S. America

143 (p. 146)

Migrates widely through interior of N.A.; less commonly westward along coast (esp. in fall)

PECTORAL SANDPIPER

Winters in S. America

144 (p. 142)

Resident in Aleutians

Not found away from coastal rocks

ROCK SANDPIPER

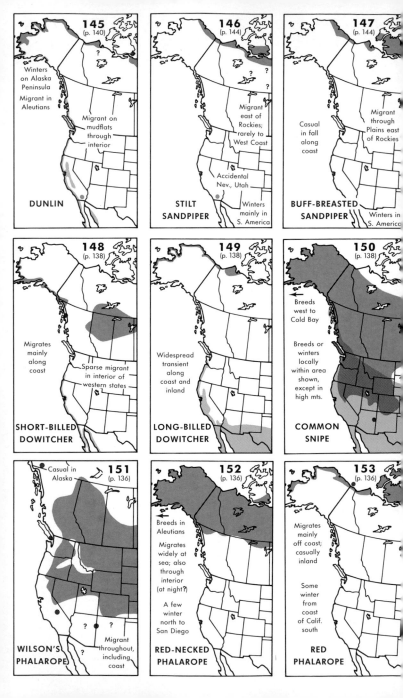

145 (p. 140)
Winters on Alaska Peninsula
Migrant in Aleutians
Migrant on mudflats through interior
DUNLIN

146 (p. 144)
? ? ?
Migrant east of Rockies; rarely to West Coast
Accidental Nev., Utah
Winters mainly in S. America
STILT SANDPIPER

147 (p. 144)
Migrant through Plains east of Rockies
Winters in S. America
BUFF-BREASTED SANDPIPER

148 (p. 138)
Migrates mainly along coast
Sparse migrant in interior of western states
SHORT-BILLED DOWITCHER

149 (p. 138)
Widespread transient along coast and inland
LONG-BILLED DOWITCHER

150 (p. 138)
Breeds west to Cold Bay
Breeds or winters locally within area shown, except in high mts.
COMMON SNIPE

151 (p. 136)
Casual in Alaska
? ?
?
Migrant throughout, including coast
WILSON'S PHALAROPE

152 (p. 136)
Breeds in Aleutians
Migrates widely at sea; also through interior (at night?)
A few winter north to San Diego
RED-NECKED PHALAROPE

153 (p. 136)
Migrates mainly off coast; casually inland
Some winter from coast of Calif. south
RED PHALAROPE

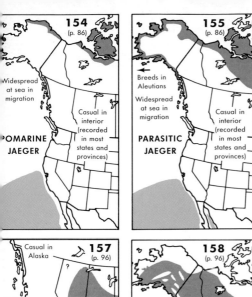

154 (p. 86)

Widespread at sea in migration

Casual in interior (recorded in most states and provinces)

POMARINE JAEGER

155 (p. 86)

← Breeds in Aleutians

Widespread at sea in migration

Casual in interior (recorded in most states and provinces)

PARASITIC JAEGER

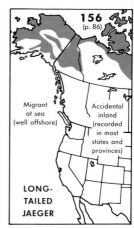

156 (p. 86)

Migrant at sea (well offshore)

Accidental inland (recorded in most states and provinces)

LONG-TAILED JAEGER

157 (p. 96)

Casual in Alaska ?

Main migration east of Rockies; some in fall to Pacific Coast

Recently expanding range

Winters in S. America

FRANKLIN'S GULL

158 (p. 96)

Widespread but local migrant inland

BONAPARTE'S GULL

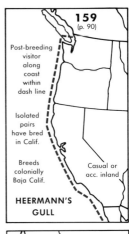

159 (p. 90)

Post-breeding visitor along coast within dash line

Isolated pairs have bred in Calif.

Breeds colonially Baja Calif.

Casual or acc. inland

HEERMANN'S GULL

160 (p. 92)

← Resident west to Unimak I.

?

?

Rare vagrant in interior states

MEW GULL

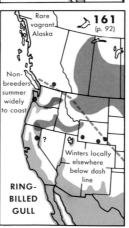

161 (p. 92)

Rare vagrant, Alaska

Non-breeders summer widely to coast

?

Winters locally elsewhere below dash line

RING-BILLED GULL

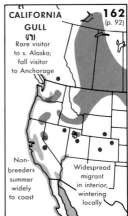

CALIFORNIA GULL

162 (p. 92)

Rare visitor to s. Alaska; fall visitor to Anchorage

Non-breeders summer widely to coast

Widespread migrant in interior, wintering locally

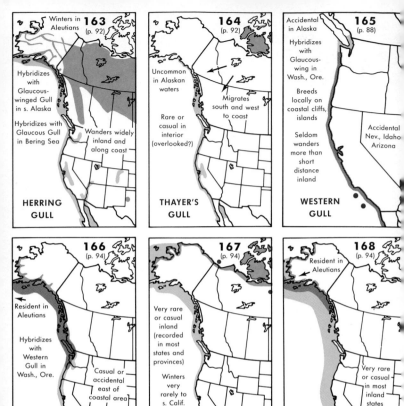

163 (p. 92)

Winters in Aleutians

Hybridizes with Glaucous-winged Gull in s. Alaska

Hybridizes with Glaucous Gull in Bering Sea

Wanders widely inland and along coast

HERRING GULL

164 (p. 92)

Uncommon in Alaskan waters

Migrates south and west to coast

Rare or casual in interior (overlooked?)

THAYER'S GULL

165 (p. 88)

Accidental in Alaska

Hybridizes with Glaucous-wing in Wash., Ore.

Breeds locally on coastal cliffs, islands

Seldom wanders more than short distance inland

Accidental Nev., Idaho Arizona

WESTERN GULL

166 (p. 94)

Resident in Aleutians

Hybridizes with Western Gull in Wash., Ore.

Casual or accidental east of coastal area

GLAUCOUS-WINGED GULL

167 (p. 94)

Very rare or casual inland (recorded in most states and provinces)

Winters very rarely to s. Calif.

GLAUCOUS GULL

168 (p. 94)

Resident in Aleutians

Very rare or casual in most inland states

BLACK-LEGGED KITTIWAKE

169 (p. 96)

Migrant off Pacific Coast to S. America

Very rare or casual inland (has been recorded in most states)

SABINE'S GULL

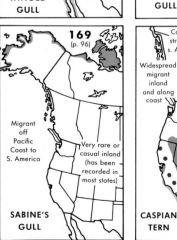

170 (p. 104)

Casual stray to s. Alaska

Widespread migrant inland and along coast

Colonies sporadic

Casual in winter to s. Calif.

CASPIAN TERN

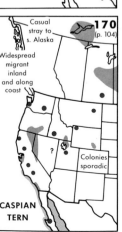

17 (p. 10

Rare in Alaska

Black-billed Asian form occurs in w. Aleutians, Pribilofs, St. Lawrence I.

Has bred se. Idaho

Widespread transient inland; mainly fall migrant on coast from s. B.C. south

Casual in winter to s. Calif.

COMMON TERN

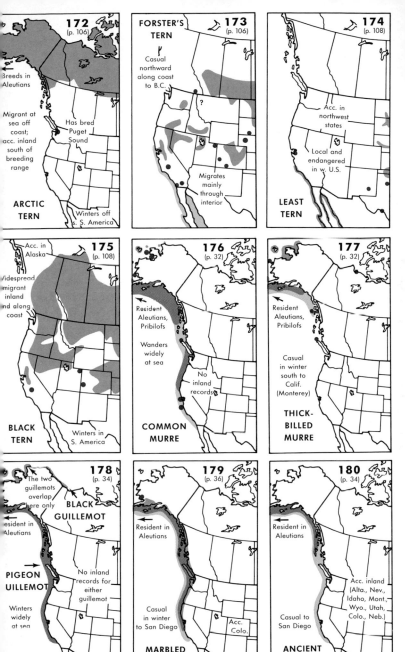

172 (p. 106)

Breeds in Aleutians

Migrant at sea off coast; acc. inland south of breeding range

ARCTIC TERN

Winters off s. S. America

FORSTER'S TERN **173** (p. 106)

Casual northward along coast to B.C.

Has bred Puget Sound

?

Migrates mainly through interior

---

174 (p. 108)

Acc. in northwest states

Local and endangered in w. U.S.

LEAST TERN

---

175 (p. 108)

Acc. in Alaska

Widespread migrant inland and along coast

BLACK TERN

Winters in S. America

---

176 (p. 32)

Resident Aleutians, Pribilofs

Wanders widely at sea

No inland records

COMMON MURRE

---

177 (p. 32)

Resident Aleutians, Pribilofs

Casual in winter south to Calif. (Monterey)

THICK-BILLED MURRE

---

178 (p. 34)

The two guillemots overlap here only

BLACK GUILLEMOT

Resident in Aleutians

PIGEON GUILLEMOT

No inland records for either guillemot

Winters widely at sea

---

179 (p. 36)

Resident in Aleutians

Casual in winter to San Diego

Acc. Colo.

MARBLED MURRELET

---

180 (p. 34)

Resident in Aleutians

Acc. inland (Alta., Nev., Idaho, Mont., Wyo., Utah, Colo., Neb.)

Casual to San Diego

ANCIENT MURRELET

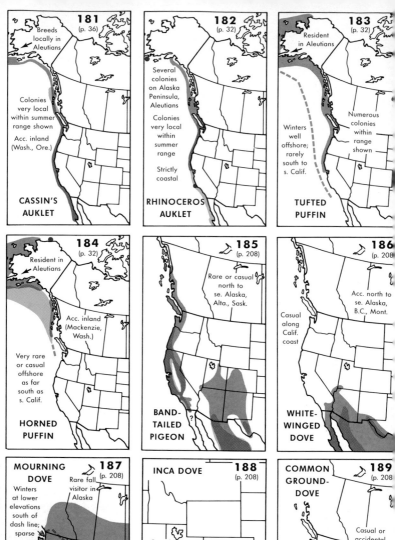

181 (p. 36)
Breeds locally in Aleutians

Colonies very local within summer range shown

Acc. inland (Wash., Ore.)

CASSIN'S AUKLET

182 (p. 32)
Several colonies on Alaska Peninsula, Aleutians

Colonies very local within summer range

Strictly coastal

RHINOCEROS AUKLET

183 (p. 32)
Resident in Aleutians

Winters well offshore; rarely south to s. Calif.

Numerous colonies within range shown

TUFTED PUFFIN

184 (p. 32)
Resident in Aleutians

Acc. inland (Mackenzie, Wash.)

Very rare or casual offshore as far south as s. Calif.

HORNED PUFFIN

185 (p. 208)
Rare or casual north to se. Alaska, Alta., Sask.

Casual along Calif. coast

BAND-TAILED PIGEON

?

186 (p. 208)
Acc. north to se. Alaska, B.C., Mont.

WHITE-WINGED DOVE

MOURNING DOVE **187** (p. 208)
Rare fall visitor in Alaska

Winters at lower elevations south of dash line; sparse or rare in North

INCA DOVE **188** (p. 208)

Casual sw. Calif., s. Nev., sw. Utah

Local; mainly in residential areas

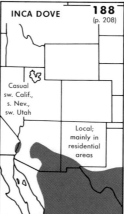

COMMON GROUND-DOVE **189** (p. 208)

Casual or accidental north to n. Calif., s. Utah, Wyo., S.D.

Probably leaves N. Mex. in winter

? ?

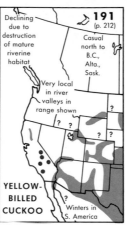

190 (p. 212)

Casual or accidental west of Rockies

?

BLACK-BILLED CUCKOO

191 (p. 212)

Declining due to destruction of mature riverine habitat

Casual north to B.C., Alta., Sask.

Very local in river valleys in range shown

?

? ?

? ?

Winters in S. America

YELLOW-BILLED CUCKOO

GREATER ROADRUNNER

192 (p. 212)

BARN OWL

193 (p. 198)

Accidental in prairie provinces

Absent in higher mts.

Some withdrawal in winter from North

?

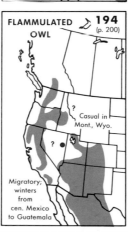

FLAMMULATED OWL

194 (p. 200)

Casual in Mont., Wyo.

?

?

Migratory; winters from cen. Mexico to Guatemala

195 (p. 200)

EASTERN SCREECH-OWL

Eastern Screech-Owl is resident east of dash line

? ?

WESTERN SCREECH-OWL

Northernmost populations partly migratory

GREAT HORNED OWL

196 (p. 200)

197 (p. 198)

Resident in Aleutians

Cyclic; winters some years to dash line; accidental farther south

SNOWY OWL

198 (p. 202)

Winters casually or accidentally south to w. Oregon, Idaho, Wyoming, Nebraska

NORTHERN HAWK-OWL

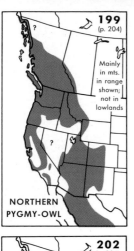

199
(p. 204)

? Mainly in mts. in range shown; not in lowlands

?

NORTHERN PYGMY-OWL

200

BOREAL OWL
(p. 202)

Resident; very rare in winter to s. B.C., n. Wash., w. Mont.

?

ELF OWL
(p. 204)
Migrates south in winter

BURROWING OWL

201
(p. 202)

Breeds very locally in fields, open country within area shown

202
(p. 204)

Local in canyons and mature forests

Casual Colo.
? ?

Declining; endangered

SPOTTED OWL

Casual se. Alaska, n. Calif.

203
(p. 198)

Some winter withdrawal in North

Extending range in Northwest

? ? ?

BARRED OWL

204
(p. 198)

Wanders rarely to n. Great Plains in winter

?

?

Casual w. Nev., Utah

GREAT GRAY OWL

Acc. in se. Alaska

205
(p. 200)

Winters locally from dash line to n. Mexico

Very local in range shown

?

LONG-EARED OWL

206
(p. 200)

Breeds to central Aleutians

Local in open habitat within range shown

SHORT-EARED OWL

207
(p. 202)

Some withdrawal from North in winter

Very local resident in highlands

?

NORTHERN SAW-WHET OWL

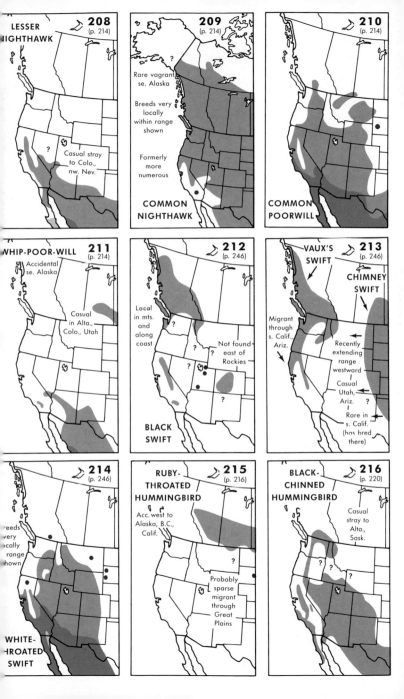

LESSER NIGHTHAWK 208 (p. 214)
? Casual stray to Colo., nw. Nev.

209 (p. 214)
? Rare vagrant se. Alaska
Breeds very locally within range shown
Formerly more numerous
COMMON NIGHTHAWK

COMMON POORWILL 210 (p. 214)

WHIP-POOR-WILL 211 (p. 214)
Accidental se. Alaska
Casual in Alta., Colo., Utah

212 (p. 246)
Local in mts. and along coast
?
?
?
?
Not found east of Rockies
?
BLACK SWIFT

VAUX'S SWIFT 213 (p. 246)
CHIMNEY SWIFT
Migrant through s. Calif., Ariz.
Recently extending range westward
Casual Utah, Ariz. ?
Rare in s. Calif. (has bred there)

214 (p. 246)
Breeds very locally range shown
WHITE-THROATED SWIFT

RUBY-THROATED HUMMINGBIRD 215 (p. 216)
Acc. west to Alaska, B.C., Calif.
?
Probably sparse migrant through Great Plains

BLACK-CHINNED HUMMINGBIRD 216 (p. 220)
Casual stray to Alta., Sask.
? ?
?

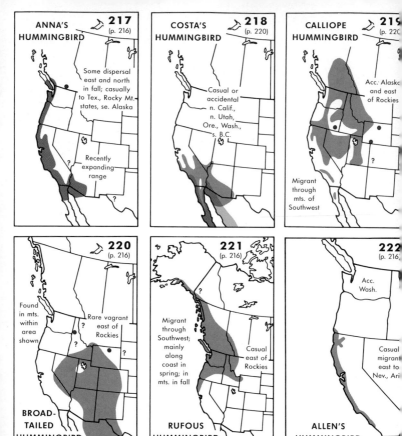

217 (p. 216)
ANNA'S HUMMINGBIRD
Some dispersal east and north in fall; casually to Tex., Rocky Mt. states, se. Alaska

Recently expanding range ?

218 (p. 220)
COSTA'S HUMMINGBIRD
Casual or accidental n. Calif., n. Utah, Ore., Wash., s. B.C.

219 (p. 220)
CALLIOPE HUMMINGBIRD
Acc. Alaska and east of Rockies

Migrant through mts. of Southwest

?

220 (p. 216)
BROAD-TAILED HUMMINGBIRD
Found in mts. within area shown

Rare vagrant east of Rockies ?

221 (p. 216)
RUFOUS HUMMINGBIRD
Migrant through Southwest; mainly along coast in spring; in mts. in fall

Casual east of Rockies

?

222 (p. 216)
ALLEN'S HUMMINGBIRD
Acc. Wash.

Casual migrant east to Nev., Ariz.

223 (p. 206)
BELTED KINGFISHER
Winters locally as far north as open water allows

?

224 (p. 222)
LEWIS'S WOODPECKER
Local; declining or absent in parts of range

Casual Sask., Man., N.D.

Wanders erratically in winter; casually south to dash line

?

225 (p. 222)
RED-HEADED WOODPECKER
Casual or acc. B.C., Alta., Idaho, se. Calif., Ariz.

Casual s. Ore.

NUTTALL'S WOODPECKER (p. 229)

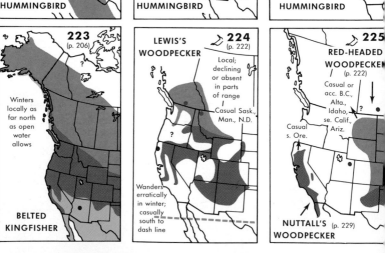

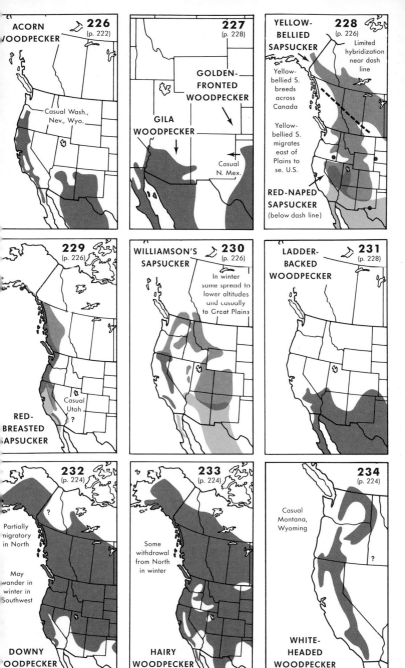

226 (p. 222)
ACORN WOODPECKER
Casual Wash., Nev., Wyo.

227 (p. 228)
GOLDEN-FRONTED WOODPECKER
GILA WOODPECKER
Casual N. Mex.

228 (p. 226)
YELLOW-BELLIED SAPSUCKER
Limited hybridization near dash line
Yellow-bellied S. breeds across Canada
Yellow-bellied S. migrates east of Plains to se. U.S.
RED-NAPED SAPSUCKER (below dash line)

229 (p. 226)
RED-BREASTED SAPSUCKER
Casual Utah ?

230 (p. 226)
WILLIAMSON'S SAPSUCKER
In winter some spread to lower altitudes and casually to Great Plains

231 (p. 228)
LADDER-BACKED WOODPECKER

232 (p. 224)
DOWNY WOODPECKER
Partially migratory in North
May wander in winter in Southwest
?

233 (p. 224)
HAIRY WOODPECKER
Some withdrawal from North in winter

234 (p. 224)
WHITE-HEADED WOODPECKER
Casual Montana, Wyoming
?

235
(p. 224)

Local in higher conifer forests; some wandering in winter

THREE-TOED WOODPECKER

236
(p. 224)

?

Some wandering in winter

?

BLACK-BACKED WOODPECKER

237
(p. 226)

NORTHERN FLICKER

238
(p. 222)

? Casual Wyo.

PILEATED WOODPECKER

239
(p. 236)

?

Transient throughout

?

OLIVE-SIDED FLYCATCHER

240
(p. 236)

WESTERN WOOD-PEWEE

YELLOW-BELLIED FLYCATCHER

241
(p. 240)

Migrates through e. U.S.

Yellow-bellied Flycatcher casual or acc. Alaska, Calif., Ariz., N.M.

Migrant through sw. states; rare along coast

GRAY FLYCATCHER (p. 240)

242
(p. 238)

Migrates east of Great Plains

Winters S. America

ALDER FLYCATCHER

Diminishing where streamside habitat is destroyed

243
(p. 238)

?

?

Formerly bred in s. Calif.

?

WILLOW FLYCATCHER

Winters in middle America

244
(p. 240)

Accidental Alaska

Rare vagrant west to Ore., Calif. (has bred), Nev., Ariz.

Migrates mostly east of Rockies

LEAST FLYCATCHER

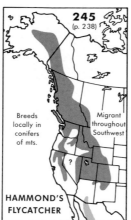

245
(p. 238)

Breeds locally in conifers of mts.

Migrant throughout Southwest

HAMMOND'S FLYCATCHER

Casual in Alaska

246
(p. 238)

Migrant through sw. states; casual along coast

DUSKY FLYCATCHER

247
(p. 240)

"WESTERN" FLYCATCHER
(now 2 species—see text)

Migrates throughout

Winters in Mexico

248
(p. 236)

Casual s. B.C., w. Wash.

BLACK PHOEBE

249
(p. 236)

Casual vagrant west to Pacific

Winters rarely Calif., Ariz.

EASTERN PHOEBE

250
(p. 238)

Sparse migrant on nw. coast

SAY'S PHOEBE

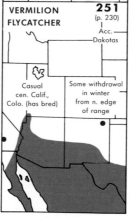

VERMILION FLYCATCHER

251
(p. 230)

Acc. Dakotas

Casual cen. Calif., Colo. (has bred)

Some withdrawal in winter from n. edge of range

ASH-THROATED FLYCATCHER

252
(p. 234)

Casual north to s. B.C., Mont.

Accidental N.W. Terr.

253 (p. 234)

Rare vagrant west to Mont., Wyo., Ariz., Calif.

GREAT CRESTED FLYCATCHER

254 (p. 232)

Casual vagrant Ore., Idaho, S.D., Neb.

CASSIN'S KINGBIRD

Casual north to Alaska

255 (p. 232)

Sparse migrant along coast

WESTERN KINGBIRD

256 (p. 232)

Rare vagrant se. Alaska

Rare migrant s. Calif., Ariz.

EASTERN KINGBIRD

SCISSOR-TAILED FLYCATCHER

257 (p. 230)

Casual or acc. throughout much of N. America; recorded in most w. states and sw. Canada

Has apparently bred in Calif.

258 (p. 242)

Restricted to open country in range shown

HORNED LARK

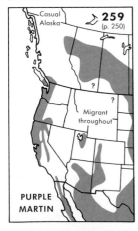

Casual Alaska

259 (p. 250)

Migrant throughout

PURPLE MARTIN

260 (p. 248)

Migrant throughout

TREE SWALLOW

261 (p. 248)

Rare vagrant further east

VIOLET-GREEN SWALLOW

Rare in se. Alaska

262
(p. 248)

Breeds locally except in high mts.

NORTHERN ROUGH-WINGED SWALLOW

263
(p. 248)

Breeds very locally in sand banks within range

Migrant throughout sw. states

BANK SWALLOW

Winters mainly in S. America

264
(p. 250)

Breeds locally

Migrant throughout

CLIFF SWALLOW

?

265
(p. 250)

Migrant throughout Southwest

BARN SWALLOW

266
(p. 256)

Some wandering beyond edges of range in winter

GRAY JAY

267
(p. 254)

Acc. eastward on Plains

STELLER'S JAY

Northern populations partially migratory; a few wander to dash line

268
(p. 254)

Extending range westward

BLUE JAY

269
(p. 254)

Casual B.C., Neb., Kans.

Some wander to lowlands and Plains in winter
?

SCRUB JAY

GRAY-BREASTED JAY

270
(p. 254)

271 (p. 254)

Irruptive or casual in winter to adjacent areas and south to Mexican borderland

PINYON JAY

272 (p. 256)

Wanders irregularly to coast and north to Alaska, east to Great Plains and south to n. Mex.

Resident at higher altitudes within range shown

?

CLARK'S NUTCRACKER

273 (p. 256)

Black-billed wanders casually or irregularly beyond edge of range

BLACK-BILLED MAGPIE

YELLOW-BILLED MAGPIE

274 (p. 252)

Casual in winter to Yukon

?   ?

AMERICAN CROW

Casual s. Ariz.

275 (p. 252)

Probable hybridization with American Crow in B.C. and Wash.

NORTHWESTERN CROW

CHIHUAHUAN RAVEN

276 (p. 252)

Some withdraw in winter from n. part of range

277 (p. 252)

Resident in Aleutians

Casual on Plains in winter

?

COMMON RAVEN

278 (p. 258)

West to Cold Bay

Wanders rarely to n. Ariz., Texas

BLACK-CAPPED CHICKADEE

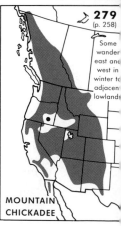

279 (p. 258)

Some wander east and west in winter to adjacent lowlands

MOUNTAIN CHICKADEE

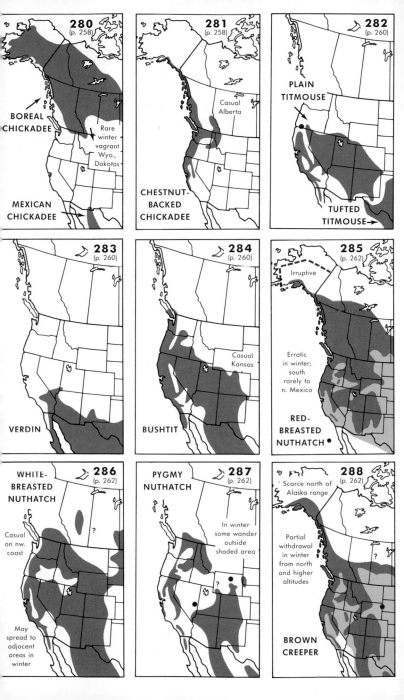

280 (p. 258)

BOREAL CHICKADEE

Rare winter vagrant Wyo., Dakotas

MEXICAN CHICKADEE

281 (p. 258)

Casual Alberta

CHESTNUT-BACKED CHICKADEE

282 (p. 260)

PLAIN TITMOUSE

TUFTED TITMOUSE→

283 (p. 260)

VERDIN

284 (p. 260)

Casual Kansas

BUSHTIT

285 (p. 262)

Irruptive

Erratic in winter; south rarely to n. Mexico

RED-BREASTED NUTHATCH

286 (p. 262)

WHITE-BREASTED NUTHATCH

Casual on nw. coast

May spread to adjacent areas in winter

287 (p. 262)

PYGMY NUTHATCH

In winter some wander outside shaded area

288 (p. 262)

Scarce north of Alaska range

Partial withdrawal in winter from north and higher altitudes

BROWN CREEPER

289 (p. 266)

CACTUS WREN

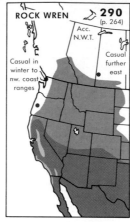

ROCK WREN

290 (p. 264)

Acc. N.W.T.

Casual in winter to nw. coast ranges

Casual further east

291 (p. 266)

Casual Sask., Neb.

CANYON WREN

292 (p. 264)

Casual Idaho, S.D.

?

BEWICK'S WREN

293 (p. 264)

HOUSE WREN

294 (p. 264)

Resident in Aleutians

Withdraws from higher altitudes in winter

?

WINTER WREN

295 (p. 264)

Casual in winter north to w. Mont., sw. S.D.

MARSH WREN

296 (p. 266)

?

Some withdrawal from higher altitudes in winter

Casual Sask., Neb., Texas

AMERICAN DIPPER

297 (p. 268)

?

GOLDEN-CROWNED KINGLET

298 (p. 268)

RUBY-CROWNED KINGLET

BLUE-GRAY GNATCATCHER **299** (p. 268)

Rare vagrant north to s. Canada

BLACK-TAILED GNATCATCHER **300** (p. 268)

CALIFORNIA GNATCATCHER

Black-tailed Gnatcatcher

California Gnatcatcher

301 (p. 278)

Casual se. Alberta

?

Spreading westward

?

EASTERN BLUEBIRD

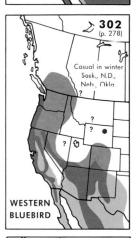

302 (p. 278)

Casual in winter Sask., N.D., Neb., Okla.

?

?

?

WESTERN BLUEBIRD

303 (p. 278)

Rare migrant along coast

MOUNTAIN BLUEBIRD

304 (p. 274)

Some winter further east on Plains

TOWNSEND'S SOLITAIRE

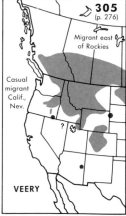

305 (p. 276)

Migrant east of Rockies

Casual migrant Calif., Nev.

?

VEERY

306 (p. 276)

Casual or accidental west to Ore., Calif.

Migrant east of Rockies

GRAY-CHEEKED THRUSH

307
(p. 276)

Widespread
in
migration

?
?

?

SWAINSON'S
THRUSH

308
(p. 276)

Widespread
in
migration

?

HERMIT
THRUSH

309
(p. 274)

AMERICAN
ROBIN

310
(p. 274)

Rare or
casual
eastward
in winter

VARIED
THRUSH

311
(p. 266)

WRENTIT

312
(p. 270)

Migrate
eastwar

Expanding
range
westward

? ?

?

Rare
vagrant
to coast

Winters in
se. U.S.,
very rarel
in sw. state

GRAY
CATBIRD

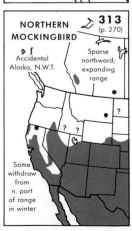

**NORTHERN
MOCKINGBIRD**

313
(p. 270)

Accidental
Alaska, N.W.T.

Sparse
northward;
expanding
range

?

? ?

Some
withdraw
from
n. part
of range
in winter

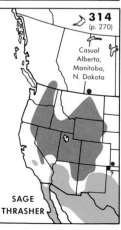

314
(p. 270)

Casual
Alberta,
Manitoba,
N. Dakota

?

SAGE
THRASHER

315
(p. 270)

Acc. to
n. Alaska,
Yukon,
N.W. Terr.

Casual
vagrant
west to
coast

?

?

Winters
se. U.S

BROWN
THRASHER

BENDIRE'S THRASHER 316 (p. 272)

Accidental Sask., Man.

?

CURVE-BILLED THRASHER / CALIFORNIA THRASHER 317 (p. 272)

California Thrasher casual in Ore.

Curve-billed T. casual in Neb., S.D.; sparse to Nev., se. Calif.

Curve-billed Thrasher

California Thrasher

CRISSAL THRASHER 318 (p. 272)

LeCONTE'S THRASHER 319 (p. 272)

AMERICAN PIPIT 320 (p. 244)

Breeds west to cen. Aleutians

Widespread in migration

SPRAGUE'S PIPIT 321 (p. 244)

?
?

Casual vagrant west to Nev., se. Calif.

BOHEMIAN WAXWING 322 (p. 282)

Very irregular in winter; absent some years

Very rare o dash line

CEDAR WAXWING 323 (p. 282)

Casual N.W.T.; widespread in migration

Irregular in winter; may be present or absent in many areas

PHAINOPEPLA 324 (p. 282)

Casual north to s. Ore., Colo.

325 (p. 280)

Breeds west to central Aleutians

Irregular or rare in winter in South

NORTHERN SHRIKE

LOGGERHEAD SHRIKE **326** (p. 280)

Casual on nw. coast (Ore. to B.C.)

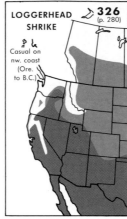

327 (p. 280)

In winter some withdraw from n. part of range

Extending range locally in Mexico

EUROPEAN STARLING

328 (p. 284)

Declining due to loss of riparian habitat

Casual or acc. north to Ore., Idaho, Wyo.

BELL'S VIREO

329 (p. 286)

Has bred in Wyo. ?

? ?

GRAY VIREO

330 (p. 284)

Casual Yukon

?

Migrant throughout

SOLITARY VIREO

HUTTON'S VIREO **331** (p. 284)

Some fall and winter dispersal

Casual Nev. and on deserts of se. Calif., sw. Ariz.

332 (p. 286)

Migrant throughout Southwest

WARBLING VIREO

PHILADELPHIA VIREO **333** (p. 286)

Migrates mainly east of Plains

Rare vagrant west to Calif.

334 (p. 286)

Rare in e. Alaska

Still extending range in West

Rare vagrant along coast and in Sw.

Migrates mainly east of Rockies

RED-EYED VIREO

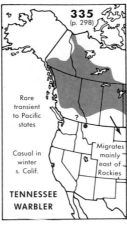

335 (p. 298)

Rare transient to Pacific states

Casual in winter s. Calif.

Migrates mainly east of Rockies

TENNESSEE WARBLER

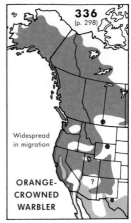

336 (p. 298)

Widespread in migration

ORANGE-CROWNED WARBLER

NASHVILLE WARBLER

337 (p. 300)

Accidental in Alaska

Winters rarely to s. Calif., Ariz.

VIRGINIA'S WARBLER

338 (p. 296)

Casual Ore., Neb., Kans.

Vagrant to coast of Calif. in fall and winter

LUCY'S WARBLER

339 (p. 296)

Winters in sw. Mexico

340 (p. 298)

Migrant throughout

Declining in Southwest

YELLOW WARBLER

CHESTNUT-SIDED WARBLER

341 (p. 294)

Acc. Alaska

Migrant mainly east of Rockies

Rare vagrant west to coast

342 (p. 288)

Casual Alaska

Rare or casual west to coast

Migrates mainly east of Rockies

MAGNOLIA WARBLER

343 (p. 294)

Accidental Alaska, Yukon

Casual west to Pacific states

Migrates mainly east of Rockies through se. U.S.

CAPE MAY WARBLER

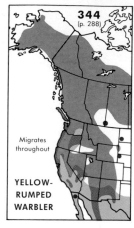

344 (p. 288)

Migrates throughout

YELLOW-RUMPED WARBLER

BLACK-THROATED GRAY WARBLER

345 (p. 292)

Casual Sask., Dakotas, Mont., Neb.

Migrant throughout sw. U.S.

346 (p. 290)

Migrant throughout mountain states

Sparse in winter in nw. states, Ariz.

Vagrant ? on Great Plains

TOWNSEND'S WARBLER

BLACK-THROATED GREEN WARBLER

347 (p. 290)

Casual Alaska, B.C., Wash., Ore.

Migrates mainly Southeast

Rare fall vagrant west to coastal Calif.

HERMIT WARBLER

Acc. Alaska

Casual Utah, Colo., Neb.

Hermit Warbler

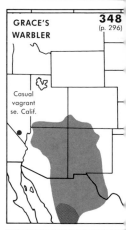

GRACE'S WARBLER

348 (p. 296)

Casual vagrant se. Calif.

349 (p. 298)

Casual in Alaska, Yukon

Rare but regular west to Pacific states in fall and winter

Migrates mainly east of Rockies

PALM WARBLER

350 (p. 294)

Acc. Alaska

Rare vagrant west to Ore., Calif.

Migrant mainly east of Rockies

Has bred in Colo.

BAY-BREASTED WARBLER

351 (p. 292)

Sparse transient west to Pacific Coast

Migrates mainly east of Rockies to tropics

BLACKPOLL WARBLER

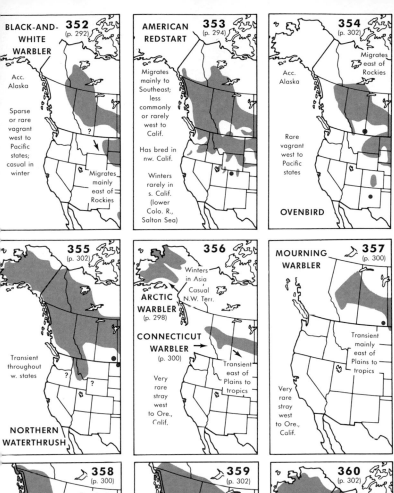

BLACK-AND-WHITE WARBLER **352** (p. 292)

Acc. Alaska

Sparse or rare vagrant west to Pacific states; casual in winter

Migrates mainly east of Rockies

AMERICAN REDSTART **353** (p. 294)

Migrates mainly to Southeast; less commonly or rarely west to Calif.

Has bred in nw. Calif.

Winters rarely in s. Calif. (lower Colo. R., Salton Sea)

354 (p. 302)

Acc. Alaska

Migrates east of Rockies

Rare vagrant west to Pacific states

OVENBIRD

355 (p. 302)

Transient throughout w. states

NORTHERN WATERTHRUSH

356

Winters in Asia; Casual N.W. Terr.

ARCTIC WARBLER (p. 298)

CONNECTICUT WARBLER (p. 300)

Transient east of Plains to tropics

Very rare stray west to Ore., Calif.

MOURNING WARBLER **357** (p. 300)

Transient mainly east of Plains to tropics

Very rare stray west to Ore., Calif.

358 (p. 300)

Transient through Southwest and on Plains

MacGILLIVRAY'S WARBLER

359 (p. 302)

COMMON YELLOWTHROAT

Migrates throughout

360 (p. 302)

Breeds west to Cold Bay

Winters rarely in s. Calif.

WILSON'S WARBLER

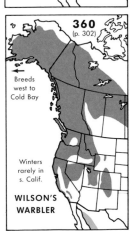

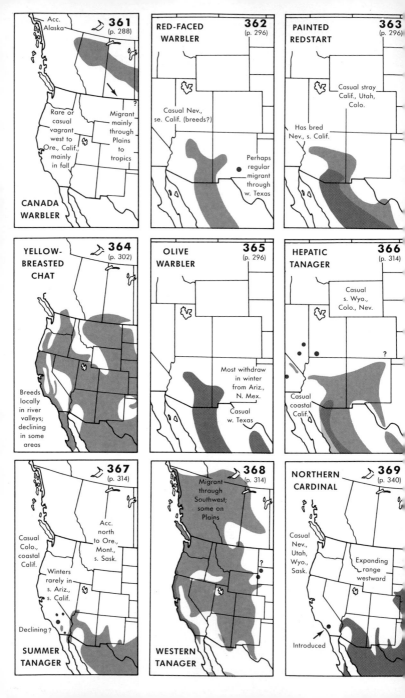

361 (p. 288)

Acc. Alaska.

Rare or casual vagrant west to Ore., Calif., mainly in fall

Migrant mainly through Plains to tropics

CANADA WARBLER

362 (p. 296)

RED-FACED WARBLER

Casual Nev., se. Calif. (breeds?)

Perhaps regular migrant through w. Texas

363 (p. 296)

PAINTED REDSTART

Casual stray Calif., Utah, Colo.

Has bred Nev., s. Calif.

364 (p. 302)

YELLOW-BREASTED CHAT

Breeds locally in river valleys; declining in some areas

365 (p. 296)

OLIVE WARBLER

Most withdraw in winter from Ariz., N. Mex.

Casual w. Texas

366 (p. 314)

HEPATIC TANAGER

Casual s. Wyo., Colo., Nev.

?

Casual coastal Calif.

367 (p. 314)

Casual Colo., coastal Calif.

Acc. north to Ore., Mont., s. Sask.

Winters rarely in s. Ariz., s. Calif.

Declining ?

SUMMER TANAGER

368 (p. 314)

Migrant through Southwest; some on Plains

?

WESTERN TANAGER

369 (p. 340)

NORTHERN CARDINAL

Casual Nev., Utah, Wyo., Sask.

Expanding range westward

Introduced

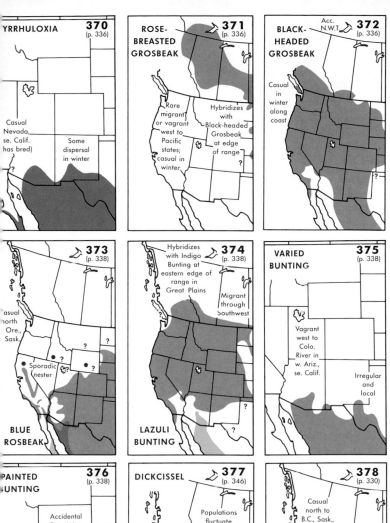

PYRRHULOXIA **370** (p. 336)

Casual Nevada, se. Calif. (has bred)

Some dispersal in winter

?

ROSE-BREASTED GROSBEAK **371** (p. 336)

Rare migrant or vagrant west to Pacific states; casual in winter

Hybridizes with Black-headed Grosbeak at edge of range

?

BLACK-HEADED GROSBEAK **372** (p. 336)

Acc. N.W.T.

Casual in winter along coast

?

373 (p. 338)

Casual north Ore., Sask.

Sporadic nester

? ? ?

BLUE GROSBEAK

Hybridizes with Indigo Bunting at eastern edge of range in Great Plains

374 (p. 338)

Migrant through Southwest

?

?

LAZULI BUNTING

VARIED BUNTING **375** (p. 338)

Vagrant west to Colo. River in w. Ariz., se. Calif.

Irregular and local

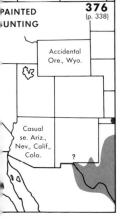

PAINTED BUNTING **376** (p. 338)

Accidental Ore., Wyo.

Casual se. Ariz., Nev., Calif., Colo.

?

DICKCISSEL **377** (p. 346)

Populations fluctuate

Sparse or casual transient west to coast; casual in winter

?

?

?

378 (p. 330)

Casual north to B.C., Sask., N.D.

Rare in fall on Calif. coast

Migrant on southern Great Plains

GREEN-TAILED TOWHEE

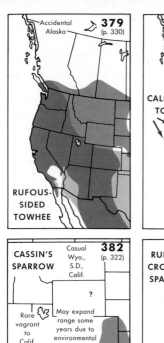

379 (p. 330)

Accidental Alaska

RUFOUS-SIDED TOWHEE

380 (p. 330)

CALIFORNIA TOWHEE

Casual Neb., Kansas

CANYON TOWHEE

38 (p. 330)

ABERT'S TOWHEE

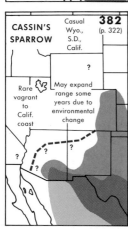

382

CASSIN'S SPARROW

Casual Wyo., S.D., Calif.

?

Rare vagrant to Calif. coast

May expand range some years due to environmental change

? ? ?
?

(p. 322)

RUFOUS-CROWNED SPARROW

383 (p. 320)

Casual Nev.

May withdraw in winter from n. part of range

384 (p. 320)

Casual west to coast (Wash., Ore., Calif.)

AMERICAN TREE SPARROW

385

(p. 320)

Declining in some areas

CHIPPING SPARROW

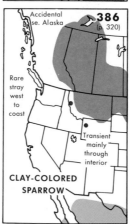

386 (p. 320)

Accidental se. Alaska

Rare stray west to coast

Transient mainly through interior

CLAY-COLORED SPARROW

387

(p. 322)

Casual nw. coast

?

Migrant w. Kans., w. Okla.; also coastal Calif.

?

BREWER'S SPARROW

388 (p. 320)

Casual Sask.

?

Acc. Calif., Nev., Ariz.

Scarce of Pecos

FIELD SPARROW

BLACK-CHINNED SPARROW

389 (p. 318)

Casual sw. Ore.

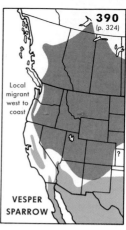

390 (p. 324)

Local migrant west to coast

?

VESPER SPARROW

391 (p. 318)

LARK SPARROW

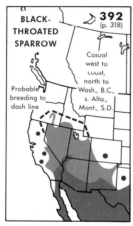

BLACK-THROATED SPARROW

392 (p. 318)

Casual west to coast, north to Wash., B.C., s. Alta., Mont., S.D.

Probable breeding to dash line

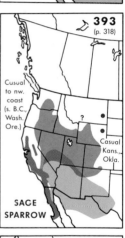

393 (p. 318)

Casual to nw. coast (s. B.C., Wash., Ore.)

?

Casual Kans., Okla.

SAGE SPARROW

394 (p. 346)

Irregular migrant to coast of Calif.; casual B.C., Wash., Ore., Nev.

May breed westward in wet years

?   ?

LARK BUNTING

395 (p. 326)

Breeds to cen. Aleutians

Widespread migrant in open country

?

SAVANNAH SPARROW

396 (p. 326)

Declining during last century due to farming

Casual Calif.

Migrates through Great Plains

BAIRD'S SPARROW

GRASSHOPPER SPARROW **397** (p. 326)

Breeding very spotty in range shown; varies in wet and dry years

?

398 (p. 326)

Casual west to Yukon, Pacific states

?

Migrant through Plains to s. Miss. Valley

Winters casually in Ariz., N. Mex.

LeCONTE'S SPARROW

399 (p. 326)

Very rare in winter to coastal Calif.

?

Migrates east of Plains to coasts of e. U.S.

SHARP-TAILED SPARROW

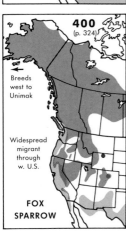

400 (p. 324)

Breeds west to Unimak

Widespread migrant through w. U.S.

FOX SPARROW

401 (p. 324)

Resident throughout Aleutians

Winters mainly south of dash line to n. Mexico

SONG SPARROW

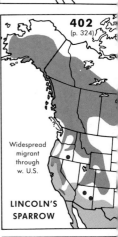

402 (p. 324)

Widespread migrant through w. U.S.

LINCOLN'S SPARROW

403 (p. 320)

Acc. Alaska

Sparse winter visitor to w. states, esp. along coast

Migrant mainly east of Rockies

SWAMP SPARROW

404 (p. 316)

Winters mainly in e. U.S.; a few migrate to sw. states and coast

WHITE-THROATED SPARROW

405 (p. 316)

?

Casual transient and winter visitor eastward

GOLDEN-CROWNED SPARROW

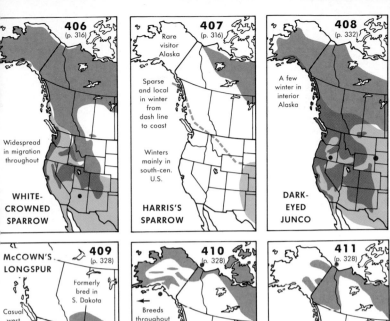

406
(p. 316)

Widespread in migration throughout

WHITE-CROWNED SPARROW

407
(p. 316)

Rare visitor Alaska

Sparse and local in winter from dash line to coast

Winters mainly in south-cen. U.S.

HARRIS'S SPARROW

408
(p. 332)

A few winter in interior Alaska

DARK-EYED JUNCO

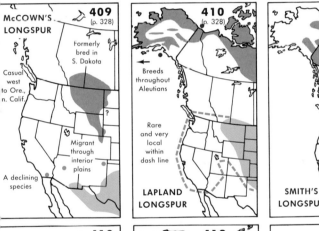

McCOWN'S LONGSPUR

409
(p. 328)

Formerly bred in S. Dakota

Casual west to Ore., n. Calif.

?

Migrant through interior plains

A declining species

410
(p. 328)

← Breeds throughout Aleutians

Rare and very local within dash line

LAPLAND LONGSPUR

411
(p. 328)

Migrates through Great Plains to south-cen. U.S. east of map area

Acc. Ariz., w. Tex.

SMITH'S LONGSPUR

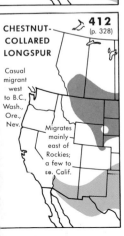

CHESTNUT-COLLARED LONGSPUR

412
(p. 328)

Casual migrant west to B.C., Wash., Ore., Nev.

Migrates mainly east of Rockies; a few to se. Calif.

413
(p. 334)

← Resident in Aleutians

Winters mostly in open country; avoids mts.

Casual n. Calif., Nev.

Acc. Ariz., N.M.

SNOW BUNTING

Acc. to n. Alaska, Yukon, N.W. Terr.

414
(p. 308)

?

?

Expanding range

Migrant mainly east of Rockies; a few along coast and through sw. states

BOBOLINK

415
(p. 308)

Winters mainly south of dash line

RED-WINGED BLACKBIRD

416

A very few migrate and winter in w. Nev.

ORCHARD ORIOLE
(p. 312)

Very rare vagrant west to Ore., Calif.

(p. 308)

TRICOLORED BLACKBIRD
?

417
(p. 310)

EASTERN MEADOWLARK

?

Some withdrawal and dispersal in winter

WESTERN MEADOWLARK

418
(p. 310)

Casual Alaska, N.W.T.

YELLOW-HEADED BLACKBIRD

419
(p. 308)

Casual Alaska, Yukon, N.W. Terr.

Migrates to coast

420
(p. 306)

Winters rarely from se. Alaska to Calif.

A few migrate west to Pacific Coast

Migrates mainly east of Rockies

RUSTY BLACKBIRD

Acc. Alaska, Yukon

421
(p. 306)

BREWER'S BLACKBIRD

422
(p. 306)

Casual B.C., Ore.

Expanding northward locally

GREAT-TAILED GRACKLE

Acc. Alaska

423
(p. 306)

Casual vagrant and winter visitor west to Pacific states

Recently expanding range
?

COMMON GRACKLE

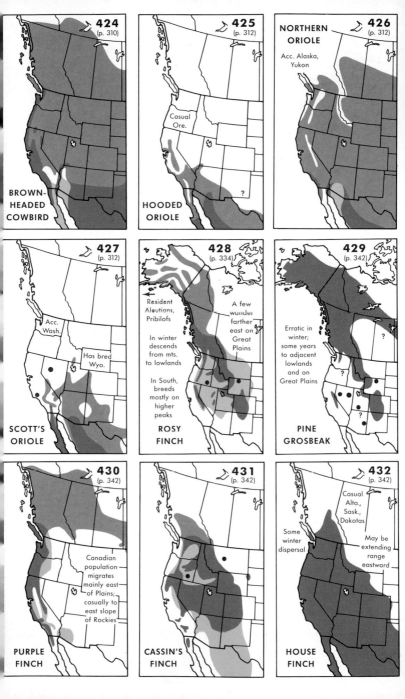

424 (p. 310)

BROWN-HEADED COWBIRD

425 (p. 312)

Casual Ore.

HOODED ORIOLE

NORTHERN ORIOLE **426** (p. 312)

Acc. Alaska, Yukon

427 (p. 312)

Acc. Wash.

Has bred Wyo.

SCOTT'S ORIOLE

428 (p. 334)

Resident Aleutians, Pribilofs

In winter descends from mts. to lowlands

In South, breeds mostly on higher peaks

A few wander farther east on Great Plains

ROSY FINCH

429 (p. 342)

Erratic in winter; some years to adjacent lowlands and on Great Plains

?

?

PINE GROSBEAK

430 (p. 342)

Canadian population migrates mainly east of Plains; casually to east slope of Rockies

PURPLE FINCH

431 (p. 342)

CASSIN'S FINCH

432 (p. 342)

Casual Alta., Sask., Dakotas

May be extending range eastward

Some winter dispersal

HOUSE FINCH

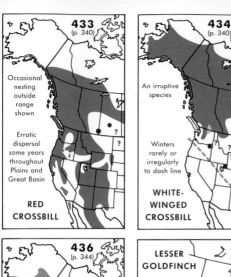

433 (p. 340)

Occasional nesting outside range shown

Erratic dispersal some years throughout Plains and Great Basin

RED CROSSBILL

434 (p. 340)

An irruptive species

Winters rarely or irregularly to dash line

WHITE-WINGED CROSSBILL

435 (p. 342)

Breeds west to cen. Aleutians

"Hoary" Redpoll (northern race) regarded as conspecific with Redpoll

REDPOLL Including "Hoary" Redpoll

Winters rarely to dash line

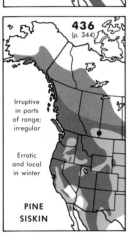

436 (p. 344)

Irruptive in parts of range; irregular

Erratic and local in winter

PINE SISKIN

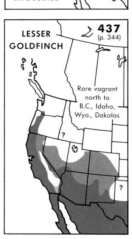

LESSER GOLDFINCH **437** (p. 344)

Rare vagrant north to B.C., Idaho, Wyo., Dakotas

LAWRENCE'S GOLDFINCH **438** (p. 344)

Casual s. Ore., s. Nev.

Erratic in winter

Rare in winter to w. Texas

AMERICAN GOLDFINCH **439** (p. 344)

Accidental Alaska, Yukon

Erratic in winter

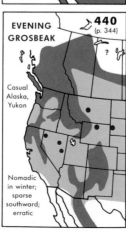

EVENING GROSBEAK **440** (p. 344)

Casual Alaska, Yukon

Nomadic in winter; sparse southward; erratic

Casual Alaska, Yukon **441** (p. 346)

HOUSE SPARROW

Systematic Checklist

Keep a "Life List." Check the birds you have seen.

This list covers the western part of the continent east to the 100th meridian on the Great Plains. It includes only those species that are described and illustrated in this *Field Guide*, but excludes most of those strays from Mexico or Asia that are shown or listed on pp. 348–358 and the escaped parrots shown on p. 211, as well as a few other accidental vagrants covered elsewhere in the pages of this book. However, space is left at the end of the Checklist for listing any such species that you may observe. *Accidentals* are defined as those birds that have been recorded less than a dozen times within our area; this is an arbitrary category that could change over the years with increased observation.

For a convenient and complete continental list, the A.B.A. *Check list*, prepared by the Checklist Committee of the American Birding Association (P.O. Box 6599, Colorado Springs, Colo. 80934), is recommended. It lists every species recorded north of the Mexican border, East and West, including the accidentals.

In the following list, birds are grouped first under orders (identified by the Latin ending *-formes*), followed by families (*-dae* ending), sometimes subfamilies (*-nae* ending), or tribes (*-ni* ending), and then species. Scientific names of genera and species are not given here but will be found in the species accounts throughout this book. The vernacular names are those endorsed by the Checklist Committee of the American Birding Association (A.B.A.). They are essentially the same as those adopted in the Checklist of the American Ornithologists' Union (A.O.U.). So that there will be no confusion, names used in the previous edition of this *Field Guide* that differ from those in current usage are included in parentheses. All scientific names are the latest official ones decreed by the A.O.U. Checklist Committee (and accepted by the A.B.A.).

Gaviiformes
LOONS: Gaviidae
—RED-THROATED LOON
—ARCTIC LOON
—PACIFIC LOON
—COMMON LOON
—YELLOW-BILLED LOON

Podicipediiformes
GREBES: Podicipedidae
—PIED-BILLED GREBE
—HORNED GREBE

—RED-NECKED GREBE
—EARED GREBE
—WESTERN GREBE
—CLARK'S GREBE

Procellariiformes
ALBATROSSES: Diomedeidae
—SHORT-TAILED ALBATROSS
—BLACK-FOOTED ALBATROSS
—LAYSAN ALBATROSS
SHEARWATERS, PETRELS: Procellariidae
—NORTHERN FULMAR

—MOTTLED PETREL
—PINK-FOOTED SHEARWATER
—FLESH-FOOTED SHEARW.
—BULLER'S SHEARWATER
—SOOTY SHEARWATER
—SHORT-TAILED SHEARW.
—BLACK-VENTED SHEARW.
STORM-PETRELS: Hydrobatidae
—WILSON'S STORM-PETREL
—FORK-T. STORM-PETREL
—LEACH'S STORM-PETREL
—ASHY STORM-PETREL
—BLACK STORM-PETREL
—LEAST STORM-PETREL

Pelecaniformes
TROPICBIRDS: Phaethontidae
—RED-B. TROPICBIRD
BOOBIES: Sulidae
—BLUE-FOOTED BOOBY
—BROWN BOOBY
PELICANS: Pelecanidae
—AM. WHITE PELICAN
—BROWN PELICAN
CORMORANTS: Phalacrocoracidae
—DOUBLE-CR. CORMORANT
—OLIVACEOUS CORMORANT
—BRANDT'S CORMORANT
—PELAGIC CORMORANT
—RED-FACED CORMORANT
FRIGATEBIRDS: Fregatidae
—MAGNIFICENT FRIGATEBIRD

Ciconiiformes
HERONS, BITTERNS: Ardeidae
—AMERICAN BITTERN
—LEAST BITTERN
—GREAT BLUE HERON
—GREAT EGRET
—LITTLE EGRET
—SNOWY EGRET
—LITTLE BLUE HERON
—TRICOLORED HERON
—REDDISH EGRET
—CATTLE EGRET
—GREEN-BACKED HERON
—BLK.-C. NIGHT-HERON
—Y.-C. NIGHT-HERON
IBISES, etc.: Threskiornithidae
—WHITE IBIS
—WHITE-FACED IBIS
—ROSEATE SPOONBILL
STORKS: Ciconiidae
—WOOD STORK

Anseriformes
WATERFOWL: Anatidae
  WHISTLING DUCKS: Dendrocygnini
—FULVOUS WHISTLING-DUCK
—BLACK-BELLIED WH.-DUCK
  SWANS: Cygnini
—TUNDRA SWAN
—WHOOPER SWAN
—TRUMPETER SWAN

  GEESE: Anserini
—BEAN GOOSE
—GR. WHITE-FRONTED GOOSE
—SNOW GOOSE
—ROSS'S GOOSE
—EMPEROR GOOSE
—BRANT
—CANADA GOOSE
  DUCKS: Anatinae
—WOOD DUCK
—GREEN-WINGED TEAL
—BAIKAL TEAL
—FALCATED TEAL
—AMERICAN BLACK DUCK
—MALLARD
—NORTHERN PINTAIL
—GARGANEY
—BLUE-WINGED TEAL
—CINNAMON TEAL
—NORTHERN SHOVELER
—GADWALL
—EURASIAN WIGEON
—AMERICAN WIGEON
—COMMON POCHARD
—CANVASBACK
—REDHEAD
—RING-NECKED DUCK
—TUFTED DUCK
—GREATER SCAUP
—LESSER SCAUP
—COMMON EIDER
—KING EIDER
—SPECTACLED EIDER
—STELLER'S EIDER
—HARLEQUIN DUCK
—OLDSQUAW
—BLACK SCOTER
—SURF SCOTER
—WHITE-WINGED SCOTER
—COMMON GOLDENEYE
—BARROW'S GOLDENEYE
—BUFFLEHEAD
—SMEW
—HOODED MERGANSER
—COMMON MERGANSER
—RED-BR. MERGANSER
—RUDDY DUCK

Falconiformes
AM. VULTURES: Cathartidae
—BLACK VULTURE
—TURKEY VULTURE
HAWKS, etc.: Accipitridae
—OSPREY
—BLACK-SHOULDERED KITE
—MISSISSIPPI KITE
—BALD EAGLE
—WHITE-TAILED EAGLE
—NORTHERN HARRIER
—SHARP-SHINNED HAWK
—COOPER'S HAWK
—NORTHERN GOSHAWK
—COMMON BLACK-HAWK
—HARRIS'S HAWK

__GRAY HAWK
__RED-SHOULDERED HAWK
__BROAD-WINGED HAWK
__SWAINSON'S HAWK
__ZONE-TAILED HAWK
__RED-TAILED HAWK
__FERRUGINOUS HAWK
__ROUGH-LEGGED HAWK
__GOLDEN EAGLE
CARACARAS, FALCONS: Falconidae
__CRESTED CARACARA
__AMERICAN KESTREL
__MERLIN
__PEREGRINE FALCON
__GYRFALCON
__PRAIRIE FALCON

Galliformes
FOWL-LIKE BIRDS: Phasianidae
__GRAY PARTRIDGE
__CHUKAR
__RING-NECKED PHEASANT
__SPRUCE GROUSE
__BLUE GROUSE
__WILLOW PTARMIGAN
__ROCK PTARMIGAN
__WH.-TAILED PTARMIGAN
__RUFFED GROUSE
__SAGE GROUSE
__GR. PRAIRIE-CHICKEN
__L. PRAIRIE-CHICKEN
__SHARP-TAILED GROUSE
__WILD TURKEY
__MONTEZUMA QUAIL
__NORTHERN BOBWHITE
__SCALED QUAIL
__GAMBEL'S QUAIL
__CALIFORNIA QUAIL
__MOUNTAIN QUAIL

Gruiformes
RAILS, etc.: Rallidae
__YELLOW RAIL
__BLACK RAIL
__CLAPPER RAIL
__VIRGINIA RAIL
__SORA
__PURPLE GALLINULE
__COMMON MOORHEN
__AMERICAN COOT
CRANES: Gruidae
__SANDHILL CRANE
__WHOOPING CRANE

Charadriiformes
PLOVERS: Charadriidae
__BLACK-BELLIED PLOVER
__AM. GOLDEN-PLOVER
__PACIFIC GOLDEN-PLOVER
__MONGOLIAN PLOVER
__SNOWY PLOVER
__WILSON'S PLOVER

__SEMIPALMATED PLOVER
__PIPING PLOVER
__KILLDEER
__MOUNTAIN PLOVER
__EURASIAN DOTTEREL
OYSTERCATCHERS: Haematopodidae
__BLACK OYSTERCATCHER
STILTS, AVOCETS: Recurvirostridae
__BLACK-NECKED STILT
__AMERICAN AVOCET
SANDPIPERS, PHALAROPES:
Scolopacidae
__COMMON GREENSHANK
__GREATER YELLOWLEGS
__LESSER YELLOWLEGS
__SPOTTED REDSHANK
__WOOD SANDPIPER
__SOLITARY SANDPIPER
__WILLET
__WANDERING TATTLER
__GRAY-TAILED TATTLER
__COMMON SANDPIPER
__SPOTTED SANDPIPER
__TEREK SANDPIPER
__UPLAND SANDPIPER
__WHIMBREL
__BR.-THIGHED CURLEW
__FAR EASTERN CURLEW
__LONG-BILLED CURLEW
__BLACK-TAILED GODWIT
__HUDSONIAN GODWIT
__BAR-TAILED GODWIT
__MARBLED GODWIT
__RUDDY TURNSTONE
__BLACK TURNSTONE
__SURFBIRD
__RED KNOT
__SANDERLING
__SEMIPALM. SANDPIPER
__WESTERN SANDPIPER
__RUFOUS-NECKED STINT
__TEMMINCK'S STINT
__LONG-TOED STINT
__LEAST SANDPIPER
__WHITE-R. SANDPIPER
__BAIRD'S SANDPIPER
__PECTORAL SANDPIPER
__SHARP-TAILED SANDPIPER
__PURPLE SANDPIPER
__ROCK SANDPIPER
__DUNLIN
__CURLEW SANDPIPER
__STILT SANDPIPER
__BUFF-BR. SANDPIPER
__RUFF
__SHORT-BILLED DOWITCHER
__LONG-BILLED DOWITCHER
__COMMON SNIPE
__WILSON'S PHALAROPE
__RED-NECKED PHALAROPE
__RED PHALAROPE
JAEGERS, SKUAS, GULLS, TERNS,
SKIMMERS: Laridae
__POMARINE JAEGER

411

—PARASITIC JAEGER
—LONG-TAILED JAEGER
—SOUTH POLAR SKUA
—LAUGHING GULL
—FRANKLIN'S GULL
—LITTLE GULL
—COM. BLACK-HEADED GULL
—BONAPARTE'S GULL
—HEERMANN'S GULL
—MEW GULL
—RING-BILLED GULL
—CALIFORNIA GULL
—HERRING GULL
—THAYER'S GULL
—SLATY-BACKED GULL
—YELLOW-FOOTED GULL
—WESTERN GULL
—GLAUCOUS-WINGED GULL
—GLAUCOUS GULL
—BLACK-L. KITTIWAKE
—RED-L. KITTIWAKE
—ROSS'S GULL
—SABINE'S GULL
—IVORY GULL
—GULL-BILLED TERN
—CASPIAN TERN
—ROYAL TERN
—ELEGANT TERN
—COMMON TERN
—ARCTIC TERN
—FORSTER'S TERN
—LEAST TERN
—ALEUTIAN TERN
—BLACK TERN
—BLACK SKIMMER
AUKS, etc.: Alcidae
—COMMON MURRE
—THICK-BILLED MURRE
—BLACK GUILLEMOT
—PIGEON GUILLEMOT
—MARBLED MURRELET
—KITTLITZ'S MURRELET
—XANTUS' MURRELET
—CRAVERI'S MURRELET
—ANCIENT MURRELET
—CASSIN'S AUKLET
—PARAKEET AUKLET
—LEAST AUKLET
—WHISKERED AUKLET
—CRESTED AUKLET
—RHINOCEROS AUKLET
—TUFTED PUFFIN
—HORNED PUFFIN

Columbiformes
PIGEONS, DOVES: Columbidae
—ROCK DOVE
—BAND-TAILED PIGEON
—RINGED TURTLE-DOVE
—SPOTTED DOVE
—WHITE-WINGED DOVE
—MOURNING DOVE
—INCA DOVE
—COMMON GROUND-DOVE

Cuculiformes
CUCKOOS, ROADRUNNERS, ANIS:
Cuculidae
—COMMON CUCKOO
—BLACK-BILLED CUCKOO
—YELLOW-BILLED CUCKOO
—GREATER ROADRUNNER
—GROOVE-BILLED ANI

Strigiformes
BARN OWLS: Tytonidae
—BARN OWL
TYPICAL OWLS: Strigidae
—FLAMMULATED OWL
—EASTERN SCREECH-OWL
—WESTERN SCREECH-OWL
—WHISKERED SCREECH-OWL
—GREAT HORNED OWL
—SNOWY OWL
—NORTHERN HAWK OWL
—NORTHERN PYGMY-OWL
—FERRUGINOUS PYGMY-OWL
—ELF OWL
—BURROWING OWL
—SPOTTED OWL
—BARRED OWL
—GREAT GRAY OWL
—LONG-EARED OWL
—SHORT-EARED OWL
—BOREAL OWL
—N. SAW-WHET OWL

Caprimulgiformes
GOATSUCKERS: Caprimulgidae
—LESSER NIGHTHAWK
—COMMON NIGHTHAWK
—COMMON POORWILL
—BUFF-COLLARED NIGHTJAR
—WHIP-POOR-WILL

Apodiformes
SWIFTS: Apodidae
—BLACK SWIFT
—CHIMNEY SWIFT
—VAUX'S SWIFT
—WHITE-THROATED SWIFT
HUMMINGBIRDS: Trochilidae
—BROAD-BILLED HUMMINGBIRD
—WHITE-EARED HUMMINGBIRD
—BERYLLINE HUMMINGBIRD
—VIOLET-CR. HUMMINGBIRD
—BLUE-THR. HUMMINGBIRD
—MAGNIFICENT HUMMINGBIRD
—LUCIFER HUMMINGBIRD
—RUBY-THROATED
    HUMMINGBIRD
—BLK.-CHINNED HUMMINGBIRD
—ANNA'S HUMMINGBIRD
—COSTA'S HUMMINGBIRD
—CALLIOPE HUMMINGBIRD
—BROAD-TAILED HUMMINGBIRD
—RUFOUS HUMMINGBIRD
—ALLEN'S HUMMINGBIRD

Trogoniformes
TROGONS: Trogonidae
—ELEGANT TROGON

Coraciiformes
KINGFISHERS: Alcedinidae
—BELTED KINGFISHER
—GREEN KINGFISHER
WOODPECKERS: Picidae
—LEWIS'S WOODPECKER
—RED-HEADED WOODPECKER
—ACORN WOODPECKER
—GILA WOODPECKER
—GOLDEN-FR. WOODPECKER
—RED-B. WOODPECKER
—YELLOW-B. SAPSUCKER
—RED-NAPED SAPSUCKER
—RED-BR. SAPSUCKER
—WILLIAMSON'S SAPSUCKER
—LADDER-BACKED WOODP.
—NUTTALL'S WOODPECKER
—DOWNY WOODPECKER
—HAIRY WOODPECKER
—STRICKLAND'S WOODP.
—WHITE-HEADED WOODP.
—THREE-TOED WOODPECKER
—BLACK-BACKED WOODP.
—NORTHERN FLICKER
—PILEATED WOODPECKER

Passeriformes
FLYCATCHERS: Tyrannidae
—NORTHERN BEARDLESS-
    TYRANNULET
—OLIVE-SIDED FLYCATCHER
—GREATER PEWEE
—WESTERN WOOD-PEWEE
—EASTERN WOOD-PEWEE
—YELLOW BELLIED FLYC
—ALDER FLYCATCHER
—WILLOW FLYCATCHER
—LEAST FLYCATCHER
—HAMMOND'S FLYCATCHER
—DUSKY FLYCATCHER
—GRAY FLYCATCHER
—PACIFIC-SLOPE FLYC.
—CORDILLERAN FLYC.
—BUFF-BREASTED FLYC.
—BLACK PHOEBE
—EASTERN PHOEBE
—VERMILION FLYCATCHER
—DUSKY-CAPPED FLYC.
—ASH-THROATED FLYC.
—GREAT CRESTED FLYC.
—BROWN-CRESTED FLYC.
—SULPHUR-BELLIED FLYC.
—TROPICAL KINGBIRD
—CASSIN'S KINGBIRD
—THICK-BILLED KINGBIRD
—WESTERN KINGBIRD
—EASTERN KINGBIRD
—SCISSOR-TAILED FLYCATCHER
—ROSE-THROATED BECARD

LARKS: Alaudidae
—EURASIAN SKYLARK
—HORNED LARK
SWALLOWS: Hirundinidae
—PURPLE MARTIN
—TREE SWALLOW
—VIOLET-GREEN SWALLOW
—N. ROUGH-WINGED SWALLOW
—BANK SWALLOW
—CLIFF SWALLOW
—CAVE SWALLOW
—BARN SWALLOW
JAYS, MAGPIES, CROWS: Corvidae
—GRAY JAY
—STELLER'S JAY
—BLUE JAY
—SCRUB JAY
—GRAY-BREASTED JAY
—PINYON JAY
—CLARK'S NUTCRACKER
—BLACK-BILLED MAGPIE
—YELLOW-BILLED MAGPIE
—AMERICAN CROW
—NORTHWESTERN CROW
—CHIHUAHUAN RAVEN
—COMMON RAVEN
CHICKADEES, TITMICE: Paridae
—BLACK-CAPPED CHICKADEE
—MEXICAN CHICKADEE
—MOUNTAIN CHICKADEE
—GRAY-H. CHICKADEE
—BOREAL CHICKADEE
—CHESTNUT-B. CHICKADEE
—BRIDLED TITMOUSE
—PLAIN TITMOUSE
—TUFTED TITMOUSE
VERDIN: Remizidae
—VERDIN
BUSHTIT: Aegithalidae
—BUSHTIT
NUTHATCHES: Sittidae
—RED-BR. NUTHATCH
—WHITE-BR. NUTHATCH
—PYGMY NUTHATCH
CREEPERS: Certhiidae
—BROWN CREEPER
WRENS: Troglodytidae
—CACTUS WREN
—ROCK WREN
—CANYON WREN
—CAROLINA WREN
—BEWICK'S WREN
—HOUSE WREN
—WINTER WREN
—SEDGE WREN
—MARSH WREN
DIPPERS: Cinclidae
—AMERICAN DIPPER
**KINGLETS, GNATCATCHERS,
THRUSHES, etc.:** Muscicapidae
—ARCTIC WARBLER
—GOLDEN-CR. KINGLET
—RUBY-CROWNED KINGLET
—CALIF. GNATCATCHER

—BLUE-GR. GNATCATCHER
—BL.-TAILED GNATCATCHER
—BL.-CAPPED GNATCATCHER
—GRAY-SPOTTED FLYC.
—SIBERIAN RUBYTHROAT
—BLUETHROAT
—NORTHERN WHEATEAR
—EASTERN BLUEBIRD
—WESTERN BLUEBIRD
—MOUNTAIN BLUEBIRD
—TOWNSEND'S SOLITAIRE
—VEERY
—GRAY-CHEEKED THRUSH
—SWAINSON'S THRUSH
—HERMIT THRUSH
—EYEBROWED THRUSH
—DUSKY THRUSH
—RUFOUS-BACKED ROBIN
—AMERICAN ROBIN
—VARIED THRUSH
—WRENTIT

MIMIC THRUSHES: Mimidae
—GRAY CATBIRD
—N. MOCKINGBIRD
—SAGE THRASHER
—BROWN THRASHER
—BENDIRE'S THRASHER
—CURVE-BILLED THRASHER
—CALIFORNIA THRASHER
—CRISSAL THRASHER
—LeCONTE'S THRASHER

WAGTAILS, PIPITS: Motacillidae
—YELLOW WAGTAIL
—WHITE WAGTAIL
—BLACK-BACKED WAGTAIL
—OLIVE TREE-PIPIT
—RED-THROATED PIPIT
—AMERICAN PIPIT
—SPRAGUE'S PIPIT

WAXWINGS: Bombycillidae
—BOHEMIAN WAXWING
—CEDAR WAXWING

SILKY-FLYCATCHERS: Ptilogonatidae
—PHAINOPEPLA

SHRIKES: Laniidae
—NORTHERN SHRIKE
—LOGGERHEAD SHRIKE

STARLINGS: Sturnidae
—EUROPEAN STARLING
—CRESTED MYNA

VIREOS: Vireonidae
—WHITE-EYED VIREO
—BELL'S VIREO
—BLACK-CAPPED VIREO
—GRAY VIREO
—SOLITARY VIREO
—YELLOW-THR. VIREO
—HUTTON'S VIREO
—WARBLING VIREO
—PHILADELPHIA VIREO
—RED-EYED VIREO
—YELLOW-GREEN VIREO

EMBERIZIDS: Emberizidae
WOOD WARBLERS: Parulinae
—GOLDEN-WINGED WARBLER
—TENNESSEE WARBLER
—ORANGE-CR. WARBLER
—NASHVILLE WARBLER
—VIRGINIA'S WARBLER
—COLIMA WARBLER
—LUCY'S WARBLER
—NORTHERN PARULA
—YELLOW WARBLER
—CHESTNUT-SIDED WARBLER
—MAGNOLIA WARBLER
—CAPE MAY WARBLER
—BLK.-THR. BLUE WARBLER
—YELLOW-RUMPED WARBLER
—BLK.-THR. GRAY WARBLER
—TOWNSEND'S WARBLER
—HERMIT WARBLER
—BLK.-THR. GREEN WARBLER
—GOLDEN-CHEEKED WARBLER
—BLACKBURNIAN WARBLER
—YELLOW-THR. WARBLER
—GRACE'S WARBLER
—PRAIRIE WARBLER
—PALM WARBLER
—BAY-BREASTED WARBLER
—BLACKPOLL WARBLER
—CERULEAN WARBLER
—BLACK-AND-WHITE WARBLER
—AMERICAN REDSTART
—PROTHONOTARY WARBLER
—WORM-EATING WARBLER
—OVENBIRD
—NORTHERN WATERTHRUSH
—KENTUCKY WARBLER
—CONNECTICUT WARBLER
—MOURNING WARBLER
—MacGILLIVRAY'S WARBLER
—COMMON YELLOWTHROAT
—HOODED WARBLER
—WILSON'S WARBLER
—CANADA WARBLER
—RED-FACED WARBLER
—PAINTED REDSTART
—YELLOW-BREASTED CHAT
—OLIVE WARBLER
TANAGERS: Thraupinae
—HEPATIC TANAGER
—SUMMER TANAGER
—SCARLET TANAGER
—WESTERN TANAGER
GROSBEAKS, BUNTINGS, etc.:
Cardinalinae
—NORTHERN CARDINAL
—PYRRHULOXIA
—ROSE-BR. GROSBEAK
—BLACK-HEADED GROSBEAK
—BLUE GROSBEAK
—LAZULI BUNTING
—INDIGO BUNTING
—VARIED BUNTING
—PAINTED BUNTING

—DICKCISSEL
TOWHEES, SPARROWS, etc.:
Emberizinae
—GREEN-TAILED TOWHEE
—RUFOUS-SIDED TOWHEE
—CALIFORNIA TOWHEE
—CANYON TOWHEE
—ABERT'S TOWHEE
—BOTTERI'S SPARROW
—CASSIN'S SPARROW
—RUFOUS-WING. SPARROW
—RUFOUS-CROWN. SPARROW
—AMERICAN TREE SPARROW
—CHIPPING SPARROW
—CLAY-COLORED SPARROW
—BREWER'S SPARROW
—FIELD SPARROW
—BLACK-CHINNED SPARROW
—VESPER SPARROW
—LARK SPARROW
—BLACK-THR. SPARROW
—SAGE SPARROW
—FIVE-STRIPED SPARROW
—LARK BUNTING
—SAVANNAH SPARROW
—BAIRD'S SPARROW
—GRASSHOPPER SPARROW
—LeCONTE'S SPARROW
—SHARP-TAILED SPARROW
—FOX SPARROW
—SONG SPARROW
—LINCOLN'S SPARROW
—SWAMP SPARROW
—WHITE-THR. SPARROW
—GOLDEN-CR. SPARROW
—WHITE-CR. SPARROW
—HARRIS'S SPARROW
—DARK-EYED JUNCO
—YELLOW-EYED JUNCO
—McCOWN'S LONGSPUR
—LAPLAND LONGSPUR

—SMITH'S LONGSPUR
—CHESTNUT-C. LONGSPUR
—RUSTIC BUNTING
—SNOW BUNTING
—McKAY'S BUNTING
BLACKBIRDS, ORIOLES, etc.:
Icterinae
—BOBOLINK
—RED-WINGED BLACKBIRD
—EASTERN MEADOWLARK
—WESTERN MEADOWLARK
—YELLOW-H. BLACKBIRD
—RUSTY BLACKBIRD
—BREWER'S BLACKBIRD
—GREAT-TAILED GRACKLE
—COMMON GRACKLE
—BRONZED COWBIRD
—BROWN-HEADED COWBIRD
—ORCHARD ORIOLE
—HOODED ORIOLE
—STREAK-BACKED ORIOLE
—NORTHERN ORIOLE
—SCOTT'S ORIOLE
FINCHES: Fringillidae
—BRAMBLING
—ROSY FINCH
—PINE GROSBEAK
—COMMON ROSEFINCH
—PURPLE FINCH
—CASSIN'S FINCH
—HOUSE FINCH
—RED CROSSBILL
—WHITE-W. CROSSBILL
—COMMON REDPOLL
—PINE SISKIN
—LESSER GOLDFINCH
—LAWRENCE'S GOLDFINCH
—AMERICAN GOLDFINCH
—EVENING GROSBEAK
WEAVER FINCHES: Passeridae
—HOUSE SPARROW

ACCIDENTALS, STRAYS, AND OTHERS

_____   _____

_____   _____

_____   _____

_____   _____

_____   _____

_____   _____

Key Sources for Further Reference

The *Field Guides* (listed on p. 1) have a basic function — to make it easier to name things. They stress *field marks*, the "trademarks of nature," by which one species can be known from another. Obviously you own this *Field Guide* and probably its eastern counterpart. Two excellent guides covering all of North America — East and West — in single, pocket-sized books, are the *Birds of North America* (Golden Press) by Robbins, Singer, Bruun, and Zim, and the National Geographic Society's *Birds of North America*. Both are illustrated with well-executed artwork. The several Audubon Society bird guides are lavishly illustrated with fine photographs and some drawings. Especially recommended is the three-volume *Master Guide to Birding* (Knopf) by John Farrand, et al. You will also profit from *The Western Bird Watcher* by Kevin Zimmer, and Paul Johnsgaard's several books on bird families. A well-written book that helps mid-level or advanced birders put their act together is *The Complete Birder* (HMCo.) by Jack Connor, and for the serious birder who is challenged by difficult identification problems, the ultimate authority is *A Field Guide to Advanced Birding* (HMCo.) by Kenn Kaufmann. Should you want more than names, the Stokes' nature guides to *Bird Behavior* are the next step.

Books on attracting birds are many and so are "where to go" *Baedeckers*, but what else might you add to your basic bird library? I cannot list all state or regional works here. No single book can give all the answers, although the massive *Encyclopedia of North American Birds* (Knopf) by John Terres goes a long way. Another good encyclopedic handbook is *The Birdwatcher's Companion* (Hill and Wang) by Christopher Leahy. The Audubon Society's *Handbook for Birders* (Scribner's) by Stephen Kress is a good general guide to observing birds. The standard species-by-species reference is the *Handbook of North American Birds* (Yale University Press) by Ralph Palmer. This covers the innumerable details in several volumes. Canadians will also want *The Birds of Canada* by Earl Godfrey. However, the ideal supplement to your favorite field guide is *The Birder's Handbook* (Simon and Schuster) by Ehrlich, Dobkin, and Wheye. It is a mine of information that is beautifully boiled down, but, handy as it is, it still won't quite fit the pocket.

In addition to the academic ornithological journals, the *Auk*, *Condor*, and *Wilson Bulletin*, and the more popular magazines such as *Bird Watcher's Digest*, *Birder's World*, *The Living Bird*, and *Wildbird*, there are literally hundreds of journals, newsletters, and checklists published by regional or local bird clubs, but every serious birder should subscribe to *American Birds*, published by the National Audubon Society, 950 Third Avenue, New York, N.Y. 10022. Bimonthly, it monitors migration, breeding, population trends, and accidentals for every section of North America. Susan Drennan, the editor, has prepared a selection of the best state and regional books in a *Special Book Supplement*. Birders who wish to keep up-to-date on the sporting or competitive aspects of their hobby might also subscribe to *Birding* (American Birding Association, P.O. Box 6599, Colorado Springs, Colo. 80934).

Index

417

Conservation Note

Birds contribute to our pleasure and standard of living. But they are also sensitive indicators of the environment, a sort of "ecological litmus test." Help support the cause of wildlife conservation by taking an active part in the efforts of the National Wildlife Federation, as well as the work of the National Audubon Society, the Sierra Club, the Nature Conservancy, and your state or local Audubon or natural history societies. On the international level, don't forget the International Council for Bird Preservation (ICBP) and the World Wildlife Fund (WWF).

The Roger Tory Peterson Institute of Natural History is oriented toward fact-finding and teaching, emphasizing hands-on field work by those who teach, rather than the methodology of the classroom or laboratory. It is not an activist organization like those mentioned above, but is supportive of their work through education and enlightenment.